"When it came to Hollywood,
I had an automatic flinch reaction."

—*Philip K. Dick*

"Sometimes the design is the statement."
—*Ridley Scott*

FUTURE NOIR:
THE MAKING OF
BLADE RUNNER

Paul M. Sammon

HarperPrism
An Imprint of HarperPaperbacks

HarperPaperbacks *A Division of* HarperCollins*Publishers*
10 East 53rd Street, New York, N.Y. 10022

Copyright © 1996 by Paul M. Sammon
All rights reserved. No part of this book may be used or reproduced in any manner whatsoever without written permission of the publisher, except in the case of brief quotations embodied in critical articles and reviews. For information address HarperCollins*Publishers,*
10 East 53rd Street, New York, N.Y. 10022.

HarperPaperbacks may be purchased for educational, business, or sales promotional use. For information, please write:
Special Markets Department, HarperCollins*Publishers,*
10 East 53rd Street, New York, N.Y. 10022.

First printing: July 1996

Cover art credits and copyright information for interior art appear on page 436.

Designed by Lili Schwartz

Printed in the United States of America

Library of Congress Cataloging-in-Publication Data

Sammon, Paul M.
    Future noir: the making of Blade runner/Paul M. Sammon.
      p. cm.
    ISBN 0-06-105314-7 (trade paperback)
    1. Blade runner (Motion picture) I. Title.
PS1997. B569S26 1996
791.43'72 --dc20   96-14196
                                                   CIP

HarperPrism is an imprint of HarperPaperbacks. HarperPaperbacks, HarperPrism, and colophon are trademarks of HarperCollins*Publishers.*

96 97 98 99 ❖ 10 9 8 7 6 5 4 3 2 1

This Labor of Love
Is For
RIDLEY SCOTT, HAMPTON FANCHER,
and PHILIP K. DICK

CONTENTS

ACKNOWLEDGMENTS

Like the film which it examines, *Future Noir* ultimately reflects the vision of one person—but it took a legion of unsung collaborators to help bring that vision into focus.

First and foremost, I'd like to thank *Cinefantastique* editor Frederick S. Clarke. Fred not only first waved me onto that career on-ramp feeding into the strange, wonderful, awful Hollywood freeway down which I find myself careening today, he also showed me what to do, and what *not* to do. Without Clarke's long-ago assignment, this book simply would not exist.

Of equal importance is Ridley Scott. Throughout this work you'll encounter certain voices critical of the man—mine is not one of them. Over the past fifteen years this talented, committed, consummate professional has been unfailingly gracious in allowing me ongoing access into what I know is one of the busiest schedules in the entertainment business. Thanks, Ridley—I've enjoyed your candor and civility. Maybe now people will stop asking us if Deckard is a replicant!

Other key participants without whom *Future Noir* would just not be are Michael Deeley, Hampton Fancher, Katy Haber, David Peoples, Ivor Powell, and Terry Rawlings. This core group provided me with critical information and documentation far beyond the call; at the same time, their unflagging warmth, cooperation and enthusiasm for this project more than once helped stop this author from flinging his word processor against a wall. Thanks for keeping me sane, all of you; I hope this book stands as a testimonial to your invaluable input (and punishing work on an amazing motion picture) for decades to come.

I would also like to thank the many *Blade Runner* cast and crew members who generously gave of their time and memory regarding their experiences on the film. My sincere appreciation to Joanna Cassidy, Gary Combs, Jordan Cronenweth, Linda DeScenna, David Dryer, Mike Fink, Harrison Ford, Terry Frazee, Rocco Gioffre, Robert Hall, Daryl Hannah, Rutger Hauer, James Hong, Brian Kelly, Brion

James, Michael Kaplan, Saul Kahan (for initially clearing my way through a very thorny path), Charles Knode, Alan Ladd, Jr., Syd Mead, Edward James Olmos, Lawrence Paull, Hy Pyke, John Rogers, William Sanderson, David Snyder, Tom Southwell, Bob Spurlock, Mark Stetson, Dave Stewart, Douglas Trumbull, Vangelis, M. Emmet Walsh (thanks for the lunch!), Marvin Westmore, Michael Westmore, Gene Winfield, Sean Young, Matthew Yuricich, Richard Yuricich, John Wash, and John Zabrucky (from Modern Props).

A special note of gratitude to Anne Lai and Cindy Pearson, for putting up with (and never blowing off) my numerous queries, requests and re-requests.

And all good things to William M. Kolb, as well. Bill was the only person connected with this project who spontaneously and unselfishly kept flooding my office with information; his professionalism, enthusiasm, and—most important of all—his scrupulous fidelity to the facts made our association a pleasant one indeed. My one regret is that *Future Noir* was unable to bring you Kolb's *Annotated BR Bibliography* (the fact that it runs over 100,000 words might have had something to do with that). Ah, well—have a better one anyway, Bill. I'm sure we'll be seeing the full shaggy beast in all its splendiferous glory soon enough.

Further thanks to Michael Arick, Cherie Buchheim, Andrew Hoy, Charles Lippincott, and Ron Yerxa for allowing me to interview them for ancillary *Blade Runner* information.

A most important technical note: *Future Noir* was written on an Amiga 2000 computer, and a number of Amiga-oriented companies graciously supplied me with various pieces of hardware to help expedite that process. These companies and their fine products (both of which I recommend), are:

CENTURY COMPUTER SYSTEMS
(Amiga hardware/software)
841 E. WHITTIER BOULEVARD
LA HABRA, CA 90631
(310) 697-6977

UTILITIES UNLIMITED
INTERNATIONAL INC.
(EMPLANT Macintosh
Emulation Module)
3261 MARICOPA #101
LAKE HAVASU CITY, AZ 06406
(520) 680-9004

Additional gratitude is extended to the various agents, publicists, managers, and assistants whose collective energies helped fuel *Future Noir*. Noteworthy participants in this respect were: Jim Cota, Jeff Goldberg, Andi Howard, Lori Jonas, Joanie's Answering Service, Audrey Kahn, Guy MacElwaine, Patricia McQueeney, Lana Morgan, Troy Nankin, Alan Nirob, Steven Spignese, Cynthia Snyder, and Susan Patricola.

A special note of thanks to Jeff Walker (who was there at the beginning) and to Don Shay, editor of *Cinefex* magazine, for both forgiving me for jumping ship so long ago and for penning what's still the best analysis of *Blade Runner*'s special effects.

Also—and we're getting close, now—my ongoing gratitude to Eric Caiden (and John Kantas) of Hollywood Book and Poster. Eric's a nice guy, runs a wonderfully well-stocked ship, and can supply many of your film-oriented needs. Give him a jingle at (213) 465-8764. Or you might want to drop in personally some day—Hollywood Book and Poster is located at 6349 Hollywood Boulevard, in Hollyweird CA. Tell Eric Rick Deckard sent you.

More help and/or inspiration was donated by Eileen Gunn, Eugene King, Larry Ortiz, Mike Stuart (and, *in memoriam*, Pete Wine). Two final inclusions: Robert Neal and Terence Oldham, who'll probably be surprised to see their names in print alongside Ridley Scott and Harrison Ford.

And many, many thanks to John Silbersack and Caitlin Blasdell, my editors at HarperCollins. During what was an unexpectedly long and sometimes bumpy trip, John and Caitlin never wavered in their whole-hearted support of the bleary-eyed driver behind the wheel.

Appreciation also goes to Lori Perkins, my agent. One more feather in our caps!

Penultimately, a posthumous note of gratitude to Philip K. Dick. Thanks for everything, Phil—rest in peace. I'm sorry you're not around to see how well they ultimately served your book.

Finally, *Future Noir* is secretly dedicated (as are all my works) to my friend, wife, and soulmate, Sherri Sammon.

Who never wants to hear the words *Blade Runner* again.

INTRODUCTION:

ONE MAN'S
OBSESSION

It's only fitting that a book examining the history of one of the most compulsively detailed motion pictures ever made should spring from one writer's equally compulsive obsession with that picture.

It's also somewhat ironic that, while director Ridley Scott and company took only two years to complete *Blade Runner, Future Noir* took fifteen.

This book, and my fascination with Scott's moody, seminal, hyperdetailed cinematic milestone, actually began before the first frame of *Blade Runner* was ever shot or sent to the laboratory. In June 1980, nearly a full year before principal photography began, I was assigned by editor Frederick S. Clarke to write a special "double issue" of *Cinefantastique* magazine on the making of *Blade Runner*. This report was to take the form of a comprehensive production history, one intended to chart every aspect of the motion picture by examining such various production minutia as the film's sets, scripts, costumes, cast, crew, and special effects.

My initial reactions on receiving this assignment? Exhilaration and apprehension. After all, *Blade Runner* was being directed by then redhot filmmaker Ridley Scott, fresh off the box-office triumph of his Gothic science fiction hit *Alien* (the somber flip side of *Star Wars'* joyous kineticism). Moreover, *Blade Runner* had been adapted from the intriguing novel *Do Androids Dream of Electric Sheep,* a complex rumination on the effects of dehumanization by a master of paranoid alternate realities, noted science fiction author Philip K. Dick. *Blade Runner* was also set to star one of the most bankable Hollywood actors (Harrison Ford) and was to be produced by seasoned veteran Michael Deeley, a man whose most recent effort (*The Deer Hunter*) had won the 1978 Academy Award for Best Picture. Furthermore, the Hollywood gossip mill was buzzing with rumors that *Blade Runner* was to be one of the most expensive genre pictures yet attempted.

All of which certainly fueled my enthusiasm. However, at this point in my career, I was painfully aware of my relative inexperience as a film journalist. My previous efforts had been primarily limited to such small (if well-received) efforts as a production history of John Milius' *Conan the Barbarian* and a career overview of the always-intriguing Canadian director David Cronenberg.

But how would the *Blade Runner* staff react to the exhaustive archaeology my *Cinefantastique* article required? How would they feel about my presence on the set? How would they respond to what I knew would be an ongoing demand for interviews, interviews, and more interviews?

How, in short, was I going to be treated after making such an ubiquitous nuisance of myself?

The answer to that last question was—well. Very well. Throughout 1980, 1981 and 1982, during preproduction, principal photography, and postproduction, virtually everyone connected with the creation of *Blade Runner*—Scott, Deeley, screenwriters Hampton Fancher and David Peoples, designer Syd Mead, special effects ace Douglas Trumbull, and others too numerous to mention—were more than happy to provide me with all the information I could possibly need.

I initially gathered so much data, in fact, that it began to overflow the boundaries of my original assignment. So by late 1980, I started to submit numerous short "production update" articles to *Cinefantastique,* some published under the pseudonym "P. B. Beene." Then I sold a series of *Blade Runner* articles to *Omni* magazine, which saw print in 1981 and 1982. This was followed by my shoehorning more and more facts into that proposed "double issue" article, simply in order to handle the information overflow.

Even more important than the endless factoids I was now receiving, however, was the manner in which I found myself embraced as an unofficial member of the *Blade Runner* team. Much to my pleasant surprise, Ridley Scott, Michael Deeley, and Katy Haber—names which will be thoroughly familiar by the time you finish this book—went out of their way to assure my virtually unlimited access to every phase of their dauntingly ambitious, nearly $30 million production.

This meant I was able to examine *Blade Runner*'s ever-changing scripts and conceptual art. That I was present the day Deeley and Scott first explored the notion of casting Harrison Ford. I also witnessed the construction of key sets; visited the then-called Burbank Studios, in order to observe *Blade Runner*'s actual filming; chatted with cast members, designers, and other sundry behind-the-scenes personnel; sat in a Spinner; toured Douglas Trumbull's Entertainment Effects Group; experienced the feuds, the tensions, the fabled T-shirt War; saw the San Diego-based *Blade Runner* sneak preview.

In short, long before the picture's enshrinement as the cult film par excellence, I was *Blade Runner*'s Boswell, who ultimately reduced an ever-enlarging databank into a 125-page manuscript for that long-in-the-making *Cinefantastique* article, published in the summer of 1982 and timed to coincide with the film's original theatrical release.

Satisfied with the manner in which I thought I'd completely covered this picture, I dusted off my hands and moved on to other things. An action which, under normal circumstances, would have ended my involvement with the film.

But *Blade Runner* is far from a "normal" film, and my involvement with it definitely did not end in 1982.

In many senses, it had just begun.

To explain, we must first remember that *Blade Runner* was a financial flop during its initial theatrical release. Further, critical reaction to the picture had been decidedly mixed, with the majority of reviews decidedly leaning toward the negative. Yet despite this public rejection—and in spite of the fact that the first time I had seen a completed cut of the picture, I'd been more impressed with *Blade Runner*'s production design and melancholic atmosphere than with its intrinsic merit as a *film*—I soon found myself returning to this motion picture. Over and over, time and again.

Why? Partly because of sentiment: everyone had put so much damn effort into *Blade Runner*, and then it had up and died at the box office. I was also curious to determine whether I'd simply been too close to the production to notice what audiences and critics kept insisting were its fatal dramatic flaws (i.e., cardboard characterizations and a simplistic storyline). Lastly, via the magic of home video, I kept rescreening the film simply to sort through its staggering visual information; if nothing else, *Blade Runner* is one of the most fully realized visions of a future society ever set on film, and repeated viewings are an absolute necessity if one wants to catch the multitude of design flourishes littering every frame.

Then something curious happened.

Like an intellectual nest of Chinese boxes, every time I opened the *Blade Runner* container, five more boxes popped out. This revelation eventually convinced me that popular perceptions were wrong—

Scott's motion picture *was* more than a kaleidoscopic accretion of detail. In fact, the *Blade Runner* I was discovering not only revealed an *adult* narrative and *complex* characters (subtle, dramatically wrenching ones at that), it also evidenced a *thematic* complexity every bit as intricate as its much discussed *visual* complexity.

At this point I found myself suffused with a growing sense of excitement. Despite Ridley Scott's repeated claims that *Blade Runner* was "only an entertainment," it had become obvious to me that this director (and cowriters Fancher and Peoples) had, in point of fact, created one of the most intelligent, thought-provoking, and metaphysically textured mainstream science fiction films since *2001: A Space Odyssey.* One which both admirably displayed the paranoid/alternate reality motifs of source author Philip K. Dick and mirrored the sophisticated sensibilities typifying much of contemporary literary science fiction.

Or, to put it simplistically, I'd discovered that there is more to *Blade Runner* than meets the eye. Much more—for this was also that rare motion picture of *ideas.*

Jump cut, past 1982 and into the future. The years roll by; Ridley Scott goes on to direct other films, none quite as controversial or memorable as *Blade Runner* (with the sole exception of, perhaps, *Thelma and Louise).* I move on from writing about motion pictures to working on them—initially as a publicist, then as a studio administrator, then a scriptwriter, Digital Effects Supervisor, and television producer.

Meanwhile—and quite unexpectedly—*Blade Runner* refused to die. If anything, as the eighties wore on, it became obvious that the film was undergoing a full-fledged renaissance.

A growing home video audience, which found the VCR format the perfect environment in which to visit (and revisit) Scott's teeming 2019 Los Angeles, treated the film's initially hostile critical response as a dim memory, ultimately making *Blade Runner* one of the all-time rental champs. Simultaneously, a burgeoning print movement subjected *Blade Runner* to everincreasing critical reassessment; scores of new articles, a semiregular fanzine (*Cityspeak),* and a book-length collection of academically oriented essays (*Retrofitting Blade Runner)* were the end result.

Next came *Blade Runner*'s frequent revival at art cinemas and midnight movie venues, as well as The Criterion Collection's letterboxed laser disc, which contained supplementary material and additional footage not seen in the U.S. theatrical release. By 1991, the groundswell of *Blade Runner* mania reached its first peak with a sold-out booking of a recently discovered *Blade Runner* "workprint" at two theaters on the West Coast. The following year, a shortened, more viewer-friendly "director's cut" was released to theaters, laser disc, and home video.

The entire time, my *Blade Runner* obsession kept apace. As I bemusedly noted the way the film was lodging in the popular consciousness, like a popcorn kernel under the gumline, I became increasingly fascinated by the manner in which *Blade Runner*'s dystopian subtexts of alienation, rebellion, and humiliation, its cautionary depictions of a disintegrating future whose institutionalized brutality was only one aspect of a overpopulated society teetering on the brink of apocalypse, uncomfortably reflected the day-to-day realities of those straining to bring these subtexts to the screen.

Therefore, I began cutting *Blade Runner* articles out of magazines and newspapers, continued to author various pieces regarding the film, bought and picked over each new version released on tape and disc. And what had begun as a professional assignment soon blossomed into personal obsession.

I now tracked down *Blade Runner* spinoffs and ad material. Found hard-to-get stills. Hoarded revised scripts. Swapped information with other *Blade Runner* fanatics. Kept in touch with most of the key *Blade Runner* personnel. Even collected actual props from the film (as I write this, a plastic, unpainted $2^1/_2$-inch-long Spinner model, cast for the picture itself, stares at me from its favored spot atop my computer monitor).

Yet all was not sweetness and light—lurking amid this enjoyable new hobby were prickles of discontent. I'd become alarmed at the manner in which misinformation on the film was being disseminated and accepted as fact. I was also irritated at the manner in which other journalists were lifting great chunks of my *Cinefantastique* article and not giving me proper credit (the "Blade Runner" article in the October 1992 issue of *Details* magazine and John Brosnan's *BR* section in his 1991 book *The Primal Screen* were two of the more blatant offenders). And I was distressed by the realization that that selfsame *Cinefantastique* piece had actually only told *part* of the *Blade Runner* story.

So one day in 1993, I picked up the telephone and called my agent, Lori Perkins. "How about something on *Blade Runner*?" I asked. The result of that query is this book.

Future Noir is based on over 100 hours of taped interviews with seventy-plus participants who helped make the film, conducted from 1980 to 1982 and 1993 to 1995. I have also referred to the many personal observations I jotted down while experiencing the 1980–1982 *Blade Runner* production process itself. In order to insure further accuracy, I undertook repeated viewings of The Workprint, the original theatrical release, the Director's Cut, and the Criterion disc version. And while some of this material may have previously appeared under my byline (in a vastly different form) in *Cinefantastique, Omni,* and *Video Watchdog* magazines, that previously published text only adds up to about twenty percent of the material incorporated herein. The rest appears for the first time.

Of course, I have never been alone in my fascination with this motion picture. Many other writers have published excellent, insightful *Blade Runner* pieces over the past fourteen years as well, and so, wherever I have utilized such sources in this book, I have credited same within the body of this text (if *no* credit is given, it's safe to assume that the quotes and/or information cited herein were gathered through my interviews). Those readers wishing to expand on their *Blade Runner* education are urged to consult the bibliography found at the back of *Future Noir.*

But enough backgrounds and brickbats—on to the book. I hope you find *Future Noir* an authoritative compendium on its subject. I also hope it broadens your understanding of the sheer, staggering amount of *work* demanded by the making of a major motion picture.

Just as I hope it somewhat reimburses the hard personal prices paid by *Blade Runner*'s army of filmmakers during their long, weary march to the screen.

—Paul M. Sammon
January 31, 1996
Los Angeles, California

"This is not like anything we have ever seen. . . . It isn't like anything that has ever been done."

—*Philip K. Dick, author of* Do Androids Dream of Electric Sheep, *after being shown footage of* Blade Runner. *From "They Did Sight Stimulation on My Brain," by Gregg Rickman.*

THE FILM

Early in the 21st Century, THE TYRELL CORPORATION advanced Robot evolution into the NEXUS phase—a being virtually identical to a human—known as a replicant.

The NEXUS–6 Replicants were superior in strength and agility, and at least equal in intelligence, to the genetic engineers who created them. Replicants were used Off-world as slave labor, in the hazardous exploration and colonization of other planets.

After a bloody mutiny by a NEXUS–6 combat team in an Off-world colony, Replicants were declared illegal on earth—under penalty of death.

Special police squads—BLADE RUNNER UNITS—had orders to shoot to kill, upon detection, any trespassing Replicants.

This was not called execution.

It was called retirement.

—OPENING CRAWL FROM *BLADE RUNNER*,
ORIGINAL THEATRICAL PRINT

BLADE RUNNER

Los Angeles. November, 2019.
A vast industrial wasteland fills the frame. From foreground to horizon, thousands of oil refineries and processing plants litter the landscape. This hellish environment is dotted by dozens of fireball-belching cracking towers cocooned in a thick petrochemical haze.

Strange futuristic vehicles zip by in the polluted sky overhead. One flies toward a pair of massive buildings looming over this Boschian inferno; the camera pushes in toward them, reveals the colossal structures to be pyramidal, Mayan-like ziggurats hundreds of stories high.

These titanic twin edifices house the headquarters of the Tyrell

The obsessively detailed "Hades Landscape" miniature. Model work by EEG (Entertainment Effects Group).

Corporation, a powerful genetic engineering firm. Near the top of one building, inside a smoke-filled room ventilated by revolving ceiling fans, sits a sweating, abrasive man named Holden (Morgan Paull). Holden is about to administer a bizarre lie-detector test. His subject? Leon Kowalski (Brion James), a lower-echelon Tyrell employee. Holden's equipment? A futuristic device called a Voigt-Kampff machine, designed to measure emotional responses through involuntary dilation of the human iris.

We know neither why this interrogation is taking place nor who either man is. All we understand is that Holden's questions are strange and hostile, and that Leon is becoming increasingly uncomfortable.

"Describe in single words only the good things that come into your mind. About your mother," Holden queries.

"My mother?" Leon replies. "Let me tell you about my mother."

Whereupon Kowalski fires an unseen handgun he's been hiding beneath the conference table. The shot strikes Holden, slams him against a wall. Leon fires again. This time the impact smashes Holden through the wall.

And thus begins *Blade Runner,* Ridley Scott's high-tech blend of a forties-style detective thriller with twenty-first-century science fiction.

Before moving on to a further examination of *Blade Runner*'s narrative, it should first be noted that *Blade Runner* is an adaptation of science fiction author Philip K. Dick's novel, *Do Androids Dream of Electric Sheep.* Then, it should—must—be pointed out that, above all else, this is a film whose primary attraction was (and continues to be) its dazzling production design.

Blade Runner presents one of the most elaborately visualized fictional environments ever constructed for an American film; each frame is bursting with an obsessive accretion of detail. Still, it's not a pretty sight. Ridley Scott's twenty-first century is a decayed, jaded, mutated place, a cheerless landscape whose meager humanity is being ground down by the microchipped jackboot of a ruthless technological *zeitgeist*. Its mean streets teem with hundreds of oddly dressed citizens (mostly Asians, some punks, street gangs, Hare Krishnas, and the ever-present police). All scurrying ratlike through concrete canyons whose confines are constantly bombarded by ubiquitous neon advertising, by the blare of unctuous announcers hawking pristine "Off-world colonies," from huge, insanely graphic-heavy blimps, and by the sodden, perpetual downpour of a numbing acid rain.

Director Ridley Scott (right) puts "Rick Deckard" (Harrison Ford) through his paces.

It is exactly this deluge of details—the striking costumes, the fantastic flying cars, the atmospheric ethnicity, the moody music, the lavish, lived-in sets—which makes *Blade Runner* such addictive eye-candy. And it is to this bewitching visual surface which most viewers repeatedly return. Like its industrial counterparts in the worlds of high fashion and architecture, *Blade Runner* is a form of ultrasophisticated "designer cinema," one whose astonishingly complex visual field has, despite a subsequent decade's worth of futuristic/alternate world spectaculars like Tim Burton's *Batman* trilogy or the recent *Judge Dredd,* remained the high-water mark against which all other big-budget SF entertainments are measured.

Amusingly, however, *Blade Runner*'s *plot* evidences a sentimental fondness for the old-fashioned *films noirs* which it so thoroughly emulates.

Following the strange, oddly tense opening sequence related at the beginning of this chapter, *BR*'s audience is introduced to Rick Deckard (Harrison Ford), the film's protagonist. A cynical, world-weary ex-cop,

Deckard exhibits all the familiar icons of the burnt-out detective: he wears a trenchcoat, drinks too much, and even, in the original version, narrates his story through a series of hard-boiled voice-overs. Additionally, while Deckard's former profession may be an exotic one (he once was part of the LAPD's elite "Blade Runner" unit, a department assigned to track down and execute rogue "replicants," short-lived, genetically-engineered human beings virtually indistinguishable from the real thing), it is certainly no less distasteful than the typical private investigator's sordid history of peephole spying and divorce cases.

Like those classic detective heroes before him, Deckard now finds himself embroiled in a seemingly routine case which turns mystifying and deadly. Unwillingly plucked from retirement by his crude ex-superior Captain Bryant (E. Emmet Walsh), Deckard is ordered to find and eliminate a cadre of four murderous replicants who recently "jumped an Off-world shuttle, killed (its) crew and passengers," and made it down to Earth. These rogue androids—exotic dancer Zhora (Joanna Cassidy), dim-witted Leon, cunning, lascivious Pris (Daryl Hannah)—are being led by Roy Batty (Rutger Hauer), a top-of-the-line combat model. All are Nexus–6 replicants, the latest and best products of Tyrell technology, endowed with physical and mental capacities far superior to ordinary humans.

Their only weakness? A temporal one—replicants are engineered to biologically self-destruct after a four-year lifespan.

Armed with these fundamentals, Deckard moves on to interview the great Eldon Tyrell (Joe Turkel) himself, who, out of seeming curiosity, asks Deckard to run a Voigt-Kampff test on a genuine human. Tyrell then persuades the exquisitely alluring Rachael (Sean Young) to volunteer as Deckard's test subject. But Tyrell is playing a cruel joke on both the woman and Deckard: the Blade Runner's test reveals that Rachael is actually an unknowing replicant, one implanted with false memories obtained from Tyrell's real niece. "How can it not know what it is?" Deckard asks.

From this point onward, *Blade Runner* follows the traditional mystery blueprint. Deckard now crosses paths with the expected *film noir* grotesques: sleazy nightclub owner Taffey Lewis (Hy Pyke), childlike genetic engineering genius J. F. Sebastian (William Sanderson). Next Deckard falls in love with Rachael and discovers puzzling clues (a discarded snake scale). Finally he tracks down, violently confronts, and ultimately triumphs over his android adversaries.

Romance among the replicants; artificial human "Rachael" (Sean Young) shares a quiet moment with real (?) detective Deckard (Ford).

Yet for all its generic conformity, *Blade Runner* commendably strives to criticize and invert its formulaic underpinnings. For example, Deckard's character is painted in ambiguous shades of gray. He is (initially) portrayed as macho, brusque, and insensitive. Deckard is shown to be ineffectual, as well; he is constantly being put upon, beaten up, and misled. Furthermore, by only killing two replicants, he technically never completes his assignment. Most tellingly, both of Deckard's "retirements" are women—and he shoots one in the back.

Obviously, *Blade Runner*'s perversion of the clichéd cinematic hero suggests ambitions beyond a clever blending of rote thriller with awesome effects. But are those ambitions genuine and justified? One can answer that query only by penetrating *beneath* the surface of *Blade Runner*'s overwhelming images. For it is precisely there, in the film's subtextual underbelly, where alert viewers will find numerous ways to validate *Blade Runner*'s credentials as a lasting, credible work of art.

Lurking under the film's pop visuals and trendy special effects is a subtle, dizzying tangle of deeply felt moral, philosophical, and sociological concerns. Take the film's title—a "Blade Runner" could also be interpreted as someone who scampers along the thin edge of life. Or witness the multiple examples of narrative mirroring (or doubling) throughout. Deckard kills two replicants; two replicants save his life. Deckard finds a reason to live; Batty wants to live. Religious parallels are also rampant: Tyrell is literally the replicant's God, and Batty, Tyrell's prodigal son, symbolically pierces his hand with a nail, suggesting crucifixion. Even the film's horizontal/vertical design scheme makes a statement; *Blade Runner*'s privileged few live in luxurious towers, literally high above the disenfranchised masses below.

All these musings are swept aside, however, by the three, key,

Ruthless replicant leader Roy Batty (Rutger Hauer): "Who am I? Why am I here? What does it mean to be human?"

simple-yet-profound questions which constitute the core of the film: Who am I? Why am I here? What does it mean to be human?

Moreover, *Blade Runner* displays virtues beyond its philosophical and ethical ones. For instance, its densely conceptualized production design launched dozens of look-alike television series and feature films, ones identified by such distinctive Ridley Scott/*Blade Runner* touches as all-intrusive shafts of light, large, slowly turning fan blades, and smoke-choked interior sets. *Blade Runner* also became something of a touchstone for a new literary movement (cyberpunk), helped boost the career of source novelist Philip K. Dick, and (most alarmingly), actually predicted the future—a simple walk through any downtown neighborhood should convince viewers that the trash-strewn, poverty-ridden, overpopulated streets of *Blade Runner* are already with us today.

So while its initial reputation may have been founded on incredible visual density, mesmerizing Vangelis music, and a popular leading man, Ridley Scott's dystopic vision of a crowded, polluted, multiethnic society is actually a supremely challenging and cautionary achievement, one far too accomplished to be blown off by such simplistic knee-jerk reflexes as the oft-heard "all form and no content." Indeed, *Blade Runner* is a serious, *mature* work, one ten years ahead of its time, both of and about the future ("of" because it was released before the widespread advent of home video, which is the only format allowing easy, repeated access to its richness).

In the final analysis, then, *BR* is much more than the (visible) sum of its parts. It is complex. Thought-provoking. Even flawed (too many narrative links were dropped and forgotten during the rewriting process, for instance). Yet, on the whole, it is also visionary, enduring, and unique. The first $30 million mainstream science fiction art film, if you will.

Make no mistake, however. For despite this author's enthusiastic endorsement, there is no middle ground regarding this motion picture—audiences either love it or hate it. Some are hypnotized by its pace, some are bored by it. Certain viewers are stimulated by *Blade Runner*'s elliptic narrative, while others are confused. Yet one topic on which both sides seem to agree is the notion that, fourteen years after its initial release, *Blade Runner* is still worth picking over, arguing about. . . and treasuring.

But where did it all begin? Who made this controversial picture? How? What was contained in the radically different "Workprint"? Why did Vangelis' soundtrack take so long to be released? Who was involved in the on-set feuding? Is Deckard really a replicant? What the hell's that unicorn doing in the Director's Cut? And why does *Blade Runner* remain so popular today?

To answer those questions, perhaps we should first pick up a Bible, and then turn to an old, old line. One which opens the Gospel of St. John and will serve as the proper introduction to *Future Noir* as well:

"In the beginning was the Word . . . "

THE BOOK

In a giant, empty, decaying building which had once housed thousands, a single TV set hawked its wares to an uninhabited room.

The ownerless ruin had, before World War Terminus, been tended and maintained. Here had been the suburbs of San Francisco, a short ride by monorail rapid transit; the entire peninsula had chattered like a bird tree with life and opinions and complaints, and now the watchful owners had either died or migrated to a colony world. Mostly the former; it had been a costly war. . . .

—FROM *DO ANDROIDS DREAM OF ELECTRIC SHEEP*

Translating a novel into a major motion picture is usually a thankless task. More often than not, subplots are flensed, characters combined, and an overall tightening of plot and dialogue is done in order to condense even the slimmest novel into a feature film's two-hour running time.

With the end result being an oft-repeated complaint: "The movie wasn't as good as the book."

Of course, such criticisms are valid when filmmakers simply dispense with the best elements of their source novel and make a poor motion picture. But the case of *Blade Runner,* and the novel from which it was adapted (*Do Androids Dream of Electric Sheep),* is not so clear cut.

First, *Blade Runner* is definitely not a failed motion picture (although, as previously noted, it still provokes its fair share of detractors). Secondly, while *BR* and *Electric Sheep* exhibit many points of divergence, this does not automatically mean the film is a shallow adaptation of the book; *Blade Runner* is merely *different,* a necessary reworking of the same basic storyline for a dissimilar medium. Finally, a careful viewing of *BR* actually reveals a surprising number of *similarities* between it and the novel on which it was based.

At which juncture I would recommend those not interested in *Electric Sheep* or Philip K. Dick to skip this section and move on to chapter III.

Those seeking more information on *Blade Runner*'s source novel, however—as well as insights into the talented, tormented author who wrote it—are encouraged to read on.

Philip K. Dick, author of Do Androids Dream of Electric Sheep?, poses with director Ridley Scott at the EEG special effects facility following the writer's first—and only—screening of some just-completed Blade Runner *special-effects footage. Less than four months after this photo was taken, Dick would be dead.*

THE AUTHOR: PHILIP K. DICK

Philip Kindred Dick was born in Chicago on December 16, 1928. While great interest has risen regarding this man and his fiction since the early 1980s—primarily because of *Blade Runner*—a quick review of the author's private side reveals a history every bit as complicated as *BR* itself.

Dick's personal life was oftentimes difficult. Born to Joseph Edgar Dick and Dorothy Grant Kindred, Philip Dick was actually a twin, sharing the same day of birth as a sister named Jane; however, Jane died only forty-one days after her delivery. The reason for her passing has been blamed on Dorothy, who reportedly refused to seek proper medical attention for the ailing baby until it was too late (Philip Dick also had an unsatisfying relationship with his mother, whom the author viewed as a cold, distant authority figure). Whatever caused Jane's death, the loss of Dick's sister was an event which obsessed the writer throughout his life, and she was never far from PKD's thoughts. Indeed, Dick would always claim to have a spiritual bond with Jane, and many of the mysterious female characters in his works were thinly veiled representations of the unreachable sister Dick never had.

As a boy, Dick's early days were typified by constant travel and ruptured relationships. In 1930, his parents moved from Chicago to Berkeley, California. Following her divorce from Joseph in 1932, Dorothy took Philip with her to Washington, D.C., in 1938. Mother and son subsequently moved *back* to Berkeley in 1940. The author thereafter lived most of his life in the Golden State, specifically San Francisco, Marin County, and Santa Ana, where Dick spent his final ten years.

As he matured, Dick's life became riddled with physical and emotional problems. Somewhere between 1944 and 1946, for example, he received intensive psychiatric treatment for agoraphobia and other psychological ailments. Also in 1946, Dick was diagnosed as suffering from tachycardia (rapid heartbeat) and became dependent on the medications used to treat this illness. Compounding these physiological setbacks was a string of broken marriages; Dick married no less than three times, for example, within a single ten-year period. First to Jeanette Marlin in 1948, to Kleo Apostolides in 1950, and then to Anne Williams Rubinstein in 1958.

Yet physical or psychological problems never blocked Philip K. Dick's artistic development. From an early age he'd evidenced a love of learning and literature, particularly the science fiction and horror tales found in pulp magazines like *Unknown* and *Astounding*. These fantastic yarns so influenced Dick that he wrote his first novel, *Return to Liliput*, when he was only fourteen years old, but the manuscript was lost and never recovered. By his early twenties, Dick had also developed a fondness for such mystery/horror/SF writers as Fredrik Brown, H. P. Lovecraft, and A. E. Van Vogt.

Surprisingly, although he eventually matured into a highly articulate, widely read, and impressively learned person, Philip K. Dick actually attended only one year of college. This was at the University of California at Berkeley in 1947. After that he concentrated on becoming a self-taught man.

Finally, at the age of twenty-four, Dick decided to become a professional writer. Working without an agent and sending various unsolicited short stories through the mail to the genre publications he loved, Dick ultimately broke through by selling his first story, "Beyond Lies the Wub," to *Planet Stories* in July 1952.

Thereafter it was Philip K. Dick's fiction—his *science* fiction—which secured him recognition as one of the outstanding talents in the field. Excellently written and wildly imaginative, Dick's stories began to appear at an astonishingly prolific rate.

Eventually, Dick would publish thirty-six novels during his lifetime. But the money he was making from writing at this early point in his life was not enough to support him, his wives, or, by now, his various children. Therefore, in order to supplement his income, Dick embarked upon the traditional struggling writer's route of numerous odd jobs. These included working in a television repair shop and being employed as a radio disk jockey who played only classical music (which was a constant passion throughout Dick's life; it's not by accident that part of *Do Androids Dream of Electric Sheep* is set in an opera house).

Despite this extra income, however, Dick's financial state was still precarious. Casting about for ways to further increase his literary output, Dick hit upon a dangerous solution: amphetamines. Massive quantities of them. This gambit initially paid off with increased productivity, but eventually levied a heavy fine on Dick's mental health, as we shall see.

Still, the author never looked upon his early drug usage as anything other than a purely pragmatic answer to money problems. While once speaking to me in 1981, Dick himself justified his amphetamine habit by stating that, "I took so much speed simply because I had to support myself by writing fiction. And the only way I could do that was to write a lot of it."

Yet despite his tremendous output, and in spite of the fact that Dick's early novelistic career saw his work relegated to the low-cost, low-paying publishing arena of the "paperback original," PKD's fiction was far from hack work. In 1962 his novel *The Man in the High Castle* (a story concerning an alternative universe where both the Japanese and Germans of World War II won the war and split America down the middle as booty) won the Hugo Award, the science fiction fan community's equivalent of the Pulitzer prize for literature. The year 1974 saw Dick's *Flow My Tears, The Policeman Said* garner the John W. Campbell Memorial Award for best novel of the year. Furthermore, Dick's peers began to increasingly laud his accomplishments. One such bit of praise came from fellow SF alumnus John Brunner (late author of the classic overpopulation novel *The Sheep Look Up*). Brunner called Dick "the most consistently brilliant science fiction writer in the world."

The reason for this praise was simple: no one wrote quite like Philip K. Dick. Although the majority of his work took place in a world mostly recognizable as our own, Dick's viewpoint was so skewed by existential observation and idiosyncratic insight, so prone to vaulting from the mundanely realistic or slyly humorous to the utterly fantastic, that anyone sampling his work over any period of time found their perceptions of that world irrevocably altered.

Contextually, Dick's early work was mostly sociological and politically left wing. It routinely used the science-fiction backdrop of a radiation-scarred twenty-first-century western seaboard to comment on such contemporary twentieth-century problems as totalitarianism, materialism, and nuclear weapons. Besides incorporating critiques of such then current affairs, Dick also addressed the notion that reality was composed of stacked or interlocking levels far beyond ordinary human ken ... as well as the fairly ominous idea that humanity was being manipulated by unfathomable higher powers.

In fact, this definite strain of paranoia was not only evident in Dick's early work, it informed *all* his work. But by the seventies, Dick's paranoid riffs had become much more evident. So had a preoccupation with mysticism, religious belief and ethics, as well as a fundamental questioning of physical and psychological realities.

As for Dick's protagonists, they had always been smart, sensitive, and flawed: fallible individuals who were more likely to be afflicted by ordinary human weaknesses (or terrifying hallucinations) than jutting jaws and skintight spacesuits. But by the 1970s, Dick's characters were becoming even *less* heroic. And the deadpan humor which had frequently popped up in his fiction was increasingly laced with dark undercurrents of troubled doubt.

What was going on?

Simply the fact that, by the early 1970s, Philip K. Dick had hit a new low in his personal life.

Ten years earlier, the author had upped his amphetamine consumption to the point where he was composing sixty pages per day, a figure he felt would keep the money rolling in. But such punishing amounts of work (and stimulants) immediately led to a series of ever-worsening mental breakdowns. Then, although Dick had taken a fourth wife in 1966 (Nancy Hackett, who gave birth to a daughter, Isolde, in 1967), she left him in 1970, not long after Dick had been stricken with a near-fatal case of pancreatis.

The writer now plunged into deep despair. This, despite the fact that during the late sixties Dick's work had escaped from the science fiction ghetto and was being enthusiastically embraced by America's counterculture. Particularly popular were such works as "Faith of Our

Fathers" (in which God is not dead, just insane), *The Three Stigmata of Palmer Eldritch* (1965), thought by many to be *the* ultimate LSD novel, although Dick maintained he had never dropped acid either before or while writing the book, and *Ubik* (1969), in which the contents of a simple aerosol container literally sprayed away reality.

But this newfound audience hardly mattered to Dick—the *real* Philip K. Dick. After Hackett left him, Dick tried to drown his despair by actively pursuing an unsavory street life rife with narcotics, frequent LSD trips, and ongoing alcohol abuse. His lonely Santa Venetia home now became filled with junkies and parasitic hangers-on; he was also burdened with a crippling case of writer's block and escalating stress.

Then, on November 17, 1971, someone broke into Dick's home. Who, it was never discovered. Dick, however, had his own ideas; he was convinced the CIA did it. Now his paranoid depression rapidly escalated. About the only bright spot in Dick's life were his fifth wife (Tessa Busby, whom he married in 1973), and two new friends, K. W. Jeter and Tim Powers, up-and-coming young writers whom Dick had met at Cal State Fullerton in 1972.

That same year, Dick tried to kill himself.

Then came 1974 and a major event which would irrevocably alter his universe.

In February and March of 1974, the author abruptly experienced a series of intense, mystical visions which he likened to a "divine invasion." Dick was never sure of the meaning or origin of these apparitions. In fact, over the next eight years he would obsessively write a confidential, eight-thousand-page, million-word document called *Exegesis,* trying to rationalize those experiences.

Other visions and bizarre phenomena quickly followed. At one point the author was certain his consciousness was experiencing life in first-century Rome and twentieth-century California *simultaneously*, a supernatural superimposition that lasted for weeks. Dick also began having vivid, incredibly detailed dreams. He saw manifestations of St. Elmo's fire everywhere he looked; heard a soft, feminine voice counseling him in times of stress; "visited" an illusionary (though beatific) palm tree garden.

These otherworldly experiences finally ended on November 17, 1980. As detailed in "Philip K. Dick: The Other Side," an intriguing essay by Paul Rydeen originally published in *Crash Collusion Magazine #5,* Dick's final vision consisted of "A confrontation [with] God . . .

[which] led him to a series of infinite stacks of punched cards being generated each time [Dick] attempted to rationalize the vision. The only thing that could save him from this infinite information regress was to not rationalize it."

Which leads to an obvious question: Was it all a delusion or reality?

Dick himself was convinced he had been touched by God and furiously threw himself into a wholehearted study of philosophy and theology. At the same time, the author was honest—or canny—enough to insist he could never fully understand this phenomenon, since what we call God is, by its very nature, incomprehensible.

Heady stuff, indeed. But others were not so convinced. As fellow author John Brunner was quoted in *The Collected Stories of Philip K. Dick: Volume 3: The Father Thing* (Underwood-Miller, 1987): "At our last meeting [in 1977], in France during one of the Metz science fiction festivals, I . . . failed to figure out how literally [Dick] intended people to regard his claims about communicating with the Apostle Paul, or having killed a cat by willing it to death."

Certainly, Dick's visions and "invasions" were essentially religious ones. But they also had their dark side, to which this author can personally attest.

During 1980, 1981, and 1982, I repeatedly interviewed Philip K. Dick about his fiction and reactions to the then ongoing cinematic adaptation of *Electric Sheep*. Most of these conversations were invariably pleasant, informative ones, with Dick usually warm, charming, and strikingly articulate. That is, until our penultimate talk, at which time the person I was talking to in no way, shape, or form resembled the Philip K. Dick I'd come to enjoy and respect.

I'd telephoned Dick to follow up on a few, nonconfrontational facts: correct spellings, dates, that sort of thing. Yet from the moment Phil picked up the telephone he was suspicious, belligerent, and evasive. Indeed, it soon became clear to me that he wasn't drunk, or stoned—Dick didn't even know who I was, despite the fact that we'd already spent many hours on the phone and, indeed, had talked only a few days previously.

As our conversation awkwardly lumbered along, Dick became both increasingly bellicose and weirdly silent, sometimes within the course of the same sentence. This demeanor was so out of line, so completely at odds with his usual affability, that, strained and uncomfortable, I finally asked if I'd inadvertently done something to offend him.

Whereupon Phil immediately launched into an irrational, unrelated rant about government spies and lapsed Christians. By the time I hung up the phone a few seconds later, Dick was in a full-blown, paranoid rage.

A week later, I reluctantly called Dick back (I had to—I still needed those clarifications). This time it was as if the previous unpleasantness had never happened; Phil was again his friendly, forthcoming self. Which prompted me to (guardedly) ask what had set him off during our last conversation.

Phil couldn't recall what had angered him.

He was also firmly convinced that our earlier conversation had never taken place.

Again, let me hasten to repeat that this erratic behavior was far from Dick's norm. The "phildickian" personality I most often encountered (and try to remember) was the appealing, intelligent, fascinating one.

In any event, because of the mystical visions and bodiless voices which Dick experienced from 1974 to 1980, he soon found himself writing again, this time with a brand-new set of obsessions. His last three novels (called "The Valis Trilogy"), saw the author transmuting his usual concerns (what is real? what is human?) into complicated metaphysical inquiries. These explorations were mostly concerned with exploring the validity of religion; *Valis* and *The Divine Invasion* (both 1981), in particular, are suffused with near-obsessive quests to discover God.

Happily, Dick also cleaned up his personal act. Much good followed. By 1977, the author had renounced narcotics, and the same year saw publication of *A Scanner Darkly*, an excellent novel which purportedly recounted dire moments from Dick's own drug experiences plus his strong denunciation of the same.

In his last years, Phil Dick was virtually drug free (illicit substances never seemed to have qualitatively affected his fiction, though; besides, Dick once claimed that the only thing he ever wrote under the influence of LSD was a portion of the 1966 novel *The Unteleported Man*). Also pleasing was the manner in which Dick began attaining a modicum of fame during the latter part of his life.

Partly because of his new mystical/religious concerns, partly because of his early science fiction efforts, Philip K. Dick became lauded throughout Europe in the late 1970s and early 1980s, particularly in England and France. He also was the subject of many flattering articles and profiles in his own country, all while he was still alive to enjoy it.

Philip K. Dick's final novel was *The Transformation of Timothy Archer*. This thinly fictionalized account of certain events in the real life of Dick's friend Bishop James Pike was posthumously published in 1982, the year of Dick's death; ironically, the same year in which *Blade Runner* was released.

A film which, like the novel fourteen years earlier, asked a familiar Dickian question: "What constitutes an authentic human being?"

DO ANDROIDS DREAM OF ELECTRIC SHEEP

When *Do Androids Dream of Electric Sheep* was first published in 1968, it was definitely a child of its times. Released during the height of the Vietnam War, *Electric Sheep* was, according to its author, "written during a time when I thought we had become as bad as the enemy.

"Alongside *Martian Timeslip* and *The Man in the High Castle*," Dick told this author in 1981, "*Sheep* is one of my three favorite novels. I liked it very much. Although it's essentially a dramatic work, the moral and philosophical ambiguities it dealt with are really very profound; *Sheep* stemmed from my basic interest in the problem of differentiating the authentic human being from the reflexive machine, which I call an android. In my mind android is a metaphor for people who are physiologically human but behaving in a nonhuman way."

Dick first became interested in this problem while doing research for *The Man in the High Castle*. Given access to prime Gestapo documents in the closed stacks of the University of California at Berkeley, Dick discovered certain diaries scribed by SS men stationed in Poland. One sentence in particular had a profound effect on the author.

"That sentence read, 'We are kept awake at night by the cries of starving children,'" Dick explained. "There was obviously something wrong with the man who wrote that. I later realized that, with the Nazis, what we were essentially dealing with was a defective group mind, a mind so emotionally defective that the word 'human' could not be applied to them.

"Worse," Dick continued, "I felt that this was not necessarily a sole German trait. This deficiency had been exported into the world after World War II and could be picked up by people anywhere, at any time. You see, I wrote *Sheep* right in the middle of the Vietnam War, and at the time I was revolutionary enough and existential enough to believe that these android personalities were so lethal, so dangerous to human beings, that it ultimately might become necessary to fight them. The problem in this killing then would be, 'Could we not become like the androids, in our very effort to wipe them out?'"

Sheep was not the only work in which Dick dealt with this problem. Time and again would the author return to the amoral ambiguities embodied in the artificial human. For example, robots, simulacra, and androids figure prominently in short stories such as "Imposter," "Nanny," "The Father Thing," and "The Defenders." In 1973 the author himself delivered a now famous speech entitled "The Android and the Human" at the University of British Columbia in Vancouver, Canada.

Do Androids Dream of Electric Sheep, however, was the work which best explored Dick's conviction that love and compassion were the crucial differences between man and machine.

But what does this slim novel (216 pages in the current Del Rey paperback edition) have in terms of a plot?

Electric Sheep opens with a dedication "To Tim and Serena Powers, my dearest friends." The story proper then begins in a crumbling San Francisco largely devoid of human and animal life. The year is 1992 (a date changed by *Sheep*'s publisher, Ballantine Books, to 2019 after *Blade Runner*'s release to coincide with the time frame established by the film).

A nuclear conflict ("World War Terminus") has resulted in omnipresent radioactive dust. This substance has destroyed most animal life, caused many humans to either die or become mental defectives (called "chickenheads"), and is threatening the remaining population with slow sterility (in a touch of dry humor, the men of *Electric Sheep* wear lead codpieces to protect their virility). Those humans who can have left the Earth altogether to find better lives on other, unpolluted planets.

Enter Rick Deckard, who's not one of the lucky ones. A petty bureaucrat employed by the San Francisco Police Department (but *not* a policeman), Deckard hasn't the resources to afford a new life. He also has marital problems. His wife, Iran, despises the fact that Deckard makes his living as an official bounty hunter. "You're a murderer hired by the cops," she bitterly tells him, after the two awaken in their near-empty apartment building during the book's opening chapter.

In one sense, Iran is right. Deckard *is* licensed to kill the organic androids of this future society (or "andys," as they're called in the book), especially if they attempt to blend in with real humans. Limited by a four-year lifespan, equipped with all human emotions except empathy, these remorseless beings were known as "Synthetic Freedom Fighters" when initially designed as weapons during the prior nuclear conflict. Then the andys' functions were modified to become, in *Sheep*'s words, "the mobile donkey engine of the (Off-world) colonization program." Now their modifications have proliferated to the point where "the variety of subtypes passed all understanding, in the manner of American automobiles of the 1960s."

Unfortunately, relatively few andys try to pass for human. And Deckard can't seem to make a decent living executing the ones who do. So, depressed and money hungry, Deckard distracts himself while waiting for his next assignment.

One of these distractions is the "Penfield Mood Organ," an electronically-operated brain stimulator. This device allows people to dial up any emotion they wish (in a second moment of phildickian humor, Deckard surreptitiously programs the sullen Iran's own mood organ to "Setting 594—'pleased acknowledgment of husband's superior wisdom in all matters'"). Another of Deckard's distractions is the wildly popular television program, "Buster Friendly and His Friendly Friends," a perpetually playing news and talk show. Yet another is the "empathy box," a variety of mechanically-induced virtual reality (described by Dick long before such devices became fact) which endlessly reconstructs the final moments of Wilbur Mercer, a much-admired prophet who was stoned to death before his teachings gave rise to a form of mass-marketed religion named Mercerism.

But Deckard's greatest comfort—his pride and joy—is his robotic "electric" sheep. This "black-faced Suffolk ewe" is penned on the rooftop of Deckard's "ConApt" (condominium–apartment). And though Rick tends to it as lovingly as if it were the real thing, Deckard cannot help but recall the time he once owned a genuine sheep named Groucho. Sadly, Groucho is no more; after receiving a scratch from a small piece of barbed wire hidden in a bale of hay, the animal contracted tetanus and died.

Now Deckard is obsessed with the idea of scraping together enough money to buy another genuine woolbearing animal. But his fixation isn't a sentimental one—in this world, real animals are the ultimate status symbol, and Deckard desperately craves that status.

Deckard's dream suddenly seems attainable when his boss, Inspector Harry Bryant, informs the bounty hunter that eight advanced Nexus–6 andys—whose brains are "capable of selecting within a field of two trillion constituents, or ten million separate neural pathways"—have escaped from a Martian colony and are now hiding on Earth. Bryant further advises Deckard that Dave Holden, senior bounty hunter of Northern California, had managed to eliminate two of the androids before a third carved "a laser track in his spine." This leaves six Nexus–6 androids loose in San Francisco.

Would Deckard like to pick up where Holden left off?

Those familiar with *Blade Runner's* plot will have already noticed a striking number of differences between it and *Electric Sheep*. What's more striking, however, is how much of Dick's novel actually made it to the screen.

It is currently fashionable to state that Ridley Scott gouged the core from Philip Dick's book and threw away the rest. But this simply isn't true. For example, the scene of Deckard accepting Rachael as human before the Voigt-Kampff machine (also a Dickian invention) proves her otherwise was a moment first laid down in *Sheep*. So was the idea of a powerful genetic engineering corporation and the fact that the androids only have four-year lifespans. Furthermore, many *Sheep*

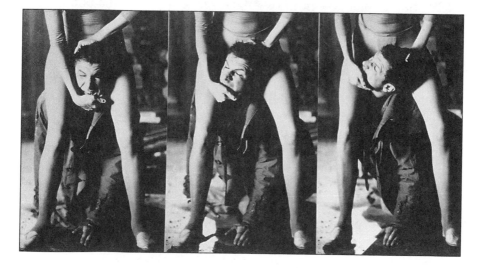

In this exciting montage, Deckard is nearly killed by the deadly thighs of Pris (Daryl Hannah). Pris and Deckard also battle in Do Androids Dream of Electric Sheep; *however, in the book, Deckard simply shoots her.*

character names were retained for *Blade Runner*, as were patches of the book's original dialogue.

Example: When Deckard in *Blade Runner* asks Rachael what she would do if she came across a photograph of a nude girl, Rachael sarcastically replies, "Is this testing whether I'm a replicant or a lesbian, Mr. Deckard?" The Rachael of *Sheep* says, "Is this testing whether I'm an android, or whether I'm homosexual?"—an almost word-for-word transcription of Dick's dialogue.

But these minor moments are nothing compared to the philosophical, ecological, and sociological concerns which *Blade Runner* faithfully transplanted from *Sheep*'s impassioned heart. Not only did Ridley Scott's film retain *Electric Sheep*'s original themes of paranoia (that huge staring eye at the film's beginning) and alienation (the cynical, disaffected Harrison Ford), it also condemned mankind's emotional sterility (Tyrell creates people for slave labor) while indicting humanity's misuse of the earth's natural resources (*BR*'s ever-present acid rain and absence of real animals).

In short, *Blade Runner* was most faithful to *Sheep* where it really counted.

Still, there's no denying the many *differences* between *BR* and Philip K. Dick's book. To begin with the obvious, Dick's novel is set in a 1992 San Francisco—not Los Angeles in 2019. And the population problem of Dick's universe is exactly the opposite of Ridley Scott's. *Sheep*'s San Francisco is *dis*inhabited, a near-vacant ghost town of eerily empty buildings and streets. Plus, the character of Deckard is also dissimilar, as his *Sheep* persona resembles a henpecked, petty bureaucrat, not a brooding, burned-out detective.

One could play this *Sheep* vs. *Blade Runner* game for pages, though. Perhaps it's more fruitful to point out that the greatest difference between Philip K. Dick's novel and Ridley Scott's film lies in this ironic fact: that what began as a militantly antiestablishment literary protest ultimately became a thoroughly capitalistic Hollywood production.

The metamorphosis from book to film, however, wasn't easy.

DEVELOPMENT

You would have to kill me and prop me up in the seat of my car with a smile painted on my face to get me to go near Hollywood.

—PHILIP K. DICK
FROM A CONVERSATION WITH PAUL M. SAMMON,
SEPTEMBER 25, 1980

"DO I LOVE HOLLYWOOD? NO."

As should be obvious from the above quotation, Philip K. Dick was not exactly a fan of the filmmaking industry. Yet his deep distaste for the movie community didn't spring from a naïve print author's arrogant ignorance of the filmmaking process. In fact, Phil Dick "touched base" with the film and television industries a number of times during his lifetime.

"Despite my personal reaction to that android factory I call Hollywood," Dick told this writer in 1980, "I must confess I do love *movies*. In fact, I have pay TV, and watch films all the time. I especially enjoy the work of directors like Scorcese, Altman, and De-Palma. At the same time, I always feel as if as if I'm at a cheap porno show when I watch a movie. So you could say I'm conflicted about the process.

Still, Philip K. Dick did attempt to author some feature films. In 1974, for example, he was commissioned by French director Jean-Pierre Gorin, who had worked with Jean-Luc Godard, to write a screenplay for a motion picture based on Dick's novel *Ubik*. "But then Gorin became ill with a liver ailment and had to give up the project," Dick pointed out. Yet even though the author's scenario was never made into a movie, it was eventually published, in 1985, as *Ubik, the Screenplay* by Corroboree Press.

Finally, *Ubik* and *Do Androids Dream of Electric Sheep* were not the only literary works of Philip K. Dick to be optioned while the author was still alive. This was made clear during my 1980 conversations with Dick, when *Electric Sheep*'s author indicated his excitement over two *other* upcoming adaptations.

One was the outright purchase (as opposed to simple optioning) of Dick's 1966 short story, "We Can Remember It for You Wholesale." This arrangement had resulted in a script being written under the title *Total Recall* by Dan (*Alien*) O'Bannon. The other pending adaptation was an option-only project tentatively titled *Claw*. Likewise scripted by O'Bannon, *Claw*'s plot had been based on Dick's 1953 novella "Second Variety."

Total Recall, of course, ultimately went on to become the 1990 box-office hit starring Arnold Schwarzenegger. And fifteen years after he wrote the first-draft script in 1980, Dan O'Bannon's *Claw* would be retitled *Screamers*, feature Peter (*RoboCop*) Weller in the leading role, and be released on January 26, 1996.

"But in both cases," Dick explained to me in 1981, "once the ink on the contracts was dry, no one from either the *Recall* or the *Claw* production companies made any attempt to keep me informed of their progress. That I found rather insulting. It's also one of the things I don't like about Hollywood.

"I do enjoy writing screenplays, though," Dick went on to say. "I would have even done one for *Blade Runner*, had they asked. But that enjoyment purely arises from a function of my being a novelist and short story writer. What I'm talking about is creating dialogue; I love to write dialogue, and since screenplays primarily consist of dialogue, that's why I would like to do more of them.

"But do I love Hollywood? No. Not in the least. In fact, I don't want to have any involvement with Hollywood."

A sentiment partly inspired, as we shall see, by Dick's negative experiences surrounding the years-long process of carrying his *Electric Sheep* to the screen.

THE FIRST OPTION ATTEMPTS

Blade Runner's long genesis from book to film began in 1969, the year after its source novel was first published. It was then that fledgling director Martin Scorcese and film critic/screenwriter Jay Cocks (cowriter of 1995's *Strange Days,* a dystopian science fiction film heavily influenced by *BR*), were both struck by *Sheep*'s visual and moral landscapes. Yet after evidencing an initial, partnered interest in Dick's book, Scorcese and Cocks never got around to optioning the novel. The final result was . . . nothing. Martin Scorcese/Jay Cocks' *Electric Sheep* adaptation became one more unrealized dream project in the blue sky of never-made Hollywood films.

Then, in 1974, *Sheep* actually *was* optioned. This deal was closed by Herb Jaffe Associates, Inc. Robert Jaffe, Herb's son, subsequently became the first person to pen an *Electric Sheep* screenplay. It was a scenario Philip Dick loathed.

"Jaffe's screenplay fell into my possession by accident," Dick pointed out. "The first thing I noticed was that he'd simplified my book by turning it into a straight action-adventure. While I wasn't pleased with that direction, I also wasn't surprised by it, given the nature of the source material. But what really bothered me was the fact that Jaffe had also turned *Do Androids Dream of Electric Sheep* into a comedy spoof, something along the lines of *Get Smart.* That was horrible. I suspect Robert felt that way too, because he wrote this script under a pen name.

"Anyway, Jaffe's screenplay was so terribly done I couldn't believe it was a shooting script," Dick continued. "Not long after I'd read it and expressed my displeasure, in fact, Robert flew down to Santa Ana to speak with me about the project. And the first thing I said to him when he got off the plane was, 'Shall I beat you up here at the airport, or shall I beat you up back at my apartment?' Robert asked me, 'Was the script that bad?' 'Yes it was,' I told him."

Yet despite his initial skepticism, *Sheep*'s author was surprised and heartened to then hear Jaffe say, "Maybe you can give me some ideas for improving the screenplay."

"We then spent a very enjoyable day together doing that," Dick concluded. "I found Robert to be a warm, affable, intelligent person. In fact, I enjoyed our day together so much I even allowed Jaffe Associates to renew their option on the book one more time."

By 1977, however, nothing further had occurred on the Jaffe front. "So they let their *Sheep* option lapse," Dick said. "Jaffe Associates went on to make *Demon Seed* instead, which I thought was a pretty decent picture."

Coincidentally, at the same time Jaffe Associates was involved with

Do Androids Dream of Electric Sheep, Philip K. Dick was approached by yet another person interested in optioning his novel.

Significantly, this man would become the prime force behind the alteration of Dick's literary *Electric Sheep* into Scott's film *Blade Runner*—not before spending six long years dealing with wariness, refusals, different studios, rotating directors, and constantly rewritten scripts, however.

This man's name?

Hampton Fancher.

ENTER HAMPTON FANCHER

Hampton Fancher was born in 1938. A casual, intelligent, and strikingly unpretentitous man, Fancher spent his early life pursuing a variety of exotic interests; poetry and dancing are two of them. However, it was ultimately upon the foundation of acting that Fancher chose to build his (first) career.

The secret heart of Blade Runner; *co-screenwriter and Executive Producer Hampton Fancher, circa 1980.*

Put under contract by Warner Brothers in the early 1960s, Hampton Fancher subsequently appeared in ten feature films—"mostly as a heavy," the former performer now notes. His cinematic credits included a turn in the wildly melodramatic Troy Donahue vehicle

Parrish (1961, with Fancher appearing as Karl Malden's son), *Rome Adventure* (1962, also with Donahue), and a number of films made in Europe. Fancher's final motion picture performance came in 1975, with *The Other Side of the Mountain.*

However, this performer was adept at other creative aspects of moviemaking. Hampton Fancher began writing screenplays when he was a teenager. He also made a series of self-financed 8mm and 16mm films, patiently learning the crafts of editing, directing, and producing, until his labors culminated in a prizewinning 35mm short, *Beach Parking,* made when he was twenty-one years old. But what about science fiction and *Blade Runner?*

"Prior to my involvement with Ridley Scott," Fancher explains, "I'd had very little exposure to science fiction. My literary tastes have always leaned more towards poetry or fine contemporary literature anyway. In fact, before *Blade Runner,* I'd only read two novels in the entire field of science fiction." One of these books was Alfred Bester's *The Stars My Destination,* a fifties SF classic which reworked and reset Alexander Dumas' *Count of Monte Cristo* in the far future.

The other was *Do Androids Dream of Electric Sheep.* Yet Fancher hadn't chosen to read *Sheep* out of a fascination with science fiction or the works of Philip K. Dick. Far from it, in fact.

"At that point, I hadn't even heard of Phil Dick," Fancher recalls. "But early in 1975, I did find myself in the unusual position of having ten thousand dollars in my pocket. I'd never had ten thousand dollars in my life before, and as I figured this would be the *last* ten thousand dollars I'd ever have, I thought, 'I've got to turn this money into something else. Maybe I should try optioning a literary property.'"

The first book Fancher thought of obtaining was William Burroughs' *Naked Lunch.* "But I knew I'd have to fly to New York to get in touch with Burroughs' agents," Fancher continues. "I just knew there was a good chance that those agents wouldn't let go of the book. Therefore, I thought the best way to maximize my New York trip was to have a *second* property in mind as a backup, in case *Naked Lunch* fell through. Which it did.

"Anyway, I began looking and calling around for other novels I could option. During that search I telephoned my best friend, Jim Maxwell, and asked him if he could think of any other books I might go after. Jim said, 'Yeah.'"

The novel Maxwell had recommended was *Do Androids Dream of Electric Sheep.* Taking his friend's advice, Fancher then tracked down an old paperback copy of *Sheep* and became excited. Not by the book's artistic concerns, however: Fancher initially responded to *Sheep*'s economic possibilities.

"Which sounds like a totally mercenary, typically Hollywood reaction," Fancher explains. "But you have to understand that I was going into this thing on a business level. I also like to think I'd had a fair amount of exposure to American literature and responded well to what I thought of as great books. *Electric Sheep*, although certainly a cut above the norm, *wasn't* a great book. Or at least I thought so at first. Here's why.

"One of the things I think fans of Philip K. Dick love about him," Fancher continued, "is his voice. It certainly is a unique one. But there's also something about Dick's artistic voice that bothers me. Not that Phil bothered me as a person; I was more than amused by him, and respected his brilliance. It's just that I wasn't sold on this particular book.

"Still, there was something about the *style* of *Electric Sheep* which I found engrossing. Its Kafkaesque quality. Its paranoia. There was also a bureaucratic weakness about its central character, Rick Deckard, which I thought felt much like Kafka. And I just basically *liked* this guy Deckard. He was so whipped. There was something kind of impotent about him, something that should have worn spectacles almost. He was thin blooded, in a way. His wife was against him and the world he lived in was dark and sewerlike and overrun with entropic ruins. Him floating through that world intrigued me very much.

"And to be fair I should also say that I liked the humor of *Electric Sheep*," Fancher went on. "Phil's satirical flourishes, like the Buster Friendly character, were terrific. But in terms of a book that you love, or one that becomes a part of your life . . . well, *Electric Sheep* wasn't that book. I never recommended it to my friends, and I'm constantly telling people to read certain books. It just didn't turn me on."

Then what besides humor, stylistic tricks, and the echoes of Franz Kafka *did* persuade Fancher to pursue his idea of turning *Do Androids Dream of Electric Sheep* into a motion picture?

"Two reasons, really," Fancher answered. "First, after I'd read it, I immediately saw a chase movie, with a detective after androids in a dystopic world. I thought, 'What a great idea for a science fiction film!' You must also keep in mind that I first read Phil's book in 1975, and in 1975, *Star Wars* wasn't even a gleam in George Lucas' eye. At the same time, there was this smell of science fiction in Hollywood, and I had the gut feeling that science fiction was going to happen in a big way, just like cowboy movies had happened."

The second reason Fancher pursued *Sheep* was his hope that optioning the novel would offer him a chance to attain a long-cherished goal. "Prior to my involvement in *Blade Runner*, I'd sort of been this frustrated underground filmmaker who'd also acted, but who'd never had the opportunity to get anything he'd written or really wanted to direct into production," Fancher explained. "I had learned, though, that one way of doing this was by acquiring a property studios would think was commercial. *Do Androids Dream of Electric Sheep*, with its story hook of a bounty hunter chasing androids, seemed commercial enough to me. Which is why I decided to option the book, really.

"But then I changed my mind about *Sheep* being a property that I could maybe write or direct. At the time, I decided that that sounded too much like wishful thinking. It also made my ultimate authorship of the *Blade Runner* script kind of ironic. Because originally, the only way I felt I'd ever get something like *Sheep* going in Hollywood was to be solely attached to it as a *producer*."

With the few dollars he had left in his pocket, Fancher now took a stab at optioning *Do Androids Dream of Electric Sheep*. Almost immediately, the process became a frustrating one.

"First I tried to get hold of Philip K. Dick himself," Fancher said. "But I had no idea of where to start. Later I found that it was just about impossible to learn anything about him. I even flew to New York to talk to Phil's agents. They were sympathetic, but they weren't much help."

Returning to Los Angeles, Fancher was ready to give up his Dick hunt when he accidentally bumped into noted science fiction/fantasy author Ray Bradbury, a man whom he'd met once before. During the course of their conversation, Fancher mentioned the difficulties he was having in finding *Sheep*'s author. To his amazement, Bradbury then withdrew a small telephone/address book from his pocket and gave Fancher Philip K. Dick's home phone number.

"Right away," Fancher relates, "the next day, in fact, I called Phil about the book and we set up an appointment to meet in his apartment. He was living in Santa Ana, then; this was still 1975."

Dick and Fancher's first meeting was mostly an amiable one (as were two subsequent encounters, all of which lasted between five and six hours). But Fancher would also sense ambiguous undercurrents during his visits with Dick.

"Actually, we got along very well," Fancher recalled for my 1982 *Cinefantastique* article about *Blade Runner*. "I liked Phil and I think he liked me. He was a lot of fun, kept coming up with these real zingers. At one point he even talked about casting the movie; I can remember Phil telling me he thought Victoria Principal would make the perfect Rachael.

"But—well, I'd be lying if I didn't say that there were also some things about Philip I found difficult. For instance, he could be manic, or self-reverential, or solipsistic.

"Right from the beginning, Phil was very evasive about anything to do with *Do Androids Dream of Electric Sheep*," Fancher explains. "Instead, he kept pushing other things on me, like *Flow My Tears, The Policeman Said*. I also had the feeling Phil thought I was some sort of Hollywood hustler. There was this sort of elusive wariness about him, a certain suspiciousness. This funny way he had of being pleasant yet sort of insulting at the same time. I tried to ignore that. Tried to get across the point that I was just a filmmaker interested in adapting his book, because I thought it'd make an interesting motion picture. In fact, I even mentioned that I really didn't have a handle on how to do an adaptation, and maybe Phil could do one, or make some suggestions along those lines. I was that naïve!

"But not only did Dick seem reluctant to get involved, he also appeared reluctant to have that particular book of his done. At that time Phil seemed, more and more, to be just totally uninterested in becoming involved with any kind of film projects."

What Fancher did not realize—and what Dick himself would later tell this author—was that the science fiction writer was also operating under a limiting set of preconceptions.

"I don't think Hampton realized I was as naïve about Hollywood as he was," Dick explained to me in 1981. "Although I got to like him very much, I don't think he ever understood that, when it came to Hollywood, I cringed. I had an automatic flinch reaction. Putting it on an anthropological basis, I represented the tribe of novelists and short story writers, while Hollywood represents the tribe that makes movies. I look at their tribe and their customs completely baffle me. I'm sure they look on me with the same confusion."

Discouraged by Dick's evasiveness and his own lack of headway, Fancher now let all *Sheep* matters drop. Ironically, what the ex-actor hadn't known (or forgotten, as Dick pointed out to this author), was that the novel had *already* been optioned by Jaffe Associates. "Maybe Hampton's memory failed him on this point," Dick would later say to me.

In any event, the end result was still the same: once again, it looked as if *Do Androids Dream of Electric Sheep* would never be adapted into a motion picture.

BRIAN KELLY CARRIES THE BALL ⸻

Two years after Hampton Fancher's meetings with Philip K. Dick, the budding producer would find those *Electric Sheep* unexpectedly bleating their way back into his life.

"In 1977," Fancher recalled, "I was about to go on a long trip when I ran into an old actor friend of mine, Brian Kelly, who starred in the TV show *Flipper*. Now, Brian had ambitions of becoming a producer, and he was looking around for a suitable property. Recalling my past fondness for Dick's novel, I told Brian, 'Why don't you try optioning this book called *Do Androids Dream of Electric Sheep.*'"

Intrigued, Kelly proceeded to do just that.

"I read it," recounts Kelly, "and thought, 'Whoa, wait a minute!' Then I read it again. Then I called Hampton and said, 'Let's meet.' We did and I said, 'Look, how do you really feel about this book?' Hamp said, 'Very strongly.' So I said, 'Okay, let's see what I can do about that.'"

What happened next came as a surprise to everyone involved, especially to Hampton Fancher, who'd fought so hard to option the book a few years before. As Fancher told interviewers Randy and Jean-Marc Lofficier in *Starlog* magazine ("Detective Future Past: Hampton Fancher Interview," November 1992, #184): "[So] I just mentioned [*Do Androids Dream of Electric Sheep*] to him, saying to do it if he could. [And Brian] succeeded rapidly! I guess Dick needed the money. There was nothing like what I went through."

Kelly agrees that his acquiring *Sheep* went smoothly, but adds, "I never met Philip Dick. Never talked to him, either. Instead, I strictly went the legal way. Had my attorney draw up a certain amount of papers, sent those off to Dick's attorney, and that attorney showed them to Phil. And lo and behold, Dick said okay. It was that easy."

Of course, by this time (1977), the Jaffe Associates option on *Sheep* had also lapsed, clearing the way for Kelly and Fancher's overtures. But whatever the reason, Dick accepted Kelly's option fee of $2000, and the former *Flipper* star now owned the motion picture rights to Philip K. Dick's novel.

The next step lay in deciding which methods seemed best for producing that motion picture.

TREATMENT AND PITCHES

Late in 1977, Brian Kelly began thinking of different ways to get his nascent *Sheep* film off the ground.

One of his first inspirations was to take the book to English producer Michael Deeley. "Michael and I had worked on a couple of pictures together in Europe before my accident," Kelly explained. "One was this cocaine smuggling story with Michael Caine called *The Brazil Story*. And after that, Deeley and I stayed in touch."

So the former actor approached the English producer with Dick's novel, told Deeley that Kelly owned the rights, and insisted that Deeley read the book. Deeley did—and promptly turned Kelly down.

The reason? Deeley felt that Dick's complex concepts would not adequately translate to film.

"After Brian took the book to Michael Deeley," clarifies Hampton Fancher, "he came back and told me that Deeley had read it and said the property was unfilmable. I actually understood that point of view; a professional filmmaker used to clarity and straightforward narrative would probably find *Sheep* maddeningly vague, or ambiguous. But then Brian surprised me. He went on to say that Michael had actually *liked* the novel; Deeley just hadn't seen how anyone could turn it into a movie.

"By then," Fancher continues, "I was so familiar with Phil's book I'd already formulated a few ways I thought somebody else could adapt *Sheep*. I was right in the middle of telling them to Brian when he suddenly interrupted me and said, 'Hold it—why don't you write these things down?'"

Persuaded by Kelly to set his thoughts on paper, Fancher now began composing a series of notes on Dick's book, ideas which Kelly eagerly passed on to Deeley.

Deeley looked them over—and passed on the project again.

At this point, Fancher says, "I was beginning to feel bad about involving Brian in this thing. So I wrote an eight-page outline of the novel, basically a simplification of the book."

Once again, Kelly brought the final result to Deeley. Once again, the producer turned Kelly down.

"By now, Brian was becoming upset," Fancher said. "And I was starting to feel even worse about suggesting that Brian option *Sheep* in the first place."

However, even though he had repeatedly negated the idea of turning *Do Androids Dream of Electric Sheep* into a film, the presentation of Fancher's eight-page summation now prompted Deeley to dangle a tantalizing offer before the budding screenwriter. "Mike was becoming more and more interested in the book," Kelly recalls, "and more impressed with what Hampton was doing with it. Then, after passing on Hampton's treatment, Mike said something that I took as an indirect way of telling me that the door was still open for us; he suggested we get together some sort of screenplay based on the book."

This was all the encouragement Kelly needed. He immediately came back to Fancher and argued that, since Fancher was a writer, and since Fancher was the one most familiar with Dick's book, it was only logical that Fancher should also be the one to compose the first *Electric Sheep* screenplay.

"But I didn't want to do it," Fancher points out. "And I refused at first. Remember, I'd gone into this project as a producer, not a writer. I *never* wanted to do that screenplay myself."

Kelly, however, wouldn't listen.

"When Hampton told me he didn't want to write the *Electric Sheep* screenplay, I said to him, 'Well, what are you reading it for then, if you don't want to write it?' I kept after him about that."

However, the person who would ultimately have the most to do with persuading Hampton Fancher to write a screenplay based on *Do Androids Dream of Electric Sheep* was Barbara Hershey.

"Barbara and I were close at that time," Fancher recalls, "and she kept saying I should do the screenplay, too. Brian had something to do with it, sure, but it was really Barbara Hershey who convinced me that writing a script was the only way to get this project off the ground. She kept saying, 'If you believe this is what you want to do, and if you want to make it happen, why don't you write it?'

"I tried telling Barbara I'd only seen myself as a producer on this project, and besides, this was going to be the first major screenplay I'd ever written! But she didn't care about those excuses, and I finally caved in."

At this point Fancher began negotiating with Kelly over credits and fees. "Basically, I made a fifty-fifty deal with Brian," Fancher recalls. "Since I'd already put so much work into this thing and was going to write the screenplay as well, I wanted to share an Executive Producer credit with him. Brian had no problem with that. That's when I sort of groaned and got to work on the first draft script."

"After Hampton finally agreed to do the *Sheep* screenplay," Kelly continues, "and I put him under contract to write it for me, he wrote and he wrote and he wrote. It took him a year, all of 1978 to finish the first draft, but he did all right on that thing."

"In one sense, Brian was just as involved with that first draft as I was," Fancher points out. "During the year it took me to write that spec script, he paid my rent and came over all the time to offer encouragement and was an audience to my writing every week. Really, Brian was the one who made that whole process possible."

"But it was *Hampton* who created the script," Kelly concludes. "And it was a pretty good one, too. So good that as soon as it was finished, I tucked Hamp's screenplay under my arm, pointed myself towards the West Side of Los Angeles, and ran it over to Michael Deeley."

THE PRODUCER: MICHAEL DEELEY ─────────────

Fancher's first screenplay bore the same title as Dick's novel, *Do Androids Dream of Electric Sheep* (not *Android* or *The Android,* as some other journalists—this one included—have erroneously stated). The man Brian Kelly was rushing to see with that script was Michael Deeley.

Born in 1931, Deeley had still been in his twenties when he cut his cinematic teeth by editing the entertaining, British-made CBS television series *The Adventures of Robin Hood* (1955–1959, starring Richard Greene). He then became a producer with his first film, a ten-minute 1956 "Goon Show" short starring Peter Sellers, titled *The Case of the Mukkinese Battlehorn.*

Deeley next produced such full-length features as *Robbery* (1967), *The Italian Job* (1969), *Murphy's War* (1970), *The Wicker Man*

(1973), *The Man Who Fell to Earth* (1975), *Nickelodeon* (1976), and *Convoy* (1978). For a time, Deeley also ran British Lion and was an upper-echelon executive at the powerful English entertainment conglomerate Thorn-EMI; he also was the producer of Michael Cimino's controversial 1978 Vietnam War hit *The Deer Hunter*, which garnered five Academy Awards (including Best Picture).

"I remember carrying Hampton's screenplay up to these offices Michael had in Beverly Hills," Brian Kelly continues. "I knocked on his door, went in and dropped the script on Deeley's desk. And I said, 'Mike, read this thing. Read it this weekend, and give me an answer by Monday. 'Cause I've got seventeen other places that want to do it.'

"Well, I didn't really have seventeen other places, of course. Mike knew that, and I knew that he knew that I knew that he knew that. Still, Michael had enough trust in me to read this thing. He must have really liked it, too, because he called me up that Sunday and said, 'You've got a deal.'"

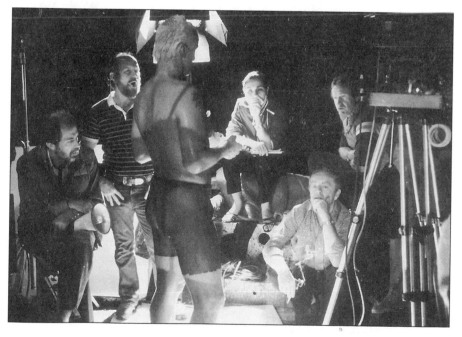

On the final night of filming, producer Michael Deeley (seated lower right, with cigarette) watches "Roy Batty" (Rutger Hauer, holding dove, center, back to camera) rehearse Batty's death scene. The dove in Hauer's hands was supposed to fly off-camera. However, the bird was too wet and couldn't fly as planned, so a pick-up shot was later filmed with another bird in England.

It was now the winter of 1978. After years of effort, Fancher and Kelly had finally completed the second step in their journey of bringing Dick's novel to the screen. However, even though Michael Deeley was at this time a hot commodity due to the success of his *Deer Hunter*, there were still many steps to go.

But what exactly attracted Deeley to the *Sheep* project in the first place? When this author posed that question in 1980 to the elegant, patrician Englishman who would eventually become *Blade Runner*'s producer, Deeley replied in this manner:

"It first caught my interest while I was reading the novel—and I did read it, by the way, all the way to the end. What I discovered was this marvelous blending of a thriller with a romance. There was also a dramatic moral problem at the heart of the book, the idea that this sanctioned executioner was becoming emotionally attracted to the one he's supposed to kill. That aspect enormously appealed to me. If you were to cast it in another genre and time period, *Do Androids Dream of Electric Sheep* could almost have been something like a World War II concentration camp movie. With a heartless Nazi commandant falling in love with his beautiful Jewish prisoner.

"Frankly, however," Deeley continued, "what ultimately sold me on the project was Hampton Fancher's script. I've read a lot of screenplays and produced a lot of pictures, but Fancher's script really was the most driving and interesting and original piece of writing I'd ever seen. That sort of ultimately pulled in Ridley Scott, as well. And he's not an easy person to seduce by writing, I'll tell you."

With much-praised screenplay and producer in hand, Fancher and Kelly now launched themselves into the next phase of traditional feature development: finding the right director, and studio, to both create and finance that feature.

IV

THE DIRECTOR
AND THE DEAL

Director Ridley Scott's follow-up to ALIEN has been set: BLADE RUNNER, based on Philip K. Dick's DO ANDROIDS DREAM OF ELECTRIC SHEEP, budgeted at $13 to $15 million by producer Michael Deeley for Filmways Pictures.

—"BLADE RUNNER: BOASTS
'HEAVY METAL LOOK,' RIDLEY SCOTT HELMS."
ARTICLE BY "P. B. BEENE" (PSEUDONYM FOR PAUL M. SAMMON)
CINEFANTASTIQUE MAGAZINE VOL. 10, #3
(WINTER 1980)

By late 1978, Michael Deeley had begun submitting Hampton Fancher's adaptation of *Do Androids Dream of Electric Sheep* to a number of different studios and film directors. "Michael was a bear on that," Fancher recalls. "He kept hustling my script all over town, getting more and more involved in trying to make this thing happen."

But what of the film's other executive producer, Brian Kelly?

"Brian was the originator of this whole enterprise," Deeley recalls. "It was he who brought Hampton in, and he deserves all the credit for that. He also deserves credit for being among the first people to recognize the validity of Dick's novel as a motion picture. Brian saw that, he really did. But to be honest, during the actual production, there was nothing for him to do. At that point it was all about just trying to keep the damn thing alive. That was my job."

Kelly, then, had fulfilled his prime function. Yet what were the deals Michael Deeley was now trying to cut? And what was it—what was it *exactly*—he was trying to sell?

FANCHER'S FIRST SCRIPT

"It was a little strange how quickly I became protective of my screenplay," answers Hampton Fancher. "As I've said, my initial attempts to option Philip's novel had strictly been a commercial maneuver. I'd thought the basic idea of a bounty hunter chasing androids in the future a clever tent pole on which to peg a movie. Now I was starting to realize that there must have been something else in the novel, something that subconsciously touched my heart. Because once I'd proven to Deeley, through Brian Kelly, that *Sheep* could be a viable motion picture, I became increasingly attached to my screenplay. *Emotionally* attached."

Despite Fancher's initial fidelity to Dick's novel, however, numerous modifications were inserted into the first draft as well.

As Fancher told Randy and Jean-Marc Lofficier in *Starlog* #184, November 1992, "I didn't really create much of a world [in the initial screenplay]. You could have pretty much taken my first draft and put it on a (theatrical) stage. There weren't many exterior scenes, there wasn't much hardware. It was basically a small drama, [one originally projected to be] done for $9 million."

Hampton Fancher's first BR *script portrayed Deckard as a "bespectacled bureaucrat," a far cry from the world-weary character played by Harrison Ford.*

Fancher's first-draft revisions included changing the novel's San Francisco locales to Los Angeles, downplaying the role of Deckard's wife Iran, and building up the part of Rachael, who now became Deckard's girlfriend. The character of Deckard himself was also tweaked. "At first I was going along with the Deckard of the book," Fancher remembers. "But as I wrote that first draft, I dug deeper into his defeated side, made Deckard more the bespectacled bureaucrat."

In retrospect, the one thing Fancher feels he *didn't* provide for his initial screenplay was an important piece of character motivation. "It sounds really foolish now," Fancher explains, "but at first, I didn't have a good reason for the androids to be on earth! They were just loose cannons, walking around whacking people."

Of all the various elements which would subsequently be altered or dropped from Fancher's first draft, however, the one he still feels most strongly about can be summarized in one word: ecology.

"At the time I wrote my first *Sheep* screenplay, I'd become increasingly alarmed about environmental matters," said the writer/producer. "Every day I was thinking, 'Where are the owls? Where are the trees? Where is our fresh water?' So those ecological concerns became critical to the first draft and, in fact, crucial to that draft's original ending.

"What I'd done was portray Deckard as becoming more and more disillusioned by the events of the story. This came to a head near the end, when Rachael killed herself by stepping off the roof of Deckard's apartment. At that point, he went kind of crazy and wandered out into this desert to commit suicide.

"Deckard just keeps walking until he drops. Then he's lying in the sand, almost too weak to move. Near his head is this turtle that's somehow been turned over and can't right itself. Deckard watches that turtle struggle for a long time. Finally, it does flip itself over, and the turtle scuttles away. Deckard takes heart from this; he staggers up and begins to walk back to where he came from.

"Then we came to the last shot in that script. It was a long pullback. It began by receding from Deckard until he was just a tiny dot, then you saw a satellite photo of the lush, beautifully blue planet that is Earth. And then you pulled back from that until you were lost in the cosmos. Fadeout.

"Everyone loved that ending," Fancher recalls with a sigh. "We all cried over it."

ROBERT MULLIGAN, UNIVERSAL PICTURES,————
AND CBS FILMS

Love it or not, Fancher soon found himself engaged in numerous rewrites as Deeley's search for a corporate *Sheep* sponsor began in earnest. "Most of that was rewriting cosmetic stuff, at least at first," Fancher recalls. "Deeley's chief concern was the title. He thought the studios might put up some resistance to something called *Do Androids Dream of Electric Sheep*, so Michael wanted me to change it before the script made the rounds in Hollywood."

At this point, in early 1979, Fancher was working with Deeley at the producer's home on Cape Cod. It was here that a second-draft screenplay was shaped, one given the title *Android*. Then, a short time later, Fancher traveled to London to continue working on his script. It was there that the screenplay which had started out as *Do Androids Dream of Electric Sheep* received its third title: *Mechanismo*.

"I actually stole that from this beautifully illustrated English paperback which was out at the time," Fancher explains. "*Mechanismo* was this gorgeous coffee-table thing, an art book chock-full of futuristic illustrations and newspaper articles and an index with all these impossible words in it. But then we discovered we couldn't get the rights to that. So *Mechanismo* got changed to *Dangerous Days*, which became the fourth title of the script."

By now, Michael Deeley had been marketing various drafts of Fancher's screenplays to as many potential buyers as the producer felt was proper. "Which was when something peculiar happened," Fancher continues. "The response we were getting from the studios was that they liked the script. They really did. But they also didn't think the story would be an interesting one to the world."

Help in countering studio resistance, however, suddenly arose from an unexpected quarter.

"From Gregory Peck, of all people," Fancher says. "Peck had somehow got one of my scripts and read it. Then he dashed off this letter to the MPAA and a few studios which said, in effect, 'This picture must be made!' But Peck didn't do that because he wanted to act in it. He sincerely felt that the script's themes of conscience and ecology were important ones.

"Peck wrote a whole page along those lines . . . under his own letterhead. He later gave a copy of that letter to Michael Deeley, to use as Deeley saw fit. What a wonderful, altruistic thing to do."

Meanwhile, as rewrites continued, Fancher, Deeley, and Kelly were engaged in an intensified search for a director to attach to their nascent film. They'd been joined in this pursuit by Katy Haber, a tough-minded, personable, thoroughgoing professional who'd begun her cinematic career as an assistant to director Sam Peckinpah. Haber was now working with Michael Deeley; the two had met during production of Peckinpah's *Convoy* (1978), which Deeley had produced, and both had recently suffered through what Deeley calls "the incredible ordeal of making [the Oscar-winning] *The Deer Hunter* together."

In Hampton Fancher's words, Katy Haber (who, like Deeley, is also English), would soon become "one of the few truly indispensable people on *Blade Runner*. Katy remembered everything, she was there for everything, and she helped make everything happen." At this early stage of *BR*'s genesis, however, Haber herself recalls that "Michael and Hampton and Brian Kelly and I were mainly watching a lot of films, trying to catch whoever was new or exciting out there. In other words, we were trying to find *Blade Runner*'s director."

Among the numerous nominees under consideration at this point were directors Adrian Lyne (*Fatal Attraction*), Michael Apted (*Gorillas in the Mist*), and Ridley Scott. "But nothing was happening," Fancher said. "Either these guys all passed on the project, or—and initially I lumped Ridley in with this second category—or else they were visually interesting but not the type of director I thought could do the kind of film I was envisioning. In fact, about the only guy I liked during this period was Bruce Beresford, the Australian director. I'd seen his *Breaker Morant* (1979) and been knocked out by that."

Beresford was unavailable. Yet unbeknown to the fledgling *Blade Runner* team, the first director to actually become attached to Fancher's screenplay was just around the corner. And he came their way almost by accident.

"I was over at this friend's house where I caught a film called *Bloodbrothers* (1978)," Fancher recalls. "It was about these big-city construction workers. And when I saw the passion and the interplay between the actors in that picture, I thought, 'Holy shit! Who directed this thing?! This could be our guy!'"

The "guy" transpired to be Robert Mulligan—a director who, to those familiar with film history, might seem an odd first choice for a downbeat *future noir* thriller like *Blade Runner*. Mulligan's prior claim to fame had been through such prestigious "relationship movies" as *To Kill a Mockingbird* (1962), *Up the Down Staircase* (1967), and *Summer of '42* (1971).

"Mulligan seemed like a dark horse to me, too," Fancher concedes. "I never would have thought of him to begin with. But he responded very well to the *Dangerous Days* script Deeley sent him. Also, my screenplay at that point was more of a 'relationship movie' anyway. The love affair between Deckard and Rachael was a lot softer. All of which, I think, appealed to Mulligan." Something must have appealed to the director, because on August 17, 1979, Robert Mulligan agreed to work with Deeley in developing Fancher's screenplay.

While Mulligan may have seemed an offbeat choice for *Dangerous Days*, choosing him offered possibilities beyond the director's chair. For instance, Mulligan had professional ties with Universal Pictures, which now expressed a (cautious) interest in Fancher's screenplay. Since Deeley still had not yet secured financing for his project, this Mulligan/Universal partnership must have looked promising.

"Having both a director and a studio attracted to this thing was very important to us," explains Fancher. "Although everyone seemed to like the scripts, we also kept hearing what we'd heard before—that my screenplays were just too unconventional for most Hollywood people. Obviously, then, the only way we were going to insure the value of this project was to have a name director and studio attached."

Fancher and Mulligan now set about reshaping the material to suit the director's personal tastes. "Overall, that collaboration was initially encouraging," Fancher remembers. "Mulligan was intelligent and very enthusiastic." But a larger number of negative factors soon crept into the equation, ultimately derailing the arrangement.

"Mulligan's was a very brief encounter," Katy Haber said. "He tried to take the material in a different direction from where Michael and Hampton thought it should go."

Fancher: "I did do one rewrite for Mulligan, but we didn't spend that much time together. Maybe two weeks, all told, spread out over three and a half months."

According to Michael Deeley, "The Mulligan relationship never really got off the ground. After we'd met—and I only met with him two times—it became pretty plain that we didn't all have a similar view as to what the material was. It wasn't his sort of picture anyway, and I guess in truth he wasn't my sort of director.

"What I'd found originally encouraging was that Mulligan really responded to the romantic relationship between Deckard and

Rachael. That was much stronger and deeper at this point. In fact, I would have welcomed him developing the material along those lines, because that's what had initially attracted me to Hampton's script in the first place. But then it seemed Mulligan *wasn't* as interested in the romantic angle as I'd thought. In truth, I never managed to really find out *what* direction he wanted to take the script in. It almost seemed as if it was more an issue of power or control that he was looking for. Which is fine. Control is okay for directors. But at that early stage, when I had $120,000 of my own money in this thing, I wasn't looking to hand it over to somebody else who'd try to shape it to their vision.

"Basically, we just weren't right for each other. That was a mutual feeling, by the way. It wasn't just us who thought that."

Nonetheless, the Mulligan relationship sustained itself long enough to produce some interesting consequences. "Other things that started happening around that time included some problems with Universal," Fancher continues. "The studio was never really willing to commit to our picture, and at the same time, they couldn't agree with us on a production budget. Universal also started insisting on a happy ending. Mulligan, to his credit, resisted that. So did I. In fact, at one point, Mulligan even suggested we pull a fast one on the studio by writing a bogus happy ending for them. Then we'd go out and shoot the ending *we* wanted."

Fancher actually did write a new ending to the Universal/*Dangerous Days* script for Robert Mulligan. It was a process, he now says, which "thrilled and terrified me like no other; careerwise, I'd never had an experience like that before."

Days' new climax dumped Fancher's original "cosmic pullback," (one which BR's writer/executive producer continued to try and retain past this point), and instead substituted "something like a shootout at the O.K. Corral. The Sebastian character got tossed out the window of his apartment by Roy Batty, Deckard came in and killed Roy, and Rachael showed up and waited for Deckard outside the building. When he came out, they linked arms and walked off together into the night. The end. All that was a smokescreen for the original, ecological ending we still intended to shoot."

This ruse became a moot point, however, when, on December 3, 1979, Robert Mulligan pulled out of *Dangerous Days*. Deeley next approached another production company which he hoped could get his stubbornly resistant project off the ground. This was CBS Films, an offshoot of the CBS television network, which had come into being solely to produce theatrical features.

Once again, things looked promising. CBS Films was then being headed by Donald March and Nancy Hardin, who would have the most to do with their company's *Dangerous Days* involvement. Also at CBS Films was Ron Yerxa, who "really loved *Dangerous Days*. It was very well-written. I actually met with Hampton Fancher at a restaurant on Beverly Glen and Mulholland to discuss his script one day; I recall him driving up in this eye-catching black speedster. I also remember getting a letter from Michael Deeley stating how proud Deeley was to be attached to this project.

"The economic beauty of Hampton's *Dangerous Days* script," Yerxa continues, "was that his futuristic Los Angeles looked pretty much like it does today. You even had some used-car salesmen around, except now they were selling animoids. I also remember a nice bit where everyone in the script was excited because the last living polar bear had just been found up near the North Pole.

"Now, as for the design, which is what everybody remembers about *Blade Runner*, at that time there was some implied devastation in the *Dangerous Days* script. But it was small-scale. Which was good, because CBS Films was a small outfit. The *Days* screenplay I read and liked didn't have any of the elaborate detailing Ridley Scott later brought to it.

"In fact, it was Ridley who later made CBS Films drop out of *Dangerous Days*. I don't mean that in any pejorative sense, because we'd already been developing *Days* for some months when Ridley came aboard. But with his arrival our potential budget outlay started creeping up towards the $11 million mark. That was because Ridley began bringing in all these different production design ideas and changing the look of it.

"*Dangerous Days* finally just got too rich for CBS Films. So we reluctantly had to pass on it."

Undaunted by the CBS Films pullout (which occurred at the end of February 1980), and dismissing it as "a situation that never came to anything," Deeley again resumed his quest for a *Dangerous Days* patron. But the loss of Robert Mulligan, Universal, and CBS Films essentially meant that Deeley, Fancher, Kelly, and Haber had been pushed back to square one.

Ironically, it was while this quartet had first been starting out from square one—in late April 1979—that Michael Deeley had sent Fancher's *Android* script to the man who would finally become the project's long-sought director.

A man who would initially turn the project down.

THE DIRECTOR: RIDLEY SCOTT —————————————

The story behind Ridley Scott's refusal and later acceptance of *Blade Runner* is a fairly complex one. It involves Italian film producers, American cult novels, and a death within Scott's own family. This complicated process began simply enough, however; Ridley Scott had always been Michael Deeley's first choice as the perfect director for Fancher's script.

Part of Deeley's reasoning undoubtedly included the fact that Scott was then a red-hot property, due to the 1979 smash success of *Alien*. Yet *Blade Runner*'s producer had other motives for pursuing Scott, as well. As Deeley himself told me in mid-1980, when this author asked him if he had any reasons for pursuing Scott beyond the obvious commercial ones, "Tell me of another director with that visual quality and that scale. Sure, you can look at something like *Heaven's Gate* and see how beautiful it is, despite all the controversy surrounding it. But even *Heaven's Gate* doesn't have the scale Ridley could have given it. At the moment, I think he has the best eye for moviemaking in the world."

The man with "the best eye for moviemaking in the world" was born in 1937 (and not 1939, as reported in many other sources), in South Shields, Tyne and Wear, England. Scott was raised in London, Cumbria, Wales, and Germany, before returning to northeast England to live in Stockton-on-Tees. According to the Ridley Scott biography released with the original *Blade Runner* press kit (which also gets his birthdate wrong), Scott, as a child, "showed little scholastic aptitude for any subject but art, so his parents encouraged him to study at West Hartpool College of Art. He excelled at painting and went on to the prestigious Royal College of Art in London, with the idea of becoming a stage designer."

While at the RCA, Scott also studied drawing, an interest which had followed him from childhood. The director still draws and paints today; as Scott points out, "these abilities are invaluable to the film-making process. A sketch is infinitely more useful than the best two-hour story conference."

But it was also while studying at the Royal College that Ridley Scott first became involved in filmmaking. After finding an old 16mm Bolex movie camera in a school cupboard, the ginger-haired budding film-maker next joined the RCA's newly formed film school. Cinema then supplanted painting as Scott's primary passion.

Director Ridley Scott (left, back to camera) rehearses Ford for the sequence where Deckard attempts to leap between two roofs . . .

. . . and the final sequence as it appears in the finished film.

His first film was a short which Scott wrote, directed, and photographed. Its title? *Boy on a Bicycle*, a brief tyro effort which starred Scott's younger brother Tony, now a director in his own right, with *Top Gun* and *Crimson Tide* among his credits.

Bicycle's plot concerned Tony's dramatic encounter with a madman, played by Ridley Scott's own father. The budget for this initial effort was a princely £65, or $100 (US). After a screening at the British Film Institute, however, the BFI forwarded a grant of another £250 to "refine" the project, and Ridley Scott was on his directorial way.

After graduating from the Royal College of Art, Ridley Scott won a traveling scholarship in design, which took him to New York. There he worked for Bob Drew Associates, where he experimented in photography and observed theater and documentary filmmakers at work. After returning to London, Scott then joined the staff of the British Broadcasting Company in 1964, first as a set designer, then as a director for such popular English television programs as *The Informer* and *Z-Cars* (pronounced "Zed-Cars"). In 1967, Scott left the BBC and crossed over into advertising. He subsequently founded Ridley Scott Associates (an ongoing concern today), under whose banner he personally supervised the direction of over 2000 commercials, many of which have been award winners.

The Duellists, based on a Joseph Conrad novella and originally conceived for French television through the auspices of France's Technisonor company, was Scott's first feature film. Starring Keith Carradine and Harvey Keitel, it was produced by David Puttnam and released in 1977.

The Duellists was set against the Napoleonic Wars and examined a futile, decades-long running feud between two eighteenth-century officers. It also won the Grand Prix at the Cannes Film Festival that year. Scott's debut feature had been so loaded with confident, beautiful imagery it was showered with superlatives, ranging from "masterful" and "a classic" to "staggeringly beautiful."

Yet *The Duellists* was poorly distributed in the United States, an oversight which still pains the English director today.

"One of the problems was that it was misunderstood," Scott says. "Contrary to what many thought and how the critics approached it, *The Duellists* was not an art film. In fact, while I was shooting, I had thought of it in terms of a western. Yet it was booked on the art-house circuit anyway. Consequently, *The Duellists* never reached the large-scale audience it was intended for."

Scott's next picture definitely reached that audience.

Alien was one of 1979's top-grossing films, taking in over $100 million. A science fiction/horror/suspense thriller detailing a bizarre extraterrestrial's murderous pursuit of unlucky astronauts through the dank corridors of a huge spaceship, *Alien* starred Tom Skerritt, Yaphet Kotto, Sigourney Weaver, John Hurt, Harry Dean Stanton, and Veronica Cartwright. It was filmed in London, produced by Gordon Carroll, David Giler, and Walter Hill, and scripted by Dan O'Bannon, who'd also scripted *Total Recall*, the Philip K. Dick adaptation previously discussed in chapter II. And by any standard, *Alien* was a huge hit. It garnered many awards from the science fiction community, won the 1979 Academy Award for Best Visual Effects, and was also nominated for a Best Art Direction Oscar.

Yet *Alien* had been a genre of film in which Ridley Scott had not been previously interested. "The only two science fiction films to make any kind of impression on me were *The Day the Earth Stood Still* and *Star Wars*," Scott told this writer in 1981. Yet *Alien* was to blend science fiction with horror, another genre the director felt unfamiliar with.

Therefore, in order to better acquaint himself with the horror field (and to prepare for the creation of *Alien*'s ominous atmospheres), Scott had surreptitiously viewed Tobe Hooper's *The Texas Chainsaw Massacre* in a screening room at 20th Century Fox during *Alien*'s preproduction period. "I didn't want Fox to know about that because I felt it might make them nervous, discovering I was watching this low-budget shocker," Scott now says. "But I came away admiring Hooper's film. It's a very cleverly constructed picture, one which skillfully avoids gore in order to better frighten an audience through suggestibility."

Ironically, although Scott applied the very same Hooperian techniques to *Star Beast* (*Alien*'s original title), few critics seemed to notice. "I'd wanted to back off the hard-core blood and gore for *Alien*," Scott said, "and I think we managed to do that. However, if I ever wanted to, I probably *could* make a cheap, extremely gory $500,000 horror film. Because I know exactly what to do. How to— not manipulate, because manipulation is a dangerous word—but how to move an audience.

"Which is why I was so angry when someone wrote that *Alien* was a manipulative piece of blood and gore moviemaking with no redeeming features whatsoever," Scott points out. "I was very upset by that comment, because I had deliberately set out *not* to do that. In fact, excepting the chest-burster sequence [an infamous moment when an alien embryo explodes from the thorax of actor John Hurt], *Alien* is almost totally devoid of blood and gore. What these critics completely missed was the total environment of that film. How artists like H. R. Giger and Ron Cobb had contributed to an environment which had been carefully designed and very carefully thought out. To a large extent, that environment was a statement. And, I think, a great piece of art work."

Though Scott insists *Alien's* shock sequences (and the more visceral moments of *Blade Runner*) were not manipulative, he does admit his background in directing commercials taught him how to hook an audience. "Commercial advertising teaches you all sorts of things that you really don't learn about when you're in school. Film schools tend to only deal with very esoteric subjects. People tend to forget that the end result has got to somehow communicate with the audience."

Alien's "environment" was the popular filmgoing public's first exposure to "layering," Scott's self-described technique of building up a dense, kaleidoscopic accretion of detail within every frame and set of a film. "To me," Scott said when this author interviewed him in 1980, "a film is like a seven-hundred-layer layer cake."

This process of layering was to continue unabated in *Blade Runner*; indeed, in certain shots, freed from the claustrophobic interiors in which most of *Alien* took place, *Blade Runner's* layering was to reach an overwhelming visual intricacy unseen in any prior Ridley Scott film (or in any prior science fiction movie, for that matter).

But all this was to come nearly a year and a half *after* Scott first turned down Hampton Fancher's *Android* script in April 1979.

Being busy at the time, Scott's initial impulse had been to dismiss Deeley's submission outright. But Ivor Powell, a close associate of the director, who had already worked with Scott on *Alien* (as well as on Stanley Kubrick's *2001*), read the Hampton Fancher script and liked it. "I recall looking at that screenplay and becoming very excited by *Android*," Powell says. "I thought it was a marvelous opportunity for Ridley, and told him so."

"Michael Deeley was actively pursuing Ridley at the same time Ivor Powell was urging Ridley to give Hampton's screenplay a go," Haber continues. "Ridley finally did—and turned us down flat."

"The reason I didn't want to do *Android*," Scott said to this author in 1994, "had nothing to do with thinking Hampton's screenplay, which at that time was a very different version of *Blade Runner,* wasn't interesting. In fact, I thought it was very well written. Although I'd never met him, I could tell how well Hampton handled prose and dialogue.

"At the same time, my plate was very full. I was developing a rather dark, fantastic adaptation of the medieval *Tristan and Isolde* story, a sword-and-sorcery type of thing. I also was committed to producer Dino DeLaurentiis to do an adaptation of Frank Herbert's novel *Dune*. [*A lavish 1984 failure ultimately directed by pop surrealist David Lynch.*] *Dune* was going to be quite a large-scale science fiction epic.

"You must remember that, with *Alien,* I'd just *finished* a science fiction picture. And here Hampton and Michael were offering me *another* sci-fi. I just didn't feel that I could immediately go into yet another one of those: it was time to move on to something else."

However, even though Scott passed on *Android*, he did not completely push the Fancher/Deeley project out of his head. Indeed, in a relatively short period of time Ridley Scott began actively reappraising his refusal.

Scott had already been laboring on *Dune* for a period of approximately seven months, until screenwriter Rudolph Wurlitzer (*Two Lane Blacktop*, and *Pat Garrett and Billy the Kid*) turned in his first draft screenplay, at which point something curious happened: Scott abruptly bailed out of the DeLaurentiis project.

The director himself now picks up the story:

"I'd worked on *Dune* for over half a year," Scott explains. "Previous to that I'd brought a writer over to London whom I considered pretty good, Rudy Wurlitzer, to work with me. In a seven-month period he'd come up with a first draft script which I felt was a decent distillation of Frank Herbert's book.

"But I also realized *Dune* was going to take more work. A lot more work. And I just didn't have the heart to attack that work. Because. . . well, I'll tell you what really happened. My older brother died. Frankly, that freaked me out. I felt I couldn't sit around for another two and a half years on *Dune*, which is how long I thought it was going to take, preparing and waiting on this thing. I needed immediate activity, needed to get my mind off my brother's death. So I went and told Dino I had to depart *Dune* and that the script was his."

By now, it was a few months into 1980. Increasingly restless to begin shooting another motion picture, Ridley Scott began looking at other projects. The director continues:

"This is why I had asked Michael Deeley to show me the latest version of Hampton's screenplay, earlier in the year. At that point it was titled *Dangerous Days,* and I hadn't been able to get that script out of my head since I'd first read it. Even though I'd initially passed on *Android,* on reading *Dangerous Days,* I decided it was an extraordinary piece of work with marvelous design possibilities.

"There were also two other reasons I accepted *Dangerous Days,*" Scott concludes. "One was the fact that I knew Michael Deeley well, and knew I could work with him. The second tied in with the grief I was feeling over my brother's death. By this time, I'd realized I needed something to get my mind off that, and that I'd better take something which would be an immediate go. *Dangerous Days* looked like that project. Which is ironic, of course. Because it wasn't immediate at all. It took another bloody *year* before I began shooting *Blade Runner.*

"Yet it all was kind of an exorcism, in a way," concludes Scott. "Accepting *Dangerous Days* helped get me through my brother's passing."

THE (FIRST) STUDIO: FILMWAYS PICTURES

By the first trimester of 1980, two more crucial elements of the film ultimately known as *Blade Runner* were being fitted into place.

One occurred on February 21, 1980, when Ridley Scott officially signed on as the director of Michael Deeley's newest project.

The second took place on April 9, 1980, when that project was finally picked up by a production company. This event was reported in such industry trade publications as *Variety* and *The Hollywood Reporter,* which both announced that Filmways Pictures had just pledged $13 million for an as-yet-untitled tale of "technological terror."*

The new motion picture, was, of course, *Dangerous Days.* As for Filmways, it was a smallish production house which had been around

---

*Although Filmways "pledged" $13 million, the actual amount of hard cash which the company invested in *Dangerous Days* was only $2,561,475.00.

since at least 1961. The company had recently expanded, however, through its buyout of American-International Pictures, home of B-movie king Roger Corman and his Edgar Allen Poe films.

Filmways had been primarily attracted to *Dangerous Days* because of the "A-List" appeal of Ridley Scott. As Hampton Fancher confirmed to *Starlog* Magazine (#184, November 1992), "He, of course, was the reason the movie got made. . . . Two days after Ridley got into town and talked to [us], every studio in town called and said, 'How much do you want, and when do you want to go?'"

Yet as far as Scott was concerned, there already was an immediate problem with his new Filmways relationship: money. "I told Filmways very early on that a $13-million production floor wasn't very realistic in terms of what I had in mind for the picture," Scott says. "That figure was then raised to a pledge of $15 million. But by my estimates, our final cost was going to be closer to the $20-million mark."

Filmways, however, could (or would) not ante up the extra cash. This forced Scott and his producer to seek additional funds elsewhere. But every prospective extra-money backer turned them down.

Prophetically, two of the earliest misgivings concerning *Dangerous Days*—underfunded budgets and commercially risky storylines—would return to haunt the *Blade Runner* company at a much later date. However, Ridley Scott and Michael Deeley had forged ahead with their new production anyway. Numbers, after all, were only numbers; this producer and director were both veteran players in the money-chasing game, and budget problems would *surely* be overcome.

Better now to focus on the fact that, after all these years, Hampton Fancher's screenplay had finally been given the green light.

"Everyone was really up about the project in those days," recalls Fancher. "Filmways had given us a firm start date for principal photography [January 12, 1981], plus a firm release date [Christmas 1981]. I had to keep pinching myself to make sure it was really happening."

Little did the writer/producer know that, before the year was out, Filmways Pictures would no longer be attached to *Dangerous Days*.

Neither would Hampton Fancher. At least, not in the scriptwriting sense.

SCRIPT WARS

DECKARD (V.O.)

Every government that could was racing to populate their colonial territory. But emigrants needed incentive. Overpopulation and the greenhouse factor didn't seem to be enough; but owning a human look-a-like had lots of appeal. It was big industry, the competition was stiff, and Tyrell was top of the line.

—DECKARD ON REPLICANTS' APPEAL TO
OFF-WORLD COLONISTS
FROM *BLADE RUNNER* SCRIPT
DATED JULY 24, 1980
UNUSED—WRITTEN BY HAMPTON FANCHER

With their Filmways backing a definite "go," the nucleus of the *Blade Runner* team now began preproduction on *Dangerous Days*. By this time Deeley's attorneys had drawn up a short-term business alliance entitled Brighton Productions, a limited partnership created solely for the purpose of producing this one motion picture.

It was under the Brighton banner that Deeley, Ridley Scott, Hampton Fancher, Ivor Powell, and Katy Haber moved into their first production offices during May 1980. These were located at the Sunset-Gower Studios in Hollywood, at 1420 N. Beachwood Drive. Affectionately known to industry insiders as "Gower Gulch," the Sunset-Gower Studios is one of the oldest standing lots in Los Angeles. Brighton Productions took up residence in the Producer's Building, Suite 300.

The *Blade Runner* preproduction offices were housed in a number of smallish cubicles located within a rambling, two-story wooden structure on the Sunset-Gower lot. Scott had one office, Deeley another. The rest of the staff shared various spaces of their own. Preproduction art and storyboards festooned the walls, and the worn carpeting cushioning the Brighton conference room floor would become even more threadbare under the constant assault of feet marching to and from endless preproduction meetings. During these conferences everything from the look of a futuristic telephone to an actor's salary demands would be discussed.

The overwhelming topic of the moment, however, was Fancher's script and how to rework that script into the movie Scott wanted to shoot.

REWRITES

"I was a bit hesitant about Ridley at first," Hampton Fancher now admits. "Before we met, I'd asked about the guy through some people who'd worked with him. Some of their comments were pretty negative—'Ah, he's a fucking machine, he's not a human being.' Which are the same things you hear about Stanley Kubrick. I also knew Ridley was politically conservative, so we stood in different corners there.

"But then we started the rewrites, and it was one of the most satisfying, maddening, and fascinating relationships of my life. I'll always be in love with Ridley. He's a brilliant, dream-driven guy who knows how to impart his images to you by either drawing a picture or just saying a word. Then, *wham!* You suddenly feel as if you're going into a whole new world. His imagination is like a fucking virus—it keeps growing and spreading and mutating. Ridley's mind is almost too fast for his own good, in a way; very often, it pulled him ahead of himself, at great speed. Then he'd stumble over it, ideas were pouring out of him so fast.

"But Ridley also knows how to just sit there. How to be silent, methodical, and circumspect. So, in showbiz terms, Ridley was a heavyweight. Someone who kept his agenda and business concerns close to his chest. Yet in our personal relationship, he was one of the two or three funniest men I've ever met in my life. There's nobody you can laugh with as well as you can laugh with Ridley."

Fancher and Scott began collaborating on the *Dangerous Days* rewrite in April 1980. "All told I spent about eight months working over that screenplay with Ridley. The first four months were the best. Intense, but positive," Fancher remembers.

"We began with an overview of the material, poking at it in the general sense. For example, if you'll remember, one of the problems I'd had with the first drafts was that I didn't have a good reason for the androids to be on Earth. But Ridley, after a few weeks' work, said, 'What the fuck are they doing on Earth?' I said, 'Uh, don't ask that question.' Which is where we added the important point of the replicants being here because of longevity, or their lack of it. They're trying to break into Tyrell's for information on how to extend their lives.

"Ridley also had a great way of conveying himself in shorthand," Fancher continues. "Another day, pretty early on, we were kicking ideas back and forth when he suddenly looks at me and says, 'Hampton, this world you've created—what's outside the window?' He really knew how to push a button on me, because I realized he was talking about the total environment, the buildings and fashions and culture we were going to have to surround the story with. Which," admits Fancher, laughing, "I hadn't come up with yet.

"So I said, 'I don't know.' '*Heavy Metal*,' Ridley replies. I said, 'What's that?' Scott explained that it was originally this adult, French comic book called *Metal Hurlant* that was now being published in America by the same company doing the *National Lampoon*.

"By the next day I'd already bought a copy of *Heavy Metal* and read it. I came back in all excited, going, 'Yeah! Let's get outside the fucking window!'"

This remark would snowball into the film's famous production design. Now "energized" and "electrified" by Scott's involvement, Fancher attacked his script. One of the first results of this full frontal assault was a title change.

Fancher recalls that in July 1980, "Ridley said we couldn't keep referring to Deckard as a detective, because that was the lazy way out. Couldn't we come up with a different name for his line of work?"

Ransacking his mind and home library, Fancher discovered a slim, little-known book by celebrated "beat" author William Burroughs. It was titled *Blade Runner: (a movie)*. After then bringing these words back to Scott, the director responded favorably to them, reasoning that a "Blade Runner unit" was a catchy term to describe the departmentally sanctioned police assassins outlined in Fancher's script.

"Ridley and I also thought that *Blade Runner* would make a hell of a new title for the screenplay," Fancher continues. "So Scott asked Michael Deeley to approach William Burroughs' representatives with the idea of buying the use of his title. Deeley did so, and Burroughs was really cooperative. That's when the film started being called *Blade Runner*."

However, shortly after these words were adopted as the production's new title, it was discovered that there existed yet *another* book with the same name. This one had been written by longtime science fiction/fantasy writer Alan E. Nourse; it concerned an impoverished future society where medical supplies are so scarce they are being supplied by smugglers known as "Blade Runners."

"That forced Deeley to go through another licensing procedure," says Fancher. But, as Deeley himself recalls, "The process was quite uneventful. We acquired both of those titles for a song, certainly for under five thousand dollars."

In spite of his initial excitement, however, as preproduction progressed, Ridley Scott's enthusiasm for the term "Blade Runner" began to cool. Instead, the director now began warming to the idea of calling his new film *Gotham City*. Comic book artist/writer Bob Kane, however, the creator of *Batman*, objected to this; Kane felt Scott's use of *Gotham City* infringed on the name of the same town that Kane had created to house his Caped Crusader.

So *Gotham City* became *Blade Runner* once again. "But that's only a working title," Ridley Scott told me in 1981. "I think it may change." It didn't—but one must admit there's a certain irony attached to the fact that what began as a working title is now the name by which *Blade Runner* is universally known.

Meanwhile, while titles were being bought and scrapped, Hampton Fancher had absorbed Scott's various screenplay suggestions and was reworking his script. One result was a draft dated July 24, 1980.

In many ways, this revision was remarkably similar to the final film. The July 24 script opens with Leon's Voigt-Kampff test, for example, and much of the dialogue between Leon and Holden is exactly the same as that heard in the motion picture. Also similar (if not exactly alike) were scenes involving Captain Bryant briefing Deckard on the escaped androids, Deckard searching Leon's hotel room and discovering the Nexus–6's snapshots, and Deckard running a Voigt-Kampff test on Rachael. Certain sequences in the July 24 script also duplicated passages found in Dick's original novel; for example, Deckard first meets Rachael at the Tyrell Corporation in an elevator, before walking with her past a menagerie of real animals.

However, if there were similarities, there were also many differences in this version of Fancher's script. For instance, Deckard is first introduced to the audience while sitting alone in a high-speed, 400-mph train roaring into Los Angeles from the desert. The role of Gaff is also smaller, while the Esper (which, according the July 24 draft, is a talking, ubiquitous police computer) has been much expanded. Fancher's script then concluded with Deckard taking Rachael out into the countryside for the first time in her life, so that the female android could see real snow, after which Deckard shoots and kills her. The last scene portrays Deckard driving his car down a lonely road as his voice-over informs us that being human means making choices—and that Rachael had chosen suicide.

The July 24 draft was also notable for its inclusion of an *extra* replicant character (in addition to Pris, Roy, Leon, and Zhora) whose subsequent *exclusion* would result in confusing *Blade Runner* audiences. Remember: in the final film, Captain Bryant (M. Emmet Walsh) tells Deckard that *six* replicants escaped to Earth. One was "fried" trying to break into the Tyrell Corporation, obviously leaving *five* living androids. Yet only *four* (Pris, Roy, Leon, and Zhora again) are featured in the film.

This missing "sixth replicant" has since become the cause of much speculation. In fact, K. W. Jeter's authorized 1995 novelized sequel to the film (*Blade Runner 2: The Edge of Human*), includes one main character who's convinced that *Deckard* is the sixth replicant. But the truth of the matter is rather more mundane.

In point of fact, most of Fancher's many scripts had featured a sixth replicant named "Mary," who the July 24 script says "looks like an American dream mom, right out of *Father Knows Best.*" Mary then survived the majority of script rewrites and was actually cast for the film. The name of the actress who was going to portray her? Stacey Nelkin, a petite woman who was Barry Bostwick's wife. But then Nelkin saw her part evaporate when budgetary restrictions caused Mary to be dropped from the film during the earliest stages of principal photography.

"The changes Ridley imposed on my scripts were constant and far reaching," says Hampton Fancher. According to the writer/producer, these changes also were responsible for making the final portion of his Scott-supervised rewriting stint strained and fractious. "Some of Ridley's revisions were good ideas—others I fought like a crazed badger."

Among the more contentious elements was a scene where the Sebastian character smuggles Roy Batty onto the Tyrell estate (called a "preserve") while delivering an artificial griffin to Tyrell's son. Scott insisted that this subterfuge be changed to the Sebastian/Tyrell "chess game ploy" now seen in the final film, a device Fancher still feels is "too easy and obvious." The writer had also originally envisioned Rachael as "morally superior to Deckard; she always had a mouthful of cutting things to say to him. That was taken away, too." Also eliminated were Fancher's ecological ending and the idea that Deckard was pursuing the replicants in order to buy an electric sheep. "Ridley did try to keep that last idea in," Fancher goes on to say. "But he finally told me he couldn't figure out a way to highlight the artificial animal theme.

"Anyway," adds the screenwriter, "in the final few months of 1980 I began to realize there was a slow process of involuntary elimination going on. Through Ridley, who was jettisoning key concepts I felt central to the story. That horrified me.

"So we began butting heads. What Scott didn't seem to realize was that the way the script had been written, if you changed one thing over here in Kansas, California would get shoved off the map. So there were endless arguments over endless story points. The weird thing was, most of time I'd thought I'd made my point; Ridley would quiet down and I'd walk away thinking, 'Well, I won that round.' It wasn't until much later that Ivor Powell came up to me and said, 'You never won once and you never will.' And he was right. Two or three weeks later, as I'd be going along my merry way, Ridley would suddenly question the same story point and the arguments would start all over again. But Ridley's like that: he's a fucking bulldog who never lets go."

By 1995, however, hindsight had mellowed Fancher's bitterness. "In retrospect, I now realize there was a certain naïveté in my refusal to give Ridley what he wanted. I was being ignorant and block-headed. When they'd tell me, 'You can't write that,' and I'd get angry, it was partly because I was still uneducated as to the realities of production. I'd think, 'Why can't you do this? You've got fifteen million fucking dollars!' But I didn't know what Ridley had in mind; I didn't know he was going to have printing presses turning out newspapers with future headlines and all that shit.

"I also have to say," Fancher continues, "that Ridley inspired me many times. I wrote many of his suggestions down because I thought they were brilliant. But my arrogance must have been insufferable to Ridley and Michael. Being English, they weren't about to sit down and have therapy with me.

"The upshot of all this was that I became more and more intractable and finally got left out in the cold. Maybe if I'd been just a hired gun on this project, I'd have been more accommodating, would have written down the things I didn't agree with. But you see, I'd already done a tremendous amount of rewriting on this film. And *I* felt the scripts were improving with each draft. Yet somewhere along the way, Ridley seemed to forget that I was not simply a hired writer; I was also a producer and part owner of the film. Anyway, we finally came to the point where we just weren't getting anywhere. Ridley had what he felt were crucial points he wanted incorporated into the screenplay—those were the ideas I actively resisted. Because I didn't think they'd work."

By mid-November, these contextual battles had crystallized into two basic disagreements. "Hampton's take on the material was very lyrical and sci-fi, in the purest sense of the word," explains Katy Haber. "But Ridley wanted more meat and potatoes; he saw the film as a detective thriller. He kept urging Hampton to provide him with more clues, more mystery, more *detecting*. Hampton wouldn't do that."

Michael Deeley viewed Scott and Fancher's dissension under a plainer light. "It's quite simple, really: Hampton saw *Blade Runner* as a romantic morality play. Ridley wanted a harder edge."

FANCHER OUT, PEOPLES IN

Feeling that they now faced a creative deadlock over Fancher's attitude, Deeley and Scott took a sudden step which caught the stubborn writer/producer off guard. "Things had gotten to the point where I'd basically said, 'You don't like this? Then fire me!'" Fancher recalls. "It was a dare, really. I thought my position was secure. What an idiot."

Unbeknownst to Fancher (at the time of their action, anyway), Scott and Deeley *had* decided to take him up on his bluff. Therefore, on November 17, 1980, Michael Deeley met with a second potential *Blade Runner* screenwriter. This scribe had been recommended by Ridley Scott's brother, Tony, who had just finished rewriting a property with a writer whom the younger Scott felt would perfectly suit his older brother Ridley's needs.

The screenwriter's name was David Peoples.

The David Peoples of 1980 had no way of knowing that his greatest triumph—a 1976 script being turned into Clint Eastwood's critically acclaimed Oscar-winning 1992 revisionist Western, *Unforgiven*—still lay before him. Still, before 1980 Peoples had hardly been idle; by then he had already coedited and cowritten (with his wife Janet Peoples and Jon Else) the Academy Award-winning documentary feature *The Day After Trinity*, which detailed the birth of the first atomic bomb. Peoples had also written the Oscar-nominated short *Arthur and Lilly*, and edited another Oscar-winning documentary, the then-perennial television favorite *Who Are the DeBolts, and Where Did They Get 19 Kids?*

After these projects, Peoples focused on writing spec (speculative) feature scripts. Then came Tony Scott and *Blade Runner*. Peoples continues the story:

"In 1980 I was working with Tony on one of my spec scripts, which was called *My Dog's on Fire*. That one's hard to describe. It was sort of a dark rock comedy, like a punk *The Commitments* thing.

"Anyway, I'd just come back from working with Tony and was in Berkeley when I got this call that said, 'Ridley Scott wants you to come down and work on this huge picture.' Wow! I was thrilled, you know, because I knew all about *Blade Runner*. There'd already been a buzz building up in the industry over it, and that just kept growing all through the shoot.

"But I hadn't seen Hampton's script and didn't really know what it was about. I'd never read Philip K. Dick then, either. So anyway, I was flown down to Los Angeles and put up in this great suite at the Chateau Marmont where a copy of Hampton's script was delivered to me. Now, this was all very big-time for me back then; I was thrilled!

Then I read Hampton's latest draft—and was immediately devastated. Because it was awesome. A knockout. Hampton had done some great writing, and you don't see that very often.

"So when Michael and Ridley came in later and asked me, 'What do you think?,' I couldn't lie to them. I said, 'It's terrific.' They looked at each other and replied, 'You can't find anything wrong with it?' I said, 'No. There's nothing I can do to make this script any better.' I would have loved to have had something negative to say, because I really wanted to work on this picture.

"But apparently I'd given them a good answer, because Ridley and Deeley both grinned and said they really liked the fact that I liked their script. Then Ridley pointed out some changes he wanted to make.

"So, in fact, I did get hired. And since I felt very honored to be working on something this well written, I thereafter tried to imitate Hampton's style, tried to write in the same tone and voice he'd established in his earlier drafts. Because it was beautiful."

However, the first job-related assignment Scott gave Peoples had nothing to do with Fancher's script. "Ridley told me *not* to read Philip K. Dick's novel; he felt it was better if I concentrated on Hampton's script and stay away from the book," Peoples explains. "So I wrote furiously over Thanksgiving and the early part of December and delivered my first draft on December 15, 1980."

The screenplay bearing this date (with Fancher's name first, Peoples' second), had actually been completed on December 11. Whatever its date of origin, a quick look through its pages proves that *Blade Runner*'s new writer had not shied away from impressing his own creativity on Fancher's script.

For instance, Peoples' December 15 rewrite opens on an "Off-world Termination Dump," a small planetoid used for the cremation of androids whose four-year lifespans have run out. Two "Dumpers" (goggle- and fire-ensuited workmen) are introduced, routinely shoveling dead androids from a huge pile of cadavers when one of the "corpses" suddenly stirs. It is a very much alive Roy Batty, masquerading as a dead android. Batty then surreptitiously pulls Mary and Leon from the heap of bodies, and before the trio attack the defenseless Dumpers, they pause to stare up at the glittering heavens—and the beckoning planet Earth—above.

Clearly meant as a prelude to the androids' murderous escape from the Off-world colony, this unusual sequence was later dropped because of budgetary constraints. Two contributions which Peoples added to his first draft, however, were not. First, it was Peoples who helped include the "detecting" angle that Scott had so unsuccessfully tried earlier to negotiate out of Fancher; the snake scale which Deckard discovers in Leon's apartment, for instance, was inserted by Peoples into the script.

"The *idea* of the snake scale, though, was Ridley's," Peoples points out. "Which brings up a good point.

"For years I've read how David Peoples saved this screenplay by adding all these mystery elements. But I honestly must say that I don't think I ever solved many of those particular script problems. Hampton had had a terrific sort of chase/adventure thing going, in which Deckard was in a lot of jeopardy, but Ridley was sort of heading toward the spirit of *Chinatown*. Something more mysterious and foreboding and threatening. And he'd wanted all these clues and things put into the script so Deckard could detect. But clues aren't my strong point; I just couldn't mesh something like puzzles and the

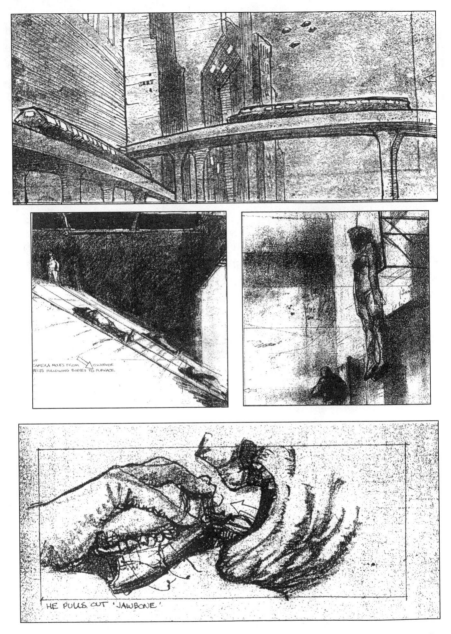

Panels from four Sherman Labby storyboards representing unshot, alternate openings and sequences for BR. (Top) Deckard arrives in 2019 Los Angeles on a futuristic train. (Middle left) Tyrell Corporation employees dispose of dead replicants on a "Furnace Asteroid." (Middle right) Pris plays dead by hanging from a basketball hoop in the unfilmed "Pris & Deckard gymnasium fight." (Bottom) Deckard removes the jawbone of a replicant he's killed on a farm in a never-shot BR opening sequence.

forward movement and the tension in there all at once. So I think it's one of the sad ironies of this motion picture that the area I'm most praised for is probably the one where I most considerably let Ridley down.

"On the other hand," concludes Peoples, "I don't think that even Robert Towne could have whipped out a *Chinatown* script under the circumstances we were facing. Not with all those sets already built and waiting for crews to shoot." *(When Peoples was hired, the projected start of principal photography was less than two months away.)*

Vexing clues aside, David Peoples did indeed make a significant contribution to *Blade Runner*. This involved the creation of a whole new name for Dick's androids—a term Ridley Scott had actively lobbied to eliminate.

"The term *android* is a dangerous one, undermined by certain generic assumptions. I don't like using it. In fact, I threatened to crack open heads with a baseball bat if I heard it used around me on the set," Scott jestingly declared to this writer in 1981. "You see, *android* is a very familiar word. Not just to science fiction readers, but to the general public. A lot of material—some good, some crap—has been touched by the term. Therefore, I didn't want *Blade Runner* to be premonitory of *android* at all. Because then people would think that this film was about robots, when in fact it isn't. I thought it was better that we come up with a new word altogether."

David Peoples was the man who came up with that new word, in his first draft rewrite. Or, to put it more accurately, it was his *daughter* who prodded the word into being.

"Knowing Ridley's detestation of the term "android," I started thinking of something else to call these artificial humans," Peoples relates. "But I came up empty. So I called my daughter, Risa, because she was doing scientific work in microbiology and biochemistry at the time. I said that I hated the word android and so on and so forth, and she said. 'How about this? Have you ever heard of 'replicating'? That's the name of the process used to duplicate cells for cloning."

"Well, I'd never heard that one before. But I liked it. So out of the word 'replicating' came 'replicant,' which I immediately inserted into my first pass through Hampton's script."

MORE REWRITES ————————————————————————

David Peoples now recalls that "I loved working with Ridley Scott. He's inspirational, and personally I like him very much. Which is odd, in a way, because there's an artistic difference between us. I'm kind of up front and obvious; Ridley tends to be a tad obscure. But that's the greatness of *Blade Runner*. Scott made something that was hidden, rich, textured, and layered.

"In any event," Peoples goes on to say, "everything was positive about my *Blade Runner* experience. Except the usual industry nonsense of a writer churning out pages that he's never quite sure somebody's read."

Other changes Peoples worked into his December 15 script included a brand-new introduction to *Blade Runner*'s hero; this time, a trenchcoated Deckard was seen walking along a crowded city street, musing, in voice-over, about his recent divorce. Further additions included the discovery (and termination) of yet another new android, (this one called Roger, who is caught hiding in a Murphy bed in Leon's hotel room); a scene of a mechanical cat lapping up oil outside Sebastian's apartment (a situation which Pris uses to gain Sebastian's trust); the discovery of Chew's frozen body in his eye lab (the body is accidentally knocked over and shatters into a million pieces); a moment when Deckard forces Gaff (whose role is much expanded here) to take the Voigt-Kampff test; and a climax which sees Deckard taking Rachael to the *beach* before shooting her.

"Ridley didn't like Hampton's ending in the snow," Peoples explains. "It reminded him too much of the climax of a film called *Elvira Madigan*.

Peoples' first 159-page December 15 screenplay then concluded with Deckard back at his apartment, calmly loading his weapon. He is waiting for a violent police reprisal he knows must come; earlier, Deckard had murdered Gaff, who'd been trying to terminate Deckard for not killing Rachael in a more timely manner.

Having now delivered what he felt "was an acceptable first draft," Peoples now found himself "astounded" when yet *another Blade Runner* screenplay suddenly appeared. This one was dated December 22, 1980—and it was a script into which Peoples had had no input.

"That December 22 script came as a real stunner," explains the second *Blade Runner* screenwriter. "In those days I was writing like a motherfucker, and I remember Ridley and Michael being surprised at how fast I was. But then I found out, somewhat to my surprise, that Ridley and Michael and Katy and Ivor had been cutting up this December 15th thing and making their own edit out of it. They'd done that by pasting in scenes from Hampton's earlier drafts with some of the stuff I'd done on the fifteenth. But Hampton and I really had nothing to do with it. And that's the story behind the December 22 script; it's got my name on it, but it really was composed of *several* drafts. Quite literally.

"Apparently," Peoples concludes, "that screenplay was very well received [laughs]. I'm not sure I've ever read it from cover to cover, though. Because I was kind of shocked that it wasn't what I'd written, or that it didn't contain all the stuff of Hampton's I'd left in."

It might be also surprising to learn that, although David Peoples had now been writing for *Blade Runner* for nearly a month, the original scripter was still on the picture. Not for long, though, and not because he was unhappy with Peoples' involvement.

"The fact of the matter is, I didn't even know David Peoples had been hired to rewrite me," recalls a bemused Hampton Fancher. "I remember finding this out just before Christmas at a dinner I went to, when I came across a copy of Peoples' first draft. I hit the ceiling—I figured they'd found some whimpering hack to give Ridley what he wanted."

Fancher officially terminated his agreement as a *Blade Runner* screenwriter on December 21, 1980. "But I did come back and do a couple of quick scene rewrites towards the end of production. Before that, though, I was fuming over this Peoples thing. I'd never heard of him, didn't know what he'd done. But then I read his December 15th script. Surprisingly, the things I had felt that couldn't be put into the script, the things Ridley had wanted, were incorporated by Peoples in tight, original, admirable ways. I really liked what he did with my script. In fact, now we're good friends. But David and I never did really collaborate on *Blade Runner*."

AN UNHAPPY DICK

Besieged by script problems, a rapidly approaching start date and dire rumors concerning the failing financial health of Filmways Pictures, the *Blade Runner* team could be forgiven for not noticing yet another, though seemingly insignificant, storm cloud gathering on the horizon.

This squall could have been averted, however, if someone had remembered to be courteous or politic. Or just plain human.

"One day I got a call from Robert Jaffe, around late April 1980," said Philip K. Dick to this author in late 1980. "And the first thing he told me was 'Congratulations!' I said, 'On what?' Jaffe then said he'd called to congratulate me on *Sheep* being made into a film. I told him I didn't know a thing about it, because I didn't. It turned out that Jaffe had read about it in the trades, but no one from the production company had taken the trouble to inform me of the fact.

"At first I was just bemused by this incident," Dick continued. "In fact, a bit later I was having dinner with Ray Bradbury—it's funny how Ray kept popping up in odd places during the beginnings of this thing—and I mentioned that I'd heard someone was making a movie out of my book by reading about it in the trades. Well, Ray just started shouting and waving his arms! He was totally scandalized. He thought that that was absolutely unacceptable behavior. I just smiled and finished my drink.

"But as time went on, that snub began to gnaw on me. That and other things."

THE (SECOND) STUDIO: ——————————————————
WARNER BROTHERS, TANDEM PRODUCTIONS,
AND SIR RUN-RUN SHAW

Although this book has not yet reached its special effects point (it will, in chapter X), by mid-December of 1980 various F/X crews had already been hired to tackle *Blade Runner*'s ambitious trick photography. Joining these magicians was a small army of designers, actors, and technicians—an entire production company, which was massing toward the film's projected start date of January 12, 1981.

But then a not entirely unexpected event nearly sank the film on the spot: the departure of Filmways Pictures and its financing.

Relations with Filmways had, up to this point, been relatively cordial. "I did spend four months trying to convince them—that's the polite word for it—that we were severely underbudgeted, though," notes Ridley Scott. Nevertheless, Brighton Productions had already begun erecting sets at The Burbank Studios, which was the home of

Warner Brothers and Columbia Pictures, as well as home base for such independents as The Ladd Company and Clint Eastwood's Malpaso Company.

Still, although The Burbank Studios would indeed be the location where *Blade Runner* was ultimately filmed, the film's original financier was now gone.

"The rumor going around was that Filmways had had second thoughts about *Blade Runner* and decided to put their money behind another project," said a source close to the production. "Gossip had it that this other project was Brian DePalma's *Blow Out*. That cost about $16 million. If it's true, someone made a big mistake, as the ultimate failure of that film more than points out."

Whatever the reasoning behind Filmways' change of heart, Scott, Deeley, and Ivor Powell first found out about the crisis in a manner which (if he was aware of it) must have struck author Philip K. Dick as poetic justice: the filmmakers confirmed that Filmways had dumped them by reading about it in the trades.

However, Ivor Powell later told this writer that he and other *Blade Runner* team members had already uncovered a number of prior "alarming" reports concerning Filmways' financial instability. Still, when Filmways confirmed that they were pulling out of the project, many on the *BR* crew expressed grave doubts that the film would ever be made.

As Katy Haber points out, "We had a full crew working, all of them on salary, and principal literally weeks away. The Filmways pullout was a nightmare."

The stall could not have happened at a worse moment. If a new backer was not quickly found, an inevitable lull of weeks or months would pose the insurmountable problem of reassembling the *Blade Runner* crew. Also to be considered was the fact that Scott was still a hot property; therefore, if a lack of funding dragged on for any length of time, *Blade Runner* could conceivably find itself without a director.

Happily, the turnaround was brief. The Filmways fiasco had occurred in late December 1980; less than two weeks later, Michael Deeley managed to secure the necessary financing from a number of various sources. "That was a major feat," Haber adds. "In less than ten days and ten nights, Michael had arranged a whole new package deal. And not one person missed a single paycheck during that period."

Deeley, however, is more pragmatic about his accomplishment. "Having got a director and having gone this far with this picture, and suddenly having to spend money but not having any finances, I really had no choice but to start pounding the pavement. One had to, if you really liked the project. And at that time, I loved it."

Deeley now approached no fewer than thirteen different companies (including 20th Century Fox, United Artists, and Universal) in his desperate race to keep *Blade Runner* alive. Finally, he hit paydirt in the form of a three-way deal involving The Ladd Company (an independent production house run by Alan Ladd, Jr., son of the famous movie star), Far East movie mogul Sir Run-Run Shaw, and an entity up until this time known primarily for its work in television, Tandem Productions, Inc.

Each participant set up a separate deal; The Ladd Company put up $7½ million through Warner Brothers, which in turn would receive domestic distribution rights to the picture. Alan Ladd, Jr., would later state that the reason he had agreed to invest in *Blade Runner* was "the good relations I had with Ridley Scott when we were both at Fox and he was making *Alien*. I had every confidence in what he could do with *Blade Runner*, as well." Ladd was referring to that period when he was president of Twentieth Century Fox; no stranger to the science fiction genre, Ladd had already produced the likes of *Star Wars, Looker,* and *Outland.*

Sir Run-Run Shaw also put in $7½ million for *Blade Runner's* foreign rights. Shaw was a renowned Asian filmmaker who had been steadily supplying product to the Far East for decades, through his powerful film production and distribution company, Shaw Brothers. "Actually, though, it was Run-Run's son, Harold Shaw, who made the deal," Deeley explains. "I just called him up and asked him. You see, when I'd been at EMI I'd done a lot of work with Japan, Hong Kong, and Singapore on certain pictures like *Convoy,* which did nothing in the States, but made magic money in foreign territories like Japan. And I'd conducted a great deal of business with Harold and Sir Run-Run Shaw in Singapore. So there was a prior history there."

The third and final participant was Tandem Productions, run by producer/director Bud Yorkin *(Cold Turkey)*, Jerry Perenchio, and Norman Lear *(All in the Family)*. Lear, however, decided not to participate, leaving Yorkin and Perenchio as the sole Tandem reps.

"Tandem essentially came in as completion bond guarantors, which meant that if we went over budget by ten percent, they would pay for it. But they could take over the picture," Deeley concludes. "Originally, they put in another $7 million.[1] This meant we now had an overall production floor of $21½ million. And again, there were essentially three deals here; U.S., foreign, and ancillary rights, ancillary being television and video and all that stuff. Which Tandem also bought."

Everything looked to be back on track. Solid (and reliable) financing had been found. *Blade Runner* had a major distributor. The only thing left to do was rearrange the schedule a bit and push back the start of principal photography.

Which is exactly when Hurricane Dick struck.

Since first hearing that his book was being made into a film, Philip K. Dick had had virtually no contact with the *Blade Runner* production company. As Dick told this writer over the telephone in late 1980, "They haven't talked to me at all; on the other hand, I haven't tried to get in touch with them, either." Dick had not been approached by Deeley or Scott, and had not spoken with Hampton Fancher since the days when the ex-actor had first attempted to option the author's book. But Dick had finally read early versions of Fancher's scripts. And he wasn't happy about it.

"I read two drafts of Fancher's screenplay, both bearing the Filmways imprint," Dick said, "and it was just one terrible script. Corny, extremely maladroit throughout. In my opinion it was doubly negative. I did not approve of what it tried to do, and I don't think it accomplished what it tried to do. In other words, they aimed low and failed at what they aimed at.

"Fancher had dropped most of the aspects of my novel and, instead, had concentrated on a lurid collision between human and android. The whole skein of the book had been simplified into a 'you or me' type of thing; only one of us, this human or an android, will survive. I should make it clear that I wasn't angered by what had been cut from my novel, because I do know that there's no way you can transfer everything from a book to the screen.

"However, what was bad was the execution of the script. Fancher had overrelied on the old cliché-ridden Chandleresque figure, and his script opened with a hoary voice-over that went something like, 'It was a dirty town, it was a dirty job. Somebody had to do that job. I was that somebody. My name's Rick Deckard.' I mean, my God! And the ending had this awful thing where Rachael mercifully, for everyone's sake, does

---

[1] Bud Yorkin has disputed this figure, stating that Tandem only put approximately $4 million, in total, into *Blade Runner*.

herself in. At which point Deckard grows in stature from the experience. 'Grows in stature' is just a sobriquet for the fact that he's really grown infinitely more cynical, which is apparently how these Hollywood people mature. There's a confusion there between world-weary sophistication, and what I would call spiritual wisdom. Anyway, Fancher's screenplay was a bumbling effort from start to finish."

Dick did not limit his anger to personal phone calls. In an article published in the February 15, 1981 issue of the Los Angeles *Select TV Guide* (a publication of a now defunct, then highly regarded early eighties Los Angeles cable television channel), Dick lashed out at the deficiencies he saw in the *Blade Runner* script. He also went one step farther, attacking Scott's *Alien* with the line that "a monster is a monster, a spaceship is a spaceship, and the only thing that saves this is its special effects."

"*Alien* was an effective film for what it tried to set out to do," Dick later admitted to me, "but I would have preferred more intellectual or conceptual content. I also thought the ending was weak; the monster lost simply because it was a monster. The same thing was going on in Fancher's script, by the way. At the end of this long fight between Deckard and Batty, the human won and the android lost simply because this conformed to that godawful generic convention which states that good must inevitably triumph over evil."

Of course, it wasn't long before Dick's *Select TV* piece got back to Warner Brothers. Dick, however, knew that it would; he sent it to them.

"I did that because, after not hearing from anyone at *Blade Runner* for all that time, I suddenly got an obnoxious call from them one afternoon, wherein they immediately said that they were angry that I had a copy of the script and demanded to know just where I had got it! This was while the property was still with Filmways, by the way. Anyway, they were so hostile that I was tempted to tell them that I'd floated over the studio one night in a helium balloon long after everyone else was in bed. Then I'd bored through the ceiling, lowered a string and a piece of chewing gum through the hole, and lifted the script off the nearest desk.

"I didn't say that, though I should have. Instead, I first pointed out that I'd gotten the script legitimately, through Michael Deeley's lawyers. But all the time I'm thinking, 'Jesus Christ! I'm the author of the novel on which this property is based! Is it so strange that I should have a copy of the script?'

"Secondly, I then told them that not only did I have a copy of it, but that I had already denounced it in print. And I shall send you a Xerox of this. I reacted this way not only because of their rudeness, but because of the fact that, at one point in the conversation, they told me that I shouldn't be using the word 'android.' That this was dangerous talk. At which point I wondered whether I was talking to a studio or the Mafia. So I told them, 'Shucks, fellas, I am *so* sorry I titled my book *Do Androids Dream of Electric Sheep.* But you know, gosh . . . now I'm sort of committed to it."

Dick's *Select TV* article was promptly mailed to the studio. But, after a cooling-off period, the author later commented that, "I do accept the word 'replicant' now, since 'android' genuinely has been overused. We also didn't have genetic engineering or recombinant DNA at the time I wrote the book. But the bottom line is that none of this had to happen. I would have loved to have given some kind of input to the production, free, gratis, or to have been able to act as a feedback loop to whoever was doing the screenplay. But this didn't happen. And the first scripts I read were on the level of 'Phillip Marlowe Meets the Stepford Wives.' I am not now and never was on the *Blade Runner* payroll, so why shouldn't I tell the truth about all this?"

Yet what Peoples had done with Fancher's scenario met with Dick's enthusiastic approval. "I asked The Ladd Company for Peoples' rewrite," Dick pointed out, "and I immediately knew things had changed when they said, 'No problem, here you go.' I got it right away. This was the February 1981 version of the script, and it immediately struck me that all the previous problems had been resolved. Peoples had done a first-class piece of work. He'd smoothed out the dialogue and reworked certain problems in some of the scenes. And the whole idea of the replicants being infused with progeria, or premature aging, was a new twist. By inserting this angle, by dropping Rachael's suicide, by rethinking the final Batty/Deckard confrontation as a moving, wonderful sequence—and by any other number of touch-ups—Peoples transformed the *Blade Runner* screenplay into a beautiful, symmetrical reinforcement of my original work."

Despite Dick's highly publicized denunciation of Fancher and his praise for the new *Blade Runner* cowriter, however, Peoples insisted that his contributions were overamplified by the *Electric Sheep* novelist. "I can't emphasize enough that Ridley Scott is really the author of *Blade Runner*," Peoples said. "His ideas and thrust were the motive force of the film. Ridley was totally involved on every level of scripting; for instance, he always felt strongly about Dick's original animal

Blade Runner *co-screenwriter David Peoples in Paris, 1995.*
(photo by Janet Peoples)

theme, that a holocaust had wiped most of the real ones out, that it was an incredible status symbol to have one, and that most people had to settle for synthetic ones. But we just never licked that, other than inserting the short Animoid Row scene.

"Other people had their input into the revised *Blade Runner* script, too. Dick probably didn't understand just how much of a committee art filmmaking is. For example, Harrison Ford and Rutger Hauer themselves contributed some very nice ideas concerning their dialogue. As for Fancher—well, I think he's been unfairly depicted as the heavy in this case. I don't know which version of the script Dick first saw, but the one I read was just terrific. Simply great. Hampton is awesome, he can really write, which is something I even mentioned in my first meeting with Ridley."

Be that as it may, Peoples obviously contributed his own material. "But you always have to remember that I was working from Fancher's script simply to make it jibe to Ridley's vision. I gather from Dick's reaction that he felt my work had turned the script back towards his novel. Well, that's really just the force of the original ideas in his book turning everybody back. And let's face it—scripts are always changing. So perhaps the last draft Dick read came closest to his book. But even that script had changed by the final days of shooting."

VI

DESIGNING
BLADE RUNNER

At virtually the same time he began laboring on his initial script rewrites with Hampton Fancher, Ridley Scott had also begun ironing out another all-important wrinkle in *Blade Runner*'s fabric—the film's overall "look."

This was because production design had always been one of Scott's greatest personal obsessions and strongest professional strengths. The trait had been apparent as early as Scott's first feature; *The Duellists* evidenced a period detail far in excess of its relatively meager production cost. Scott's next film, *Alien*, had a larger budget, and the corresponding intricacy of its gothic celluloid portraiture established Scott as a world-class visualist. (*Alien* also turned heretofore relatively unknown artists H. R. Giger and Ron Cobb into much sought-after motion picture designers.)

Blade Runner offered Scott an even larger canvas to draw upon—yet Michael Deeley knew his director was up to the challenge. "In a sense, no major art director would ever work with Ridley, because Ridley wouldn't let him do what he wanted," Deeley points out. "But Ridley would be right in doing that. He started out in design, you know, and he always knows what he wants. Frankly, Ridley Scott is one of the best art directors ever. He draws well, has an incredible flair for detail, and a brilliant eye."

A collage of "Ridleygrams," quick sketches drawn by Ridley Scott showing some of the director's design ideas for Blade Runner. *(Top left) Scott's drawing of Deckard's apartment, influenced by the architect Gaudi. (Top right) A Scott storyboard for an used idea of inter-building freeways. (Bottom) A BR street scene by Scott.*

Much of that "eye" evolved during Scott's early professional training. "I was a designer, trained as a painter, then an art director, and then from art direction drifted into graphic design," Scott told *The American Cinematographer* ("*Blade Runner:* Production Design and Photography," by Herb A. Lightman and Richard Patterson, July 1982). "Graphic design opens up all sorts of things, because it's photography, film, and editing."

With his intensive visual background it's not surprising that Ridley Scott believed (in 1981, at least) that a film's design can be just as important—and in some cases, perhaps more so—than the actual narrative. As such, he still tends to closely control as many of the visual elements of his films as possible, preferring *not* to simply turn a film over to a production designer, cinematographer, or special effects supervisor.

"I think there's a great tendency for a certain type of director to walk in and never be involved with his art department or with his camera crew," Scott elaborates. "This is the type who's only involved with the actors and the script. Which means he then tends to be dictated to by what he's going to get. This sort of director will just point a camera at his action and shoot it. If he's lucky enough, or has had the good sense or taste to choose a good cameraman, the cinematographer will then take over. At which point this kind of director strictly works with his actors.

"I find that is doing half the job," Scott continues. "There should be a total integration on a film, a complete synthesis running through the hands of a director who is involved in everything. That includes all the design elements. Certainly, there are moments in movies when the background of a shot can be as important as the foregrounded actor, whether that background be a figure or a landscape. Because every incident, every sound, every movement, every color, every set, prop or actor, is all part of the director's overall orchestration of a film. And orchestration, to me, is performance. Just as performance is everything."

Yet Scott still had to decide on the overall look of his new film. What was that to be? Setting *Blade Runner* in the year 2020, as was originally intended,[1] posed specific design problems.

As Scott points out, logic dictated many of the decisions in this area. "The most difficult problem for all of us involved the look of the film. The nightmare in my mind was that this 'look' would merely become an intelligent speculation concerning a city forty years in the future, and nothing more. Believe me, designing *Blade Runner* was more of a challenge than *Alien*, simply because it's much easier to create the environment for a space film rather than a project detailing life on Earth. In any event, I insisted that *Blade Runner*'s final look be authentic, not just speculative.

"For instance, take clothes and cars," Scott goes on. "What if you could take someone, a contemporary man, and whisk him back to the Times Square of forty years ago? He wouldn't, I think, have that many shocks in store for him. Except perhaps for the signage; neon in 1940 must have been much more impressive. A contemporary

---

[1] A later decision, made well into postproduction, pushed the film's time frame back to the year 2019. This was done after it was noticed that "2020" triggered too many associations with eye charts and the term "20-20 vision."

man wouldn't be puzzled by forties clothing, either, since we're seeing something of a resurgence in forties fashions right now *[in late 1981, when this interview was conducted]*. Fashion is always cyclical.

"So you're going through a rather frightening process every time you make a design decision," Scott concludes. "Whether it's a telephone, or a bar, or the shoes a character will wear, once it has been designed, it must be lumped in with everything else in the film. For better or for worse."

Scott's extremely complex stylistic sense was applied to *Blade Runner* via a number of methods. One was his self-described habit of "pictorial referencing"—omnivorously ingesting every image and artistic influence Scott can lay his hands on before he shoots a film. "I always spend a great deal of time building a library of weird and wonderful illustrators," Scott explained in that same 1982 *American Cinematographer* article. "That's usually where I begin a project. [*Blade Runner*'s look] began haphazardly, but I found myself totally enthralled with this unusual world, and [that] led me to the path of collecting odd illustrators, odd pictorial references to things. So I try to dig out those individuals first and that becomes, along with the development of the script, the design side of the film."

One early and key *Blade Runner* visual influence was artist Edward Hopper's hauntingly lonely painting "Nighthawks." This famous work depicts a group of nocturnal urban dwellers frozen in silent meditation under the stark fluorescent light of a sparsely populated all-night diner. "I was constantly waving a reproduction of this painting under the noses of the production team to illustrate the look and mood I was after in *Blade Runner*," Scott said.

Further "atmosphere" filtered through Scott in the form of thirties photographs, Hogarth engravings and, most importantly, the skewed, hallucinatory landscapes of the then popular graphic arts magazine *Heavy Metal*.

"I'd always been a fan of that magazine, which dealt with what I term 'half-fantasy,'" Scott goes on to say. "In fact, I first encountered it in its original French appearance, which is called *Metal Hurlant*. And I particularly enjoyed the work of the French artist known as 'Moebius,' whose real name is Jean Geraud. He was one of the best *Heavy Metal* illustrators, without question. I'm still knocked out by the stuff he does. And yet, I can't put my finger on why, or what it is about the way he handles himself. Perhaps it's the way Moebius juxtaposes familiar elements with the fantastic, to make some sort of architectural or fashion statement. Or it could simply be his graphic insolence."

Yet despite his saturation in such visuals Ridley Scott had still yet to meet the one man, after the director himself, who was to exert the most sweeping design influence over *Blade Runner*.

That meeting would soon come about. And it would arise partially through visual impressions burned into Scott during mundane business trips to New York.

SYD MEAD, "VISUAL FUTURIST" ━━━━━━━━━━━━

Two of *Blade Runner*'s most impressive design elements are its overcrowded streets and flying cars. Yet these did not totally spring from the imagination; instead, both were influenced by actual experiences in Ridley Scott's life. As the red-haired director told writer/publisher Don Shay in Shay's excellent *"Blade Runner—2020* Foresight" article (which comprised the entire contents of issue #9 of Shay's *Cinefex* magazine in July 1982)[2]:

"The city we present is overkill," Ridley Scott admitted. "But I always get the impression of New York as being overkill. You go into New York on a bad day and you look around and you feel this place is going to grind to a halt any minute—which it nearly does all too often. All you need is a garbage strike or a subway strike or an electrical blowout and you have absolute chaos.

"So we took that idea and projected it forty years into the future and came up with a megalopolis—the kind of city that could be where New York and Chicago join, with maybe a hundred million people living there. Or maybe San Francisco and Los Angeles. In fact, at one point we were going to call the city San Angeles, which would of course have suggested that the eight-hundred mile-long Western seaboard had been transformed into a single population center with giant cities and monolithic buildings at either end, and then this strange, kind of awful suburb in the middle. I thought the idea was

---

[2]This issue of *Cinefex*, a technical magazine dealing with the nuts and bolts of cinematic trick photography, is the single most comprehensive examination of BR's special effects.

interesting, but the city's now been moved to the East Coast because it's raining so much.[3]

"Anyway, it seemed to me that in such a proscenium there would be a lot of air traffic. I picked that up from the fact that I used to fly in and out of New York a lot over a period of about five years back before they stopped the helicopters landing on top of the Pan American Building. It was seven minutes from the airport to the roof and I could remember coming in in January or February—in blizzards and high winds—and landing on the Pan Am Building. We used to drift in over the city, very close to the buildings, and it felt like the way of the future.

"So we proceeded in that direction. [Our idea was that] the first [flying] vehicles would be police. The police, by then, will be paramilitary—they're already paramilitary in Los Angeles. Then there'd be corporate and other official vehicles and already you'd be creating a helluva traffic jam in the air. But we all agreed and felt that that was pretty much the way the cities will go. And for us, it was a very nice visual notion."

Now that Scott had arrived at the idea of a congested, broken-down, flying-vehicle-choked metropolis, his next step lay in assembling a team of artists who could turn that vision into three-dimensional reality. But where to start?

It's already been noted that Scott often relies on his "pictorial referencing" process while designing a motion picture. Part of this process involves either the director or his staff combing through bookstores for hours on end, buying any and all art, comic, or picture books, and then stacking them, library fashion, on Scott's desk. After which Scott spends an equal amount of time studying the volumes for interesting artists and imagery.

It was while engaged in such a reference binge that Scott stumbled across the first collection of an artist named Syd Mead. That book's title was *Sentinel,* and it was published by Dragon's Dream, a small

---

[3]After dropping the San Angeles idea, Scott decided to set *Blade Runner*'s action in New York. But the film was finally relocated to occur in 2019 Los Angeles. Explains Katy Haber, "That was due to the simple, pragmatic fact that we ultimately cut a deal to shoot on the Warner Brothers lot, in Burbank, and on a few locations throughout L.A. You couldn't set a film laid in New York and then show Harrison Ford driving up to the Bradbury Building without people in Los Angeles laughing us out of the theater."

London-based publishing house run by noted rock 'n' roll record album cover artist Roger Dean, in 1979.

"A lot of the art in *Sentinel* was a bit too futuristic for what I had in mind for *Blade Runner*," Scott points out. "But from his photographic, specific style, and the other elements I could already see in his art, I had the feeling Syd Mead would be able to pull back on his 'Flash Gordon' tendencies and place his visions within our own film's time period. I was specifically impressed with his automotive designs; since Fancher's script placed emphasis on certain futuristic vehicles, I felt I might be on to something. Then, when I did a little more research, found out about Mead's background and the fact that his artistic reasoning is always based on sound industrial speculations, we formally approached Syd with the idea of working on *Blade Runner*."

Mead was called in to the Gower Gulch preproduction offices in April 1980 by Ivor Powell and by John Rogers (who had just joined the *Blade Runner* team as the film's production manager). At the time, Scott's new venture was still being called *Dangerous Days* and was still under the production umbrella of Filmways Pictures.

Mead had been asked by Rogers to come in for a meeting with Ridley Scott. The artist agreed. Mead and Scott met, and the rest is history; soon afterwards, Syd Mead would become the most highly visible artist attached to the production.

Mead brought with him a set of uniquely impressive credentials. First, surprisingly unlike most of the other *Blade Runner* personnel, was the fact that Mead was a hardcore science fiction fan. "I'd been a avid reader and appreciator of science fiction long before my involvement with this project," Mead elaborated. "In fact, in 1948, when I was still in high school, I personally met Robert Heinlein, who of course was the author of *Stranger in a Strange Land* and *Starship Troopers* and many other fine works. I'd already read everything he'd written up until then. I've also always been fascinated by the work of Isaac Asimov and Arthur C. Clarke. I think they're the grand deans of science fiction, mainly because their visions are so realistically based on hard science: chemical engineering, biomechanics, satellite communication systems and so on. In a sense, science fiction has been one of the defining principles of my life."

That life began July 18, 1933. In June of 1959, Syd Mead graduated from the prestigious Pasadena, California, Art Center; he began his professional career that same year by working for the Ford Motor Company, at its Advanced Vehicle Studio in Deerborn, Michigan.

Two years later Mead placed with the Chicago-based Hansen Company, designing lavish promotional booklets for such clients as U.S. Steel and the Sony Corporation. Then, in 1970, he formed his own company, Syd Mead Inc. That year also saw Mead embark on a ten-year relationship with the Holland-based Philips Electronics group as a consultant. "That experience gave me a tremendous amount of exposure to electronics," Mead recalls, "particularly to the consumer product/hardware end of that stuff." Mead has also provided the concept for a Norwegian/Caribbean cruiseliner, worked on mass-transit projects, did wide-body jumbo jet interiors, and helped design the supersonic Concorde airliner for Air France.

However, despite extensive design experience across the entire spectrum of the transportation field (particularly in the engineering aspects of the general vehicular market), Mead's primary concerns lay in what he calls "future studies."

"Actually, despite the downbeat philosophical atmosphere permeating *Blade Runner,* I'm an optimist about the future," Mead points out. "And my futuristic interests were actually why Ford Motor Company hired me in the first place. Not only could I come up with advanced designs that weren't impossible, but I could also project them into a complete, imaginary scenario, a full lifestyle overview which surrounded and complemented the basic object. In other words, I was producing little self-contained worlds, automobiles that were placed into fully functioning futuristic environments, as opposed to an isolated airbrush rendering of a single car on a white board."

With these imagistic skills, then, it is not surprising that Mead would eventually gravitate toward the film industry. However, *Blade Runner* was not the artist's first brush with Hollywood. In 1979 Mead had been hired to conceptualize the mammoth alien "V'Ger" ship of *Star Trek: The Motion Picture.* He found himself working on that film with both the *Apogee* special effects company (founded and run by award-winning illusionist John Dykstra), and with effects ace Douglas Trumbull (*2001* and *Close Encounters*), through Trumbull's own company, the Entertainment Effects Group (EEG).

As for *Blade Runner,* working with Scott was, in Mead's words, "Nice. Inspiring. Very cooperative. Ridley is good to work for, because I'm very visual and he is, too. He can actually sit down and draw out an idea. He did that quite a bit during *Blade Runner*, which gave me an immediate insight into what he was thinking about."

The drawings Scott was primarily producing at this point concerned the futuristic automobiles of *Blade Runner*. Designing *Blade Runner*'s cars became Mead's first official assignment, and it was a job to which he applied his customary diligence.

"Although I eventually assumed broader artistic responsibilities and wound up creating props, street scenes, and buildings," Mead explains, "I was originally hired just to design the automobiles that would appear in *Blade Runner*. And I did five of them.

"As I started designing the automobiles I simply could not help but place them in a surrounding environment which I felt mirrored the industrial aesthetic which had produced these cars. Consequently, I might do a drawing of a single car, but it would be firmly grounded by a palpable environment—a real street, with real buildings and people dressed in believable future fashions. Ridley became more and more excited by this."

As Mead goes on to say, "These futuristic surroundings gradually began to illustrate and were based on Ridley's idea of 'retrofitting,' which became one of the significant design schemes of the film. It also became the word most associated with the picture; 'retrofitting' simply means upgrading old machinery or structures by slapping new add-ons to them."

Once Mead had decided on a *Blade Runner* production design (whether it be vehicle, prop, or set), he would then do a color tempera illustration 10" x 15" in size, with enough detail to not only satisfy Ridley Scott but also allow the art department staff to build that object.

"Ridley had his own particular vision for the cars," Mead said. "He'd wanted somebody who could visualize believable mechanical objects, to complement his own ideas. But at no time did he want these vehicles—or any piece of machinery in the film, for that matter—to dominate the proceedings. Scott would always say we weren't making a 'hardware' movie, like *2001*. What he wanted were backgrounds that reflected an everyday, workaday level of technology, yet backgrounds that would still be sufficiently impressive to interest an audience."

Part of these Mead-induced backgrounds included *Blade Runner*'s "star car"—the sleek blue spinner—a word coined by Hampton Fancher—first seen as that streamlined land/air police vehicle used by Gaff to fly Deckard away from the Noodle Bar.

The Spinner was actually the first design concept discussed at

Mead's initial meetings with Ridley Scott. "The starting-off principle for my work on the film was that this futuristic society could produce a car that could fly," Mead pointed out. "Therefore, not only is the interior instrumentation unique, but the configuration of the Spinner is totally different from any other vehicle in the film, simply because it *can* fly."

Scott had originally conceived of the Spinner as a fairly compact coupe. However, Mead himself subsequently designed a larger, "Chevrolet scale" model, which would lend itself to visually impressive full-scale takeoffs. The artist further decided against the helicopterlike blades and folding wings, which had become the stereotyped cliché of other flying film automobiles. "Instead of unwieldy folding propellers or H. G. Wells-like appendages," Mead said, "I suggested designing the Spinner as an aerodyne, which is a heavier-than-air craft with an internal enclosed lifting system built into it, like the British Harrier jumpjet. The Spinner would also look like a car all the time, whether it was flying or just rolling down a street. Although it would be equipped with bigger windshield wipers and glass cleaning systems, because the air of *Blade Runner*'s time is supposed to be so heavy with pollutants.

"One further aspect of my police Spinner design was the fact that I conceived of it as a restricted vehicle. It can only be used by authorized personnel; in this case, the LAPD. Again, because it could fly at faster speeds than other Spinners, and therefore would be involved with a whole new set of complicated travel patterns."

In addition to incorporating hydraulic sections which allowed the police Spinner's front wheels to fold up inside the craft (for its conversion into a flying car) and collapsible headrests installed with self-contained speaker systems (which can be glimpsed behind Harrison Ford's head during his flight to Tyrell's pyramid), Mead's most unusual Spinner detail was a hydraulic, "twist-wrist" steering device. The traditional automotive steering wheel was replaced with two in-dash holes into which operators placed each hand. By grabbing a handle recessed within each hole and turning their wrists, drivers could then effectively guide both the left and right sides of the vehicle.

"I set up the design format for each vehicle type and then let the draftsmen and builders make changes as they went along, as they had or wanted to," Mead continues. "I liked that sense of collaboration. What we ended up with was a curious accumulation of detail, a heuristic growth of odds and ends that the original concepts didn't include. Which, I think, made the cars look that much more believable."

Despite Mead's capabilities and qualifications, however, it soon became evident to the *Blade Runner* accounting department that the artist didn't come cheap. Since he was not a part of the Hollywood union system, Mead was able to ask for—and receive—his then usual rate of $1500 per day. "I hadn't been a professional illustrator for twenty years just to bump down my price because I was working in my first major capacity on a big production," Mead explained. "I felt I had no choice but to exact my going fee. I would have done that whether my client were NASA or Volvo or a motion picture company."

LAWRENCE G. PAULL, DAVID SNYDER, AND THE ART DEPARTMENT

Of course, Syd Mead was only a conceptual artist. Hired to staff *BR*'s Art Department were:

Lawrence G. Paull (Production Designer) and David Snyder (Art Director). These men would hold two most crucial positions in regards to creating a three-dimensional Los Angeles circa 2019, a job constantly helped by numerous $1\frac{1}{2}''$ by $3''$ illustrational sketches (dubbed "Ridleygrams") drawn by Ridley Scott, which showed exactly what the director was looking for in a scene. Other important Art Department contributors included Sherman Labby (Storyboards), Mentor Huebner (Production Illustrator), Linda DeScenna (Chief Set Decorator), and Tom Southwell (who designed many of the film's futuristic graphics and neon signs).

According to Michael Deeley, however, "It was really Ridley who was the overall Production Designer/Art Director on *Blade Runner*. It wouldn't be fair to say otherwise."

VII

THE CAST
AND CREW

"Other than Harrison Ford—who was a complete professional, intelligent, and quite focused—we decided early on not to choose familiar faces for **Blade Runner.** *Particularly in the case of the replicants. This made for quite adventurous casting; we had to find new people so that audiences wouldn't say, 'Oh, look, there's old so-and-so playing an android. Isn't that sweet?'"*

—MICHAEL DEELEY

LOOKING FOR THE LEAD

With the assistance of casting directors Mike Fenton and Jane Feinberg (a prolific, wildly successful team which cast many of the most high-profile films of the eighties), Scott, Deeley, Katy Haber, and Hampton Fancher now commenced trying to match up appropriate performers with their counterparts in *Blade Runner.*

The most critical role was, of course, Rick Deckard, a part Fancher had begun thinking of five years before production actually began.

"Way back in 1975, when I was first trying to option Phil's book, I'd already decided that Robert Mitchum was perfect for the role of Deckard," Fancher recalls. "The last thing I'd seen him do was *Farewell, My Lovely* (1975), where Mitchum played Philip Marlowe. He had a certain vulnerability in that film I really liked. I also liked the fact that Mitchum played Marlowe as a guy with insomnia and a constant hangover. The age issue was there, of course, but at that time Mitchum still looked like he was only fifty. A *tough* fifty. Mitchum could wrestle and kiss and fight with the best of them."

Four years later, however, Fancher's conception of Deckard had changed. "By 1979 I was more sold on the idea of Deckard as he was portrayed in the book: bland, nondescript, a bureaucrat. That ruled Mitchum out." Fancher was also aware of the demands of the box office, however, and realized that Deckard "would probably end up looking like the sort of tall, hard-bitten private eye that figured so prominently in classic film noir, no matter what I said." Therefore, Fancher's first suggestions regarding Deckard's casting included such names as Tommy Lee Jones and Christopher Walken.

But by August 7, 1980, Ridley Scott had already approached and intrigued a superstar talent whom Fancher had "never, ever dreamed of as Deckard": Dustin Hoffman.

"I'd always adored Dustin Hoffman," Scott explains. "His is an amazing talent. And I figured, unlikely though he may be in terms of his physical size as a sci-fi hero, as an actor Hoffman could do anything. Therefore, it really didn't matter. For me to get an actor of that power would have been incredibly and enormously valuable to the project. It also would have given what otherwise could have been perceived as a fairytale story a certain gravity. Hoffman would have grounded Deckard in reality."

Fancher, however, was not so convinced. "The whole Dustin Hoffman thing came up during one of those alarmed moments when we needed a star to keep the picture's momentum going. At which point Ridley came up with the idea of Dustin. I hated it. Yet even though I was still in the production mix strongly at that point, they told me they were still going to go ahead with Hoffman. My response was, 'You guys do that, I'm outta here!'

"But they did anyway. Next thing I knew, I was being asked to go over to Dustin's house for the evening so we could review the script. I went, but with a chip on my shoulder. But Hoffman surprised me. He liked the project, was very talented and formidable, and asked very intelligent questions. I went away impressed."

"The first time I met Dustin was in New York City; he was, in fact, with Michael Deeley," Scott continues. "Dustin had read Hampton's latest draft and was obviously intrigued by it. I knew that because he'd just moved into this large apartment on the Upper West Side, and there was not a stick of furniture in it. Except one table, around which we all sat. Here we were in the corner, on three little chairs. The whole scene looked like something out of an Edward Hopper painting. It was so stark and empty.

"Anyway, Dustin then proceeded to talk about Hampton's script for the next six hours. His wife finally came in, carrying some shopping. And she said, 'My God, Dustin, these men haven't even had coffee!' He looked at her and said, 'Oh? Oh!' He'd completely forgotten. But Dustin forgets about everything when he's on a roll. So I could see how interested he was.

"Now, it's not easy to get to Dustin Hoffman. You've really got to present him with something that genuinely interests him. Otherwise there's a bailout."

One way in which Scott and Deeley intended to keep Hoffman interested involved making another pass on the *Dangerous Days* script. As Fancher now explains, "One of the things that amazed me about Hoffman was how candid he was in acknowledging that he wouldn't be accepted as this particular hero. He really could step back from himself and talk about his personality in the third person; he knew what his audience would and wouldn't accept. So Hoffman said if he was going to be involved, there'd have to be a rewrite. I had no problem with that. Stars always make changes anyway.

"Ridley and Michael now began panting for me to make those changes," Fancher continues. "So I went away for a couple of days and came back with the idea that Deckard was a selfish guy who wants what he wants, and nobody had better get in the way of what he wants. He'd become one mean little motherfucker, in other words. That would have made Deckard's moral transformation at the end of the picture even more affecting, I thought."

Pleased at this change in character, Hoffman now engaged in a series of extensive story conferences with Scott, Deeley, and Katy Haber. Most of these occurred during the month of September 1980, during which Hoffman would ask many questions and throw out numerous suggestions concerning his character and the script.

For example, at this time Fancher's screenplay still contained a scene of Batty slaughtering Tyrell's entire family. But upon reading a meeting memo dated September 29, 1980, one can see that it was Hoffman who raised the point that he "did not like the killing of the family. Therefore, [we] should consider the lone God image." This story point would indeed be changed and result in the release print's sole murder of Tyrell.

With a superstar like Dustin Hoffman onboard, however, Scott and company felt sure they had found their leading man. Yet, as had occurred so many times in the past on this project, problems loomed ahead.

"Hoffman was involved for a couple of months," Fancher continues. "But during that time I started seeing parts of the story veering into what I thought were overly familiar areas. Dustin was enamored of cryogenics, for example. He began talking about how freezing people with deadly diseases before they died and then being able to successfully thaw them out was really going to happen someday. He was a big fan of that. Ridley got off on the idea, too. I didn't. I resisted these changes in the script—I felt we were getting too far away from our original concepts.

"But then Dustin Hoffman abruptly dropped out of the production. So did that scene."

Hoffman did indeed leave the production, on October 16, 1980. "Frankly, I think it might have been something as simple as money," explains Ridley Scott. "Also the fact that Dustin was trying to change the basic content of the story into a more socially conscious picture," adds Deeley. "None of us really wanted to see the film pushed in that direction."

HARRISON FORD

The pressure to find a leading man increased. With less than three months before the start of the projected Filmways-financed, January 1981 principal photography, the need to cast Deckard became an urgent priority.

At which point actor Harrison Ford, like his character Indiana Jones, suddenly came to the rescue.

"No one can remember who finally came up with the idea of casting Harrison Ford," begins Fancher, "but I do recall his name being in the air over Hollywood at the time. Don't forget, this was still a year before *Raiders of the Lost Ark* was released—*Raiders* came out in 1981. The perception of Harrison Ford in a lot of people's minds at that point was still that he'd done some good work in the *Star Wars* pictures but was basically a terrific character actor."

However, events then transpired to persuade Fancher otherwise. "Barbara Hershey was talking on the phone one day to Steven Spielberg, who was over in London shooting *Raiders*," Fancher goes on. "And Spielberg seemed really hyped on Harrison; Barbara told me Steven told her Harrison Ford was going to be the biggest star in

Hollywood. Scott and Deeley must have heard something like that, too, because the next thing I knew they had flown over to England. Spielberg showed them some *Raiders* rushes, Michael and Ridley talked with Ford, and that was that."

Ridley Scott still remembers the day he first met Harrison Ford—and not for the reason a reader might think, either. "Harrison signed onto *Blade Runner* in late October of 1980. But I first met him straight off the set one night," the director recalls. "He drove into London, and I think he still had the goddamn hat on he wore as Indiana Jones. I thought, 'Oh, shit!' Because up to that point, we'd seen *Deckard* wearing the same kind of hat. The kind they used to sport in those old noir thrillers.

"So there went Deckard's hat. I thought, 'Okay, if that's out the window, we'll give him a crew cut.' Which is where Deckard's brush cut came in."

Hats aside, the important fact of the moment was that Ridley Scott was now convinced that he'd finally found his Rick Deckard.

Harrison Ford was born on July 13, 1942, in Chicago, Illinois. After dropping out of Ripon College in Wisconsin, where he did some acting and later summer stock, Ford moved to the Los Angeles area. Then, in 1963, after appearing in a Laguna Beach Playhouse production, he was signed by Columbia Pictures as a member of their "new talent" program.

Ford made his screen debut in 1966's *Dead Heat on A Merry-Go-Round* as part of his Columbia contract. Bit parts in such features as *Luv, Getting Straight,* and *The Long Ride Home* followed, along with a new contract at Universal, where he guest-starred in such episodic television fare as *The F.B.I., The Virginian, Ironside,* and *Gunsmoke.*

But frustration over the lack of growth in his career caused Ford to quit the acting business for four years. During this hiatus he worked as a professional carpenter, with some of his jobs involving remodeling homes of famous movie stars. By 1973, however, Ford had returned to the acting game. That same year marked the turning point of Ford's career: he had an accepted an offer to play car freak Bob Falfa in George Lucas' mega-smash nostalgia film *American Graffiti.* Meeting Lucas was a godsend; Harrison Ford would now not only go on to create his well-received role of Han Solo in Lucas' ensuing *Star Wars* trilogy, but he would attain even greater popularity as the fedora-wearing archaeologist-adventurer in the Lucas-produced Indiana Jones films.

Harrison Ford as Rick Deckard, Blade Runner.

Yet Lucas was only one of the so-called "USC Mafia" with whom Ford would have a fruitful association. Francis Ford Coppola's *Apocalypse Now*, for example, featured Ford in a distinctive cameo, and in that same director's *The Conversation*, Ford had his best supporting role yet as a menacing and absolutely appalling company man. In 1983, Ford married successful screenwriter Melissa Mathison (*E.T.*, and *The Indian in the Cupboard*); the couple now live with their children on an 8000-acre ranch in Montana.

Other pre-*Blade Runner*, Ford-starring vehicles would include such features as *Force 10 from Navarone*, *Hanover Street*, and *The Frisco Kid*. Beyond this cinematic experience and the 1980 buzz surrounding his work on the still-unreleased *Raiders*, however, there were also other reasons why Deeley and Scott felt Harrison Ford would make a perfect Rick Deckard.

Blade Runner's producer and director were in unanimous agreement that Ford had thus far been given ample public exposure as a *personality*, but little opportunity to showcase his true talents as an *actor*. "Ford had not been given much of a chance, particularly since *Star Wars*, to show what he was made of," Deeley underlined to this writer in 1981. "Both Ridley and I felt Deckard's curious mixture of emerging sensitivity and hard-boiled bureaucracy would offer an excellent chance for Harrison to do that."

During one of my occasional visits to the *Blade Runner* set in May 1981, this writer happened to stumble—almost literally—across Harrison Ford sitting in a chair in a corner of the Warners back lot between setups. After introducing myself, I then informed the actor that I was writing a series of articles on the film for a number of magazines. Ford seemed uncomfortable with this fact until I stressed that I was approaching my project more as a film historian than a typical (scumbag) journalist (a statement I hope this book has finally verified). At which point the actor seemed to loosen up a bit.

I then asked Ford if he could tell me anything about the part of Deckard that appealed to him. He mulled the question over for a moment, and then replied, in a serious tone, "One of Deckard's innate qualities is that he's struggling with a job-oriented fear. That involves killing; shooting people is not something he likes to do. So although he might be a pretty good Blade Runner, Deckard's also a reluctant one. That conflict, that ambiguity, makes for an interesting character. He also," the actor added, with his wry, trademark grin, "gets kicked around a lot."

The physicality of the Deckard character was obviously not a prospect that worried the actor—Ford has always been known, and admired, within the film industry for the assured manner in which he does many of his own stunts. But the prospect of losing *Blade Runner*'s principal player to serious injury certainly frightened Michael Deeley.

"Harrison's a wonderfully agile, coordinated man," states *Blade Runner*'s producer. "He's also intelligent and professional enough to know when to stand back and let the stuntmen do their work. But he does like to get physically involved. That can be worrisome. For example, one evening we were shooting the scene where Deckard hunts Zhora down through these crowded streets. And Harrison did a number of takes where he went tearing at a full gallop across the tops of these vehicles that were stalled in traffic. I remember feeling terrified that Harrison was going to fall off the top of one of those buses or taxis or things and break both his legs. Or worse."

As for Ridley Scott, the director felt Ford embodied the very essence of *Blade Runner's* cross-genre melding of forties *film noir* with contemporary sensibilities.

"Our main character, Deckard, is a detective, like Sam Spade or Philip Marlowe, a man who follows a hunch to the end," Scott related in the original *BR* pressbook. "He's in trouble because he's begun to identify with his quarry, the replicants. [Harrison] possesses some of the laconic dourness of Bogey, but he's more ambivalent, more human. He's almost an antihero."

When I later asked Harrison Ford that same night what he thought of Ridley Scott, the quiet, unpretentious star said, "The really successful films I've done always have had something new about them. *Blade Runner* has that freshness too, I think. Just look around you—Ridley's created a world unlike any I've ever seen."

Sadly, the cordiality between Ford and Scott suggested by the above quotes would not endure. That unfortunate situation, however, is a story for chapter IX: *Blood Runner*.

Now it was time to cast the remaining citizens of *Blade Runner's* futuristic cityscape.

THE ACTORS AND THE CREW

Picked for the crucial role of blond, black-jacketed Roy Batty—the second key part in the film—was Dutch actor *Rutger Hauer.*

Hauer was born in Amsterdam on January 23, 1944. In 1959, when he was fifteen years old, Hauer ran away from his home in Breukelen, Holland. According to the original *BR* pressbook, Hauer did this in order to "follow a tradition set by his great grandfather, captain of a tea schooner that sailed the Caribbean. Hauer headed for the seacoast, where he signed aboard a freighter as an ordinary seaman. Like his grandfather, another generation of seaman, his sailing career was cut short when he discovered he was colorblind."

Hauer's parents were both actors. After being sent to an acting school by them, Hauer then served a short five-month stint in the

Rutger Hauer as Roy Batty, with his symbolic dove. Note nail protruding from Hauer's right hand.

Dutch Army, studied theater in Amsterdam, and worked at a theater in Basel, Switzerland, where he "learned all the fundamentals—I was a stagehand, a gardener, a carpenter, you name it." At this point in his life the actor enjoyed racing motorcycles and mountain climbing.

From 1967 to 1972, Hauer toured the Netherlands with an experimental theatrical group. He then segued into film work, with his first role being a radical sculptor in Paul (*RoboCop*) Verhoeven's *Turkish Delight,* which was nominated for an Academy Award in 1973. Hauer then specialized in lusty, free-thinking characterizations. Before starring in *Blade Runner,* Hauer had already appeared in over seventeen films, including a stint as the despicable terrorist Wulfgar (a most hissable screen villain) in the Sylvester Stallone action-adventure film *Nighthawks.* The actor was also featured in two other Paul Verhoeven-directed projects: *Spetters* and the Oscar-winning *Soldier of Orange,* in which Hauer played an heroic World War II resistance fighter. This latter film was the project that caught Scott's eye, convincing the British director to sign the Dutch actor on for *Blade Runner.*

When I spoke to Hauer on his gleamingly spotless sailboat moored in a Los Angeles harbor one damp October night in 1995, the actor (who looks just the same offscreen as on, with the exception of his hands—they are enormous and powerful), the actor revealed himself to be fascinating. "Rutger is a nice man," Ridley Scott fondly recalls. "A very nice man."

Indeed. Initially wary, as the soft-spoken Hauer relaxed he progressively revealed himself to be thoughtful and well-educated, warm yet genuine, with a devilish sense of humor and a rebellious glint in his eye. His Dutch accent has been mostly erased by a utilitarian American one; only an occasional slip serves as a reminder of his European origins.

Sitting in the gathering dusk, surrounded by a restful silence punctuated only by the occasional cry of a gull or the clang of a ship's bell, I asked Hauer why Roy Batty has remained such a mesmerizing characterization to audiences the world over. Smiling, Hauer replied:

"The best trick Ridley played with Roy and the other replicants was that he told us early on—the androids, that is, Daryl Hannah and Joanna Cassidy and Brion James and myself—to relax and be comfortable. To have fun and to make the replicants likable. And we did. That, I think, is their underlying appeal."

"The central problems in *Blade Runner* are essentially moral ones," producer Michael Deeley points out. "Should the replicants kill to gain more life? Should Harrison Ford be killing them simply because they want to exist? These questions begin to tangle up Deckard's thinking . . . especially when he becomes involved with a female replicant himself."

The name of that replicant is Rachael, and for many *Blade Runner* fans, *Sean Young* has become a noirish icon: impossibly beautiful, cool yet emotional, mysterious yet sensitive.

The actress who brought Rachael to life was born a native Kentuckyian on November 20, 1959, in Louisville. Young spent her childhood in Cleveland. A "rabid moviegoer," Young attended high school at the Interlaken Arts Academy in Michigan. She then moved to New York, worked for seven months attending to cancer patients at Sloan Kettering Hospital, and studied dance and acting. Previous to *Blade Runner*, Young had appeared in such films as James Ivory's *Jane Austen in Manhattan* and the Bill Murray comedy *Stripes*.

"We auditioned at least fifty actresses for Rachael," says Ridley Scott. "Of those we only screen tested three. One was Barbara Hershey: Hampton was very keen that Rachael should be Barbara Hershey. Another was Sean Young.

"Now, there were any number of reasons why I was interested in Sean for this part. First I felt the girl had to be young, and that she ought to be beautiful. Particularly as the part involved a love relationship with

Harrison. Secondly, in my mind I had always had an image of Rachael looking like either Vivien [*Gone With the Wind*] Leigh or Rita Hayworth. Partly because Vivien Leigh was such a powerful, spunky kind of woman, partly because I was looking for somebody who was a brunette."

Scott also felt that Young conceptually fit the part. "I'd felt that Rachael needed to be very fresh," Scott concludes. "Perfect, in fact. As if she'd just stepped out of the replicant vat. I couldn't get that from a thirty-five- or forty-year-old actress, no matter how talented they were. It just wouldn't work. It'd become a different kind of film. Sean was exactly right for the part."

Sean Young as Rachael during her Voigt-Kampff test. Rachael's glowing eyes betray her replicant status; this was BR cinematographer Jordan Cronenweth's favorite shot in the film.

In recent years, Sean Young has garnered some notoriety for eccentric behavior, which included dressing up in a Catwoman costume while director Tim Burton was casting *Batman Returns*, marching into his office, and declaring that she was perfect for the part (which she didn't get). However, this author met Sean Young while he was working on *Dune* in Mexico City in 1983. In that film, Young played the romantic lead, "Chani." The young woman I remember was more restless and utterly unselfconscious than strange.

In any event, *Blade Runner* continues to loom large in Young's life. Witness this statement by the actress, who, when I talked to her some years after *Blade Runner*'s initial release, had this succinct comment to make regarding her thoughts about the picture:

"Are you kidding?" the actress said. *"Blade Runner* is still my favorite movie!"

Another fetching replicant—the seductive yet cunning Pris—was portrayed by *Daryl Hannah,* who has moved on to a world-class acting career.

Living doll toys with a real one; Daryl Hannah as Pris.

During the compilation of this book, Hannah proved to be one of its most gracious, unpretentious, and down-to-earth participants. Born Daryl Christine Hannah on December 19, 1960, (also in Chicago, making her and Harrison Ford citymates), Hannah first attracted notice as upper-class schoolgirl "Pam" in Brian DePalma's 1978 psychokinetic thriller *The Fury* (which was *filmed* in Chicago). The athletic, 5'10" tall actress then appeared in a variety of smaller films (including the little-seen "Let's go camping and get picked off by that madman in the woods" horror flick *The Final Terror*, 1981), before signing onto her first major production that same year. The picture in question? *Blade Runner.*

Since 1982, of course, the actress has scored major applause by starring in such popular features as *Splash, Steel Magnolias,* and *Wall Street.* Yet, like Sean Young before her, *Blade Runner* still retains a special niche in Hannah's heart.

"*Blade Runner* is the only movie I've ever been a part of that came even close to my expectations of what filmmaking was all about," Hannah told me by telephone from her mother's home in Colorado in 1995. "In fact, that experience was the whole reason I moved out to the West Coast in the first place. It was an incredible, extraordinary experience. The sets, the costumes, the production design, the meticulousness of Ridley's vision, the professionalism and dedication of the other actors and the crew—it really was unbelievable. I've said this many times, but *Blade Runner* is still my favorite film. And one of my favorite performances."

Rounding out the *Blade Runner* cast were *Edward James Olmos* as Gaff, *Joanna Cassidy* as Zhora, *M. Emmet Walsh* as Captain Bryant, *William Sanderson* as J. F. Sebastian, *Joe Turkel* as Tyrell, *Brion James* as Leon, *Morgan Paull* as Holden, *James Hong* as Chew, and *Hy Pyke* as Taffey Lewis. As Daryl Hannah has already pointed out, each, in their own way, was extraordinary.

Lest the reader assume that I am giving the first four performers in this chapter privileged status over the other actors mentioned herein, never fear; each *Blade Runner* performer will be given equal time under the spotlight in the ensuing chapters to come.

Now, however, it's time to move on to those equally important laborers who toiled on the other side of the camera: *BR*'s crew.

These personnel included Cinematographer Jordan Cronenweth (who says,"we reasoned that *BR*'s intrusive 'shafts of light' emanated from futuristic aircraft"); Editor Terry Rawlings; Property Master Terry Lewis (who transformed part of an Austrian-made, Steyr/ Mannlicher rifle into Deckard's handgun); Wardrobe Designers Charles Knode/ Michael Kaplan; Gene Winfield (who built twenty-five full-size functional vehicles for *BR*'s streets); Floor Effects Supervisor Terry Frazee; Sound Effects, Peter Pennel (who, at Scott's urging, revised a "humming sound" heard in *Alien* for Deckard's apartment; Stunt Coordinator Gary Combs; Makeup Supervisor Marvin G. Westmore (assisted by Peter Altobelli and Jack Obringer). Uncredited *BR* prosthetic makeups were supplied by Michael Westmore (Marvin's younger brother) *and* John Chambers, Oscar-winner for *Planet of the Apes*

The supporting actors of Blade Runner. *From left to right: (Top row) Morgan Paull (as Holden), Brion James (Leon), M. Emmet Walsh (Bryant); (Center) Joe Turkel (Tyrell), William Sanderson (Sebastian), James Hong (Chew); (Bottom row) Joanna Cassidy (Zhora), Edward James Olmos (Gaff).*

VIII

THE SHOOT

Making a film is like going to war. You've heard that one, right? One of the oldest expressions in the book. Yet making Blade Runner *validated that cliché—every day, I felt as if I were engaged in an unprecedented military action.*

—RIDLEY SCOTT TO PAUL M. SAMMON
JUNE 12, 1982

Making a movie is the awful chore at the end of a successful negotiation.

—MICHAEL DEELEY TO PAUL M. SAMMON
OCTOBER 15, 1995

With *Blade Runner*'s cast, crew, and financing now in place, Brighton Productions next relocated from The Sunset-Gower lot to the Burbank Studios on February 13, 1981—a move not without its consequences.

"Before we switched offices from Gower Gulch to Warner Brothers," explains Katy Haber, "I'd packed up a number of boxes with all the paperwork pertaining to the film's preproduction period—*BR*'s early scripts, its memos, meeting notes, the lot. What I'd done was empty everything out of our filing cabinets before the switch to make it easier for the movers to transport those cabinets. Unfortunately, by the time we got to Burbank, all the paperwork boxes had been thrown away; the movers apparently thought only the cabinets were going. So we lost just about everything. That was a disaster, and one reason why documentation on the early phases of the film is so hard to come by today. It was all lost before shooting even began."

Yet Brighton's loss of *BR*'s preproduction documents was a minor nuisance compared to its newest task—*Blade Runner*'s principal photography.

The first and most important step in that phase, of course, would be deciding just where that photography would take place.

RIDLEYVILLE

Ridley Scott had initially conceived *Blade Runner*'s futuristic, Asian-dominated metropolis as being a vast urban center composed of two giant cities which had grown together. One was to be New York. In fact, Syd Mead had had the Manhattan skyline in mind while creating his original preproduction designs, and Scott was eager to feature the Chrysler Building (an Art Deco structure for which the director had a particular fondness) in one *Blade Runner* shot.

Therefore, based on this "megalopolis" concept, and Scott's original desire to film *Blade Runner* on actual urban streets, he and producer Michael Deeley scouted a number of different cities as possible shooting sites. These potential locations included New York, Atlanta, London, "and a huge housing estate not far from Logan Airport in Boston, which turned out not to have the height Ridley wanted," Deeley says.

However, it soon became apparent that the complicated logistics and relative lack of control such location shooting would impose—plus the risk of local residents damaging or dismantling the elaborate sets which would have to be erected on the three or four genuine city blocks Scott felt necessary to properly film *Blade Runner*—posed too great a fiscal risk to the production company. Thus, by September

A rare daylight shot of Warner Brothers' Old New York Street Set being transformed into Ridleyville.

1980, it was decided that most of the film's exteriors would have to be shot on a studio back lot instead.

This decision resulted in one of *Blade Runner*'s minor claims to cinematic history: the film's primary setting would soon encompass one of the largest and most detailed exterior sets ever erected within a major studio.

Ironically, *Blade Runner*'s primary location was actually "retrofitted" over a preexisting one—the Old New York Street, a back lot area located within what was then known as The Burbank Studios (now Warner Brothers). Eventually to serve as *BR*'s chief filming site throughout principal photography, the Old New York Street had a long and venerable history. It had been built in 1929 and witnessed the original filming of such detective classics as *The Maltese Falcon* and *The Big Sleep*. This coincidence was sure to stir any *film noir* buff's palpitating heart, since it meant Harrison Ford would be chasing murderous replicants down the same studio streets once trod by the fast-talking Jimmy Cagney and wise-cracking Humphrey Bogart.

Now came the task of scheduling. It had already been decided that *Blade Runner*'s principal photography would begin on March 9, 1981. Since most of *BR*'s scenes took place at night, this likewise meant that the *Blade Runner* crew would have to typically arrive at The Burbank Studios in mid-afternoon, take their lunch at 12:30 A.M., and then wrap their "day's" work at around five or six A.M. Furthermore, certain *BR* sequences also required the presence of large groups of people, so at least 300 extras were now recruited for the various crowd scenes shot on the Old New York/*Blade Runner* Street.

It wasn't long before this location acquired an affectionate nickname bestowed upon it by *BR*'s cast and crew: "Ridleyville." Yet above this touch of humor hung something ominous—a threatened Directors Guild strike. This shutdown was tentatively scheduled to start July 1, 1981. Consequently, the *Blade Runner* team would be under constant pressure to finish principal photography before that deadline to avoid the possibility of Scott having to withdraw from the picture because of the strike itself.

Such a disaster, however, still lay in the future. For now, the *BR* production team concentrated on the realities at hand. One such objective involved deciding how to best transform Old New York into the Los Angeles of tomorrow. "Once we decided we'd be shooting on the Old New York Street," Lawrence Paull told this author in 1981, "I had a number of photos taken of the existing façades on that part of the back lot. Then Syd Mead studied these photos and began laying the retrofitting piping and tubing and all that other detail over some tempera sketches he'd made based on the photographs of those façades. That's the way we detailed the street."

As for lighting Ridleyville, this was primarily accomplished through dozens of neon signs the *BR* production team had assembled for the shoot. "There was so much neon, in fact," says cinematographer Jordan Cronenweth, "that we had a seven-man team whose sole responsibility it was to take care of those signs. Those guys were necessary because, whenever possible, I tried to light the New York set—all those bazaars and crowd scenes and street chases—with available light."

Along with the crowds, the neon and the intricate props used to fill in the corners of the Old New York set (which, topographically speaking, formed a rough "X" shape and comprised a total of eight different city blocks, most fronting one another), it was also decided to litter Los Angeles' futuristic avenues with a number of high- and low-tech vehicles. This assignment fell to Gene Winfield.

The teeming Ridleyville set, built on the Warner Brothers backlot Old New York Street set.

A longtime film/TV car supplier, Winfield was originally contracted to build fifty-seven full-scale vehicles for *Blade Runner*, a number that was subsequently scaled back to twenty-five.[1] Most of the full-scale automobiles seen on Ridleyville's streets were constructed around a Volkswagen chassis; virtually all of them were artificially aged. "Dirtied down," Winfield says, "to make them appear five or ten years older than they really were."

Yet not all of *Blade Runner*'s cars were provided by Winfield. "The

---

[1]Winfield ultimately delivered only twenty-three vehicles. An arson fire at Winfield's shop on the night of May 14, 1981 destroyed two *BR* vehicles (a van and a car), which were not rebuilt.

production company was using a big hangar out at the Burbank airport as a warehouse for the various props and bits of material they used in the film," the automotive ace continues. "And mixed in with all this stuff were about a half-dozen vehicles that we had had nothing to do with. These weren't custom jobs in any sense of the word. Instead, they were old cars from the sixties—Plymouths, Cadillacs, and so on—that had been all crutched up with tanks and tubes and stainless steel gimmicks. The idea was to make them look beat-up and awful and retrofitted. And the best time to look for these older vehicles is during the big traffic-jam scene, where Deckard chases Zhora; you'll see them mixed in with my own cars."

Such details were, of course, scrutinized very closely by *Blade Runner*'s money men. At the highest level, *BR*'s financial structure comprised Alan Ladd, Jr. and Warner Brothers. The fiscal troops in the trenches, however, those controlling the cash flow on a daily basis, included Michael Deeley, Katy Haber, and Ivor Powell. Tandem's Bud Yorkin and Jerry Perenchio also had a vested interest in keeping tabs on *BR*'s production costs.[2]

Costs that very much centered on Ridleyville itself.

STREET SCENE 2019: A VISIT TO THE
BLADE RUNNER SET IN 1981

Ridley Scott had already demonstrated an obsessive eye for detail in *Alien*; in fact, the director's visual passion on that production had even extended to the words "Weylan/Yutani" stenciled on the underwear which Sigourney Weaver strips down to before her final confrontation with the film's titled creature ("Weylan/Yutani" was the name of the corporation for which *Alien*'s characters worked). Yet nowhere was Scott's fascination with "layering" more tangibly evident that on *Blade Runner*'s set.

This writer, who visited Ridleyville a number of times during *BR*'s principal photography, can testify to that fact; texture was everywhere

---

[2]Around the time of *BR*'s production, Perenchio owned the rights to the Embassy Pictures film library. He would later sell these rights to Nelson Entertainment; among the titles included in this transfer would be *Blade Runner* itself.

on this set. In fact, it even *smelled* like a sleazy metropolis—Ridleyville was permeated by the aromas of burned coffee, wet trash, and boiling noodles.

At which point I must interrupt *Future Noir's* narrative, turn back the clock, and take the reader on a guided tour around *Blade Runner's* primary set.

Blade Runner's most oft-used location was a complex one. Although primarily representing the "bad" part of town, Ridleyville was also constantly being redressed to suggest a number of other 2019 neighborhoods and businesses. Among these were the red-light and nightclub districts, the Noodle Bar where Deckard is arrested at the beginning of the film, Little Tokyo, Animoid Row (also called "Animal Row" and "Animoid Emporium" in the shooting notes, referring to that bazaarlike area where replicant animals are sold), Chinatown, and the shopping arcade where Zhora bursts through numerous windows before dropping dead on the sidewalk. The Old New York Street/Ridleyville set comprised recognizable (though considerably altered) characteristics of Hong Kong, New York, Tokyo's Ginza district, London's Piccadilly Circus and Milan's business area as well.

As this author strolled through Ridleyville in 1981, he could see that Mead, Paull, and Scott's 2-D design work had been faithfully carried out into three dimensions. Great wet clumps of paper (retrofitted trash) lay everywhere. Subway entrances descended a few feet down into the pavement before abruptly ending at thin plywood walls. Retrofitting was also in ample evidence, with thick corrugated pipes snaking up from the sidewalks and writhing across and through the façades of the buildings. Over the babble of shouted instructions from electricians and grips, extras playing New Wave punks (some of them carrying umbrellas with lighted handles), were nearly engulfed by the larger crowd of Asian extras. Many of these were wearing old, threadbare, quilted pajama suits, an indication of their lowly status in this futuristic metropolis.

Continuing his walk down Ridleyville's streets, this writer also noticed that further detailing had been added to Gene Winfield's full-scale vehicles. The interiors of the many autos, for instance, were actually dusty, their rear-exposed electronics (for easy repair access) suitably oily. Gazing at the back of a flying police car, I could also see that a metal plate reading "Spinner" had been riveted onto the auto's framework, much in the way our own contemporary Camrys, Accords, and Lexuses are identified. Next an enormous yellow street cleaner roared by, the word "Disinfectant" stenciled on its bumper in highly stylized script. And Los Angeles' 2019 bus system—represented by two heavily retrofitted public transport vehicles—was identified by signs on the buses proclaiming them part of the "Megatrans" group (smaller signs by these vehicles' front doors warned, "Driver Is Armed; Carries No Cash").

This decidedly inhospitable tone had even been carried out to include such usually innocuous artifacts as parking meters (which, on Ridleyville's streets, were made from molded fiberglass). These squat bulky objects were topped with plastic domes that glowed green while time remained on the meter, red when that time had expired. Meter payments were made by the insertion of metal-stripped credit cards. Inflation, however, has kept pace with the future; one minute's parking time was worth $3.00. But it was the fine print on these parking meters that captured this writer's attention. Bending closer, I read these words; "WARNING—DANGER! You Can Be Killed By Internal Electrical System If This Meter Is Tampered With."

Not all of *Blade Runner*'s traffic-related items were so lethal. Ridleyville also featured thick metallic pylons sporting multiple video screens strategically placed at street intersections. These were called "Trafficators" by the *BR* crew, had been built by the Warner Brothers prop department, and were four-sided stoplights of the future. The Trafficators not only told pedestrians and vehicles when to halt and when to move forward, but also poured out a constant flow of video-screened information pertaining to traffic conditions, news, and weather reports.[3] A few of these props were actually rigged to receive on-set video input during the *BR* shoot, resulting in yet another example of Scott's mania for detail. As to their construction, the Trafficators were mainly composed of surplus airplane parts, missiles, and radar units salvaged from Monthan Air Force Base. Covered in sculpted high-density polyurethane, the Trafficators' video-screen frames were cobbled up from a bomber pilot's radar scope machinery.

Another highly visible communications device on the Ridleyville set was the VidPhon, 2019's amalgamation of a pay phone and a television set.

---

[3]At one point during Deckard's pursuit of Zhora, the female replicant takes refuge in a subway entrance while Deckard, hanging from a bus, frantically scans the teeming crowds. A Trafficator can be quite clearly heard over this scene mindlessly chanting, "Cross now" and "Don't walk."

"The VidPhons, which are used by both Deckard and Batty in the film" [although Batty's use of the VidPhon was ultimately cut; see chapter XIII], were totally designed from scratch," says Larry Paull. "Some of the parts were surplus material, but a lot of the detailing resulted from taking a number of parts from Japanese tank kits and retrofitting them on to pay phone surfaces, giving them interesting textural qualities. Conceptually, the VidPhon is nothing more than a forty-year-plus version of a touch-tone pay phone. Of course, after Ridley was through with it, the VidPhons were the dirtiest graffiti-smeared objects on the block. Just like the pay phone around the corner."

On further examining the Ridleyville set, this author noticed that the production crew had built many of the film's arcades and shops right out onto the street. Cylindrical bubbles on the second floor of Taffey Lewis' club ("The Snake Pit"), for example, extruded four feet into the air. Within these bubbles were poised mannequins wearing kinky S&M leather outfits and large, stuffed, oversized pythons. The shops lining Animoid Row were even more impressive, especially one which sported a stuffed swordfish, transformed by foam and surplus mechanical parts into a retrofitted icon. This swordfish (the handiwork of *Blade Runner*'s set decorator, Linda DeScenna) can be seen in the film hanging near Deckard's head as he asks the Cambodian saleslady to examine Zhora's snake scale.

Turning down the block and ducking into a futuristic newsstand revealed the most humorous touches of layering. For it was here that this author immediately noticed that a number of faux twenty-first-century magazines had been stuffed into racks mounted on the newsstand's walls, and that many of them sported decidedly tongue-in-cheek covers.[4]

These publications had been designed by *BR* art department member Tom Southwell. Periodicals of note included *Krotch* (going for $29 a copy!), *Zord* (at $30), *Moni, Bash, Creative Evolution,* and *Droid. Horn,* the "skin mag" of the future, had a cover which offered articles such as "The Cosmic Orgasm" and "Hot Lust in Space." *Kill* (whose logo was "All the News That's Fit to Kill") sported cover stories like "Multiple Murders—Reader's Own Photos." The cover of

---

[4]All of these periodicals were stamped with the year "2020"; during most of its principal photography period, *Blade Runner* was still set in the year 2020.

A Ridleyville News-
stand, which displayed
Tom Southwell-
designed magazines of
the future.

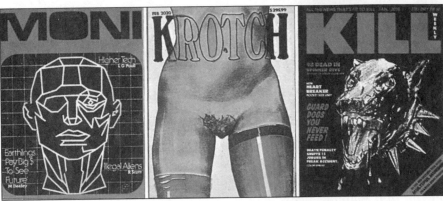

another magazine sported an in joke: a blurb for an article entitled "Illegal Aliens," bylined by one "Ridley Scott." Yet riffling through these magazines proved something of a disappointment—only the covers had been redone. The *interior* of these magazines were standard 1981 publications like *Omni* and *Playboy*.

The one Ridleyville detail which overloaded the eye, though, was the vast amount of neon sculpture and advertising liberally splashed around the set. In fact, everywhere one looked there were signs advertising products like Atari, Jim Beam, Trident, Michelob, Jovan, TDK, and Shakey's—all of which were dominated by a nearly life-sized neon image of a girl wearing a cowboy hat, one whose left leg continuously moved in wanton invitation above the teeming street below.[5]

"We promoted nearly four dozen bits of neon from various compa-

[5]Interestingly, since *Blade Runner*'s release, many of the (real) companies whose products were advertised in the film have gone out of business (Pan American Airlines is one example). This oddity has led some of the production members to even today believe in what they call a "product-placement *Blade Runner* curse."

nies for the film," Paull says. "These companies didn't actually donate signs, but were kind enough to give us the money to make them. And all the neon signs which we had specifically constructed for *Blade Runner* were made by American Neon, in Burbank, which spent five and a half months building them for us. But American Neon didn't build everything, only about two-thirds of the signs you see in the movie. We inherited the rest of our neon from Francis Ford Coppola's *One From the Heart,* after they were finished filming their Las Vegas sets. That kicking cowgirl, for instance? She came directly to us from *One From the Heart.* "

Besides neon, the dominant feature of the Ridleyville set was its precipitation. Lots of it. Scott's vision of the future included a near-perpetual acid rain, one caused by out-of-control industrialization and the worst kind of Greenhouse Effect. In order to convincingly simulate those torrential downpours, an elaborate overhead sprinkling system had been erected about twenty feet above the outdoor Old New York Street set. But where most productions are content to use a single sprinkler head to drop rain on their actors, Scott and company utilized more than *seven* such rapidly spinning devices to simulate a heavy downpour (necessitating long periods of waiting between shots while all the rain effects were synchronized and set up). The constant starting and stopping of this rain system also resulted in a damp, perpetual chill being felt on the set.

One final watery touch was that during many of *BR*'s *rain* scenes Scott had slow, eerie music fed through overhead loudspeakers to help pull his cast and crew into the moody atmosphere he'd had so painstakingly constructed. A melancholy ambiance which perfectly transferred from Ridleyville to *Blade Runner* itself.

Future Noir will now examine, scene by scene, the manner in which *Blade Runner* was constructed during principal photography. This is the longest chapter in *Future Noir*; therefore, I have decided to jettison the orthodox manner of presenting the mass of information to follow. Instead, the remainder of chapter VIII will alternate between descriptive paragraphs and numerous "bulleted" quotes in order to better convey the full range of endeavors accomplished during principal photography by *BR*'s cast and crew.

Think of this chapter as a *Blade Runner* "data file," then. One through which the reader may browse or return at leisure.

LEON'S VOIGT-KAMPFF TEST————————————————

"The set where Holden runs a Voigt-Kampff test on Leon was called 'The Interrogation Room,'" says *BR* production designer Lawrence G. Paull. "Actually, we reused that same set *[located on the Burbank Studio's Stage 4]* three different times. Once for Leon's V-K test, once for Tyrell's office, and once for Tyrell's bedroom. We just re-dressed it for each different scene."

One of the most critical devices in Ridley Scott's film (as well as Philip K. Dick's book) is the Voigt-Kampff analyzer—the only sure way to uncover the subtle empathic differences between human and android.[6] But how was the V-K machine transformed from printed suggestion to three-dimensional prop?

"Ridley gave me a small, rough sketch of the Voigt-Kampff analyzer he'd done one day," Syd Mead begins. "Then he explained what it was all about and specified that the design direction he definitely didn't want to go in was high-tech. 'Make it menacing,' he told me. 'But also make it delicate.'

"So I'd kicked around a number of possible directions when a startling image suddenly came to me; I imagined the picture of a giant

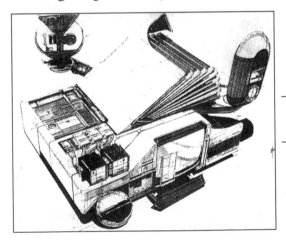

Syd Mead's design for the Voigt-Kampff machine.

[6]The Voigt-Kampff machine Holden uses to interrogate Leon measures Leon's emotions by involuntary fluctuations of the iris, capillary dilation (blush response), and changes in body chemistry (pheromones), sniffed out by its black, pumping bellows. The questions Holden asks are designed to provoke an empathic response, which replicants presumably have difficulty imitating.

tarantula on a desk lamp. That was weird, but it made me realize that what could give this sophisticated lie detector a definitely threatening air was to suggest that it was alive. Taking it from there, I devised a small rectangular lens on a stalk that would focus on your eye. People are probably more body-conscious about their eyes than any other organ in the body. That certainly gave the Voigt-Kampff analyzer an air of intimidation. I also designed a set of bellows on the side of the device; it breathed. Actually, this breathing had a functional aspect, as the machinery was taking air samples of its subject for analysis. When you're nervous, you sweat and exude a distinctive airborne chemistry.

"But essentially, the Voigt-Kampff machine is a retinal scan. It focuses on the human eye, blows that image up on a self-contained video monitor, and then analyzes it by measuring the pupil's dilation and contraction under the pressure of various emotional triggers. Specifically, the questions the Blade Runners ask the replicants."

The human irises seen on the V-K machines were not those of *BR*'s actors. Instead, they were "stock shots," library footage of human eyes supplied by an English company named Oxford Scientific. Some test close-ups of certain *Blade Runner* cast members' eyes actually were filmed (including Brion James'), but it was then decided that it would be less expensive to secure stock footage than to have to shoot customized close-ups—which is why James' blue-green eyes appear brownish-green on the V-K monitors.

As for the graphics seen on the Voigt-Kampff analyzer, this was video imagery designed by EEG's John Gilman.

BRION JAMES portrays Leon Kowalski, a replicant with a "C-Level Mentality." "But even though Leon had only a C-level mental capacity, I always thought C-Mental was still about fifty percent above anything that was human," James points out. "I think that comes across during Leon's interrogation; in that scene, I'm fucking with Holden, playing mind games with him."

Born in 1945, in Beaumont, California, Brion James grew up around the movies—his father built the Beaumont Theater, owned a local drive-in, and son Brion helped him project. "I was at the movies every night of my life from the time I was two years old," James says. "The one that inspired me to be an actor was *The Hunchback of Notre Dame*."

James began his acting career by studying in Manhattan under famed drama teacher Stella Adler, ("along with another guy named Tim Thomerson, who's my best friend,") before segueing into stand-up comedy at New York's Improv comedy club. Moving to Los Angeles, James snared roles in such television programs as *Gunsmoke, The FBI, BJ and the Bear, Battlestar Galactica,* "and a lot of TV movies." His first film appearances were in 1976's *Nickelodeon* and *Harry and Walter Go to New York.* James' breakthrough part came as a one-armed Cajun in *Southern Comfort* (1981), and he has since appeared in such critically well-received feature productions as Robert Altman's *The Player* (1992, in which he portrayed a studio head) and many straight-to-video productions.

"The way I got cast for *Blade Runner* was kind of interesting," James recalls. "At first they were thinking of Leon as a black man; in fact, they'd almost decided on Frank McRae, an actor who'd played this big police captain in *48 Hours*. But then I went in to audition and read through the interrogation scene for Ridley and his secretary. When I was done, Ridley asked her, 'Were you scared?' And she said, 'This guy scares me to death!'

"That was good to hear, but I was actually pretty scared myself. Because shortly before I went in to see Ridley, I was in a motorcycle accident. My head was open, my hands had turned into hamburger, I had big scabs on my face. And I thought, 'Oh fuck, I'm going to get fired from this fucking movie before I'm even on it!' But then when I went to see Ridley, he took one look at me and said, 'Ah, man, that's fucking great! Use that look for the whole movie!' He was such a sick fuck that he loved it!" James says, laughing. "The fact that I was scarred up and scabbed actually worked for me."

"Holden" was portrayed by MORGAN PAULL. Prior to his appearance in *BR*, Paull had also been featured in such films as the Robert Redford-starring *Brubaker* (1980), *Patton* (1970), and *Norma Rae* (1979).

Paull no longer acts—his latest industry job was as an agent. He was unavailable to be interviewed for this book, since he was sailing a boat around the world while *Future Noir* was being written.

During Leon's V-K test, his eyes can be (faintly) seen glowing, a tip-off that he's a replicant. But this effect is very hard to see; it primarily appears when Leon is seated and acting nervous. The reason for this difficulty was that Brion James' V–K scene was shot early in the production with pin lights: Ridley Scott later refined the "glowing android eyes" effect by bouncing light off a half-mirrored glass mounted at a forty-five degree angle on the camera (the giant staring eye at the start of *BR*, according to EEG Effects Supervisor David Snyder, belonged to EEG Optical Lineup man Richard Ripple).

"When Leon shoots Holden, there's this big flash of blue-white light," says Terry Frazee. "That was supposed to be from this heavy-duty gun Leon was using. But that light was actually caused by these enormous flashbulbs we'd scrounged up, bulbs that are used by the government for photographing missiles going down range. They stayed lit for a good length of time; Ridley wanted you to think, by the amount of light that weapon threw off, that Leon's gun really could blow a guy through a wall."

After shooting Holden once, Leon's second shot slams the (soon to be revealed)) Blade Runner through an adjoining office's wall.

BR Stunt Coordinator Gary Combs explains, "That's me in the chair doubling for Holden being blown through the wall. If you look real close, you'll see I've got a gun in my hand; Holden was trying to outdraw Leon, but he couldn't.

"Anyway, Holden's chair was attached to a cable that was mechanically activated by a mechanism designed by Terry Frazee to yank me through that wall, which had been prescored. They didn't undercrank on that shot, either. It was filmed at normal speed.

"It was also a lot harder to do and rougher on me than it looks. In fact, they put some acid on my coat to make it look like Leon's bullet had gone through Holden's back and made a smoking hole. Some of that stuff ate right through the cloth, though, and blistered my skin. That kinda hurt."

"The gun I fired at Holden was a real weapon that's made in Compton, California," James adds. "It looks space-age, but it's real. And it has four barrels on it. That way you can shoot four shots one right after the other; it's sort of like a quadruple-barrel pistol."

THE NOODLE BAR ——————————————————————

The Noodle Bar sequence, where Harrison Ford orders dinner at the beginning of the film, was the first *BR* scene to be shot on the Old New York Street set. It was filmed the night of April 23, 1981.

Says Lawrence Paull, "The idea for the Noodle Bar came from this hamburger chain I used to love eating at as a kid. That was called the White Castle. We called our version the White Dragon. That's what that neon sign with the dragon on the Noodle is all about—it's that place's logo. In fact, we even put a bunch of 'White Dragon' signs up on the food stand itself, but I don't think you can see them in the picture."

Regarding the teeming masses of lower-class humanity seen in *Blade Runner*'s opening Noodle Bar scenes, Hampton Fancher states, "Those crowds reflected the rigid social hierarchy of our own world. But that whole dystopic idea in *BR* was entwisted right from the beginning, because it was in Philip Dick's book. I just retained that for my screenplays.

"But *Blade Runner* was always meant to be cautionary. For instance, *BR* was shot during the dawn of Reaganism. And I was flabbergasted by Ronald Reagan and everything he stood for. So the cruel politics portrayed in the film were my rebuttal of Reaganism, in a sense."

According to *BR* makeup supervisor Marvin Westmore, "One of my biggest challenges was coming up with makeup for all the extras they used in the crowd scenes. Many of them were supposed to be Asians, so I came up with something called 'Asian Blade Runner Blue." That was applied by a crew of about forty people—the biggest-sized team I had in my makeup department on *BR* at any one time. It was sort of a greasepaint with a light blue cast to it.

"We also detailed the crowds around the Noodle Bar with a lot of grime and some great hairstyles. Ridley wanted everybody to look a little different."

Jordan Cronenweth told this author in 1981 that the illuminated umbrella handles carried by *BR*'s extras served a dual purpose—to

The White Dragon Noodle Bar, which was patterned by Production Designer Lawrence G. Paull after the White Castle hamburger chain. Note White Dragon signs in rare still of Noodle Bar at bottom.

illuminate their faces for filming, and (storywise) to act as built-in flashlights, to help their carriers pick their way through 2019 LA's dark and rainy streets.

As for the science-fiction architecture surrounding the Noodle Bar, *BR* special effects supervisor David Dryer says that, "Someday, I want to take shots from Fritz Lang's *Metropolis* and shots from *BR* and run them back to back. Because there's an awful lot of *Metropolis* in *Blade Runner*. Those cityscapes you see before being introduced to Deckard and the flashing lights in Tyrell's office, for instance. I was even using stills from *Metropolis* when I was lining up *Blade Runner*'s miniature building shots [which is explained in more detail in chapter X]."

Harrison Ford is first seen in the film reading a newspaper. Its headline is "Farming the Oceans, the Moon and Antarctica." This same paper will appear two more times in *Blade Runner*: as the lining of a drawer in Leon's hotel room, and as Deckard's reading material while he waits for Zhora outside her dressing room.

Even a futuristic detective must have a trenchcoat, of course. According to the 1982 *BR* press kit, Rick Deckard's outerwear consisted of "a new, oddly proportioned version of the traditional trenchcoat . . . a russet-colored full-length cotton, with multipintuck collar, raglan sleeves, deep pockets, and French seams."

One character who makes an immediate impression during the Noodle Bar scene is the so-called "Sushi Master," or manager of the White Dragon. This character argues with Deckard over the amount of food the Blade Runner can receive.

The Sushi Master was portrayed by ROBERT OKAZAKI. This Asian-American performer also appeared in two thrillers by maverick film director Sam Fuller: *House of Bamboo* (1955, as "Mr. Hommaru"), and *The Crimson Kimono* (1959, as "Yoshinaga").

> *Sushi Master* (in Japanese): "Come, come. Welcome, welcome.
>   Please [be seated]. What shall it be?"
> *Deckard*: "Give me four."
> *Sushi Master* (in Japanese): "Two is plenty."
> *Deckard*: "No, four! Two—two, four."
> *Sushi Master* (in Japanese): "Two is plenty!"
> *Deckard*: "And noodles."
> *Sushi Master* (in Japanese): "Please understand!"

While Deckard is eating, he is approached from behind by two men. One is a bulletproof-vested policeman, who taps Ford on the shoulder. This policeman says, (in Korean), "Hey, come here."

The second man—who is sharply dressed, has yellowish-brown skin, and light blue eyes—is further described in the 1982 *Blade Runner* press kit as "(A) Police Lieutenant . . . [who favors] iridescent shirts, metallic-threaded vests, and silk suits with loud bow ties, fedoras, and pointed shoes, topped by a long knit coat with leather appliqués."

This is Gaff, Rick Deckard's fellow Blade Runner—and a shadowy, bitterly competitive sidekick.

"Gaff was originally a very minor character in my early scripts," explains Hampton Fancher. "I'd just glommed onto a real word—a 'gaffe,' or a mistake—and then came up with a character to match that. I made him part-Mexican because I'm partly Chicano myself. Eddie Olmos and David Peoples are the ones who really fleshed him out."

As Fancher indicates, Gaff was portrayed by EDWARD JAMES OLMOS.

A Mexican-American born February 24, 1947, in East Los Angeles, Olmos had, prior to his appearance in *Blade Runner,* been mostly known for two projects. One was 1981's *Wolfen* (a "thinking man's" werewolf movie), where Olmos appeared as an Amerind steelworker. The second project was Olmos' featured role as "Ed Pachuco" in the film (also 1981), Broadway, and Los Angeles theater versions of *Zoot Suit,* which concerned the Los Angeles-based, late 1940s, Mexican-American "Sleepy Lagoon" riots.

As for Gaff, he is one of *Blade Runner's* most memorable characters, despite his brief screen time. Yet Gaff was "almost nonexistent in terms of character in the script," Olmos recalls. "We were really flying by the seat of our pants on that one. Gaff was so undefined, I was making him up as we went along.

"First I asked Ridley if I could embellish the character, make him more interesting to the audience. Ridley respected me enough as an artist to trust me with building up an entire history for Gaff. So the backstory I came up with was that Gaff was primarily Mexican-Japanese, and that his lineage in America stretched back at least five generations. Gaff was quite proud of that, as well as the sense of his past culture.

"Gaff was also a terrific linguist. He could speak ten languages, fluently. Gaff's morally interesting, too—he begins as an ambitious, slightly shifty character, but by the time the film's over, he's gone through a total character arc. You see that he's capable of sympathy for both Deckard and the replicants.

"I then came up with the idea of Gaff being so well-dressed," Olmos continues, "in conjunction with Charles Knode and Michael

Kaplan of the wardrobe department. Then I began to feel that, despite his mixed blood, Gaff was more Asian than anything else. So I asked Marvin Westmore to make up my skin in yellowish tones before every shot. Yet I also felt Gaff had some other nationalities in him, too. So we gave him a French-Spanish mustache, an Italian punk haircut, and China-blue eyes."

In order to transform Olmos' normally brown eyes into Gaff's shocking blue ones, a set of custom-ground contact lenses was created by Dr. Morton Greenspoon, the most often used "special contacts" man in the film industry. "Greenspoon personally fit me for those contacts himself," Olmos remembers. "They were of excellent quality, but still tough to work with. Very uncomfortable. These were the old-style hard lenses, not the soft ones you can get today. I could only keep them in for twenty minutes at a time, because you had to let the eyes breathe.

"Plus, they were very hard to see through," Olmos concludes. "It was like looking through a little pinhole. Walking around those cluttered *Blade Runner* sets with blinders on—you can imagine what that was like."

When Gaff first talks to Deckard at the Noodle Bar, he speaks to him in a nearly indecipherable tongue. This strange language is identified in the February 23, 1981 *BR* script as "Cityspeak."

According to Hampton Fancher, "Cityspeak has an interesting pedigree. When I first created Gaff, I was thinking about how some of the Latino guys in East L.A. speak this slang that's all their own. So I gave Gaff a little bit of his own street *patois*. But Cityspeak, that gutter language Gaff talks, that came from Peoples and Olmos."

David Peoples: "In my scripts, I expanded the role of Gaff, who was a very minor character in Hampton's draft, and created a certain personality for him in order to allow Gaff to express a whole bunch of expository material. Gaff was looking for a promotion and always badgering Deckard about his personal appearance in my scripts. And in the course of all this badgering, he'd tell some of the story to the audience.

"I was kind of proud of what I'd done, because I felt Gaff's exposition wasn't in any way dull or boring; it was coming from a character who really had an agenda, and it was disguised within his agenda. But then came the day when Ridley suddenly decided that this guy should speak Japanese! So I went back and underlined everything Gaff said and changed some of it into Japanese; the plan was to provide that dialogue with subtitles. In fact, I even remember going to a sushi bar with Ridley at one point for research.

"However, Ridley and Ivor Powell next started throwing out the idea that maybe Gaff should speak in some sort of weird, futuristic gutter language. That clicked with me, because at one time I had lived in the Philippines Islands, and I could still remember sitting in these public taxicabs called Jeepneys there and listening to the Filipinos speaking in Tagalog, their native language, with all these other English words stuck in."

Peoples did not, however, come up with the mishmash of languages that Olmos speaks in the film. "That was pretty much all Eddie's doing," Peoples recalls. "All I'd done was indicate that Gaff was speaking some funny language in the script and then translated that into English."

According to Olmos, "Cityspeak was already a word being tossed around when I came onto the picture. I'm not sure who came up with the actual word—I think it was David Peoples. But I guess I'm the guy who literalized it.

"My first idea was to put a mixture of genuine Spanish, French, Chinese, German, Hungarian, and Japanese into Cityspeak. Then I went to the Berlitz School of Languages in Los Angeles, translated all these different bits and pieces of Gaff's original dialogue into fragments of foreign tongues, and learned to properly pronounce them. I also added some translated dialogue I'd made up myself. All that was a bitch and a half, but it really added to Gaff's character."

But what is the *English* meaning of the dialogue Gaff speaks at the Noodle Bar? According to both David Peoples and Edward James Olmos, Gaff's Cityspeak changed considerably during shooting. Today neither man remembers nor has records of exactly what Olmos was saying.

However, based on comparative conversations this author had with Peoples, Olmos, and other *BR* personnel in 1995, and by studying the

Deckard (Harrison Ford, center) is accosted by a Korean-speaking cop (left) and Gaff (Edward James Olmos, right) who berates Deckard in Cityspeak.

February 23, 1981, *Blade Runner* script, I feel that the following is a close—but certainly not complete—translation of Gaff's Cityspeak at the Noodle Bar (thanks to Bill Kolb for the Cityspeak breakdown itself):

> *Gaff* (in Cityspeak): "Monsieur, ada-na kobishin angum bi-te." (in English) "You will be required to accompany me, sir."
> *Sushi-Master*: "He say you under arrest, Mr. Deckard."
> *Deckard*: "Got the wrong guy, pal."
> *Gaff*: (in Cityspeak—but partly Hungarian!) "Lo fa, ne-ko shi-ma, de va-ja blade . . . Blade Runner." (in English) "Horse dick! So you say. You are the Blade . . . Blade Runner."
> *Sushi-Master*: "He say you Blade Runner!"
> *Deckard*: "Tell him I'm eating."
> *Gaff*: (in Cityspeak) "Captain Bryant toka. Meni-o mae-yo." (in English) "Captain Bryant ordered me to bring you in."
> *Deckard*: "Bryant, huh?"

LIFTOFF

Among the four full-scale Spinners which Gene Winfield and his crew constructed for *Blade Runner* was what came to be known as "the Flying Spinner." This lightweight, full-scale prop cost approximately $30,000 and was hung from cables on an off-camera crane to simulate flight.

"Some critics over the years have thought the Spinner was some kind of antigravity car," explains Syd Mead, "but it's not. Again, it's an aerodyne. That's a valid aerodynamic principle that uses forced air and movable jet turbines for enclosed lift.

"As for the Flying Spinner prop," Mead continues, "that was designed with a fully operational hydraulically controlled front-wheel section. The wheels folded up into a ball in front and covers folded down around them. There were flaps that opened and closed in the back and there were two other movable rear body sections that could channel out jets of steam or carbon dioxide to suggest flight. When it was first delivered to Ridley, he thought it looked too shiny, so the Flying Spinner was then aged with rust, dirt, and grime. We also heavily detailed the bottom of the Flying Spinner with tubes and lines and other paraphernalia so the camera would have something interesting to look at.

"Then we constructed the floorboards out of clear Plexiglas. This was done so that anyone in the passenger compartment could look down at their feet and see the city flying away beneath them. This, I thought, was a nice idea, suggesting a simple, practical navigational aid. If the instruments conked out, you could always fly by the soles of your feet."

"Just before Gaff takes off," notes Terry Rawlings, "there's a cut to a close-up of a monitor on his Spinner that says 'Purge.' That was a bit of footage which had been created for a TV screen in *Alien*, when Sigourney Weaver blasts away from the Mothership in an escape vessel. Ridley liked the way that 'Purge' graphic looked, so we used the original negative of that shot to make a new positive print and then ran it into a mock-up of Gaff's Spinner using three-quarter-inch videotape."

In order to create the illusion of movement within the Spinner cockpit mock-up, Jordan Cronenweth positioned two eight-foot-long panels of programmable strip lights on either side of the cockpit during the live-action shoot. These panels were each equipped with twelve color-dyed photofloods that could be fired off in random order to suggest exterior light sources spilling into the cockpit during Deckard and Gaff's flight to police HQ. Additional off-screen flashing lights, smoke and water effects then convincingly suggested that Gaff's Spinner was in flight.

During their journey to police HQ, Gaff's lips can be seen moving—but his words are not heard. Olmos says that his dialogue was indeed recorded for this shot, but "dropped at the last moment" due to Scott's decision to overlay mood music and make the flight a more lyrical sequence instead.

"Gaff was basically putting Deckard down during that shot," adds David Peoples. "I'd written those lines in Japanese originally, but that got changed to Cityspeak after Eddie came on the picture. Anyway, Gaff was saying that he could do a better job than Deckard, that Deckard looked sloppy, and that Deckard's bad grooming reflected poorly on the police department."[7]

BRYANT'S BRIEFING————————————————

Mark Stetson: "Ridley Scott always wanted a shot of the Chrysler Building somewhere in *Blade Runner*. But when the locale of the film shifted from New York to Los Angeles, he had to lose that. So we model department guys deliberately designed the exterior of the miniature police department to echo the Art Deco look of the Chrysler Building instead."

Most of the police headquarters interiors were shot at Union Station, downtown L.A.'s central train terminal (located at 8 N. Alameda Street).

Union Station had been the one *BR* location, according to Lawrence Paull, "that Ridley had been in love with all during preproduction." Three days were spent lighting and dressing this venerable old train terminal; the *BR* crew then spent four nights shooting a

---

[7]Gaff's last Cityspeak lines to Deckard in this edited, unheard scene were, according to the February 23 shooting script, "Whatta jerk! If I wasn't up for promotion I'd put this baby in a hot spin and leave your dinner all over the glass!"

number of scenes in Union Station's long, echoing corridors. Most of these centered around Captain Bryant's office, a set which had been constructed inside Union Station—right next to a women's rest room.

Captain Bryant was played by M. (Michael) EMMET WALSH. Born in 1935, Walsh is of Irish descent, has been deaf in his left ear since he was three, and was raised in a small town on the Canadian border. After receiving a college degree in marketing, Walsh then focused on the theater, his first and still-greatest love ("Although my father wanted me to be a businessman," Walsh says).

Years of work on the New York stage were followed by a number of mid–1960s television commercials. Walsh made his film debut in 1970's *End of the Road*. He then appeared in other pictures like *Midnight Cowboy, Cold Turkey* (directed by Bud Yorkin), *Alice's Restaurant*, and 1978's *Straight Time* (where Walsh's portrayal of a by-the-book parole officer convinced Ridley Scott to cast him in *Blade Runner*), before his breakthrough performance as a sleazy private eye in 1985's *Blood Simple*.

As for *BR's* Captain Bryant, "I based him on my family," says Walsh (who, unlike his sometimes slimy characters, is a funny and unpretentious man—and a marvelous raconteur). "I come from a long line of civil servants—both my father and grandfather were customs officers on the Canadian border—so I had no trouble playing a bureaucrat. And Bryant liked his job. He lived in that office. That's why I played him so cheerfully."

Walsh says that Ridley Scott had definite ideas on the character of Bryant as well; it was the director, for example, who told Walsh to grow sideburns and a mustache for the part. "Ridley also told me Bryant's stomach was shot all to hell. That's why he offered Deckard two glasses of whiskey in his office. Bryant liked to see other people drink because he couldn't."

At one point Bryant refers to the androids as "skin jobs." Deckard's narration (in the theatrical release) then dryly comments that, in older times, Bryant was "the kind of man who would call black men niggers."

"But nobody ever told me 'skin jobs' was bigoted while we were shooting," Walsh recalls. "They made that a racist slur after the fact, during postproduction, when they wrote the narration. As far as I knew, 'skin jobs' was just slang; I thought it was a substitute word for replicant and meant something like putting flesh over an erector set.'"

The small anteroom where Walsh shows Ford various videos concerning the escaped replicants (videos which the production crew called "Incept Tapes") was not shot at Union Station. Instead, it was built on a soundstage at The Burbank Studios. This anteroom was known to the cast and crew as the "Blue Room," due to the chilly blue light under which Scott filmed the scene.

"One of the more interesting concepts in Hampton's and Peoples' scripts was the Esper," comments Terry Rawlings. "That was supposed to be this talking supercomputer run by the police. Originally, it was going to be everywhere—inside cars, out on the sidewalk, everywhere. But that got whittled away during rewrites until the Esper only made two appearances. One was as the small terminal in Deckard's apartment through which he runs Leon's photograph. The other was in the Blue Room; we called the monitors screening the replicant's Incept Tapes the 'Esper Wall.'"

"They shot those Incept Tapes by putting nylon stocking caps on the heads of Joanna Cassidy, Daryl Hannah, and [me], and then standing us on a turntable at Warner Brothers," remembers Rutger Hauer. "Then they individually filmed us while we kept blank expressions and rotated in a circle."

Brion James: "Some people have asked, 'Why did Holden have to run a Voigt-Kampff test on me if the police already had tapes of Leon and knew what he looked like?' The answer to that one was that those tapes didn't get to the police until *after* I shot Holden. During my V-K test, the cops didn't have that much information on us. Holden was just on a fishing expedition."

The Incept Tapes display a different batch of written serial numbers and letters for each replicant. Although they might seem a jumble, this is actually identification data, and summarizes the vital statistics on each android.

For instance, Leon's serial number—"N6MAC41717"—stands for Nexus–6 ("N6"), Male ("M"), A-Physical, ("A"), C-Mental, ("C") and the android's birthday ("incept date")—April 17, 2017 ("4/17/17"). (Leon's birthdate is contradicted, however, both in this Incept Tape and when Brion James tells Ford later in the film that Leon was born on April 10, 2017.)

Here are the vital statistics shown for each replicant in the Blue Room. Note that Pris' Incept Date is Valentine's Day:

Replicant (M) Des: LEON
Nexus–6 N6MAC41717
Incept Date: 10 APRIL, 2017
Func: Combat/Loader (Nuc. Fiss.)
Phys: LEV. A Mental: LEV. C

Replicant (M) Des: BATTY (Roy)
NEXUS–6 N6MAA10816
Incept Date: 8 JAN., 2016
Func: Combat, Colonization Defense Prog
Phys: LEV. A Mental: LEV. A

Replicant (F) Des: ZHORA
NEXUS–6 N6FAB61216
Incept Date: 12 JUNE, 2016
Func: Retrained (9 Feb., 2018) Polit. Homicide
Phys: LEV. A Mental: LEV. B

Replicant (F) Des: PRIS
NEXUS–6 N6FAB21416
Incept Date: 14 FEB., 2016
Func: Military/Leisure
Phys: LEV. A Mental: LEV. B

"People ask me—a lot—if Captain Bryant knew that Deckard was supposed to be a replicant," concludes Walsh. "I tell 'em, 'Uh-uh.'

Nothing like that ever came up while I was shooting or preparing for the part. None of the scripts I looked at indicated Harrison was supposed to be an android, either."

HOLDEN AND THE HOSPITAL ━━━━━━━━━━━━━━━

Following Bryant's briefing, *Blade Runner* was originally supposed to cut to one of two scenes showing Deckard visiting Holden (who did not perish from Leon's attack) in a futuristic hospital.

The first hospital sequence (identified as Scene 13 in the February 23, 1981 *BR* shooting script) introduced Holden lying encased in a fully-enclosed, sarcophaguslike "iron lung" while reading an electronic copy of *Treasure Island*. Holden and Deckard were then to have the series of conversations concerning Holden's interrogation of Leon, Holden, being shot by Leon, and the fact that an autopsy performed on one of the replicants killed while breaking into the Tyrell Corporation revealed that the android was physiologically almost identical to a human being.

However, although these hospital scenes had been written, staged, and filmed, the "Holden and the Hospital" sequences were ultimately cut from *BR* because Ridley Scott felt that they were "redundant." They have never been seen by the general public. Some disagreement exists, however, among the *BR* filmmakers as to whether the hospital scenes were included in the Denver/Dallas sneak previews (anyone who saw these sneaks is welcome to pass along reliable confirmation regarding these scenes to this author care of his publisher).

The "Holden and the Hospital" scenes were filmed in late April, 1981 on Stage 4 at The Burbank Studios. This author briefly visited the hospital set during filming and beheld an eerie healing chamber which bore a slight design resemblance both to *Alien's* "Autodoc" and that same film's lotus-shaped "Sleep Chamber."

"I wanted a hospital room that was octagonal," Lawrence Paull says, "one with drawers containing patients that could be slid out of the walls like coffins. Syd originally did a sketch of this, but Ridley and I decided that what he had done was too slick and *Star Wars*-y."

Confirmed Mead, "There were definitely a number of times on this production when the designs I submitted were rejected as 'too futuristic.'"

Paull continues: "So we decided to use some of our retro-foam to roughen up the walls and give them some interesting design textures. What was really interesting about the hospital set was Holden's enclosed medical capsule, which we dubbed the 'sleighbed.' That was actually the sink from Deckard's apartment! We simply decided to recycle it for another go-round."

Three shots from Blade Runner's *deleted 'Holden & the Hospital' scene. (Top right) A wide shot of the Hospital set, showing Deckard visiting the wounded Holden enclosed in a futuristic iron lung dubbed "The Sleighbed." (Top left) A closer shot of Deckard leaning over The Sleighbed and conversing with Holden. (Bottom) The BR crew readies The Sleighbed between shots.*

The second Holden/hospital sequence was originally supposed to take place immediately following the scene of Batty plotting his "chess strategy" in Sebastian's apartment. It was identified as Scene 88, occurred on pages 92–94 of the February 1981 script, and began with Holden laughing hysterically at the thought of Deckard almost being killed by the snake-dancing female replicant Zhora. However, the reason Deckard has actually visited Holden is to inform him that Deckard has also "retired" Leon.

This scene then ended with Holden angrily reminding Deckard that the replicants are only machines, certain that Deckard had somehow made love to Zhora before shooting her (an action which Holden feels has prompted Deckard's newfound conscience concerning replicants).

Also during this scene in the February 23, 1981 version of the *BR* script, the encapsulated Holden tells Deckard that the replicants have come back to Earth to find "God." A pullback was then to reveal Deckard and Holden being spied on by Bryant and Gaff on a monitor.

RACHAEL AND TYRELL

Tyrell's office, where Deckard first meets and then tests Rachael (SEAN YOUNG) on a V-K machine, was among the most impressive of *Blade Runner*'s forty-seven sets. "Tyrell's office was gigantic," recalls Lawrence G. Paull. "The only comparable set I can remember in this context was Edward G. Robinson's office in *Little Caesar*."

Ridley Scott (standing left) confers with Harrison Ford and Sean Young (seated) between takes on the immense Tyrell's Office Set.

Vast, stark, and intimidating, Tyrell's office served as the physical manifestation of the commanding influence wielded by the Tyrell Corporation, the genetic engineering firm that's become one of 2019's most powerful corporate monopolies. Boasting twenty-foot-high columns and a huge picture window, the entire office measured eighty by eighty feet. "The scale of Tyrell's office was inhuman," Paull continues. "It dwarfed the people within its space, which is what we were trying to say about the central character that inhabited it."

The design of Tyrell's office can also be read as a social statement. This set contains a great amount of empty space—yet far below the

Tyrell Pyramid, the street-level masses jostle for every square inch of their own "living room."

Tyrell's office was built on Stage 4 at the Warner Brothers lot. The scene shot within it was also the first to be filmed for *Blade Runner*; cameras rolled on the Tyrell office sequence beginning Monday, March 9, 1981.

"We first talked of doing Tyrell's office as an entirely marble room," continues Lawrence Paull. "But this soon proved to be economically unfeasible, as was our original idea of erecting this set in one of a number of buildings we'd scouted in downtown Los Angeles.[8] I then rethought things and tried an approach featuring raw concrete and granite, which reflected the motif of the pyramid in which Tyrell's office was contained.

"To this end I did a lot of research in the *moderne* style. I also wanted Tyrell's office to smack of a neofascist or 'Establishment Gothic' look, because that was the character of the man. He was omnipotent, a member of a rich, powerful class who had so cloistered himself away from the masses that he literally ran his empire from a tower."

Although it now seems incomprehensible to think of anyone but Sean Young as Rachael, Ridley Scott originally wanted to cast Dutch actress Monique Van De Ven (*Turkish Delight*) in the part.

The 1982 *Blade Runner* press kit book quotes Sean Young as saying that "I didn't approach [BR] as science fiction. It's a romantic thriller, like *Casablanca*. But instead of Africa, we're in the future.

[And when] we first see [Rachael], she's a cool executive, in complete control. Deckard penetrates her smooth-running façade, and she becomes an innocent little girl."

---

[8]Among the real downtown LA structures initially considered as locations for Tyrell's office were the Title Insurance & Trust Building (which was also considered for Bryant's office), the Arco Tower, the Crocker Bank Building, the Security Pacific Bank Building, and the Bonaventure Hotel.

Tyrell's owl, first seen flying across the length of Eldon's office, is identified in the film as a replicant. Yet this bird was originally meant to be a *real* animal.

According to the *BR* screenplay dated February 23, 1981 (which served as *BR*'s shooting script), when Deckard asks Rachael whether the owl is artificial, she replies, "Of course not." In the film itself, however, Rachael answers, "Of course it is." Yet Sean Young's lip movements indicate she's still saying "Of course not."

Why this confusion?

"Sean's line was relooped in postproduction from 'Of course not' to 'Of course it is,'" explains Michael Deeley, "because, first, the owl's eyes glow in a later scene. And only replicants have glowing eyes. Secondly, Sean's line was changed in order to add credibility to the idea that Tyrell could manufacture perfect imitations of living things—remember, that owl's the first animal you see in the film. So we changed Rachael's dialogue to support these things."

JOE TURKEL portrays Eldon Tyrell, head of the vast corporation which bears his name.[9] He is first introduced wearing a severely fitted, two-piece, blue sharkskin suit, a pair of trifocal glasses (subtly continuing *BR*'s "eye motif"), and a white bow tie.

Turkel had previously appeared in films such as 1955's *The Killing* and 1957's *Paths of Glory* (both by Stanley Kubrick), the bizarre lavender western *Warlock* (1959), *King Rat* (1965), and *The Hindenburg* (1975). His most recent credit came via the low-budget, 1990 science fiction film *The Dark Side of the Moon*.[10]

"Joe Turkel was cast in *BR* because Ridley loved his 'look' as the supernatural bartender in *The Shining*," Michael Deeley says.

"Actually, Tyrell was a disappointment to me," Hampton Fancher continues. "I'd wanted Sterling Hayden (*The Killing*) for that part,

---

[9]In the December 22, 1980 *BR* script, the Tyrell Corporation was originally called "The Nekko Corporation."

[10]This author was unable to locate or interview Joe Turkel for his thoughts on *Blade Runner*. But in 1995, a rumor surfaced that Turkel had passed away. I have been unable to verify his death, however.

because I'd originally conceived Tyrell as someone huge, someone who couldn't be resisted or beaten. Hayden was perfect for that.

"Of course, the part's now become an institution with Joe Turkel. But I was still really shocked when the bartender from *The Shining* showed up."

Katy Haber: "In the technical sense, Joe Turkel was a nightmare. He didn't tell Ridley, but he was totally incapable of learning lines. So every set he was on had to be filled with cards with his dialogue written down on them.

"In fact, watch Turkel's eyes in every scene that he's in. They're not looking at anyone—they're looking at huge cue cards that were literally hung around the entire room."

The large, fat, yellow cigarette which Rachael smokes during her V-K test was real. According to Michael Deeley, "It's actually a French brand called a 'Boyard' (*BOY-yah*). They come with dark, nicotine-stained paper wrapped around them."

Holden and Pris also smoke Boyards during the film. Apparently, not all the influences in 2019 Los Angeles are Asian ones.

"My favorite close-up in the film is the shot of Sean in the Voigt-Kampff interview," Cronenweth said during an interview for the *American Cinematographer* ("*Blade Runner*: Production Design and Photography," by Herb A. Lightman and Richard Patterson, July 1982). "She is holding a cigarette in her right hand, and the key light was at such an angle so as to strike only her hair, neck, hand, and the smoke of the cigarette."

Scott also intentionally inserted a subtle audio clue to Rachael's replicant status during her V-K test.

Immediately after Deckard asks Rachael his "nude girl picture" question, Ford can also (faintly) be heard saying, "Bush outside your window . . . orange body, green legs." This is a foreshadowing of the upcoming "Mama spider memory" Rachael will relate to Deckard in his apartment, a memory artificially implanted in Rachael but actually belonging to Tyrell's niece.

(Top) Deckard prepares to give Rachael the V-K test. (Bottom) Rachael coolly answers Deckard's questions (note her glowing eyes).

LEON'S HOTEL ROOM

Deckard and Gaff now visit "1187 Hunterwasser Street," site of the Yukon Hotel and Leon's room. The room itself and the corridor outside it were filmed in downtown Los Angeles at the Pan-Am Building. "I never understood why that place had such a dignified name," Michael Deeley relates. "It was such a squalid little building. Shooting there was awkward; the room was very small."

In earlier scripted versions of this scene, Gaff and Deckard first walked through the Yukon's corridors, passing such strange tenants as sumo wrestlers, Mato Grosse Indians, and semipsychotic men. This scene was cut because of budget limitations.

A shadowy Deckard now enters Leon's bathroom, eventually finding a small, scaly object stuck to the side of the replicant's bathtub.

"If you watch closely during the scene where Deckard is in Leon's bathroom, you'll realize you never see Harrison Ford's face," Ivor Powell divulges. "That's because the actor in that scene *isn't* Harrison Ford! Ridley shot that entire bathroom scene as an insert on a set built in Pinewood, England, after principal photography wrapped. Harrison's stand-in was Vic Armstrong, a stunt double from *Raiders of the Lost Ark.*

"There was initially a bit of worry that audiences would realize this guy wasn't Harrison. But Ridley said, 'Don't worry, I'll silhouette him so nobody will know.' And nobody did—until now."

Brion James: "One bit got dropped from that bathroom scene I was really sorry to see go.

"Ridley had come up with the idea that when Harrison walked into the bathroom, the camera would tip up and you'd see me wedged up near the ceiling. The idea was supposed to be that Deckard had caught me at my house; Leon was hiding by pushing against the four corners of the room with his hands and feet. I'd be hanging there like a spider and looking down, but Deckard wouldn't know I was there. That would've been the scariest fucking thing in the world.

"So they built a false ceiling into the Pan-Am bathroom where I could stick my arms and legs into these hidden recesses and hang there all night, if I wanted to. But then they ran out of time and couldn't go back to that location. So I was filmed outside on a street in the Burbank lot instead, looking up like I was staring at my hotel room window."

As Deckard searches Leon's room, Gaff amuses himself by making another origami sculpture: a matchstick man with an erection. "The stickman was funny because he had a boner," says Edward James Olmos. "Gaff was always making these origami as a commentary on Deckard's state of mind. This time, the stickman meant Gaff thought Deckard had a hard-on because of the way he went after a case," (*BR's* prop department made most of Gaff's origami: Olmos, however, made the chicken seen in Bryant's office).

Exiting the bathroom, Deckard discovers a small stack of photographs in a drawer. These photos were, according to Brion James, "supposed to show you that Leon thought of the other replicants as his family. That's why I played him acting so pissed that he'd lost his snapshots. Those were photos of his clan! We wanted the audience to think that replicants missed having a real family, so they all hung together among themselves and made up a surrogate family, instead."

"IF ONLY YOU COULD SEE WHAT I'VE SEEN ———— WITH YOUR EYES"

"There's a funny story concerning how Rutger Hauer got his part," continues Katy Haber. "When we got around to casting Batty, I said, 'Ridley, there's one person you've got to cast in this role. I mean, he looks like an android, he's just right. His name's Rutger Hauer.' Ridley said, 'Who?'

"So I set up some screenings for Ridley of Rutger's previous films—*Turkish Delight, Kitje Tipple, Soldier of Orange*. Ridley liked what he saw, and Rutger was signed without Ridley ever meeting him.

"But now comes the day for Rutger to have his first meeting with his new director. I'll never forget that, because Rutger had already dyed his hair bleached-white and cut it in a very high crew cut. He was also wearing these enormous Elton John sunglasses, brightly-colored pink satin pants, and a huge white sweater with a fox design that had two beady red eyes.

"Ridley, I swear to God, went white. He looked at me like I'd killed him—he must have thought Rutger was a two-hundred-pound raving queen! But Rutger wasn't. He'd just wanted to really blow Ridley away. And he did."

Rutger Hauer: "Speaking about *Blade Runner* after all these years is funny," Hauer told this author in 1995, "because it deals with memory. And our memories are emotional; we remember things based on feelings rather than fact most of the time.

"But I do recall being concerned about what these replicants were to look like. The cliché at the time was pasty-faced *Star Trek*-type things, which I had real problems with. But then Ridley convinced me the replicants would be presented as more normal human beings.

"Roy Batty was a complex and important role for me. I enjoyed the challenge of portraying this four-year-old thing, enjoyed the marvelous sets and atmosphere and Ridley's particular brilliance. Yet Ridley and I hardly ever talked about my performance. He'd occasionally say something like, 'Could you be a little less nasty, or little more?' But we really didn't need to talk very much, since we had such a good understanding between us."

As Roy and Leon leave the VidPhon booth, they pass by a square pillar banded with blue neon. On their left is a string of electrified parking meters with glowing red domes; on their right, deep in shadow, are an Asian "shoeshine boy" and his customer, wearing round, wide-brimmed hats. All are throwaway examples of Ridley Scott's "layering" technique.

Chinese graffiti covers the outer wall of and a trash can standing before Chew's Eye Works, the laboratory at which the replicants now stop. These Chinese characters were genuine—they express hope for prosperous days ahead and wish passersby a safe journey (thanks to Phil Ching for the translation).

Although the Eye Works exterior was constructed on Warner Brothers's back lot, the interior of Chew's lab was another non-Burbank *BR* location. Dubbed "Chew's Ice House" by the crew, this set was shot in early May 1981 within a functioning meat locker in Vernon, California (a municipality of downtown Los Angeles). Temperatures within this location dipped seven degrees below zero; ironically, the temperature on the street outside this cold-storage facility had soared to an unseasonable ninety-eight degrees. "It was so cold in there, everyone was wearing snow suits and parkas," Brion James recalls. "Except Rutger and Hong and I. So after every take, we'd run outside to warm up, because we were freezing to death."

The *Blade Runner* crew spent two days in this frigid environment, first having to wait four days for various parts of the set to form an appropriate icicle buildup. These icicles were painstakingly formed by

Terry Frazee's crew by adding successive layers of water, by hand, to objects scattered around the room.

As for the many eyeballs on display in Chew's Ice House, these were a mixed bag; those closest to the camera were actual sheep's eyes purchased from a nearby slaughterhouse, while those not needed to be subjected to the camera's intense scrutiny were artificial orbs purchased from Max Factor of Hollywood. Standard aquariums were then utilized as the tanks Chew used to store his eyes.

The scene within Chew's Eye Works begins with the camera coming upon the elderly Chinese happily engaged in microsurgical work, plucking replicant eyes from a plastic storage box with a pair of chopsticks. As previously mentioned, Chew is played by JAMES HONG, one of the hardest-working character actors in Hollywood.

Born in Minnesota, he was raised in Hong Kong until he was in the fifth grade. "My family then moved back to Minneapolis," Hong says. "I was a very quiet teenager from a strict Chinese family. So, when I discovered that I liked doing plays in my junior high years, I also realized I'd found a wonderful way of expressing myself."

Hong moved to Los Angeles in the late 1940s to attend the University of Southern California for a degree in civil engineering. "At the same time, I loved doing stand-up comedy and impersonations," Hong continues. "In fact, I had an acting partner back then named Donald C. Parker, and we were a stand-up comedy team much like Martin and Lewis. Don and I worked a lot of different, second-tier places: strip clubs, VA hospitals, intermission shows."

In 1953, Hong was tapped for a small part in the Clark Gable film *Soldier of Fortune*. "That's when I got my first SAG *[Screen Actor's Guild]* card. So I asked for a year's leave of absence from the job I had then with the L.A. County road department—which was so boring—and I never went back. I think I'm just about the only civil engineer that has movie status."

After *Soldier of Fortune* Hong continued to work steadily and often in films and television; some of his many credits include *Love Is a Many Splendored Thing* (1955), *The Satan Bug* (1965), *The Sand Pebbles* (1966), *Colossus: The Forbin Project* (1970), the TV-movie *Kung-Fu* (1972), *Chinatown* (1974), *Big Trouble in Little China* (1986) (in which Hong played three roles), and *Wayne's World 2* (1993).

But what are Hong's thoughts on his *BR* character? "I played Chew as a brilliant scientist who was on the edge of senility," Hong explains. "Being in that refrigerator and working so hard, sixteen, twenty hours a day, had probably gotten to him. I think his job might have even frozen part of Chew's brain!" Hong says, laughing. "Ridley and I also saw Chew as constantly inventing all these gadgets to help him stay in that refrigerator, like those stupid heating pipes in the back of his coat. The reason he's got all that paraphernalia is that he can't bear the thought of leaving his eyeballs—which Chew considers his children—any longer than he has to. In fact, I asked Ridley if I could speak Chinese to those eyes during the opening of my scene. And I did. Chew was making sweet talk to his kids: 'You good little children, how are you today?' Things like that."

In English, part of Chew's dialogue during the opening Eye Works scene (translation courtesy Phil Ching/William Kolb) is:

Chew: (In Chinese) "Ha, yes! So little time."
(Chew examines an eye under a microscope.)
Chew: (In Chinese) "Ha, ha! So beautiful."
(Then Batty and Kowalski enter the lab.)
Chew: (In Chinese) "Ha, ha! Beautiful indeed!"
(Leon tugs at the hoses connecting Chew's heated fur coat.)
Chew: (In Chinese) "Where did you come from? What the hell do you think you are doing?!"
(Chew speaks into his coat-lapel microphone.)
Chew: (In Chinese) "Ah-Chong, come quickly!"

"I did an old-age makeup on Hong using the same stretch-and-stipple technique I used on Bill Sanderson," says Marvin Westmore. "I also stuck a fake little chin piece on James to make him look like a Mandarin. But the touch nobody ever asks me about is that tattoo on Chew's left cheek.

"Ridley wanted something different on Chew's face, so we put a little mark there, possibly as an identifying number—a lot of things we did on *Blade Runner* were 'possibly it's this' or 'possibly it's that.' Anyway, the tattoo itself is just the last four digits of my home telephone number, combined with a barcode type of thing. I drew that on with what we call a tattoo-colored inkpen.

———

After gaining Chew's attention, Batty's first words to the angry eye-engineer are a poem:

"Fiery the angels fell,

"Deep thunder rolled around their shores,

"Burning with the fires of Orc."

This piece of dialogue is actually a slightly altered extract from William Blake's epic poem "America: A Prophecy," an allegory concerning the struggle for independence fought in the American Revolution. But why would a replicant quote Blake to a Chinese?

"Because Ridley, that inimitable man, asked me to," recalls David Peoples. "During my rewrites, I'd done a scene where Batty discovers that the Tyrell he kills isn't the real one, but a replicant—the real Tyrell is in a state of cryogenic suspension. And somewhere in that scene I'd slipped in a reference to a poem by Shelley called 'Ozymandias.'

"Now, Ridley is a culturally alert guy. He said, 'That's good. There ought to be a reference to Blake, too. Let's give that to Batty.' But I'm not a Blake fan—in fact, I'd never read him before. So I dutifully went out and purchased a book of Blake, came across that 'America' poem, rewrote it a bit, and gave the lines to Roy as a piece of dialogue. Which seemed to work; Batty was certainly the type of person who could surprise you."

After Batty quotes his poem, Chew speaks a mixture of Chinese and English. Translated, these lines are:

(Chew, in Chinese) "How can this be!? It can't be!" Then (in English), Chew continues with, "You not come here! Illegal!" At which point the curious Leon plunges his hand into a tank full of a sub-zero viscous material, meant to represent Chew's eyes in a liquid state. Chew now says (in English) "Hey! Hey!" Then, in Chinese, "What are you doing?" Chew concludes his shouted warning by speaking in English again: "Cold. Those are my eyes. Freezing!"

"Sticking my hand in that solution and then sniffing it, I'm like a kid in a candy store checking things out," says Brion James. "That's part of Leon's C-level intellect—he's very inquisitive."

"We filled that tank by buying hundreds of these little Cyalume sticks—you know, those plastic sticks that you snap and shake to get 'em glowing?—and emptying those into Chew's eye tank," Terry Frazee recalls. "I'd found out that that solution was safe to stick your hand into. Then we hit that tank with a black light to make Brion's hand glow an even weirder color."

Batty's pleasant demeanor now hardens as he demands information on, "Morphology. Longevity. Incept dates." Chew responds with, "I don't know about such stuff. I just do eyes!"

According to Hong, "Chew had never before seen his eyes come back to him in a living body before. Batty was his first experience with that; it frightened him to see his kids looking at him in such a threatening way."

Rutger Hauer: "I still like what Batty says next—'Chew, if only you could see what I've seen with your eyes.' *Blade Runner* had an uncommon amount of memorable dialogue."

"I agree," adds Brion James. "One of the greatest lines in the movie came out of that scene. That's a classic."

James Hong: "While I thought *Blade Runner* was an incredible, mesmerizing film, I have mixed emotions about actually working on it. One thing I was sad about was a scripted scene that was never filmed. Harrison Ford was supposed to come to Chew's lab later in the picture with some other policemen and find me frozen solid. Then one of them accidentally knocks me over and I shatter into a million pieces.

"But that's just an actor wanting to have one more scene. What I found more uncomfortable were the working conditions and general atmosphere—we were performing under circumstances that were among the most tense I've ever worked in my life. The *BR* guys were trying to squeeze five days of shooting into two, because I understand by that point they were under extreme pressure from the front office to hurry up. So it was just constant turmoil on that set. Not only were the cameras starting to freeze, but when they closed the door, the big lights they were using gave off this gas and everybody started getting sick. Then, at the end of the second day, we were running late, and all the freezer trucks were impatiently waiting in a line outside to bring their meat back in! Yet we still did that scene in spite of the hardships."

DECKARD'S APARTMENT —————————————————————

The tunnel through which Deckard drives on the way to his apartment was a real location. This passageway is situated on 2nd Street between Hill and Figueroa Streets in downtown Los Angeles, one locally known as the "2nd Street Tunnel." The strangely glowing, glazed ceramic tiles seen within it were not installed by the *BR* production team but are an integral part of this still-existing tunnel, which was built in 1924 and has also served as a location for such films as *The Terminator*.

According to the 1982 *Blade Runner* pressbook, Deckard's car (which had its own "stand-in") is "a turbine-powered, maroon and bronze sedan with a solar-energy converter at the lower-right corner of the front windshield. The vehicle has 'twist-wrist' steering, four interior read-out screens, and gull-wing doors which open sideways."

The exterior (first floor only) of Deckard's apartment complex was shot at a real house designed in 1924 by controversial architect Frank Lloyd Wright. This structure is called "The Ennis-Brown house" and is situated in the hilly Los Angeles suburb of Los Feliz; it can be found at 2655 Glendower Avenue, just off Western Avenue above Los Feliz Boulevard.

"We looked at a lot of sites for Deckard's apartment building," says Lawrence Paull, "realizing all the time that we had to turn a single structure into a cantilevered condominium complex that was not only hundreds of stories high, but that would also appear as if it were about ready to fall over on its side at any minute. We further realized that a matte painting by Matthew Yuricich [*Blade Runner*'s chief matte artist: see chapter X] would be involved in later adding on a hundred extra stories to the exterior of Deckard's apartment complex.

"So after securing the necessary location permits, we simply filmed

Harrison driving up to the exterior of the Ennis-Brown house one night. That exterior features a Mayan cast-stone motif, by the way. And that's what we used for the entrance to Deckard's apartment building."

Continuing with Lawrence Paull's notion that "every *Blade Runner* set was designed to generate an emotional aura," the interior of Deckard's apartment (whose number is 9732, and was erected on Stage 24A of The Burbank Studios) was built to reflect both the idea of Deckard's bachelorhood and the enclosed, oppressive atmosphere of his manner of employment.

Deckard's apartment was designed by Syd Mead. The set representing that apartment was composed of an entry hall, bathroom, bedroom, living, and dining room. To help select the apartment's fixtures and furnishings, Lawrence Paull used an early 1980s book of futuristic illustrations, *High Tech*, as "an inspirational guide."

As Deckard walks into the various rooms of his dwelling during Rachael's first visit, astute viewers will notice that the lights in each room automatically turn themselves on as he enters. Jordan Cronenweth calls this "an energy-saving device of the future."

Rachael tries to convince Deckard that she's not a replicant by showing him a childhood photograph and recounting a youthful memory about hatching baby spiders eating their mother. But then, during one of the most emotionally wrenching moments in the film, Deckard brutally informs Rachael that these are false memories implanted by Tyrell.

"The scene I liked the best [in *Blade Runner*] was where Harrison tells me I'm a 'replicant,' a robot with emotions, and I cry right on cue," Young told the *Washington Post*. "Yes, they're real tears" (*Washington Post*, August 14, 1982).

After Rachael leaves Deckard's apartment, the Blade Runner picks up her discarded snapshot, which shows Tyrell's niece as a child with her mother. During a subsequent close-up, moving shadows can be seen within this photograph, accompanied by the faint sound of laughing children.

During an interview for the English science fiction film magazine *Starburst*, Ridley Scott said, "I wanted the photograph to have such a reality to it because Deckard gets drawn into Rachael's 'memory'—it's a little bit like a woman showing a picture of a refugee to people and asking, 'Have you seen this child?' . . . [That moving photograph] is [also] kind of an enhancement of what's happening to [Deckard] at that particular moment, when he gets sucked into, 'Is it real, or isn't it real?' I thought it was nice that that frame, for a second or two, came alive, and you also have the sound of children playing on the soundtrack, which is our memories." (Interview with Phil Edwards and Alan McKenzie, *Starburst* magazine, No. 51, 1982).

PRIS AND SEBASTIAN

Pris, played by DARYL HANNAH, is first introduced walking down a night-shrouded city street and passing two strange objects. The item on screen left is a Trafficator; the one at the right is a futuristic street cleaner (the same prop vehicle was later used for the scene where Leon punches through the side of a truck during his alley fight with Deckard).

This scene, like the next few to follow, was shot in downtown Los Angeles, at the intersection of 3rd Street and Broadway (across the street from the Bradbury Building).

A number of different exteriors and interiors representing Sebastian's home were staged in and around downtown Los Angeles's historic Bradbury Building (located at 304 South Broadway). This much-filmed, architectural anomaly is a structure which has seen service in a number of other genre projects, including Harlan Ellison's classic *Outer Limits* episode, "Demon with a Glass Hand."

Built in 1893, the Bradbury Building is a local historical landmark whose architectural purity had been threatened by a series of safety code modifications at the time of the *BR* shoot; in fact, the structure had fallen into a serious state of disrepair (however, it was completely renovated in the early 1990s). Commissioned by millionaire Lewis Bradbury, it was designed by architect George Wyman (who had been inspired by reading Edward Bellamy's *Looking Backward,* an early utopian novel set in the year 2000 and featuring descriptions of numerous futuristic commercial buildings).

Inside the building, the *BR* crew chose to stage scenes featuring the building's geometrically patterned stairways, wrought-iron railings and open-cage elevators (still functional today), by filming on the interior ground floor, top floor, central court, lobby, elevators, and stairways. Additionally, Scott paid particular attention during interior filming to the center court's glass-block roof, known to some on the crew as "Sebastian's atrium."

The interior of the Bradbury was then "dirtied down" by adding varying amounts of trash, smoke, revolving xenon spotlights, dripping water, and mannequins. A false wall and door were also erected before one of the Bradbury's offices to stand in for the entrance to Sebastian's apartment (the interior of J. F.'s apartment, however, was an elaborate set built inside soundstage 25 on the Warner Brothers lot).

Despite a personal fondness for the Bradbury and Million Dollar Theater, however, Hampton Fancher initially tried to convince Ridley Scott *not* to shoot at the Bradbury.

"In the late 1950s, I used to live in downtown L.A. and knew the Bradbury quite well. I'd also been a Flamenco dancer when I was young, and in 1955 I actually performed at the Million Dollar, which was then part of the Latin vaudeville circuit.

"But when Ridley decided to use the Bradbury, I was against it," Fancher continues. "He'd come back from seeing the place with the location manager (Michael Neale) and was all excited. I told him, 'Ridley, you can't use the Bradbury Building. I know you're from England and you think it's a great place, and it *is* a great place, but it's already been done. Overdone. I've seen it already in a ton of movies. And even though I never watch TV, I've been told that the Bradbury's been used for cop shows every week for the past ten years.'

"Now, I was trying to make the point that Ridley was from out of the country and didn't realize that everyone already knew this building. But then Ridley looked at me and said, 'Not the way I'll do it.' At the time I thought that was incredibly arrogant. But then I went to see

Blade Runner and thought, 'My God! Ridley was right! No one's ever seen the Bradbury like this before!'"

As for playing a female replicant, "That was very interesting," says Daryl Hannah. "Ridley had given us a short history of them, which mainly told us which replicant did what job Off-world. This history also said that the replicants were made to last only a certain number of years. We'd basically been manufactured like a car, to last only a short time so that people would have to buy a new one. But the mistake our makers had made was to implant feelings and memories in us, which gave the replicants a righteous indignation to extend their life.

"There's a tragedy and pathos to that kind of knowledge of one's own mortality. At the same time, even though she was built as a pleasure model, Pris was a young character; my idea of her was that she was very naïve, almost like a four-year-old child. But you know, Pris is always described by my friends as being very sly and cunning. Well, children are very good at that, aren't they? Besides, since the replicants knew they were going to die in a very short time, they realized they'd have to figure out a way to save their lives even more quickly. That kind of expediency required them to lie, cheat, even kill. Pris didn't have the time to relax and be genuine with Sebastian, even though she really *liked* the guy. She was working on a deadline."

J. F. Sebastian now arrives at the Bradbury via a strange armor-plated vehicle which designer Syd Mead dubbed "The Armadillo Van," from its resemblance to that animal.

Mead envisioned Sebastian's van as an asymmetrical pickup truck/jalopy made by its inventive owner out of spare parts. According to the 1982 *Blade Runner* press kit ("The Futuristic Cars of Blade Runner"), the Armadillo Van featured "oval bubbles on each side of the roof and Plexiglas panels that extend[ed] from the roof to the rear bumpers."

J. F. Sebastian had been conceived by Fancher and Scott as a painfully shy but gifted genetic engineer afflicted with a rare aging disease.

Sebastian also spent his leisure hours producing astonishingly realistic toys as playthings for the upper strata of 2019's rigidly defined society, and as mechanical companions to offset his own loneliness.

As for the actor who portrayed him, William Sanderson has made a notable career by portraying both gentle eccentrics *and* vicious villains. He started acting (in plays) while attending law school in Tennessee, where he received a Juris Doctor degree. After graduation Sanderson moved to New York, studied acting under William Hickey, and "did plays—off-off-*off* Broadway plays!" Sanderson's stage work enabled him to snare an agent. By the mid-seventies, he'd begun working in such low-budget independent films as *Hootch* (a "moonshiner movie" that was Sanderson's first screen role) and 1980's *Savage Weekend*. The actor then racked up an impressive list of other screen credits, including *Coal Miner's Daughter* (1980), *Raggedy Man* (1981), the striking made-for-TV film *The Executioner's Song* (1982), the 1985 theatrical release *Fletch*, the wildly popular miniseries *Lonesome Dove* (1989), and the successful John Grisham-bestseller-based *The Client* (1994). Sanderson's latest venture (as of 1995) is the John Frankenheimer-directed telefilm *Andersonville*, a 1996 drama concerning the Civil War's most notorious POW camp.

Yet viewers are probably most familiar with Sanderson through his continuing role on the 1982–1990 television series *Newhart;* here the actor portrayed the only speaking member of a trio of bumpkinish brothers. "We're still friends after ten years, those two guys and I. There's always talk of reprising that show, too. *Newhart* was a lot of fun. It was also nice just to have a regular job."

Despite his varied resumé, though, Sanderson credits *Blade Runner* for a pivotal turning point in his career.

"Ridley, who I think is a real visionary, is responsible for opening up the range of parts I get today. Before *BR* I'd exclusively played bad guys or bums and renegades. Ridley, for some reason, let me play a sympathetic guy. That changed everything."

As for the character of J. F. Sebastian, Sanderson created him from a number of differing elements.

"One was the physical image of Einstein. I figured Sebastian had some elements of genius in him, so I used that. I also watched a video of a child with progeria, this terrible disease that prematurely ages children. This boy walked like he had sore heels or something, so I was able to pick up a little bit of that walk and use it for Sebastian, too.

"But primarily I just listened to Ridley. So one day when he softly gave me a piece of direction—'This is a totally innocent man,'—that unlocked a lot of things for me. Because I spent a lot of my life alone. Most actors spend some time alone struggling anyway, but I did it excessively. And I have bad skin to begin with, so maybe Ridley thought I could relate to a self-conscious guy who lived alone.

"Now, I don't mean to suggest that mine was an Academy Award—winning performance. It's just a small part. Besides, *Blade Runner* was really Ridley's show; if there is such a thing as a visionary, Ridley's the guy. He's got the eye and the passion for that.

"On the other hand, I am in *BR,* and it is a film that's in the archives, right? The Library of Congress? So it's nice to be in a cult film." (*BR* was inducted into the National Film Registry on December 14, 1993.)

After accidentally dropping his keys, Sebastian "startles" Pris, who jumps up from her hiding place beneath a trash pile and makes a frantic dash for the street. A moment later her forward momentum carries Pris into the side of Sebastian's van, where she breaks the van's window with her arm (an unscripted moment where Hannah accidentally slipped on the wet pavement and chipped her elbow in eight places).

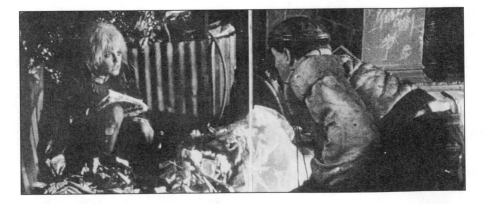

Sebastian startles a hiding Pris. Moments later, actress Daryl Hannah accidentally collided with the window of Sanderson's van—and chipped her elbow in eight places.

William Sanderson: "Daryl was a classy lady. Very athletic, real down to earth and nice. Sharp, too. I was very fond of her. In fact, I remember Daryl waltzing in when I was getting made up as Sebastian one day, and she sort of shyly gave me a drawing she'd done of my character and hers. Like a kid she said, 'It's not too good, Bill, but I want you to keep it.' But it was good—drawing's another talent of hers. I still have that pencil sketch of the two us to this day."

"I'd originally written a whole different sequence to explain how Pris got into Sebastian's place," Peoples explains. "J. F. had stepped outside his apartment to feed a kitten. But he gave it a bowl of something thick and black, not milk. Then it suddenly froze while it was lapping this stuff up. You didn't know what was going on until Sebastian opened the cat up to replace a battery and it continued to drink this stuff—which turned out to be oil. In the meantime, Sebastian had forgot to lock the door behind him, and Pris slipped into the Bradbury. That was one version."

After Pris and Sebastian enter the lobby of the gloomy Bradbury Building, the huge advertising blimp drifts over the building. According to William Kolb's *Blade Runner: Film Notes* article (printed in *Retrofitting Blade Runner*; see the bibliography in appendix H), the piece of Japanese music heard from this dirigible is "'Ogi no Mato' ['The Folding Fan as a Target'] . . . [a] famous piece for voice and Biwa . . . based on a complex legend similar to that of William Tell, in which a folding fan, instead of the famous Swiss apple, serves as the target."

Unlocking his apartment door, Sebastian cheerfully calls out, "Yoo-hoo! Home again!" Pris is surprised and delighted to find herself greeted by a pair of walking, talking dolls—a miniature Kaiser Wilhelm with a very long nose, and an upright teddy bear dressed as Napoleon. "Home again, home again, jiggety-jig. Gooood evening, J. F.!" this mechanical duo chant.

The Kaiser and Bear dolls were actually two "little people." These performers' names were John Edward Allen (Kaiser) and Kevin Thompson (Bear). Thompson has also appeared in such motion pictures as *The Ewok Adventure* (TV movie, 1984), *Weird Science* (1985), *Night of the Creeps* (1986), *Munchies* (1987), and *Spaced Invaders* (1990).

(Left) Sebastian's mistakes; the walking, talking Kaiser and Napoleon Bear dolls. (Right) Sebastian's dolls out of costume; Kevin Thompson (left) as Bear and John Edward Allen (right) as Kaiser.

According to *BR* makeup supervisor Marvin Westmore, "The Bear was just a costume that the actor slipped into, with a pull-over head. The Kaiser's nose was a last-minute idea that Ridley came up with, and a straight makeup job that took about an hour and a half to apply. No prosthetics. It was made from latex by my brother Mike, with holes in the nose for the actor to breathe through."

William Sanderson: "Ridley told me, 'These walking dolls are mistakes that you made.' That's why the Kaiser hits the door on his way out—he's a mistake."

The Pris/Sebastian relationship is another example of *Blade Runner's* fascinating "doubling effect" (previously mentioned in chapter I), a persistent mirroring of characters and situations which occurs throughout *Blade Runner.*

For what is Pris and Sebastian's pairing if not the dark, tragic echo of Rachael and Deckard's own romantic relationship?

William Sanderson again: "Ridley once said something interesting anout *Blade Runner.* He told me, '*Blade Runner* is an adult cartoon.'"

THE ESPER

At the beginning of the scene where Deckard digitally scans Leon's snapshot in the Esper, two intrusive "shafts of light" come streaking in through the Blade Runner's apartment window. The illumination source for these beams was xenon spotlights, commonly used for night advertising and sporting events.

The Esper itself was the largest prop built by EEG's Mark Stetson and his miniature-making *BR* model crew. This machine was supposed to be Deckard's personal, in-apartment extension of the police

Deckard scans Leon's photo with the Esper.

department's own Esper machine. A construct described in the 1982 *Blade Runner* production notes as "a high-density computer with a very powerful three-dimensional resolution capacity and cryogenic cooling system [which can] analyze and enlarge photos, enabling investigators to search a room without even being there."

During Deckard's examination of Leon's photo, the image of a sleeping Zhora (Joanna Cassidy) is revealed.

However, the "Zhora" discovered in this photograph is *not* Joanna Cassidy, but an anonymous, stand-in substitute for the actress. Cassidy is also not in the hard-copy photograph Deckard obtains from the Esper after scanning Leon's picture.

"It's not me, and I couldn't believe it when I saw the film," affirms Cassidy. "I didn't even know they were using a stand-in when they shot that scene. They did this after the fact. I could have killed Ridley. I would have come down to do that even if it'd been shot two years after I was done working on the picture."

"Harrison examining that photograph is one of my favorite sequences in the film, because it says, 'Watch me create a lie,'" comments Rutger Hauer. "You see, the outcome of this process is a blur. An image of a person who really could be anybody. A man, a woman, somebody wearing a wig, anybody.

"And the lie? There are many. One lie is that there are two Roys in that room, I and a stand-in. Another is that there's a false Zhora. A third is that the photo itself is a lie—you only think one person's in that room, but there are two.

"So that whole Esper sequence shows how you can play with images and tell a story and, at the same time, completely bullshit someone. Which is just like making a motion picture, come to think of it. But the truth of that photo is—there is no truth."

Before Scott came up with the idea of Deckard scanning Leon's photo in the Esper, another (unfilmed)) scene was written by David Peoples to serve the same purpose. In this sequence, Deckard returns to the Noodle Bar and suddenly realizes that the scales on a customer's fishhead are very similar to the scale Deckard found in Leon's bathtub.

This connection then inspired Deckard to visit the Cambodian lady in Animoid Row, and the story proceeded from there.

ANIMOID ROW

Deckard now takes his Esper photo of Zhora and clue he found in Leon's bathtub to Animoid Row, a section of shops and stalls that specialize in the manufacture of artificial animals. The Animoid Row set, built on the Old New York Street, cost over 1 million (1982) dollars to construct.

David Dryer: "When Deckard's on Animoid Row and the Cambodian woman examines his scale under a microscope, what you're seeing is a real electron microscope photograph. But it's not a closeup of a snake scale—it's the bud on top of a female marijuana plant! That was provided by a man named David Scharf, who finds all kinds of small, interesting things for micro-photography—molds growing on sponges on his kitchen sink, that sort of thing. And the serial number you see on that so-called snake scale, the one that leads Deckard to the Egyptian, was, I think, done by David himself. Just by retouching his original marijuana photograph."

After leaving the Cambodian woman's stand, Deckard pushes his way through a crowd of replicant animals and human customers streaming through Animoid Row. He then steps aside for two replicant ostriches.

A photo caption in the *Blade Runner Souvenir Magazine* claims that these ostriches were mechanical birds specifically built for the film. However, according to Terry Frazee, *BR*'s floor effects supervisor, "That's not true. Why that magazine said that, I don't know. We never built any mechanical birds for the picture—those are real ostriches."

When Deckard converses with the fez-hatted Abdul Ben-Hassan, replicant snake-maker, the dialogue between these two men does not match the movement of their lips. However, in the *BR* workprint it does. Terry Rawlings explains, "The reason that changed between the workprint and release print was because certain producers felt the original dialogue exchange [found in chapter XVI] was confusing. The higher-ups wanted to clarify things and give the audience more of an explanation about what Deckard was after and what this snake scale meant. So new words were looped in during postproduction. That didn't really work, though, did it?"

THE SNAKE PIT

Working on information given him by Abdul Ben-Hassan, Deckard enters The Snake Pit, a crowded, smoky, decadent nightclub populated by dozens of slumming upper-class citizens, some of whom are smoking opium pipes or sipping exotic cocktails.

The Snake Pit interiors were filmed on the same set and soundstage previously used to represent Sebastian's apartment.

In previous versions of the script, The Snake Pit was going to be a decrepit opera house instead of a nightclub. A location was scouted for this scene, as well: the interior of Los Angeles' Art Deco Wiltern Theater.

Deckard now speaks with The Snake Pit's owner, Taffey Lewis, who was portrayed by HY PYKE.

A longtime comic, stage performer, and character actor, Pyke has appeared in such low- and medium-budget films as *Nightmare in Blood* (1978), *The First Nudie Musical* (1976), and *Vamp* (1986). He can also be seen in the exploitation mindboggler *Dolomite* and the well-done, little-seen 1973 "adult fairytale" *Lemora: A Child's Tale of the Supernatural* (in which Pyke plays a zombified rural bus driver).

As for Taffey Lewis, Pyke took this role seriously, even though the part was a small one. "First I decided the Snake Pit was the sort of place where rich, important people go to do their sinning," Pyke says. "And I'd worked in nightclubs for a long time—even ran one at one point. So Taffey became kind of a composite of all the bar owners I'd ever performed for. That's why you see him planted at the bar when

Deckard comes in—that's Taffey's roost. I'd noticed other club owners do that. They plant themselves so they can watch their bar, watch their show, and watch their club. Taffey was the same way."

Abdul Ben-Hassan, replicant snake-maker of Animoid Row.

Despite the brevity of his part, however, Pyke feels the process by which he was cast for Taffey was an interesting one.

"I'd been originally sent by my agent to read for a bartender at Taffey's club *[a role ultimately going to Leo Gorcey, Jr., son of famed "Bowery Boys" actor Leo Gorcey]*. I thought that was stupid, because they wanted a big gorilla of a guy and I'm fairly small. Anyway, Ridley said he was going to audition me for this bartender part. But I had to wait for him most of the day because he was shooting.

"So while I was waiting I got a copy of the script, came across the part of Taffey, and memorized that instead. Then another man came in the room and I read Taffey for him. But this guy didn't like my interpretation; he told me this was very different from the Taffey Lewis they had in mind. At that point I got a little angry. I said, 'Look, I've been waiting here all day for Ridley and he hasn't shown up yet. Ridley Scott said he was going to read me, so let *him* send me home.'

"I was very tough on this guy, stood right up to him. He just looked at me in a strange way and said, 'Well, maybe you should stay.' It turned out that this man was Michael Deeley, the producer! I'd thought he was just some sort of clipboard carrier, an underling who can screw you up. But Deeley evidently thought my toughness was what he needed for the part, because I got Taffey after all."

The Snake Pit, decadent nightclub of 2019. Sitting (with bow tie, third from right, girl's forearm on his shoulder) at his bar is Taffey Lewis (Hy Pike), the club's owner. Note clay opium pipes.

Pyke's relationship with *BR*'s director ultimately proved a rewarding one, however.

"Ridley had all this publicity about shooting everything over and over again," Pyke recalls. " But when it got time for my scenes, he did my master in two takes and my close-up in one. Then he said, 'That's a wrap.' And everyone's jaws sort of dropped.

"Ridley looked around and said, 'I don't know why you're all so surprised. I'm a perfectionist, yes. But when I see perfection the first time, I take it.'

"That was the nicest compliment anyone ever gave to me."

Deckard now decides to call Rachael to apologize for his past behavior and invite the replicant to The Snake Pit for a drink. He dials Rachael's number—555–7583—on a graffiti-smeared VidPhon and has a short conversation with the beautiful young woman before she hangs up on him (this brief call costs Deckard $1.25).

Sean Young's conversation had actually been prefilmed for this scene. After being transferred to videotape, it was fed *via* a three-quarter-inch tapedeck into the working VidPhon screen; Harrison Ford simply delivered his dialogue into the pauses already built into Young's end of the conversation.

Back at the bar, Deckard picks worms from his mouth that were floating in his drink. An unseen club announcer now says, "Ladies and Gentlemen, Taffey Lewis presents Miss Salome and the snake. Watch her take the pleasure from the serpent that once corrupted man."

Terry Rawlings: "Ridley had very much wanted to then cut to a spectacular scene of Joanna Cassidy involved in an erotic dance with a snake. He kept fighting and fighting for that; in fact, Zhora's stage set was actually constructed, but the producers wouldn't let him shoot it. They thought it was an unnecessary strain on the budget. Ridley even said he could shoot it in the corner of a soundstage somewhere. But Tandem wouldn't budge."

Two preproduction drawings by Mentor Huebner illustrating Zhora's dance, which was to utilize Claymation and a snake. However, this sequence was budgeted at over $200,000, and deemed too expensive to film.

"Zhora's dance number was going to take place on this elevated platform covered in sand dunes," Joanna Cassidy says. "First you'd see little rivulets of sand starting to break down off one of the dunes like they were being blown away by the wind, then the camera would pull back, and those particles would coalesce into a human shape—me. I'd step away from the dune and reach towards a snake coming out from underneath the sand. Then the snake's tongue would start flicking towards my hand, I'd pick it up, and begin Zhora's dance."

ZHORA ————————————————————————

JOANNA CASSIDY plays Zhora, the beautiful but deadly exotic dancer. She is tall, athletic, and flame-haired, and her career has spanned nearly thirty years of important theatrical and television work. On the big screen, she has appeared in such films as *Bullitt* (1968), *The Outfit* (1974), *Stay Hungry* (1976), *The Late Show* (1977), *Under Fire* (1983), and *Who Framed Roger Rabbit?* (1988). On the small screen, Cassidy has had continuing roles in such well-received series as *Buffalo Bill* (1983) and stand-out parts in critically-acclaimed telefilms like *Barbarians at the Gate* (1993).

In addition to her acting talents, Cassidy has always maintained a second passion in her life: sports. "When I was in high school," the actress explains, "I played basketball, baseball, and field hockey. I was a total jock. Still am, in fact."

Speaking of her preparation for the role of Zhora, Cassidy relates that, "My imagination is a wonderful source of information for me. And I've always meditated, because I believe that in meditation we can reach sources of information we don't consciously have. Using these tools, I started exploring the situation Zhora was in, and decided she was a rebel going up against the majors. Zhora wanted something different from what all the other replicants had—second-class status was not acceptable to her. So I started reading about other women who'd walked a different road, like Queen Victoria and Joan of Arc.

"I also always felt that Zhora was an independent—she didn't really belong to anybody. Certainly not like how Pris was with Roy. I further presumed that previous replicants before the Nexus–6 line weren't programmed like Zhora, and didn't have thoughts about their short life spans. But the Nexus–6s did. I began imagining the pain they must have started to feel when those thoughts and their feelings started to leak in. I really sympathized with them, those replicants."

Why, however, did an established actor like Cassidy agree to such a relatively small part?

"One of the aspects of the character that most fascinated me was Zhora's snake. Because I myself kept snakes at one time; in fact, I had more than six of them. I used to roller skate down the Venice board-walk with one on my shoulders.

"In any event, I thought, 'Hmm, life imitates art'. . . And I real-ized that with my combination of athleticism and knowledge of rep-tiles, nobody else could play this part as well as I could. Certainly not with the comfort and the ease with which I handle snakes. And that's what a large part of Zhora was all about. I'd also already read a lot of information about exotic dancers who work with snakes. I knew, for instance, that some of these dancers used to tape their snake's genitalia and anuses to make sure there were no accidents during their acts. Which I thought was horrible; it makes the snake very angry.

"But if you combine all these elements between the character of Zhora and my own life, it seemed inevitable I'd accept."

A waiting Deckard soon spies the scantily clad "Miss Salome" (Zhora) walking backstage after her act. Claiming to be from "The American Federation of Variety Artists," Deckard follows Zhora into her dressing room.

The scene in Zhora's dressing room took three nights to film. Cas-sidy's "costume" essentially consisted of tanned body paint, a snake draped over her shoulders, numerous sequins pasted on her body, and little else. According to Marvin Westmore, this makeup process took four people three hours each day to complete.

Cassidy's nipples and groin were covered by three small pieces of plastic, and a "body makeup" girl then applied a coating of coffee-brown greasepaint to Cassidy's entire frame. "Then three of us created that celestial body with three different-sized sequins that were held in place by a latex compound," Westmore concludes. The final touch was the application of liberal amounts of hair-styling gel to grease down Cassidy's normally free-flowing locks, which were combed straight back from her forehead.

Asked how she felt having to play the first part of Zhora's scene while mostly in the nude, Cassidy told this author, "Are you kidding? It was mortifying. Walking around the stagehands, people all over the place—absolutely mortifying. But there were enough other naked women around, the ones playing the showgirls in Taffey's club, that I kind of got used to it. Interestingly enough, the makeup made me feel a little covered."

Claiming to be from "The Confidential Committee on Moral Abuses" (and using a high-pitched, affected voice), Deckard tells Cassidy he's been assigned to interview Zhora to make sure she isn't being exploited by the club. "Are you for real?" Zhora asks sarcastically, after taking her snake off her neck and hanging it on a coatrack.

"I really enjoyed that silly voice Harrison used in our scene together," Cassidy recalls. "It was wonderful because it annoyed me so much. It was so irritating, so ingratiating. This disgusting peon of a man."

As for the snake which Zhora placed on the coatrack, "That snake's name was Darling, and he belonged to me," Cassidy continues. "He was my own snake. A male Burmese python, four years old at the

Deckard questions the exotic snake dancer Zhora (Joanna Cassidy) in her dressing room at The Snake Pit. The snake around Cassidy's shoulders was the actress' own pet, a Burmese python named 'Darling.'

time. We had a little trouble with him because all that smoke they used in the dressing room set was bothering him. Darling was getting uncomfortable and very annoyed. Anytime I put him on anything, like the coatrack, it was a pain in the neck to get him off again. He didn't want to leave."

Following her shower, Zhora inserts her head into a transparent, globular hairdryer. However, this futuristic appliance (which many fans of *Blade Runner* wish they had in their own homes—this author included), was not a twenty-first-century prop.

"That hairdryer was *my* hairdryer," Marvin Westmore explains. "The production company destroyed it and then never paid me for it, them turkeys. You see, I had a small beauty salon back in the early 1980s, so I gave the *BR* unit one of the hairdryers we had in the salon. Which they dismantled, and just used pieces of. People think it's some kind of sci-fi thing, but it was real. Once you took that globe and drying unit off its neck and stand, you didn't relate to it as a hairdryer. It became something different."

According to Joanna Cassidy, her hair was already dry when she inserted her head into this device. "The air they'd rigged to blow through it wasn't warm, either," Cassidy adds. "It was cold."

Now almost fully dressed, Zhora asks Deckard to dry her back. He begins to comply when Zhora suddenly attacks him. The resultant battle nearly costs Deckard his life. "Zhora was definitely suspicious of Deckard from the start," says Cassidy. "Besides being endowed with amazing physical attributes, the replicants had been given a set of instincts that were pretty powerful. They were programmed to survive; flags came up if they smelled anything off-key. And even though Harrison played like a wuss, if you really looked at him, he wasn't. He had the bend and all that, but he was a good-looking guy. It just didn't fit. Zhora smelled something very off there, so she tried to eliminate him."

During Zhora and Deckard's fight, the replicant elbows Ford in the abdomen, karate-chops his neck, and begins strangling Deckard with his own tie. No doubles were used for this fight; Cassidy and Ford performed all their own stunts.

"Harrison really needed to get some stress out," Cassidy says of the scene. "He enjoyed fighting with me because I'm strong and capable. I've taken karate in the past, and I don't hold back—when I fight, I fight. I'm not at all sissyish about really getting into it."

"The fight in the dressing room was blocked out mainly by me and Joanna and Harrison," adds *Blade Runner* Stunt Coordinator Gary Combs. "We did it in slow little pieces here and there and they did it all themselves. Harrison's well coordinated and very good at stunts, and Joanna was just as good as he was. In fact, Joanna was probably the best actress I've ever worked with in terms of athletic ability and listening to what you wanted them to do."

Interrupted in her murderous activities, Zhora bolts from The Snake Pit through the club's stage door. A groggy Deckard chases after her, only to find himself swallowed up by the insane crush of bodies representing street life of the future—soldiers, Asians, hard-core punks, slumming society folk, even a group of Hare Krishnas. This was the largest crowd scene in the film. It employed 300 individually-costumed extras, most of Gene Winfield's full-scale automobiles, and an elaborate mosaic of steam, neon, and sound effects.

Cassidy again refused a stunt double and did numerous takes of Zhora running over the tops of various vehicles stalled in the ultra-congested street herself. Her one request was that the wardrobe department replace Zhora's high-heeled boots with black, flat-bottomed running shoes, so that Cassidy could maintain her footing while filming the chase (a request that resulted in a minor but noticeable continuity error between what Zhora pulls on in her dressing room and what she wears on the street).

"That chase scene was really something," Joanna Cassidy enthuses. "It was suspenseful, long, and made Zhora very sympathetic. I mean, the woman was obviously terrified, and here she's being cold-bloodedly stalked through the streets. I tried to communicate her fear of being killed through body language and little cries of terror. It was important to me that Zhora come across as sympathetic there; I wanted the audience to feel for her."

———

Also filmed during this chase were some shots of Harrison Ford scrambling over a number of vehicles during his pursuit of Zhora (resulting in an iconic still of a gun-drawn Ford perched atop a futuristic taxi). For reasons of pacing, however, these moments were cut from the film.

A momentary opening in the crowd allows Deckard to now shoot Zhora in the back. Not once, but twice—and in the same spot (see appendix C for an explanation of this superior marksmanship).

"Even the most cynical forties *film noir* hero didn't do that," Cassidy comments. "A man shooting a defenseless woman in the back seems rather unfair to me. But that was an unusual choice on Ridley's part. I might not have liked it, but I also knew it certainly would do something interesting to the audience."[11]

Deckard's killing shots are delivered to Zhora while the woman is breaking her way through a series of large glass panes separating various cubicles within a futuristic shopping arcade (which were lit by removing a number of neon signs from the street and placing them in these cubicles, each of which depicts a different environment: nearly-nude mannequins in one section, genteelly covered dummies in another, falling snow in a third).[12]

Although Cassidy and Ford had performed all their own stunts up to this point—including the scenes of Zhora being shot in the back—a stunt double was now deemed necessary for Zhora's "Arcade Sequence," due to the obvious danger facing Cassidy from falling shards of glass.

---

[11]"Harrison Ford was always around when I did my stunts and was very protective," Cassidy notes. "He always wanted to make sure I was okay. 'Can you do this?' he'd ask. 'How many times do you want to do it again?' He was very good with me. I loved working with Harrison."

[12]In the shooting script, Zhora crashes through this arcade, but is not killed by Deckard's shots. Instead, she actually regains the safety of the street—and is promptly hit by a bus.

The woman doubling for Joanna Cassidy was Lee Pulford, a stunt person specifically requested by Cassidy because Pulford had previously doubled for the actor many times in the past. As for the glass panes, these were a mixture of various compounds (including plastic) known in the film industry as "breakaway glass." According to Terry Frazee and Gary Combs, these were manufactured within the Warner Brothers prop department, and at the time of the *BR* shoot, they were also the largest panes of breakaway glass ever made for a film.

"We did two takes of that, in real time, all the way through the arcade," Combs remembers. "Ridley decided to shoot Lee crashing through in slow motion. It was a fairly complicated gag to set up and shoot, requiring a lot of coordination between the actors and every department working on the film. I think we spent all of one night on that—it took a long time to replace all that glass. Another problem was that those sheets had been made a little bit thicker than normal, to hold their shape. Lee hit them pretty hard, and cut her leg up a little, but it worked."

A complaint voiced by many *Blade Runner* aficionados is that the woman seen crashing through the arcade windows is plainly a stunt double and not Joanna Cassidy. Gary Combs defends this visually off-putting moment by stating that, "Whenever a director decides to use slow-motion in a sequence like that and hold the camera on it a long time, there's always the danger of the audience spotting a stand-in."

"It was pretty obvious to *us* that that stunt double wasn't Joanna," adds Katy Haber. "In fact, I thought she looked terrible. But we didn't have a lot of leeway there. By the time we shot that, Tandem was breathing hard down our necks, and we didn't have the time or money to reshoot the whole thing."

Zhora now lies dying on the sidewalk surrounded by shards of beautifully reflective glass. Her amplified heartbeat—which suddenly stops—is very prominent on the soundtrack. When a passing policeman turns her head, we see the same tattoo on Zhora's neck noticed by Deckard in Leon's photograph.

A dead Zhora
'retired' by
Deckard.

"WAKE UP! TIME TO DIE!" ─────────────────────────

Brion James: "You know that reaction shot of me looking horrified after Harrison's smoked Joanna? We put that in because Leon had been tailing Deckard in the hopes of getting his pictures back. But then when he sees what happens to Zhora on the street, Ridley wanted to do a reaction shot of me, because Leon sort of had a crush on her.

"And I'm mumbling to myself in that shot. It's almost imperceptible. I'm muttering under my breath, 'He must die, he must die.' Can you tell that? That's what I'm saying when I'm standing there and I see her get shot. Even though we were these rogue androids and knew that the police were hunting us—that's how Leon knows Deckard's a Blade Runner at that point—Zhora's death really had me distressed. That's why I go after Deckard in the alley. Once again, you could see how much feeling these replicants had."

Just before he's attacked by Leon, Deckard buys a bottle of Tsing-Tao (a Chinese alcoholic beverage) from a sidewalk bar. For some time, a cut on Ford's right cheekbone is clearly visible. Yet during Deckard's fight with Leon in the alley, this cut disappears (so does the bottle of Tsing-Tao). Moments later, however, both items are visible again!

Please turn to appendix C for Terry Rawlings' more comprehensive explanation of the reasons behind the reediting of this scene.

──────

Gary Combs: "Harrison and Brion did that fight in the alley themselves. No stuntmen. We padded them up and tried to make everything that Harrison hit as soft as we could, but that was really Brion really flingin' Harrison around. Ridley made them do it again and again, though. That's why Harrison got so sore and so stiff. You can do something two or three times and survive, but after you do something maybe seventeen, eighteen, or twenty times, it finally gets you."

During this battle, Leon slaps Deckard's (rubber prop) gun out of his hands. This effect was achieved by merely snipping a few frames of film out of the shot just before James' hand connected with Ford's weapon.

As for the moment when Leon throws a punch at Deckard's head and punctures a truck behind the Blade Runner instead (allowing a jet of steam to escape), this was accomplished by inserting a soft lead panel in the side of the vehicle through which James could punch with little trouble (to protect his hands, James was wearing gloves). Terry Frazee also installed a hose leading to a tank of liquid nitrogen behind this panel of lead; when the actor punched through it, an off-screen effects technician opened the shuttlecock on the nitrogen bottle, resulting in a convincing burst of "steam."

Leon about to retire Deckard by poking out the Blade Runner's eyes.

"I really got jacked up for that fight scene," Brion James continues. "It took us three nights to shoot, but I was adrenalized the whole time. Harrison was on a little trampoline before I picked him up by the belt and threw him on the car. That way he could bounce a little bit and help me toss him through the air. All that stuff really sold the idea of this replicant's superhuman strength."

"I'm the one who came up with the line, 'Wake up, time to die,'" claims James. "That wasn't scripted. Here I'd spent three nights kicking the crap out of Harrison and finally Ridley said, 'Okay, how do we end this?' The shooting script said Leon got shot in the neck by Rachael, but Ridley wanted a little more. So I said, 'Since he's just about unconscious, why don't I wake him up and tell him I'm going to kill him?' I'd been Leon for four or five months by that time, so that line didn't really come from me. That was Leon talking."

David Dryer, co-special effects supervisor for *Blade Runner*: "The one scene we special photographic effects guys were sorry to lose was supposed to occur during the fight between Leon and Deckard. The idea was we were going to do a matte painting of a giant building above Ford and James with an oriental woman on an animated billboard looking down on them and reacting to what they were doing. She was going to be puffing on one of those big cigarettes and acting as if she was watching a televised fight.

"That bit was supposed to give this feeling of oppression, that these billboards are always watching everyone everywhere they go. But Harrison Ford wasn't happy about this. Ridley and I both wanted to get a master shot of most of that fight in a single, unbroken shot with our 65mm special effects camera. We needed to do that in order to incorporate the billboard effect later on. Which meant Harrison had to do the whole fight all the way through for us many times, which was tiring.

"But then, the negative we had for the master shot got accidentally exposed to white light at the MGM lab that night and was destroyed. So we were unable to do the sequence. That was unfortunate; it would have been the capper for the movie, actually."

RACHAEL LETS DOWN HER HAIR————————————————————

Back with Rachael at Deckard's apartment, the shaky Blade Runner takes a drink from a shot glass full of Tsing-Tao; a small cloud of blood pours back into the glass, and blood flows into a (bathroom) sinkful of water Deckard uses to rinse out his mouth. In both instances, Ford already had some stage blood in his mouth and simply let it slip back into the two liquids.

One of *Blade Runner*'s best lines occurs near the head of this sequence. Following the discussion the couple now has regarding the psychological hazards of Deckard's profession, Rachael says, "I'm not in the business—I *am* the business." This was written by David Peoples.

According to *BR* editor Terry Rawlings, "After Deckard washes his face, he steps out of the bathroom and, for just a brief moment, you see his eyes glowing. Like a replicant's. The front end of that scene originally went on much longer; Rachael just stood there watching Deckard as he cleaned and washed up. Studying him, analyzing him, until he left the sink. But because of length considerations, we had to cut this out. That was too bad, because it was a wonderful moment."

As for the tune which Rachael plays at Deckard's piano, this melody has an interesting history. According to Rawlings, who laid the temporary music over this scene and kept track of its soundtrack counterpart:

"The temp music I laid in there was actually a variation on the slow movement of Ravel's Piano Concerto," Rawlings clarifies. "I'd played that piece to Sean and Ridley before they shot that scene, and Sean imitated it visually, so I could make it work in the editing room. But then they had Vangelis do a piano piece for her instead, which changed the music even more. Because Vangelis then did a variation of Chopin's Thirteenth Nocturne for that scene as it's heard in the final film.

"There's also a nice little off-camera story associated with Harrison Ford and that moment," Rawlings goes on to say. "I remember running footage for him one day on the Moviola because he just wanted to see some stuff. So I ran the sequence when he takes Rachael back to his apartment after the killings in the street. And by then I'd put in my temp-music Ravel stuff when Harrison and Sean were sitting at the piano. Harrison was so bowled over by that. He kept saying, 'This is so sensitively done.' You could tell the man was really involved with it."

After Deckard attempts to kiss the replicant, Rachael panics and again tries to leave Deckard's apartment. But Ford shuts the door in Young's face, keeping her in.

The lighting in this scene displays hot white light and diagonal shadows raking across Deckard's face, patterns that are supposed to be cast by a nearby Venetian blind. This author was told by both Jordan Cronenweth and Michael Deeley during *BR*'s principal photography in 1981 that the lighting scheme here was Scott's homage to both the Expressionism of forties' *films noir* and to a similar lighting effect seen in director Bernardo Bertolucci/cinematographer Vittorio Storaro's 1971 film *The Conformist*.

"But I thought that was the wrong time to be pulling that effect in *Blade Runner*," Deeley adds today. "It tends to take the eye away from the emotions of the scene."

Emotions ran high during the filming of Deckard and Rachael's love scene . . . but not pleasant ones.

"What I hear," says Hampton Fancher, "was that Harrison did not like Sean [see chapter IX]. But he used those feelings in his artistry for the love scene—where Harrison corners Sean against the door and finally breaks her down into a kiss—and it worked. That surprised me. The way I wrote it, that was a very tender, erotic moment. I was shocked and attracted by what turned up on the screen instead."

Katy Haber: "Harrison hated Sean. That was not a love scene, that was a hate scene. When he pushes her up against those blinds? Uh! He hated her, hated her."

Sean Young, during an interview with the *Washington Post* (August 14, 1982), said:

The love scene between Deckard and Rachael, which was lit as an homage to Forties film noir and the lighting schemes of Bernardo Bertolucci's The Conformist. . . .

"A lot of people like the scene where I say, 'Kiss me, kiss me,' to Harrison. Personally, it's not one of my favorites. How would you like to have somebody grab you and throw you around a room? I had bruises all over me. And Harrison's beard was all grown out, and scratched my face. The whole scene just reminded me of a woman getting beaten up. I didn't see how my character, Rachael, could go up to his room after that . . . I was a wreck. I had three or four weeks off after that scene."

"I've always thought of that so-called love scene as 'the rape in the corridor,'" continues Michael Deeley. "It's true that Sean and Harrison didn't get along. But actually, that roughness was the way Ridley intended it to be shot all along, even if Harrison and Sean had gotten on together."

"The anger Ford shows in that scene is also partially understandable in the story sense," concludes Terry Rawlings. "Rachael had already run away from Deckard once before, and now she's gotten up

... was also known as 'The Hate Scene' to some of the BR crew, since Blade Runner's two leads did not get along. Pictured to the right is a shot cut from the sequence, which originally ran somewhat longer; in this moment, replicant Rachael is about to wrap her legs around her human lover.

and run away from him again on the piano bench after they've been close for a moment. That pisses Deckard off."

Blade Runner's controversial love scene originally ran much longer than what's been seen by the general public. Terry Rawlings informed this author that there was a shot of Rachael's legs wrapping around Deckard as he caressed her thighs; no nudity was featured, however. And Model Supervisor Mark Stetson recalls, "It went on and on and got very erotic, and became much more of a sympathetic scene. What was left in the film was quite a violent encounter. That was a mistake. Instead of a relationship, that scene became this sort of sadomasochistic encounter between the two of them. But that might have had something to do with eighties sensibilities as opposed to nineties sensibilities, too. The sexual and political environment today is much different than it was then."

But how was this love/hate sequence originally conceived?

"The way that came about was sort of fun," Hampton Fancher relates, "because I didn't want to do it. There'd been this big meeting, as there was every day, and I was angry. Because they wanted a sex scene in the movie and here they were, kind of giggling about that. I said 'No, no, *no*! I detest that kind of shit.' But they kept pushing and pushing and I kept arguing. I was up on my feet, I was angry, I was being sardonic with them and condescending, but they wouldn't give up.

"Michael Deeley was sitting at one end of this long conference table, and Ridley at the other. Suddenly there was this long pause. Finally Michael said, 'Well couldn't you just try it?' And I very cuttingly said, 'Fine. I'll do it. How about this? Michael, you're Rachael. And I'm Deckard.' And," Fancher says, laughing, "I kneeled down in front of Deeley, knowing he was embarrassed to be touched. I had one hand on his thigh and the other hand up on the side of his face. And I said, 'What about this? What about . . . kiss me'. . . I just was making up these lines, and they were horrified. They said 'Okay, Hampton, fuck off.' Everybody was embarrassed and didn't like me for doing that.

"But I'd made my point. Yet by the end of making my point, I had a secret. Because I realized what I'd been saying and doing was great. So I went home right away and wrote it all down and came back the next morning and triumphantly put this scene in front of everybody. They went, 'Whoa, thank you! You fucking did it!' And I was really happy. That was a lovely moment for me."

BREAKFAST FOR THREE

Back at the shy genetic engineer's apartment, Sebastian's fascination with toys and automatons is grandly revealed as Pris prowls through the man's apartment, which is full to bursting with mannequins, dancers, soldiers, cuckoo clocks, and clockwork figures.

Many of the various automatons that litter the halls and rooms of Sebastian's apartment (including a fat, laughing man doll which will later chuckle throughout the sequence of Deckard discovering Pris) were actually genuine *objets d'art,* some centuries old. But where did the *BR* filmmakers find the over one hundred unique and genuine playthings that are showcased in this scene?

"We built very few of the toys in Sebastian's suite," Lawrence Paull said. "Most of them were real."

The majority of the toys seen in Sebastian's apartment were obtained by Set Dresser Linda DeScenna from a local Los Angeles toy/train/automaton collector living in the San Fernando Valley, Benny Marvin. Paull had already been aware of Marvin's collection (specializing in automatons reaching back to the seventeenth century) and suggested that DeScenna approach the man with the idea of leasing out the bulk of his acquisitions for use in a major film. After reassurances that the *Blade Runner* team would treat his collection with the utmost respect (a promise kept), Marvin agreed.

During the wide shots of Sebastian's toy-laden worktable, real rats can be seen scurrying across the tabletop. These were tame animals brought onto the *BR* set by a "rat wrangler." Also visible is a miniature toy unicorn, which can be seen at upper screen right (but only in theaters or on letterboxed videotapes/laser discs).

In the Director's Cut, this unicorn touch carries added significance, given the reverie Deckard indulges in at his piano (see chapter XVII).

According to Marvin Westmore, the "Kabuki Raccoon" mask Pris is seen painting across her face in this scene was an idea that originated with Ridley Scott.

"Ridley wanted some kind of twenty-first–century makeup. And the only tool we could think of at the time that would look futuristic while Pris was applying it was an airbrush. So first we covered her face in a clown-white foundation, and then I created some hypoallergenic airbrush face makeup. I had already done this once before, when I'd come up with an airbrushed eyeliner for a girl for a Maybelline commercial. But she couldn't see to apply it—she'd been shooting that stuff right in her eyes.

"I knew Daryl was going to have the same problem," Westmore continues. "So what I did was to ask if I could help out on that shot. Ridley said yes. So I had a little TV monitor installed beside me that was hooked up to the movie camera to watch what was going on. Then, out of frame, I held Daryl Hannah's elbow to guide her hand while she was spraying that black makeup on. I was moving her arm, and she was letting me move that arm while I watched what was happening on the monitor. So, really, I was directing Daryl there. Like a puppet."

———

"That raccoon makeup was supposed to be a punk, New Wave look of the future," Hannah herself adds. "I also thought it made me look like a doll, which fit in with all the other ones around Billy Sanderson's place. But you know something? They filmed kind of a cool shot just before you saw me applying that makeup.

"Pris was sitting in front of a mirror at Sebastian's apartment preparing for her doll-stage, and she's smoking another one of those cigarettes—ack! She also has live rats crawling all over her. It doesn't bother Pris, though; I'm frozen like the mannequins in there. Those rats were just everywhere. On my cigarette, in my hair . . . one even crawled right up into my face. But Pris didn't react. They shot that, but then they cut it out."

At this point in the film is a shot of the Kaiser doll sitting on Sebastian's worktable. Its mouth is encased in an unexplained breathing apparatus, and the Kaiser continually shoots a series of urgent looks between the female replicant and the toymaker.

"He was my buddy, and he was trying to warn me about Pris. He didn't trust her," says William Sanderson. "I also think that that whole thing where the Kaiser's tied up and sitting on the table was Rutger's idea; he was always making suggestions like that."

A rain-dampened Roy now unexpectedly appears at Sebastian's apartment. When the toymaker is out of earshot, Batty tells Pris, "There's only two of us now."

"We're stupid and we'll die," Pris responds.

"No, we won't," Batty consoles her.

This moment raises a question: how did Batty know Zhora and Leon were dead?

"There are all kinds of holes in *Blade Runner*," comments Hampton Fancher. "I think the main reason was because the script was rewritten so often that various narrative bits either got forgotten or ignored during the preproduction process. For example, in one of my early drafts, I'd shown the replicants tapping into the police computer. That's how Batty knew Leon and Zhora were dead, even though he wasn't around to witness the events.

"But Ridley got away with murder lots of times that way. You really don't notice those things, though, unless you poke at them—there's a kind of dream logic operating there. In fact, Robert Mulligan came up with an interesting line when we were working on a scene like that. I said, 'Oh, how am I going to justify this?' And Mulligan said, 'Don't. There are some things you don't want to scratch, because you'll fall through the tear.'"

Throughout this second scene in Sebastian's apartment, Pris and Batty are constantly affectionate: kissing, sitting close to one another, passing secret looks, etc. When asked for their takes on the Batty/Pris relationship, Daryl Hannah replied, "I thought that Pris was eternally grateful to Roy, because she'd been designed as a pleasure unit and he'd saved her from a life of prostitution. There was also a strong bond between them because both of their lives were running out at the same time."

Rutger Hauer, however, saw his bond somewhat differently: "I felt it was a somewhat incestuous relationship. As if Pris were almost his sister. They were pals, though, no doubt."

During this same scene, faint whispering can be heard from the surrounding automatons in Sebastian's apartment (especially on the Criterion *BR* laser disc). This low-key audio touch helps give Sebastian's creations a ghostly life of their own and imbues J. F's apartment with an eerie ambiance. Ridley Scott added these whispers during the post-production process in England.

Another subtle audio cue occurs during this moment as well. When Batty notices J. F.'s chessboard and makes a move, Sebastian says, "No, knight takes queen. See? Won't do." Immediately after his comment, a ghostly whisper reinforces Sebastian's line by adding, ". . . will mate you."

Batty and Sebastian now have a short conversation about chess (Sebastian is identified as a Grand Master in chess in one version of the script—notice, in the film, that Sebastian's chess figures are all birds, a visual motif already attached to Tyrell through his replicant owl). Further dialogue has Batty admitting that he and Pris are

Nexus–6s; the genetic designer side of J. F. is delighted by this revelation. "There's some of me in you!" Sebastian enthuses.

An interesting speculation raised on Murray Chapman's *Blade Runner* FAQ page (see appendix D) raises the possibility that "when Sebastian says to Roy, 'There's some of me in you,' there's an ironic double meaning: perhaps Tyrell intentionally has infected his Nexus–6s with the same genes responsible for J. F.'s Methuselah Syndrome."

Pris now demonstrates her superhuman abilities by plunging her hand into a container of boiling water to retrieve an egg. "That water wasn't even hot," says Terry Frazee. "We ran a hose into the bottom of it and shot compressed air through it first, then added some calcium chips to the water to make it give off vapors like steam."

"Those eggs were already hard-boiled, too," adds Daryl Hannah. "Did you notice the close-up of my hand when I grab one? My fingernails are blue. Like Roy's. That was a little touch of Ridley's to show we both didn't have long to live. And right after I toss the egg over to Sebastian, you see me eating these long strips of something off a plate. Those were really marinated peppers, but I think in the story they were supposed to be slabs of fish. Not worms!"

Sebastian has already told Pris that he suffers from a glandular condition called "Methuselah Syndrome" which, although he is only twenty-five years old, has prematurely aged him. Batty plays off of J. F.'s condition by claiming that the replicants share a similar problem. "Accelerated decrepitude," Pris clarifies.

"Sebastian's old-age makeup was of course was very hot," William Sanderson remembers, "since they were shooting in June by that point. It was designed by Marvin Westmore, but actually applied by Pete Altobelli. That took a lot of work. It took Pete two hours each day to put it on. But I didn't mind. I just closed my eyes and sat there and enjoyed it."

Sebastian agrees to smuggle Roy into Tyrell's headquarters by using a chess subterfuge.

Hampton Fancher states that, "That whole ploy of using a chess game to get Batty into Tyrell's wasn't my idea. It was Ridley's.

Because we were looking for ways to infiltrate the Tyrell Corporation, and I originally had this very complicated but interesting dramatic series of events that I thought were realistic in terms of ways you could get in. What I'd finally come up with in my last draft was to have Sebastian deliver Tyrell a gift of a knee-high unicorn he'd made. J. F. was going to be picked up by an automated Spinner and flown to Tyrell, who at this time wasn't in the pyramid, but at his big family estate. But Batty would be hiding onboard that Spinner, too; he was going to disable the security cameras on that so nobody would know he was there.

"I was very naïve about money, though. I hadn't liked Ridley's chess game idea because I thought it'd be laughed off the screen. I mean, why would this brilliant guy, Tyrell, let down his security just because of a chess game? But Ridley and Michael said 'Hampton, you don't understand. It's going to cost us another half-million dollars to shoot this your way. Not to mention the cost of some more miniature Spinner effects.' But I wasn't really listening. I wasn't embracing reality at all. All I cared about was my elegant idea.

"Then, when David came on, he wrote the chess scene in the way Ridley wanted. Which, I must admit, given the way Ridley staged it, worked pretty well after all."

"I WANT MORE LIFE . . ." ━━━━━━━━━━━━━━

The Pyramid, late night. A solitary Tyrell is still awake, however, and seen sitting in his luxurious bed, swathed in a quilted brocade robe, surrounded by tall candles.

Paull and Scott's ideas on Tyrell's monolithic persona even extended to the furnishings found in this boudoir: Tyrell's bed was modeled after the genuine bed of Pope John Paul II.

At the top of this scene, Tyrell, as he was in his office, is introduced by first showing his replicant owl. Birds are a consistent visual motif associated with the head of the Tyrell Corporation: Eldon's owl (a standard symbol for wisdom—but since Tyrell owns an artificial owl, this could imply that Tyrell has "false wisdom"), the stuffed eagle beside Tyrell's bed, the herons glimpsed on a screen behind that bed, an eaglelike motif on the flying buttresses surrounding the Tyrell Pyramid, the bird statues in Tyrell's office, the owl emblem on Tyrell's robe.

As previously noted, one interesting aspect of Hampton Fancher's original *Electric Sheep* screenplay was its strong "ecological" approach. Intriguingly, this concern also manifested itself in *Blade Runner*, but in so subtle a manner that most viewers miss it.

"When I first saw the picture, I noticed that each major character in *Blade Runner* was identified with an insect or animal," Fancher comments. "That's interesting, because my first screenplay centered around Deckard's hunting down these androids to get money for a living sheep. Which must have made some kind of an impression on Ridley, because that idea—the linkage between man and animal—stayed intact. Tyrell and his owl is one example of that. So it seems like that theme must have been embedded and extended from the origins of this project on, from Phil's book to my and David's scripts to Ridley's final film. The animal references were pretty blatant in the first few drafts; the way they are now, though, might have been more the result of a subconscious impulse than a worked-out idea."

Subconscious or not, this linkage between man and animal is readily apparent throughout *Blade Runner*. For example, during Leon's V-K test, Holden asks the replicant about a tortoise. Tyrell's entrances are signified by the appearance of an owl. Rachael relates a memory concerning spiders. Sebastian's apartment is crawling with rats. Pris paints herself up to look like a raccoon. Zhora dances with a snake. Batty howls like a wolf (and grabs a dove). Deckard dreams of unicorns.

All this in a world where most animals are extinct!

When Roy Batty unexpectedly appears in his bedchamber, a started Tyrell finally hears the angry replicant verbalize the meaning behind his heretofore violent actions: "I want more life, fucker," Roy says.

Batty and Tyrell, next conversation is a remarkable dialogue exchange concerning Batty's suggestions for extending his life.

> *Tyrell*: "The facts of life. To make an alteration in the evolvement of an organic life-system is fatal. The coding system cannot be revised once it's been established."
> *Batty*: "Why not?"

Tyrell: "Because by the second day of incubation, any cells that have undergone reversion mutations give rise to revertant colonies like rats leaving the sinking ship. Then the ship, sinks."

Batty: "What about EMS recombination?"

Tyrell: "We've already tried it. Ethyl Methanesulfonate is an alkylating agent and a potent mutagen. It created a virus so lethal the subject was dead before he left the table."

Batty: "Then a repressive protein, that blocks the operating cells."

Tyrell: "Wouldn't obstruct replication, but it does give rise to an error in replication, so that the newly formed DNA strand carries a mutation and you've got a virus again."

The preceding conversation not only impresses through the way it adds a patina of scientific plausibility to *Blade Runner* while simultaneously showcasing Batty's A-level mental abilities, it also contains a nugget of truth—Ethyl Methanesulfonate is indeed a mutagen (as described in *The Merck Index, 11th Edition,* Merck Publishing, 1989, pg. 602).

Yet when this author pointed out to Hampton Fancher—the writer who composed Batty and Tyrell's scientific exchange—that his description of EMS made sense, Fancher replied, "It does? That's the weird thing. You know, there's a psychiatrist who's doing this book on *Blade Runner*, and his thesis is that the individual perceptions of it by its creators actually resulted in a kind of unconscious synergy. Everybody had different ideas about the film, yet underneath that we were all part of the same song and didn't know it.

"For instance. I'm totally dyslexic and untechnical. I have learning disabilities, can't remember anything. And I just made up that entire dialogue between Batty and Tyrell, about the recombination. Basically, I was just writing shit down that came out of my head. I must have come across *something* about EMS at one time or another, though, and then forgotten it, because some people on the *BR* team checked it out at UCLA and it turned out to be right. But I *never* researched that; I was just humming in the dark. Sometimes, though, you dream a new reality, and everybody kind of unconsciously joins the same club."

Tyrell next tells Batty that their conversation has been academic, because, "You were made as well as we could make you."

"But not to last," Roy responds.

"The replicant's four-year lifespan had been deliberately designed into them by Tyrell," Fancher continues. "That was a conscious decision on my part from the very first scripts; in fact, I wanted to show this corporation including the same kind of built-in obsolescence in the androids that auto manufacturers put into their cars. I even had a line that Tyrell says about Roy in my *Dangerous Days* script where he compares him to a Ferrari. 'A high-strung racing car—built to win, not to last.'

"A lot of that, I think, came out of an experience I had a long time ago. I'd run into Dennis Hopper, who owned a Checker cab at that point, and I said, 'That's a wild car.' And Dennis said, 'Yeah, its not a Detroit job, it doesn't have the built-in obsolescence.' That was the first time I'd heard that term, and the concept appalled me.

"So the idea from the beginning was that Tyrell had purposefully built in this breakdown so people would have to buy a new replicant every few years. He did that to keep his commerce running. Of course, that also suggests Tyrell might have known a way to work around that problem, and that he was lying to Roy when he said he couldn't extend his life. We didn't really get into that in *Blade Runner*. But that's certainly one of the approaches I'd like to use for a sequel; I like the thought of exploring this limited lifespan."

After being told by Tyrell that "the light that burns twice as bright burns half as long," Batty murmurs, "I've done questionable things." Tyrell demonstrates his callousness (as well as his foolishness), by sitting down next to Roy and putting an arm around his shoulder. After another brief dialogue exchange (including Batty's wonderful, "Nothing the god of biomechanics wouldn't let you in heaven for" line), the replicant tenderly kisses Tyrell on the lips.

Rutger Hauer: "Part of my profession is to have within a character a relatively clear picture of what that character's life is all about. What his relationships are, his little games, all that. And here's something I had a little fun doing with Roy that's never been picked up.

"When we shot *Blade Runner*, I was in L.A. for the first time for five months, and I began to notice that everybody at the time was so into his or her own sexual code. Every person in this town seemed to walk around with a little neon sign over their head saying "I *am* a 'heterosexual,' or 'I *am* a homosexual'. So I played Roy as though his sexuality was totally unimportant. And that decision created behavior for Roy, as do all of the decisions an actor makes.

"One of those decisions was that Roy kisses anybody, because he likes the feel of it. And that's why Roy kisses his 'father,' Tyrell, at the end of the film. That wasn't scripted. It was something that came out of the character. And it's not a Mafia kiss of death thing, either. It's just, 'Good-bye, Pa . . . '"

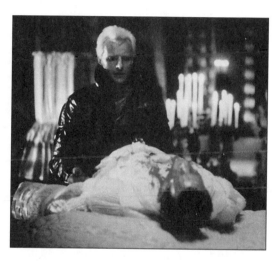

A rare shot not seen in the film of Batty standing over Tyrell's lifeless body sprawled on Eldon's bed.

After Roy's kiss, Batty suddenly and brutally crushes Eldon's head with his bare hands.

Marvin Westmore: "For the live-action shot of Rutger squeezing Turkel's head, we used blood tubes and a couple of quick cuts. We placed those tubes to run hidden through Turkel's hair, and then Rutger had small sponges loaded with blood in his palms. It looked pretty good, I thought."

Horrified by the sight of Tyrell's death, Sebastian moves his lips in soundless terror and darts in panic as Batty ominously advances on him. "You know, at one point we were supposed to kill Sebastian on the screen, but the higher-ups agreed there was already too much violence, so we never shot my death scene," begins William Sanderson. "I think Rutger probably fought that—he didn't want to make himself any more hated by the audience than he already was.

"But can I tell you another story? When I was watching Rutger mash out Tyrell's eyes, the bit of direction Ridley gave me had to do with his own children.[13] Ridley said, 'They like to watch horror movies, but I don't let them watch too much. But they will stand at the doorway and peek in at the TV with a combination of revulsion and fascination.'

"That was very helpful, for Ridley to tell me that, because I actually wasn't on the stage with Rutger and Joe when they filmed the shots of me looking through the candles at what Rutger was supposed to be doing. They filmed that stuff of me watching all in close-ups on another day. And Ridley talked me through what I was supposed to be seeing. The whole time, I kept that thought of his kids being fascinated and repulsed at the same time."

Rutger Hauer now reveals that: "When I initially I came on the picture, there was a big, surprising sequence following my murder of Tyrell that was scripted and supposed to be shot. But it never was. That was unfortunate, because it was one of my favorites.

"After Tyrell says he can't make me live longer than four years and I kill him, originally I was then going to say, 'Now take me to the real maker.' And Sebastian and I were going to go up one more floor in the Tyrell Pyramid, Sebastian was going to take a key from around his neck and open a door, and that whole level was going to be revealed as a huge freezing chamber. And inside of it, the real Tyrell lay dead and frozen.

"That was going to be the moment where Batty finally snaps. Because the real maker is dead, and he can't do anything to extend Roy's life. So I had to mentally incorporate that cut scene into my performance while I was killing the real Tyrell, to suggest Batty's feeling of lost hope.

"But if we'd had that cryogenic scene I would have done Tyrell's murder quite differently. Because if Roy knew this Tyrell was only a replicant, I would have just crushed him like a bug. I wouldn't have had to kill Sebastian, either, although that cut scene had been written that way. Why do that? Sebastian's just a pawn, and a nice guy besides. I didn't need to kill him."

David Peoples explains that "The cryonic chamber sequence was one of the things Hampton hadn't wanted to write, I think. But Ridley

---

[13] Jake Scott, Ridley's son, is now directing television commercials himself.

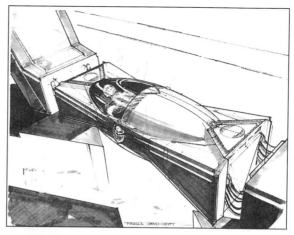

Two Syd Mead sketches for a scripted but never filmed BR scene—the discovery of the real Tyrell's frozen body in an elaborate 'Cryo-Crypt.'

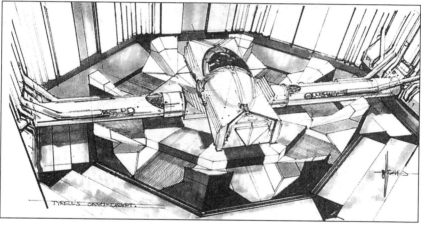

really wanted that in. So what I came up with was a scene where Sebastian takes Roy into this huge frozen room and you see the real Tyrell lying in state in a capsule. J. F. tells Roy Tyrell had suffered a fatal disease, so he'd had himself frozen to wait for a cure. Roy then tells Sebastian to wake him up. But J. F. breaks down and confesses that he screwed up somehow in the past and accidentally killed the real Tyrell while the guy was in frozen suspension. Then Batty freaks out and smears Sebastian all over the wall of this crypt.

"That's what I put down on paper. But I'd had another idea for that scene, too. Instead of going with the cryogenics, I'd suggested that Roy would discover that Tyrell's brain had been transplanted into the body of a shark housed inside a giant aquarium, with all sorts of leads coming out of it. An idea I was surprised to see turning up this year [1995] in a very similar scene in the film *Johnny Mnemonic*."

Blade Runner now shows a dazed Roy back in the Pyramid elevator descending—alone—away from Tyrell's bedroom. The replicant stares up in shock through the elevator's glass-topped roof at a night sky full of receding stars—the only time we see stars in the entire motion picture.

"One of the interesting things about the conclusion of that sequence with Batty alone in the elevator is that, as he's descending, he shivers," observes Fancher. "Almost a postorgasmic kind of shiver. Like, 'What have I done? I'm going to die for this, but I'm going to be immortal for it, too.' And the expression on Rutger's face is so—well, I've never seen anything like it on film before.

"That's also the only shot in the whole movie where you see stars. And they're moving away from him, as if he's some kind of fallen angel. That was so perfect."

Stills from this "shudder scene" show Batty clutching Sebastian's jacket. However, the cropping usually associated with theater screenings, video, and laser reproductions cuts this image off from the bottom of the frame. Yet Rutger Hauer confirms that this detail was indeed filmed for *Blade Runner*.

"Yes, I was holding Sebastian's jacket in the elevator as it descends. I took that as a souvenir, and as a token of guilt."

DECKARD PHONES PRIS ———————————————————

Following a brief shot of him driving his sedan through the 2nd Street tunnel, Deckard is next seen parked on a rain-lashed, deserted city street. This parking shot was filmed on the Old New York Street set.

Unbeknownst to Ford, a street gang composed of a teenage girl, another person, and two "little people" is walking down the same street, speaking German. Part of their translated conversation (supplied to this author by William Kolb and Rick Conner) runs as follows:

"Hey look, someone left us a small gift. "
"Anybody in it?"
"Naw, wait until the cops are gone. Wait until the cops are gone. "

A police spinner now descends from the sky, causing the street gang to scurry into hiding. According to Terry Frazee, *Blade Runner*'s floor effects supervisor, "The most complicated thing I did on the show was flying the full-scale Spinner down that street, with the rain and the German midgets and all that. To get that gag working between two cranes and coordinating how we were going to make that Spinner take off and hide the supporting cables at the same time was tough, though. Because I'm still of the old school that believes you should try to hide things so that you don't have to optically remove them later."

Both Hampton Fancher and David Peoples deny writing the anonymous Spinner cop's parting phrase, "Have a better one," a catchy 2019 farewell which is also one of the film's more memorable bits of dialogue.

"I think that was dreamed up during postproduction when Ridley was looping dialogue," Peoples recalls. "Nobody seems to know anymore who actually wrote it."

Deckard now uses his in-dash VidPhon to telephone Sebastian's apartment. Pris can be seen on a small screen answering the call before she abruptly hangs up.

Daryl Hannah: "That was shot as a close-up on a little stage on a day when Jordan *[Cronenweth]* was out sick. Haskel Wexler *[director and cinematographer]* came over and shot it for Jordan instead. Then they transferred that film onto videotape and ran it into Harrison's car."

DECKARD KILLS PRIS ────────────────

After driving away from the scavenging German street gang (which brazenly strips Deckard's sedan—while he's still sitting in it!), the

Blade Runner pulls up before the darkened Bradbury Building. Ominous, low-key Vangelis music is heard on the soundtrack; Ford cautiously approaches the eerie building. At the same time, a series of quick intercuts show close-ups of Pris (wearing a veil) making odd, darting movements with her head.

"The Bradbury was supposed to be this big, abandoned building," says Daryl Hannah. "And the replicants were supposed to have heightened senses. That's what my head movements were all about; I'd heard Deckard coming and was reacting to the sound of him getting close to the building and then climbing up the stairway to Sebastian's apartment."

Gun drawn, Deckard cautiously enters Sebastian's apartment. The film now cuts to a very strange close-up of Pris; her eyes roll back up into her head, leaving only their whites exposed.

"We played with a lot of strange things about Pris," explains Hannah. "My eyes rolling back in my head? That was something I'd done in the screen test; I'd thought that would make me seem mechanical. Like the way dolls' eyes roll up when you lay them down.

"Ridley also shot a lot of my close-ups during this scene with an undercranked camera, which made me look like I was capable of these quick, inhuman movements. Almost like a bird's."

Warily stepping into Sebastian's workroom, Deckard is surprised to discover it filled with dozens of automatons. One of them is Pris, sitting perfectly still on the edge of a table with a veil covering her body.

Hannah wore a nude-colored Spandex unitard (with a breastplate vacuformed into the fabric for a sculptured look) during this moment and during the subsequent Pris/Deckard fight. Cinematographer Jordan Cronenweth heightened Deckard's discovery of Pris by bathing the scene with rose-colored light.

After exploring the object-cluttered room, Deckard warily approaches the veiled Pris, not sure whether she is a toy or not because of her perfect immobility. "That's me sitting on the table," says Hannah, "and I'm not in a body rig or anything. The reason I was able to hold so still

Deckard discovers Pris (left, under veil) masquerading as an automaton in Sebastian's workroom.

was because I'd discovered a little trick; if you breathe very shallowly, you can hold still for a long time. I didn't try holding my breath, because then your body will start shaking."

After Deckard bends forward for a closer look at Pris, she promptly kicks him in the chest and sends him flying across the room. "Harrison did that gag himself, just threw himself backward after the kick," says Gary Combs. "But you know, I doubled for Daryl there a moment, 'cause Ridley wanted to see what it would look like if I kicked Harrison instead of her although the shot that ended up in the fiilm was of Daryl kicking Harrison.

"Let me tell you, I really didn't want to double for Daryl then, because of that form-fitting thing she had on. But Ridley insisted I get into her costume. I said, 'Ridley, please! It's too damn tight!' But he wouldn't budge. So I made them set up a little portable dressing room with screens right in the corner of the stage where I didn't have to walk down the studio back lot in that thing. And I said, 'The first time anybody whistles at me in this thing I'm out of it!'

"But I didn't have to wear falsies or anything. They shot my scene way over my back where I just had to have the bottom part of that leotard on and this veil type thing over my head that hung down into the shot. And I kicked Harrison across the room. That's the only time I doubled Daryl!"

Pris now ferociously attacks Deckard, executing a series of spinning cartwheels to approach the man.

"The cartwheels were sort of my idea," Hannah says. "When I had my audition, the fight scene took place in a gymnasium, but gymnastics wasn't a part of it. But I'd mentioned to Ridley that I could do gymnastics and I showed him a couple of things and those cartwheels got incorporated into the fight."

Gary Combs: "Daryl Hannah was athletic, but she wasn't anywhere near as athletic as Joanna Cassidy was. Most of those cartwheels and things Daryl does during the fight were done by a double. That's another story.

"Ridley wanted these cartwheels during the scene where Daryl beats up Harrison, and then Pris is supposed to land up astraddle of Harrison on his shoulders. But Daryl had banged her elbow pretty bad when she ran into Sebastian's van, so the only cartwheels she could do without a lot of trouble were the easy ones. Like the one you see her do before she tosses that egg at Bill Sanderson.

"So I had this female gymnast I was working with for about two weeks who was gonna double for Daryl during the fight. Me and this girl would go to a gym every night, and she'd practice those cartwheels and trying to land astraddle of me—and every night she'd land flat on my chest. We kept trying to work this routine out and work it out but it just wouldn't come together.

"Now, another thing was, I never worked with a director who rehearsed so much in my life as Ridley did. For Ridley, you might as well figure you're going to do the stunt all the way through every time you rehearse it, because Ridley didn't want to see you fake it or walk or talk your way through it. He wanted to see you do it!

"Here comes the day we're supposed to shoot this thing. About forty-five minutes before lunch, Ridley started rehearsing the cartwheel scene with this gymnast girl. And within that forty-five minutes, this girl was over in the corner with her tongue hanging out. Couldn't do it anymore before we even got to the shot! I thought, 'Oh boy, I'm in trouble here!'

"So I went to the first A.D. and said, 'You've gotta go to lunch now, and try to give me a little extra time. I gotta find another double—quick!' Now, it wasn't this female gymnast's fault, she was in great shape. But the way Ridley rehearsed just wore her down—she was out of gas! So I brought in a small guy I knew who was also a gymnast—Mike Washlake. We put Daryl's leotard and wig on him and Ridley rehearsed with him after lunch. Then he shot this guy the rest of that day and all the next day, too, and he couldn't wear Mike out. Believe me, this guy was just like a machine. He'd say, 'Want to see that again?' and—bang! There'd he'd go. Cartwheelin' over that stone fountain in Sebastian's place or up against the wall or whatever you wanted. Mike was sort of like the Energizer bunny rabbit in those commercials—he kept going and going and going.

"Anyway, I'll bet this is something your readers didn't know about. That when Pris cartwheels towards Harrison durin' that fight, she's really a man!"

After Deckard blows a hole in Pris' stomach, the replicant hits a wall (upside down) and falls to the floor, where she begins screaming and flailing her hands and feet. Deckard shoots her again. Pris' body arches up off the floor, and the one-time "pleasure model" dies a shrieking death.

"The guy who doubled for me during that fight is the same one who went upside down and actually hit the wall," Hannah explains. "Look at his legs in that shot—they're squat and short.

"But that's me having the seizure and screaming and arching up off the floor after Harrison shoots Pris again. Ridley filmed that seizure with an undercranked camera to make it look like Pris was moving insanely fast and desperately trying to fight off her death. And you know what? The production had made up these mirrored, silver contact lenses that we replicants were supposed to wear after we were dead. Those were supposed to show how the androids looked when they died. But nobody ever used them."

TEARS IN RAIN

Unexpectedly arriving back at Sebastian's apartment, Batty discovers Pris' dead body with her tongue protruding from her mouth. Tenderly, Roy kisses the corpse; when his mouth withdraws from hers, Pris' tongue is back in her mouth.

"That was Rutger's idea," explains Daryl Hannah. "He just pushed my tongue back in with his own. He didn't eat it," she says, laughing.

"By pushing Pris' tongue into her mouth, Batty buries her," Hauer adds. "It's a way to make her presentable. He waxes Pris up. Makes her look decent again."

As for the suspenseful cat-and-mouse chase between Batty and Deckard which now climaxes *Blade Runner*—one of the longest such segments in any genre film—this begins when Ford fails to ambush Hauer because of the replicant's superior reflexes.

"I wanted to determine Batty's physical superiority from the first moments of the chase," Ridley Scott says. "In order to demonstrate his speed, I first posed Harrison in an ambush position near a door in Sebastian's apartment. Then Rutger entered through another door at a normal camera speed. However, before he could exit the frame, I had the camera undercranked. Hauer had rehearsed his movements for this scene, and as soon as we undercranked, he began to physically slow down, exaggerating his movements very, very carefully. We then snipped out a frame or two. This combination of editing, undercranking, and slow movement on the part of the actor did, I think, result in a rather convincing burst of speed."

Seeing he's missed, Deckard takes up a new firing position beside a rain-dampened wall. But Batty punches through this barrier, grabs Deckard's gunhand, and, while saying, "This is for Zhora, and this is for Pris," savagely breaks two of Deckard's fingers (Michael Westmore made a prop Deckard hand for this shot, but it only appears in the Workprint).

Batty smashes his hand through a wall to grab Deckard's gun at the beginning of their climactic cat-and-mouse chase; also pictured are director Ridley Scott's storyboards for this sequence.

Terry Frazee notes that this effect was achieved through the use of a breakaway wall partly composed of Styrofoam and "Pyracil" (a soft plaster). After rehearsing Hauer and Ford a number of times and showing the actors where exactly to stand for this shot, careful camera placement and the addition of plaster dust at the exit area did the rest.

After breaking Ford's fingers, Hauer gamely hands Deckard back his gun—whereupon the Blade Runner promptly blows the tip of Batty's ear off.

Michael Westmore explains, "We did a cast of Rutger's right ear and then cast up the little piece that gets shot off out of latex. That ear tip was actually attached to a piece of fishing line; Ridley filmed a shot where you saw the piece blowing off Rutger's head, but he cut it out. What we'd done is just yank it off with that monofilament at the same time Harrison fired his gun.

"Then, in close-up, we showed Rutger's ear bleeding. How we did that was to run a little tube through Rutger's hair, glue it down with K-Y Jelly, and attach that tube to a hypo filled with stage blood. Again, that was a timing thing. Ridley had to shoot it a couple of times so that the timing of the blood running off Rutger's car and the tip getting blown off happened simultaneously.

"By the way, I still have the mold of Rutger's ear," Westmore said in 1995. "Everything else I did for *Blade Runner* is gone, but I still have that little mold."

For the shot where Batty returns to Pris' corpse and dips his fingers into her bloody stomach wound, Marvin Westmore made up Hannah's own stomach with an entry hole composed of makeup-based, flesh-colored highlights "and a lot of stage blood."

Batty now actively begins chasing Deckard through Sebastian's rotting apartment. The suite of seven rooms which make up Sebastian's home was constructed on the Burbank lot. But finding the proper furniture and decorations for the sprawling set was difficult.

"There just wasn't enough money on hand to manufacture all of the furnishings for Sebastian's suite," Lawrence Paull explains. "So we ended up renting, borrowing, and stealing objects from all over town. In fact, we even got to the point where we were forced to rent existing units from past films like *Darling Lili*. The nicest touch, though, is this: two of Sebastian's rooms are actually set up with units from *My Fair Lady*."

Rutger Hauer: "The only thing that bothered me about the end fight was that Ridley had first seen it as a Bruce Lee-type showdown in a gym. I told him, 'Look at me. I'm not Bruce Lee. And it doesn't really matter what the fuck I do as far as working out or studying karate, because I will never get there.' So while talking this over, I suggested, 'Why don't we make it more of a chase, based on the Game of Life? Try and make it a silly dance based on Batty's celebration of his last drops of energy? Like a wicked game?' Ridley really liked that, and we sort of got that idea down on storyboards first before it was written up. So Batty's behavior during the whole ending, in a sense, came from me. Which I'm quite proud of. It's more playful and strange than simply witnessing the last swan song of a machine."

According to an excellent article by William Kolb in *Retrofitting Blade Runner* ("*Blade Runner* Film Notes"), after Deckard has painfully reset his broken fingers he now "passes a mannequin in an old-fashioned ball gown waiting eternally with a bottle and glass at a deserted bar. The cameraman's shadow can be seen for an instant on the wall behind Deckard as he hurries from the room."

Spotting a small hole in the ceiling, Deckard climbs up an armoire, dropping his gun in the process. He then pokes his head through, next to an overflowing toilet bowl.

Gary Combs adds, "Harrison climbed that thing himself. The only climbing stuff I doubled him for—and I did that stunt myself— was when you see Deckard crawling up the side of the building. I remember Jordan Cronenweth bein' crouched up on top of that armoire, too. Scrunched down below the ceiling shooting Harrison with a hand-held camera, as he hauled himself up that piece of furniture."

Jordan Cronenweth (with camera) films Ford's attempt to escape Batty by climbing through a hole in the ceiling.

At this point in his pursuit, Batty's hand suddenly begins to cramp up, indicating his built-in demise is only a short time away. In order to revitalize himself, the replicant pulls an old nail from a rotting piece of wood and jams it through his clenching hand.

The actual shots of the nail piercing Batty's palm and reemerging from the back of his hand (a special courtesy of a Michael Westmore-built prosthetic) were seen for many years on American tapes and laser discs utilizing the so-called "International Cut." However, the Director's Cut of *Blade Runner* drops these shots altogether.

Having now "nailed" an extra packet of energy, Batty completely butts his head through a tiled bathroom wall in order to both frighten and taunt the detective. Staging the head butt took, as Lawrence Paull explains, "First building a section of the bathroom wall and then finishing it with real tiling. The interior of that wall was another story. All of the studding and lathing was balsa wood. We aged and stained that, and then squeegeed in a brittle, foamlike material on the wall's outer surfaces. The tile was applied over this with a substance named emastic, and when Rutger banged his head through the other side, all the materials within the wall just flew all over the place. It was a very convincing illusion."

Rutger Hauer: "I had a long talk about Batty's superhuman powers with Ridley, because I felt we had to be really delicate in showing how strong this guy really was. Because if he was superhuman, there'd be no comparison to a human's weakness.

"So I had a big problem with sticking my head through the wall at Harrison; I felt we went over the top there. But it looks great and it does seem to work. It's a fun moment. But there was a certain amount of freedom we took. I never wanted Batty to be Superman. He couldn't fly, he had to take the elevator."

Taking advantage of Batty's momentary power failure, Deckard whacks Batty across the face with a (rubber) pipe. Ford next kicks out the slats from a boarded-up window and finds himself teetering on a Bradbury ledge, with a matte painting showing the street far below.

Cautiously inching himself around a corner of the building, Deckard almost falls when he grabs onto a swinging triangle of rusted iron (a stunt done by a safety-tethered Harrison Ford only ten feet off the ground).

As Roy leans out of a window into the driving rain, lights from the surrounding structures show that the replicant's chest is covered in a series of strange markings.

When asked if this interesting pattern of asymmetric shapes was supposed to represent tattoos, Ridley Scott replies, "No. That was a half-developed idea we never really cracked.

"You see, I've always liked what Jean Giraud, the French artist and illustrator, does. His characters almost seem to be built up of varying plastic parts, with odd divisions in their flesh. I couldn't do that to Rutger, though; the daily makeup process would have been impossible. So we experimented with some tattooing that was supposed to suggest something like demarcations in an engine. The idea really was that they indicated an alignment to certain socket points. I'd thought that when Roy was in battle in outer space, he'd probably put on a war suit and attach plugs to that suit at those markings. But it kind of dropped away, this whole idea, and never really worked. It is interesting, though. And a curious detail."

According to Marvin Westmore, makeup artist Freddy Blau of Reel Creations (which specializes in body tattoos) created these markings by silk-screening them onto Hauer's body and then hand-finishing them where necessary. The entire process took four hours.

Deckard finds his escape route on the Bradbury ledge blocked by Batty.

Stymied in his attempt to break back into the Bradbury, Deckard now begins a dangerous, tortuous climb up the side of the Bradbury to the building's roof. This sequence (and the resulting chase on the roof) had been originally planned to be filmed on the sides of real buildings and rooftops in downtown Los Angeles.

However, after such an exercise was deemed too impractical, it was decided to film this sequence on the Warner's back lot instead. This decision necessitated building a huge, movable, twenty-two-foot-high mobile set, one equipped with wheels and stage jacks, standing in for the last three stories and rooftop of the building on which the final minutes of the Deckard/Batty pursuit take place.

But now the *BR* crew was faced with another problem: building a camera platform that was high enough and stable enough to be able to shoot these sequences. Scott decided to use a high camera boom for some shots and to also build an enormous, thirty-foot-high, reinforced steel filming platform for others. This custom shooting tower had special reservoirs installed in its bottom that were filled with hundreds of gallons of water to give this structure added stability.

Harrison Ford smiles for the camera between setups of the ledge scene.

The *Blade Runner* crew spent approximately two weeks on the top and side of this "Rolling Roof," which was occasionally turned around on its installed wheel-base to allow cinematographer Jordan Cronenweth to vary the backgrounds behind some shots. Cronenweth and Terry Frazee also added various rain, lightning, smoke, and lighting effects to break up the texture of the numerous shots filmed here.

Batty and Deckard's confrontation climaxes on two rooftops, an episode composed of a number of different elements. Although the final chase was, as previously mentioned, staged upon the "Rolling Roof" set located on the Burbank lot, further steps were taken in order to enhance the visual authority of this sequence. To this end, certain castings of real cornices located on downtown Los Angeles' Rosalind Hotel and nearby Rowan Building were obtained by the *BR* crew and then added on to the top and sides of the set.

Rutger Hauer: "Those little windmills you see on the roofs? They were supposed to be wind generators, for electric power. But they

A safety-cabled Ford confers with Ridley Scott (squatting) during filming. The climb up the side of the Bradbury and action on the roofs were staged upon the side of the 'Rolling Rooftop,' a movable, 22-foot high exterior set built on the Warners backlot.

Rutger Hauer and Harrison Ford race to the scene of the girder on the Rolling Rooftop set, a sequence shot during the last night of principal photography. The windmills were supposed to represent malfunctioning power generators.

weren't working anymore—people had put them up there a long time ago, they'd broken down, and then they were just left there. Those were Ridley's ideas, as I recall. He was very specific about showing one more detail about how this culture was collapsing in on itself."

Ford, as usual, did most of his own stunt work during this final rooftop sequence (excepting Deckard's heart-stopping leap between two buildings and his subsequent grabbing onto a projecting iron beam, which was doubled by Gary Combs). However, the actor didn't quite call his physical stunt that. "I term what I've done in *Raiders* and *Blade Runner* 'physical acting,' Ford told this writer in 1981. "Stunts are falling off a tall building or crashing a car, something you're silly enough to think isn't going to hurt the next day." Whatever he called it, Ford actually did do most of Deckard's punching, running, climbing, and just plain hanging on himself.

For example, when Ford loses his grip while dangling from the iron beam jutting over eternity, the only thing holding him in place was a waist tether which had been placed just outside camera range. An air bag had also been placed ten feet below the actor to insure his safety should Ford inadvertently fall during the filming of this scene.

Prior to making his own leap across space, Roy Batty is shown clasping a live dove.

"Again, that was my idea," Rutger Hauer explains. "My justification for suddenly appearing with it was that Batty had already explored the rooms of Sebastian's apartment before Ford came there, and Batty knew there were wild birds roosting in some of the empty ones.

"So I said to Ridley, 'As I go through these rooms during the chase at the end, I could grab a dove. What do you think about that?' Ridley said, 'What do you want to do with it?' I said, 'A couple of things. First, Batty's dying, so he wants to grab onto something, hold something that's still alive. And rather than acting out with my body at the end of the film the idea that Batty's batteries have gone dead, I could just release the dove. That will tell the story.'

"Of course, there's a lot of symbolism there, too. And I don't necessarily mean Christian ones. The dove could represent Batty's soul, freedom, wings, a liberation from a certain lifestyle, all that. There's a lot of interesting connections to birds in mythologies and religions other than Christianity."

Having now given this author his rationale for the dove's appearance and metaphors in *BR*, I then asked Hauer to clarify that moment in the film where Batty pauses with folded arms and is seemingly lost in thought, just before making his two-building leap.

"Batty was thinking about something," Hauer replied. "What I decided was going through his head was, 'Yeah, here's my chance to fuck with Deckard again.' That's all Roy was pondering, and that's why he jumped across. To mess with Deckard a little more."

Following his graceful leap between buildings, Batty kneels before the perilously hanging Deckard, whose grip is beginning to slip from a girder. Following a brief dialogue exchange, Deckard almost falls—but Batty grabs Deckard by the wrist and hauls him to safety.

Hauer's one-armed lift of Ford was done by running a cable from an unseen harness under Ford's clothes. This cable then ran above the actors' heads to a minicrane positioned out of camera range, which lifted Ford up as Hauer rose holding his wrist (again, both actors performed their own stunts here).

Batty's last-minute change of heart has confused some viewers. In the British science-fiction film magazine *Starburst* in 1982, Ridley Scott opined that Batty's saving of Deckard's life "was an endorsement in a way, that the character is almost more human than human, in that he can demonstrate a very human quality at a time when the roles are reversed and Deckard may have been delighted to blow his head off. But Roy Batty takes the humane route. But also in a way, because [Batty] wants a kind of death watch, where he knows he is going, dying. So in a sense he is saving Deckard for something, to pass on the information that what the makers are doing is wrong—either the answer is not to make them at all, or deal with them as human beings."

In 1995, however, Rutger Hauer told this author a completely different story.

"The reason I saved Harrison's life? In talking with Ridley, I'd asked him, 'Can I put stuff into this computer called Batty things that don't really belong?' And he said, 'Absolutely. What do you want to put in?' That's when we started coming up with Batty's sense of poetry and fun and the idea of a four-year-old experiencing a lot of things for the first time in life, like the way Roy's so impressed with Sebastian's toys.

"But Ridley insisted that one thing Batty had to have was absolutely no sense of hesitation. He doesn't reflect, he reacts. He's faster than anybody. A characteristic of the Nexus–6. So, if you follow that thought, you reach a point where you realize that if somebody falls, Batty grabs. It has nothing to do with how he feels about Deckard; it's just a reactive moment. That's what Roy's built for.

"In fact, while we were shooting this moment of Roy grabbing Deckard, we had a problem with the rain machines and had to wait around for them to be fixed. And I actually asked Scott, 'Ridley, what do you think? Why does Roy save this fucker?' And Ridley looked at me and said, 'It's purely a reflex. Other than that, I don't know. . . .'

"This reply might bother some people, because so many folks have read a lot of meaning into Batty saving Deckard's life. But actions always come first. *Then* we think about them, later. Roy doesn't know why he saves Deckard or grabs a dove. He just does it."

For one final opinion on this crucial scene, we turn to its original author: Hampton Fancher.

"Batty saving Deckard's life was something Ridley and I discussed before I stopped writing for the picture, and something I set down before I left. Roy's move may have been partly reflexive, sure. But Ridley and I had also talked about Batty as a character who was fascinated with life, even though he deals in death. And here, at the last moments of Batty's life, is this little man, Deckard, who literally spits in the face of death. Roy appreciated that, this last, defiant, life-affirming gesture. That's why he saved Deckard—he repaid Deckard's defiance with a moment of largesse.[14]

---

[14]Despite the nearly overwhelming favor with which Batty's climactic soliloquy has been received, it does have its critics. One is Producer Charles Lippincott (*Judge Dredd*) who read an early *BR* script and strongly feels, "There are a lot of people sold on the ending that Rutger convinced Ridley to do for the film. And even if you tell them that it's not good commercially, or wasn't the original intention, it doesn't make any difference. They're so sold on what Rutger pulled off. . . . And what Rutger pulled off was actually one of the things that the cult fans love about the film.

"I don't know why Ridley told Rutger what he did, though. Maybe he'd just forgotten by that point."

The astonished Blade Runner now watches helplessly as a tired-looking Batty slumps down in a lotus-position before him. Still cradling his dove, Batty smiles, almost bashfully, before saying:

"I've seen things you people wouldn't believe. Attack ships on fire off the shoulder of Orion. I watched c-beams glitter in the dark near the Tanhauser Gate. All those . . . moments will be lost . . . in time. Like . . . tears . . . in rain. Time . . . to die."

This unexpectedly moving soliloquy is one of *Blade Runner's* most tender pieces of dialogue; so touching, in fact, that those watching this scene being filmed were just as moved as the members of *BR's* ever-growing audience.

For example, in Lance Loud's 1992 *Blade Runner* article in *Details* magazine, *BR* art director David Snyder said, "As soon as Rutger finished his beautiful soliloquy, everyone just wept. I mean, I can hardly talk about it now, almost twelve years later. It was the combined effect of his words and the strain and struggle of working on this masterpiece."

"I'm still proud of Batty's last speech," adds Hauer. "That's a beautiful moment, isn't it? But originally it was a bit longer, like a half-page of dialogue.

"So I said to Ridley the night before we shot it, 'This is way too long. If the batteries go, the guy goes. He has no time to say good-bye, except maybe to briefly talk about things he's seen. "Life is short"—boom!'

"I truly felt that the ending of this picture should be done very quickly. I mean, we'd already seen this opera of dying replicants; I

"But the *Dangerous Days* script I read had a completely different climax. There was no poetry from Batty, no moving last words. In fact, Batty was literally dead weight. A corpse whose dead hand was clamped around Deckard's wrist and dragging him over the edge of the roof. The original intention of the *Days* ending wasn't 'Look how human the replicants are,' it was that a human under a great deal of physical and emotional strain can pull himself out of a jam despite overwhelming odds. No matter how intelligent but unemotional your enemy is. That was the point Philip K. Dick was trying to make in his book, and Hampton Fancher had retained that in the screenplay I read. That was the whole point!"

didn't think the audience would stand another protracted death scene. So I said to Ridley, 'Let's do it very fast, and do it as simply and profoundly as possible. But also, let Batty be a wiseguy for a second.' Ridley said, 'Yes, I like it.'

"So when we filmed that speech, I cut a little bit out of the opening and then improvised these closing lines: 'All those moments will be lost, in time. Like tears in rain. Time to die.'

"But you know, everyone always writes about me and that speech, and ignores the screenwriter. I thought David Peoples, the man who wrote that version of Batty's soliloquy, really did a beautiful job. I mean, I loved those images he came up with—'c-beams glittering near the Tanhauser gate, attack ships on fire off the shoulder of Orion.' I thought they were really interesting, even if you didn't understand them."

At the moment of Roy Batty's death, the replicant finally releases his dove, which flies away into the brightening sky. "Ridley and I came up with that," Hauer notes. "The whole idea there is that once he stops talking, the dove flies. You never really see the moment of Batty's death . . . the dove says it for him."

Director Ridley Scott has the last word on Batty's bird, however.

"I had Rutger holding onto a pigeon during the last few moments of that sequence," the director said. "What I wanted him to do was release the bird at a prearranged moment, letting it fly out of frame an instant later. Naturally, we had our inevitable rain effects going on just before this. I had also arranged Harrison so that he was sitting with his back against a wall with one of his knees drawn up.

"Well, the scene was going fine. Rutger made his wonderful speech, he brought the pigeon up, and opened his hand. At which point the bird flapped its wings a couple of times, calmly hopped onto Rutger's knee, carefully jumped to the ground, and walked away! We then learned that pigeons can't fly when they're wet. So I had Terry Rawlings cut away from the bird on the rooftop just as it flapped its wings. Later on, I reshot that outside Elstree Studios in England during post. We got a dry bird, kept it dry and, this time, ended up with a take."

In all versions of *Blade Runner* except the Director's Cut, Deckard now recites a short piece of narration about the replicant's love of life as Ford watches Hauer die on the roof. Two different versions of this narration were recorded for use in various versions of *Blade Runner*; one is quoted in chapter XVI.

However, a persistent rumor claims that a *third* version of Deckard's "watching Batty die narration" was recorded and screened. This was first reported in a 1982 *Starburst* magazine article by Phil Edwards ("The *Blade Runner* Chronicles 2," *Starburst* #51, November 1982). In this article, Edwards claims to have seen a preview version of *BR* in England during which Deckard simply says, "I sat for six hours and watched him die."

Blade Runner editor Terry Rawlings, however, disputes this.

"You know, I'm glad you're writing this book to set the record straight," Rawlings begins, "because there's a lot of misinformation about *Blade Runner* that's been spread around and accepted as fact over the years that just isn't true.

"Like that 'six hours' line. Now, I don't remember that line, and I don't see how it could have been included in a British sneak. For some movies you do occasionally change the *release* print for various territories, and the International Cut (*explained in chapter XV*), which was seen overseas, does indeed have a few extra seconds of violence that weren't included in the American theatrical release.

"But I'm almost positive that that 'six hours' line was never done for the film. I don't remember it and, after all, I did cut the picture. Besides, it certainly wouldn't have only been heard in a British preview print. Because at that point there was only one cut made of the film that was shown in both England and the United States, and that was the Workprint [see chapter XVI].

"It's always possible my memory might be hazy on this, of course," Rawlings concludes. "In which case I apologize. But I don't think I'll have to. I very clearly recall the two different versions of Deckard's rooftop narration which were seen at the previews and in the theatrical release, but I don't remember Deckard ever saying anything like, 'I sat for six hours and watched him die.'"

GAFF ON THE ROOF

As the first rays of dawn brighten the night sky, a Spinner slowly rises behind Batty's dead body. It is Gaff's—who now throws Deckard the firearm he dropped while climbing Sebastian's armoire (suggesting that Gaff has been secretly following his fellow Blade Runner throughout the film). Gaff compliments Deckard for doing "a man's job." Then, as he turns to leave, Gaff says something strange: "It's too bad she won't live. But then again, who does?"

M. Emmet Walsh: "According to the script I got, Bryant was supposed to be the one who ended up on the roof at the end of the film. Not Gaff *[the February 23, 1981 screenplay confirms this]*. The dialogue was different, too. But that got changed during production."

Having unexpectedly spared the Blade Runner's life, Batty dies before the dazed Deckard.

Katy Haber: "I seem to recall that the Bryant character was replaced with Eddie Olmos for that scene because Ridley wanted to tie a line of dialogue—"It's a pity she won't live"—into the origami Gaff leaves outside Deckard's apartment. Gaff had left that tinfoil unicorn to prove he'd been there, so it made sense to also have him up on the roof and say that line to let Deckard know he *had* been there. Besides, it was Gaff you always saw following Deckard around. Not Bryant."

Edward James Olmos: "By the end of the film, Gaff's changed. He's been watching Deckard from the sidelines during the whole show, but now he's come to a point where he empathizes with him. Gaff understands a little more about life and death. That's why he lets Rachael live.

"There's also a line I like a lot that very few people pick up on, up there on the roof," Olmos continues. "That's the one where Gaff says, 'You've done a man's job, sir.' You know what that was supposed to be? Ambiguous. A reference to Deckard maybe being a replicant. In fact, I saw one script where Gaff made this even more explicit. He said the same thing—'You've done a man's job'—but then Gaff went on to say, 'But are you a man? It's getting hard to tell around here.' But I'm glad they cut that out. The line as is is a lot more subtle."

TINFOIL UNICORN

Deckard rushes back to his apartment, fearful that Gaff's cryptic words on the roof may mean that Rachael is dead. His suspicions seem justified when Deckard discovers his front door is open; as he cautiously unholsters his firearm, we notice that the broken fingers on Deckard's left hand are now bandaged.

Yet another persistent rumor has it that a *Blade Runner* scene was shot and later dropped from the film showing Deckard in a Medi-Van having his hand bandaged after Batty's death. A diagnostic screen behind Ford then supposedly displayed a scan of Deckard's fingers, while the word "Replicant" flashed on the screen.

However, when this author asked Rutger Hauer if such a scene was ever shot, the Dutch actor said, "Never. How do these rumors get started?"

Editor Terry Rawlings agrees with Hauer: "I never saw a sequence like that, and I saw all the film."

Deckard now warily hunts through his apartment for his replicant lover, calling Rachael's name but getting no reply. The entire time, we can see that his face is puffy and bruised. Marvin Westmore achieved this effect with traditional facial makeup, a scab made from Pep cereal flakes, and by putting a small amount of cotton into Ford's cheeks to slightly bulge them out.

Deckard enters his bedroom and notices a tangle of sheets on his bed, eventually discovering a sleeping Rachael.

The scene later moves to the corridor outside Deckard's rooms as the couple hurries toward an elevator. On their way, however, Rachael's

*Deckard awakens
Rachael with a kiss.*

shoe knocks over a small tinfoil origami unicorn. Deckard picks it up, recognizing another one of Gaff's creations. The words which Gaff told his fellow Blade Runner on the roof—"It's too bad she won't live. But then again, who does?"—echo faintly on the soundtrack.

According to David Peoples, "The tinfoil unicorn was totally Ridley's idea. I remember him getting excited over the whole notion of Gaff's origami, because it meant Eddie Olmos could leave that unicorn sculpture behind at Deckard's apartment at the end."

Hampton Fancher: "The unicorn was definitely Ridley's, that sculpture and the full-sized one that showed up in the Director's Cut. I'd initially rejected that concept, you know. But when I saw the movie, I was kind of happy about how Ridley had handled it. That tinfoil origami hit a lot of levels.

But what is the significance of Deckard's *nod* after picking up Gaff's unicorn? In the strictest sense, Deckard's nod simply means that he realizes Gaff was at his apartment and let Rachael live.

However, the inclusion of a *live* unicorn in the *BR* Director's Cut adds a whole new dimension to Gaff's origami calling card: the possibility that *Blade Runner*'s "hero," Rick Deckard, is actually a replicant. Olmos and Hauer address this possibility:

Edward James Olmos: "Ridley wanted to put a shot of Harrison at his piano dreaming of a unicorn into *Blade Runner*. And that dream was supposed to be known by Gaff. Which is why he left the tinfoil sculpture behind in the first place."

Rutger Hauer: "I always felt the subject of Deckard being a replicant was a matter of an emotional understanding. He certainly behaves like a replicant, because he's so programmed. Ironically, through their very actions, you understand that it is the replicants who are free."

Blade Runner was originally conceived to end with the elevator doors closing on Rachael and Deckard. Yet when Hampton Fancher attended his first screening of the film—only to discover a new climax showing Deckard and Rachael driving through a pristine wilderness— he was, "Beyond shocked. It speaks well for the film that I didn't just kill myself or die or something because of that ending. I mean, the film was good enough in every other aspect so that, okay, we can forgive this. But I'm glad it came at the end.

"Still, I could not fucking believe it. That happy ending, was like waking up from a nightmare—and then you didn't wake up!"[15]

Most of *Blade Runner*'s live-action filming officially wrapped June 30, 1981. However, since the threatened director's strike had never materialized, Scott continued to shoot a number of pickup scenes until the second week of July. But for the majority of the film's cast and crew, their *BR* experience was over.

An experience which was perhaps best encapsulated by Joanna Cassidy: "I have never been on a set that was so charged, so exciting, so volatile and so passionate as that one in my life."

"Volatile" indeed, as the next chapter points out.

---

[15]Rutger Hauer: "Forget the happy ending. I didn't even like the fact that Deckard ran off with Rachael at the end. Deckard loving replicants didn't make any sense to me. Frankly, I thought Deckard was a little sick, because he ran away with a vibrator that *looked* like a woman.

"Some people get angry with me when I tell them that. They say, 'Rutger, you missed the point. You really should read Philip K. Dick's book.' Well, they don't know that I read the book. Whose whole moral, I thought, boiled down to this: 'Does a computer love you? No, a computer does not.' End of story."

"BLOOD RUNNER":
FRICTION ON
THE SET

We're not a studio, but unfortunately we were placed in the position of the heavy that a studio would take.

—BUD YORKIN, TANDEM PRODUCTIONS
"BLADE RUNNER 2," BY KENNETH TURAN
LOS ANGELES TIMES MAGAZINE, SEPTEMBER 13, 1992

One of the basic rules of filmmaking I learned early on is that very happy units usually produce very bland films.

—MICHAEL DEELEY

"Will Rogers never met Ridley Scott."

—*BLADE RUNNER* CREW T-SHIRT

By most accounts, making *Blade Runner* was a miserable, exhausting, and decidedly unhappy experience.

And that's putting a gloss on the situation.

"On one level, *Blade Runner* was an incredibly contentious production, even when measured against the typical horror that's called making a motion picture," states Katy Haber. "Tandem was furious with Michael and Ridley, Ridley and Michael were battling Tandem, and our leading man and director got to the point where they were barely speaking to one another. Ridley was also exasperated by the crew, and many on the crew hated Ridley. It was just wretched awfulness, really; *Blade Runner* was a monument to stress."

Not everyone recalls *Blade Runner* with such dread, however. Daryl Hannah, for example, still speaks of the experience with genuine fondness. "I knew there were a certain amount of problems going

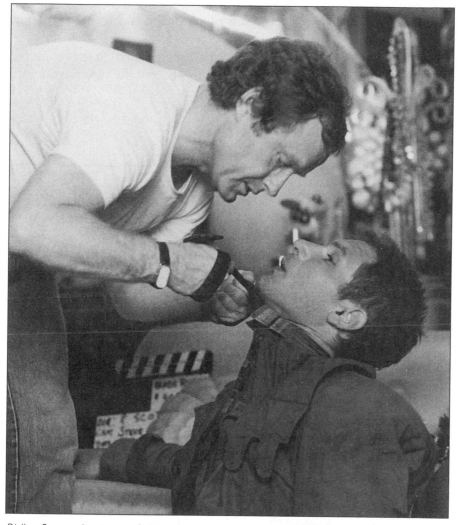

Ridley Scott rehearses a fight with Harrison Ford—a conflict that was mirrored in real life on the set.

on," the actress recalls today, "but I just tried to stay out of the way of the politics and enjoy myself. Which I did, very much."

As for this author, who visited the *Blade Runner* shoot a number of times during principal photography, I did indeed notice a palpable air of tension hanging over the set. But as Daryl Hannah points out, that's only part of the story; I was also always treated with extreme cordiality and professionalism.

However, such were the demands and strains placed upon other members of the *BR* team that some of the crew sarcastically referred to the film as "Blood Runner." Still others, even fourteen years after the fact, continue to convey a noticeable note of anger when talking about the experience. And a few more had such a terrible time making this motion picture that they voluntarily decided to never work on another movie again.

FIRED?

It is no secret (among industry insiders, at any rate) that film professionals often wear two faces: the publicly affable one, in which every production is a warm, supportive joy, and the privately candid face, in which each personal grievance or on-set mishap is bitterly passed on to a small circle of trusted associates. It's also no secret that the filmmaking process itself is a brutally punishing one—the so-called "glamour" of moviemaking is perhaps the public's single greatest misperception of the arduous reality behind the physically and psychologically demanding process of making a motion picture.

As a major studio production, then, *Blade Runner* would be expected to have had its usual share of conflicts. Yet it was only a few weeks after principal photography began that troubling rumors started leaking off the *BR* set, ones stating that the physical and emotional tolls being levied against the *Blade Runner* participants were escalating far beyond the expected quotas of abuse. The leads were unhappy, the whispers went, and the crew was nearing revolt. The workload was hideous, the director unreal.

Such mutterings probably would have remained within the closed circle of Hollywood filmmakers, however, if not for a number of articles printed in such industry trade papers as *The Hollywood Reporter* and *Variety* (in July and August 1981), which reported a startling fact: Ridley Scott and Michael Deeley had both been "removed" from *Blade Runner*.

"To understand that falling out," explains Michael Deeley, "you first have to understand a great many things. First, the film's deal structure.

"Tandem Productions, who essentially meant Bud Yorkin and Jerry Perenchio, had basically entered into an arrangement with us that placed them in the position of a completion bond guarantor. An entity, in other words, which guarantees that if a production goes wildly out of control or over budget, that same entity will step in and take over the production, to cover any costs such problems have incurred. Of course, the implementation of such a takeover essentially means that your film has been taken out of your hands and handed over to these people.

"Now, the deal we had cut with Tandem was that they would take over only if we went over budget by ten percent. Ridley and I had every reason in the world *not* to do this. Our own deal included a tidy back-end profit if we brought the film in at its projected costs. So we definitely kept a steady eye on the cash flow."

Despite Deeley and Scott's best intentions, however, cordiality between Tandem and *BR*'s producer and director began eroding during the first week of filming.[1]

"It was while we were shooting the Tyrell office scene that things began to grow uncomfortable," Deeley continues. "By day three of our first week we were already over budget and behind schedule. Fourteen days later, we then had to literally stop everything in its tracks, turn back, and completely reshoot the first two weeks all over again. This was primarily due to the fact that Ridley felt that the original lighting in Tyrell's office was much too dark; pitch-black, in fact. Ridley was very plain about that. Which of course generated a clear conflict between Ridley and Jordan Cronenweth, the cinematographer. So now we had that personality issue to deal with as well.

"However, that reshoot actually benefited the picture in some respects," Deeley adds. "Sean's performance, for instance, had been a little stiff those first couple of weeks. This return allowed her to loosen up. It also gave Ridley a chance to start over again, which is what every director would like."

As for Deeley's own reaction to this initial hiccup, *Blade Runner*'s producer goes on to say that, "I was concerned. Yet since *Blade Runner* was such a huge undertaking, I'd somewhat expected these problems. But all of us, even myself—well, maybe not Ridley—weren't quite sure what we were doing at that point, because this was such a complicated picture.

"In any event, by day three it had become clear that *Blade Runner*

---

[1] Bud Yorkin had even sent Michael Deeley a memo dated March 9, 1981, the first day of principal photography, which read, "Dear Michael: I know that you are embarking upon a project that you have worked a long time on and that it is going to be everything you have dreamed of. You have my best thoughts all the way."

wasn't going to be a smooth shoot. Since we were already over budget and behind schedule, our money men got jumpy. This is the point when they first started to say to Ridley, 'Why do you need all this detail? We're not playing Seurat *[the French pointillist painter]* here. Why are you painting in every little dot?' The answer, of course, was, 'That's what Ridley does.'"

In fairness to Bud Yorkin and Jerry Perenchio, however, it should be noted that their displeasure arose from very personal reasons: the Tandem producers had put their *own* money into *Blade Runner* and now saw the possibility that this investment might suddenly have to double or triple before the film was finished.

As Yorkin himself told film critic Kenneth Turan in Turan's essential "Blade Runner 2" article (*The Los Angeles Times Magazine*, September 13, 1992): "Jerry [Perenchio] and I didn't go into this naïvely. We knew it would be a very difficult shoot. . . . [But we were still only] two guys taking [money] out of our own pockets or going to the bank and borrowing it ourselves. Going on the set and watching someone take five hours longer to set up a shot, seeing a lot of money go out of your pocket, that kind of thing one doesn't need unless you have a very good heart."

"There's another factor to consider regarding Tandem that's only tangential to the money issue," says publicist-turned-producer *Charles Lippincott* who'd worked on *Alien* (and who at this point, like most participants in the small, insular world of Hollywood, had also begun hearing dire rumors from the *Blade Runner* set). "I'm sure when they were first pitched this project, Yorkin and Perenchio probably thought they'd be buying into another *Star Wars*. After all, here was this hot British director who'd just made a smash sci-fi picture, and he was working with one of the fastest-rising action stars in Hollywood.

"But once the cameras started rolling, what did Tandem see on the *Blade Runner* set? Rain, gloom, a woman being shot in the back, and a relentlessly perfectionist director who'd shoot the same sequence over and over again, all day long, if that's what he thought he had to do in order to get it right."

Scott's habit of filming the same take fifteen or twenty times before he was satisfied with the result quickly became a major point of contention with the Tandem financiers. "'Why are you taking so much time to set things up? Why so many takes? We don't have the money for this!' That sort of became a constant pressure from the Tandem side during principal photography," Katy Haber recalls. "What they didn't understand about Ridley was that he was not going to print a take until he felt he'd gotten what he was after. That attitude was commendable—just look at the film that resulted—but it was also very, very expensive."

By the time *BR*'s four-plus months of principal photography came to an end, the rift between Tandem on the one side and *Blade Runner*'s above-the-line personnel on the other had widened to the size of the Grand Canyon. The picture was now nearly five million dollars over budget, and the increasingly tight financial situation had not only led to escalating pressure from the film's completion bond guarantors, it had also forced Scott to either simplify certain sequences or drop them altogether.[2]

"I still tell my friends that working on *Blade Runner* was like doing a Cannon picture," recalls M. Emmet Walsh with a laugh. "Cannon was this low-budget outfit in the eighties that made a lot of cheap action pictures. And whenever Golan and Globus, the guys who ran Cannon, would hit a budget crunch, they'd just rip a page out of the script and yell, 'Shoot the next page!'"

This financial dwindling wasn't sitting well with Scott, either. Ivor Powell sums up the director's general budgetary discontent when he notes, "Ridley used to tell me that every time he sneezed on this picture, it cost him another ten thousand dollars."

Budget crunch or no, *Blade Runner* finally did manage to stagger across the principal photography finish line on July 9, 1981. Yet only two days later, the classic Hollywood battle between art and the dollar which had been embodied by the Tandem, Scott, and Deeley split reached critical mass.

"On July 11, 1981, I received a letter from Tandem's attorneys," Michael Deeley continues, "saying to the effect that Ridley and I were in default of section so-and-so of our production agreement, because the picture had gone over budget. For that reason, *Blade Runner* would now be completed by Tandem Productions. We were, quote, 'off the picture.'"

---

[2]Stacey Nelkin's scenes as Mary had been cut early on because of the budget squeeze. Other slashed segments included the proposed but never shot opening escape of the three replicants from the "furnace asteroid." The Deckard/Pris fight was pared down from an elaborate battle in a gymnasium to simple hand-to-hand combat in Sebastian's apartment, and the opening shot of Deckard entering Los Angeles via a futuristic train.

In other words, Tandem had taken *Blade Runner* away from Deeley and Scott. The two men had been fired.

"It is my opinion that Yorkin and Perenchio believed that money has total control over every aspect of making a movie," Deeley now says, by way of explaining this serious event. "Yet that isn't always quite the case. Any good director worth his salt will usually not let a balance sheet compromise his picture. I'm not defending overspending—as a producer myself, that would be lunacy. What I am saying is that Tandem never understood that Ridley and I had always hoped that Bud and Jerry would be in for a smooth ride on this production. Because they had made a deal that was *worth* that to us. Unfortunately, that's not the way it turned out."

Tandem's legal gauntlet now resulted in two critical events. One was the surprising fact that, despite their firing, Scott and Deeley remained on the picture anyway.

"Although this formal letter had been written and we'd been formally notified that our services were no longer required, obviously we still *were* required," Deeley explains. "We'd come this far and still wanted to do the picture, so we did. There was nothing actually very nasty about that firing. In a way it was almost amusing, because it was sort of a technical process, not a real process. It's my assumption that Tandem sent that letter out of frustration and a certain amount of ignorance concerning the reality of the filmmaking process. Because nobody wanted a situation where everybody was going to start screaming, 'Okay, I'm going to drop out of this picture!' or, 'I'm going to insist that a credit read, '*Blade Runner,* invented by Jerry Perenchio and codirected by Bud Yorkin.' Tandem knew better. Or at least I think Warner Brothers or Alan Ladd, Jr. must have told them that this would be a very bad situation. Because after a few weeks, things had more or less settled back down to normal."

Unfortunately, this firing also had a secondary effect: according to Deeley, Tandem now began to attempt to exert more artistic control over the production. "What happened at this point was that a certain amount of decision proposing began coming from the Tandem side," *Blade Runner's producer continues.* "That resulted in a tremendous amount of disagreement over very specific story points, like the voiceover and the unicorn shot *[both of which are explained in chapter XII: Sneaks and Panic].* But when it came right down to it, a lot of these proposals really weren't going to happen."

Stuck in the middle of this tense situation was *BR* Production Executive Katy Haber, who now found herself in the awkward position of maintaining her loyalty to Deeley and Scott while acting as a sort of unofficial liaison to Tandem, who'd begun working more closely with her in order to insure that their own agenda was met. "That was an uncomfortable situation," Haber now says of the hassles which would continue to plague the production well beyond the July 11 takeover. "But you know what I think the fundamental problem was? Personalities. Yorkin's, in particular, was a bottom-line mentality. I don't think he liked or understood what Scott was doing with *Blade Runner*. Ridley, on the other hand, was a sharp, talented, incredibly tenacious visionary. He was willing to cling to this picture until they sawed his fingers off."

An uncomfortable situation now became worse, as an outright war for control over *Blade Runner* erupted. It was a battle which would not only involve Scott, Deeley, Haber, Yorkin, and Perenchio, but other *BR* workers as well.

"Ridley got fired from the film," recalls Terry Rawlings, "but they couldn't make it stick. And I knew they couldn't make it stick because of the way the rules work—Ridley certainly hadn't gone over budget because of any intention or neglect. Nevertheless, there still was a short period of about two weeks or something right after this firing had occurred where Ridley was away in London doing inserts with Ivor Powell. That's when one of the Tandem people came to me and said, 'Well, now we can finally get this film the way we want it!'

"I realized he meant recutting the picture. His way. So I said, 'Well, that's not possible at the moment, because I've got the film scattered around in pieces.' Which I didn't have! [laughs] I kept saying, 'I can work on this sequence with you but I can't work on that one because it's all been broken down for other people to work on. Plus the effects are being inserted and that segment's not quite right yet,' and so on and so forth. I did some fancy tap-dancing for a couple of weeks before Ridley came back, in the hopes of at least helping to keep the film in one piece. Which I did. At least while I was still on the picture myself." [Rawlings was not suggesting that he too was fired, but that his schedule forced him to leave the picture in early March 1982.]

An exhausted Harrison Ford listens to Ridley Scott atop the 'Rolling Rooftop' set during the last day of filming.

UNHAPPY ACTORS

As if this ongoing tension between completion guarantors, producer, and director was not enough, the punishing *Blade Runner* shoot had already been aggravated by a more personal problem: a falling out between Harrison Ford and Ridley Scott.

The Ford/Scott relationship had begun cordially enough. Scott now recalls their initial exchanges as "enjoyable. Harrison is a complete professional, a remarkably talented, witty, and intelligent man." Yet as soon as the *Blade Runner* crew hit the production floor, that relationship changed.

One minor participant who noticed this shift in attitude was Paul Roessler, a rock musician who had been recruited as an extra (background player) to portray one of the punks glimpsed on *BR*'s busy streets. As Roessler told writer Lance Loud in a *Details* magazine article entitled "Blade Runner" (October 1992): "*Blade Runner* was one of the first movies to ever use punk rockers as extras. On the set, we punkers would watch Harrison Ford. He usually looked pissed off. I heard him once say to Ridley something like, 'What are we doing here? This is ridiculous! You're going overboard!'"

Roessler was not the only fringe *BR* figure to notice Ford's unhappiness. In the same *Details* article, Alan Raymond, a filmmaker who had visited the *Blade Runner* set to tape a story on the film for ABC News, was quoted as saying that, "On the set, Harrison sat off to the side and pretty much kept to himself. I never once saw him talk to Ridley. [Though] he [did say] he respected Ridley because he was willing to go over budget and do extra takes and all that."

What had happened? Whatever caused this rift, the scars were still obviously there ten years later, when Ford was interviewed in 1991 by a variety of publications covering the excitement attending the recently resurfaced Workprint and rumors that a new *Blade Runner* Director's Cut was on its way. "I played a detective who did no detecting," Ford told the *Boston Globe* on July 14, 1991. "There was nothing for me to do but stand around and give some vain attempt to give some focus to Ridley's sets. I think some—a lot—of people enjoy it, and that's their prerogative." The star's comments in Lance Loud's 1992 *Details* article was even more succinct: "*Blade Runner* was not one of my favorite films. I tangled with Ridley."

Yet none of this rancor surfaced during the time of the film's release. Why?

"Both Harrison and Ridley are professionals," observed Katy Haber. "Ford may have spent nearly the entire shoot in his trailer, but he wasn't about to tell the press that. And Ridley, at the time, I think, was so battered from the process of making *Blade Runner* that he couldn't have said anything negative about Harrison even if he'd wanted to. Which he didn't."

Then what was the cause of the Ford/Scott split? These days the tabloid press would assume such frictions are caused by egos, money problems, or power struggles. But the truth behind this matter was far simpler, and far more human.

"I'll tell you what it was between Ridley and Harrison," says Michael Deeley. "Basically, this was the first time since Harrison Ford had been a significant actor that he'd worked with a director who wasn't yet completely comfortable around actors. Or perhaps that's the wrong answer—at that time in his life, I think, for whatever reason, Ridley didn't really want to deal with people on the emotional level. He has changed to a significant, more positive degree since then.

"But at the time, I think Harrison perceived Scott as cold and uncaring. He wasn't, really; Ridley had a million balls in the air during that shoot, and he had taken it as his personal responsibility to insure that none of them hit the ground. Yet Ford would see Ridley perched way up on a crane thirty feet in the air peering through that perfect eye of his and creating a perfect frame, which is Ridley's hugest strength, and all Harrison wanted was to be told what to do. But Ridley didn't want to tell Harrison what to do. Yet Harrison *wanted* to be told what to do. Which is something you should be grateful to actors for, actually," adds Deeley, laughing.

"In any event, their styles at that stage were completely different. Oddly enough, many of the women who worked on *Blade Runner* seemed to have very few problems with Ridley. Which was also an annoyance to Harrison Ford: he would see them continually conferring with Scott when he couldn't even get the man's ear for a moment, and it drove him crazy."

If Scott and Ford weren't getting along, however, just about all the other *Blade Runner* actors enjoyed their working relationship with the British director (as has already been noted through the positive comments of Rutger Hauer, Daryl Hannah, Edward James Olmos, William Sanderson, Brion James, and Hy Pyke). One other *BR* performer did have a few awkward moments with Scott, though: M. Emmet Walsh.

"The first thing I shot was at Union Station," Walsh recalls, "for the scenes at Bryant's office. I'd show up about five or six in the evening, because we were supposed to shoot all night long. But we wouldn't shoot all night long. Ridley would spend all night fiddling and diddling with the lights and props and things, and all the sudden it would be close to six A.M, which was when we'd have to clear out of the station because the commuters were coming. Which meant we had about ten minutes left to do these perfect takes, or there would be enormous problems. It was like that all the time.

"Then, months after we'd finished shooting, Ridley called me back to loop my entire performance. At first he wanted Bryant to sound like he had emphysema, because of all the bad air. So he had me hacking and gasping out each word. That spooked me, because having to dub in my entire performance made me feel as if Ridley hadn't liked my acting.

"Then Bud Yorkin took over for a little while and made me loop Bryant's lines all over again. After I did that, I made a ten-dollar bet with Yorkin that I'd be coming back. Yorkin said, 'You ain't coming back.' Sure enough, I had to come back two months later for Ridley and do it again. This time to change the number of replicants who'd died breaking into the Tyrell Corporation, from one to two. But then Ridley didn't like the way my lips matched up to the dialogue or something, and my 'two' line got changed back to 'one' again!

"But the worse thing was when I was in what Ridley called 'The Blue Room,'" Walsh continues. "That was the place where Harrison and I watch those monitors that introduce the replicants to the audience. Ridley wanted me to smoke a cigar during that scene. But I don't smoke a cigar. Ridley said, 'Smoke it anyway.' So we're doing this shot and I'm smoking this awful thing and this rotten tobacco juice is rolling down my throat and I'm coughing and hacking and generally getting sick. I got angry at Ridley then, especially since we kept doing the scene over and over again.

"Finally, I muttered under my breath, 'You son of a bitch. You should be hung by your balls and left to twist in the wind.' There was silence for a moment and Ridley said, 'I feel that way now.' He'd heard me!

"That's my *Blade Runner* story."

If Walsh felt occasional irritation toward Scott, however, he felt none of that emotion toward Harrison Ford. "Harrison was a terrific guy," Walsh remembers. "In fact, we used to fool around between setups in Union Station. One night we even jammed ourselves into one of those little 'Four Photos for a Dollar' booths and had our pictures taken."

In point of fact, nearly everyone this author spoke with during the course of writing *Future Noir* had nothing but good things to say about Harrison Ford's talents and character. Some members of the crew even felt an admiration beyond Ford's personality or theatrical talents. One such crew member was Stunt Coordinator Gary Combs, who witnessed an astute business side of Ford.

"Harrison was a great guy. Everybody liked him," Combs told this author in 1995. "He was also pretty smart. In fact, let me tell you a little story about how sharp he was.

"Now, Harrison's not only a great actor, he's good at doing his own stunts, which he calls 'physical acting.' [laughs] On *Blade Runner*, Ford did a lot of stuff—running after Zhora, fighting with Pris and Batty, jumping over cars, fighting Brion James in the alley, all that.

"But then Harrison came to me one night to ask a question about what he was doing. Because to do something once is one thing, but Ridley did things over and over and over. That's the only complaint I had about Ridley. He came from the commercial era, and he wasn't afraid to do things fifteen, sixteen, seventeen times, you know? Until he got it the way he wanted it.

"Anyway, one night Harrison came to me, because I was there to double him all the time. Ford was all skinned up and everything. He wasn't hurt bad, and he didn't mind doing things, but he didn't want to do them more than he had to. So Harrison said, 'Shouldn't I be getting adjustments [*extra pay for stuntwork*] for all this?' I said, 'Technically, yes. We belong to the same union. You should be getting adjustments for the things you do.' So Harrison said, 'Well, what do you think I should get for all this?' And I told him some amount after we'd figured out all he'd done on the show so far. It was a fair figure, too, because we weren't overpricing it.

"Then I said, 'Now, you and I never had this conversation.' And Harrison said, 'That's right.'

"So he left. About twenty minutes later, here comes John Rogers, the production manager. He's in a big tither. John says, 'I gotta talk to you! Harrison wants an adjustment!' And I said, 'Oh, really?' [laughs] The way things ended, John asked me if I thought Harrison had asked for a fair deal. I said yes, and they paid him. Sharp guy, Harrison."

There were two exceptions to this overall admiration of Ford, however: one minor, and one major.

The minor qualification came from Rutger Hauer. "It's not that Harrison and I ever clashed," recalls the Dutch actor. "In fact, we only worked together a short time, during those scenes at the end of *Blade Runner*. It's just that I never really got to know him. Even though he was very polite and professional, I always felt as if there was a three-foot sheet of glass between us."

Hauer's reservations were nothing, however, compared to the conflicts Sean Young felt toward her leading man.

"Harrison and I just don't get along," the actress told me on the *BR* set late one night in 1981. "Why, I don't know. I don't want to bad-mouth the guy, but this really bothers me."

"Again," says Katy Haber, "I think the reason there was friction between Sean and Harrison was clashing personalities. You also have to remember that Harrison is the consummate professional, and here he was working with someone who was very green. That couldn't have been easy for him, given the other stresses Harrison was under."

This author was unable to reach Sean Young for her reflections on the actress' conflict with Ford. But the following excerpt from Lance Loud's *Details* piece is, I think, worth reprinting here:

> SEAN YOUNG: The first scene I shot was the one in which Rachael meets Deckard. My first line was, "Do you like our owl?" But Ridley told me I was saying "ow-el," not "owl." He made me reshoot that line twenty-six times. But *Blade Runner* was a good experience—everything, except my leading man. What happened? I could dish for days but I have a rough enough reputation as it is. Suffice it to say I wouldn't call Harrison Ford generous.

MICHAEL KAPLAN: Sean was fun and down-to-earth—
she used to hang around wardrobe and tap-dance and do
shtick. Nobody disliked Harrison either; he was very professional and had a wonderful, dry sense of humor. But
between them, something didn't work. Whenever Harrison
would come onto the set he wouldn't speak to her. Totally
ignored her [in fact].

EXHAUSTED CREWS

At the same time Ridley Scott was dealing with actor and producer
problems, yet another roadblock was thrown in his path: his own
crew.

"Most of the people on *Blade Runner* had never worked with a
director of Ridley's caliber before," Katy Haber says. "Here was a man
trying to fill up the frame with a massive amount of what he felt was
carefully considered, important visual information. In order to get
that kind of incredible detailing, he had to be deeply focused. Certain
parties misinterpreted that, I think, for him being cold and uncaring."

A weary Blade
Runner *crew
wraps the last
morning of film-
ing (Harrison
Ford is center; a
partially
obscured Rutger
Hauer is at left).
Note T-shirt
worn by crew
member in
upper right.*

"Ridley was very tough on his crew," agrees Hampton Fancher. "But that was because he was toughest on himself. He had a very clear vision of what he wanted on *Blade Runner.* A lot of the crew didn't understand that."

One way in which Scott's perfectionism manifested itself was a relentless refusal to accept anything but the best from his fellow coworkers. For example, Syd Mead told this writer in 1981, "The only difficulty I can think of regarding Ridley is, believe it or not, his imagination. It's always about twenty steps ahead of everybody else's. So if he's made you think he's decided on one thing, by the time you execute that idea, he'll have changed his mind and come up with a better one. And you'll have to start over. But frankly, I find that extremely stimulating, because it invariably helps the film."

Turning to Loud's *Details* piece one final time, *BR* Art Director David Snyder recalls one other incident that perfectly illustrates the director's demanding attitude.

> DAVID SNYDER: We worked like hell for months to get the street set right. We must've bought every piece of pipe, plastic, steel, and wood in a five-thousand-mile radius. [Then the] day came to show it to Ridley. Larry [Paull] and I were standing there—shaking, of course—when Ridley drove up to the back lot. The set was already way over budget and cost over $1 million. He got out of the car, looked around, took [a] cigar out of his mouth, and said, "This is a great start!" Then he got in his car and drove off. Larry and I stood there in complete silence for five minutes and then said, "What the fuck are we going to do now?"

"Ridley made it clear early on that he was willing to fight for every frame of film in that picture," Katy Haber told me in 1995. "And most of the time he had a very well-reasoned, articulate rationale behind every moment he was attempting to create. He could be very persuasive. And stubborn. Then we'd move onto the next setup, and the lighting or smoke or rain or whatever would take forever to set up in order to achieve the look Ridley was after, and the arguments would start all over again."

Yet another factor adding to the overall tension on the shoot was its grueling pace and surroundings. Because so much of the film would be shot on Warner's open-air back lot at night (for scenes which had been written to occur in the evening), a typical work "day" would begin in the late afternoon, last throughout the night, and only wrap when the dawning sun made the illusion of darkness impossible to hide. Overtime soon became an issue as well, as Scott attempted to pack the maximum workload into each day's limited twenty-four-hour period.

The director, in turn, found himself only able to snatch a few hours' sleep at the end of each "day," before he had to screen the previous day's rushes. Then there were the damp, dirty, trash-strewn and gloomy sets; these eventually became saturated by the constant rain and smoke effects, and the depressing surroundings—which were not helped by the suffocating "street crowds"—slowly began to gnaw on everyone's nerves.

In short, the film had not been in production very long before *Blade Runner* became a kind of psycho-physiological endurance test.

"Things got especially brutal towards the end," recalls Joanna Cassidy. "Ridley was under constant pressure to hurry up, hurry up, hurry up. In fact, my death scene, which was one of the very last sequences to be shot, was done under extraordinary stress. Luckily, we had had a couple of previous nights to film the shots of Harrison stalking me through the crowd. But by the time we got to the moment where I'm running away from him and he shoots me in the back, it was almost dawn and the sun was about ready to come up.

"We'd gotten word that if we didn't have that scene in the can by then, too bad; everything would be struck and we'd have to move on to Rutger Hauer's final fight and death scene. Ridley's solution was a multiple-camera setup, to film Zhora getting shot. It all had to be very carefully timed out, since some of the cameras were shooting at different speeds. Anyway, I ran past the cameras, triggered off the hidden controller I had in my hand to explode the blood-bag under my raincoat, and then fell out of frame at a precise spot so that Ridley could later intercut Lee Pulford crashing through the plateglass windows. All of that was filmed in a single pass. One take! That was *it*. Talk about nerve-racking! The pressure was unbelievable."

"The last night was the worst," agrees Katy Haber. "By then, we'd all been up for at least thirty-six straight hours. Yet we still had to film a lot of stuff on that rolling three-story roof set: portions of the Deckard/Batty fight, and Rutger's death scene. Somehow we managed to blast through most of it. But by then the sun was coming up. You can see the sky turning blue, in fact, behind Gaff's spinner as it rises into frame behind Roy's body.

"Anyway, that was supposed to be it. The last day's work. But Ridley still had a few shots left to do. So we rolled that roof set into a soundstage, redressed it, and lay poor Harrison Ford down on this wet garbage while they shot some close-ups of his face. He was supposed to be watching Rutger die. People have told me since that Harrison's particularly convincing during that moment. That he looks beaten up and exhausted. Let me tell you, Harrison *was* beaten up and exhausted. He was also half-asleep!"

THE T-SHIRT WAR——————————————————

All these tensions finally boiled up late in principal photography, during an infamous incident which later became known as "the T-Shirt War." According to Makeup Supervisor Marvin Westmore, the outburst had been long in coming.

Mementos of the 'T-Shirt War, manufactured to express the Blade Runner *filmmakers' displeasure with one another. (Top) The crew T-shirt, bearing the words 'Yes Guv'nor My Ass!' (registering the crew's unhappiness with an impolitic interview given by Ridley Scott) and (bottom), the counterblast made by Scott, Katy Haber, and Michael Deeley—'Xenophobia Sucks.'*

"The T-shirt thing was a way of letting off steam without getting fired," Westmore recalls, a trace of resentment still in his voice. "What got me going—what got a lot of us going—was the way Ridley operated. Yes, he shot a lot of film, but some of us felt his managerial style was too abrasive. That he kept people a little off balance so they'd work that much harder. The main problem, though, was that we felt Ridley disrespected his crew. And he had one hell of a crew, let me tell you.

"Anyway, things just kept getting worse and worse. In fact, the crew made up an honor roll—for people who'd had enough guts to quit that show. And I'd even begun airbrushing the inside of my trailer with all this anti-Ridley graffiti. The last straw, though, was that 'Yes, Guv'nor' thing."

What Westmore is referring to was an incident sparked off by an indiscreet interview Scott had given to a Manchester, England, newspaper.

"Ridley had told this English journalist that he enjoyed working with British crews better than American ones, because all he'd have to do was ask for something and the British crews would say, 'Yes, Guv'nor' and he'd get it," Katy Haber explains. "Saul Kahan, the unit publicist, then left a copy of that newspaper in Ridley's trailer. The next thing we knew, somebody else had found it and spread it all over the set."

"Somebody photocopied that article," Marvin Westmore says, picking up the story. "When I read it, I knew I'd had enough. I figured somebody on the crew had to express an opinion as to how a lot of us felt.

"So I designed and paid for about sixty T-shirts that said, 'Yes, Guv'nor My Ass!' on one side. On the other side it said either, 'You soar with eagles when you fly with turkeys,' or, 'Will Rogers never met Ridley Scott.' They could have canned me at that point for doing that, I suppose. But I'd assumed they were too deep into the production.

"The next thing I had to worry about, though, was that now that I'd made up these shirts, who was going to have the balls to wear them? Well, I put one on. The next thing I knew, sixty guys came by and picked them up!"

"There was even more tension than usual that day," Haber recalls, "because of a threatened Director's Guild strike. That would have shut us down; Ridley would have had to stop shooting. So no one was in a good mood at that time. Then these T-shirts showed up."

"The funniest part of this," Westmore continues, "was that the first person to see me wearing one of those shirts was Ridley. He sort of laughed and disappeared for awhile. Not more than an hour went by, though, before he and Michael Deeley and Katy Haber showed up back on the set. And now they were wearing their *own* T-shirts!"

"That was my idea," Haber says, concluding her part of the incident.

"I'd felt all along that the Americans didn't understand us. So I had these shirts printed with the words, 'Xenophobia Sucks.'"

"The T-shirt War had nothing to do with Ridley being British or with a fear of foreigners," Westmore contends. "I'm of English descent, and very proud of that. What it did concern was our frustration at what we on the crew called assholes. That's all it boiled down to. Without anyone quitting, the T-shirt thing was just a way of getting rid of excess negative energy."

WITNESSES FOR THE DEFENSE

Despite all these derogatory statements, however, the reader is urged to remember that there are always two sides to every story.

Ridley Scott himself gave this author an insight into his own frustration with filming *Blade Runner* when he told me, for my 1982 *Cinefantastique* article, that for all the resources at his command on this big-budget production, he was never completely happy with the *Blade Runner* technical situation.

"This is the first film I've shot in the United States," Scott said in 1981, "and overall I enjoy Los Angeles very much. In fact, I'm thinking about moving over here to live for a while. As for the differences in filmmaking between England and America, there really aren't any. It's mostly a matter of scale.

"But I must say that I encountered a certain amount of frustration in dealing with certain Hollywood union regulations," the director continued. "One of the rules here in America that has no equivalent in Britain is the fact that an American director cannot operate his own camera. What bothered me about this was that more than even being a director, I am a camera operator. That's how I've always worked. Having my camera taken away from me is illogical, like taking Arnold Palmer's golf clubs away from him. It's also inefficient. Fortunately, in England there are ways to work around this."

"I think the problem on *Blade Runner* was that Ridley had just come off *Alien*, where he was allowed to operate the camera, and *BR* was the first picture where he wasn't operating," confirmed Katy Haber in 1995. "And he panicked. He'd never looked at a set this way before—he'd always looked at it through a viewfinder."

When asked for his own take on the cause of the friction between

Scott and crew, Ivor Powell went on to say, "That was one of the sad things that happened on that picture. Part of the reason for it, I think, was that *Blade Runner* was such a big show. There were also so many unbelievable pressures bearing down on Ridley throughout. And there were small things.

"For instance, here Ridley and I were, fresh from England, and not really aware of the American system. Or that we'd not always be able to get what we needed. For example, in England there are prop houses with literally *centuries* worth of objects you can choose to use for a film. American prop houses were very meager in that respect. This is understandable, because America is such a young country. But that's just a minor example of one of the many, many surprises that took us off guard while we were shooting in Los Angeles."

Ridley Scott's further views on the problems he encountered during the making of *Blade Runner* can be found in his interview in appendix A. However, as previously stated, not all of the cast or crew did clash with the director. As Rutger Hauer told me, "Ridley was always on top of everything. He was brilliant a hundred times over in that picture. Yes, he had that British arrogance and attitude, that way of constantly saying, 'Can't you do a little better?' Yet that was ultimately *good* for the film. Besides, he was just pulling you over the edge, to see how far you could go."

Yet perhaps the final, and best, witness for Ridley Scott's defense is Terry Rawlings—who put the entire matter of warring producers, unhappy actors, and exhausted crews into perspective by noting:

"Ridley is a hard taskmaster when he's shooting, I suppose. He's very tenacious about what he wants. Yet I've always gotten along well with him. I like him.

"I also have a tremendous regard for talent when I see it. It doesn't have to be a talent that stands up and shouts out what it can do. Just to watch someone like a performer or a director or an artist or a musician or anyone with that special gift doing what they do best moves me beyond words. I can burst into tears sometimes, watching someone that good doing something perfect.

"Ridley has that talent. Plenty of it. Which goes a long way towards soothing whatever temporarily ruffled feelings I might have during a shoot."

THE SPECIAL EFFECTS

After more than a year of intensive labor, the visual effects craftsmen at Entertainment Effects Group have produced the definitive urban future for Blade Runner— *Ridley Scott's stylish homage to film noir.*

"BLADE RUNNER—2020 FORESIGHT," BY DON SHAY
CINEFEX #9
JULY 1982

DOUGLAS TRUMBULL AND EEG

Although he had been officially fired from the production on July 11, 1981, Ridley Scott was back at work on the extensive special effects needed for *Blade Runner* by July 21. And, though Hollywood F/X circa 1982 had not yet become as computer-dependent or as (relatively) streamlined as they are today, Scott was not daunted by the tremendous effects workload facing him during this important phase of the production.

"After I finished with *Alien*," noted Ridley Scott to this writer in 1981, "I had a fairly thorough grounding in some special effects areas, and a certain naïveté about others. Working with Douglas Trumbull's EEG crew on *Blade Runner*, however, has helped me to shade in some of those previously blank areas. This was an absolutely necessary education for me; the film director of the eighties and nineties will have to be able to do everything, and special effects and computers are going to become as much of a tool as the Mitchell camera."

Scott had no idea of just how omnipotent a special effects tool the computer would become—a tool used for *BR* in a much smaller capacity than what would be done today. Yet the effects produced by Trumbull's EEG company for Scott's film would still go on to become a benchmark by which many subsequent effects-oriented films would be measured for years to come.

Before he turned his attention to the special effects of *Blade Runner,* however, Ridley Scott first had to tie off the live-action filming. This had officially wrapped on June 30, 1981. However, since a threatened Director's Guild strike had never materialized, Scott continued to shoot a number of live-action pickup scenes until the second week of July. Following his brief Tandem dismissal, Scott then concentrated on bringing *BR*'s various Spinners, giant Asian billboards, and various cityscapes to life.

From the outset, it had been *BR*'s director's intent to employ a number of sophisticated optical and miniature effects for the film. But Ridley Scott wanted more than flash and dazzle; he wanted visuals that would seamlessly fit with the gritty, ultrarealistic look that characterized the rest of the film. To this end, Scott, Deeley, and company began casting about for an appropriate effects house that would not only supply the sizzle but the steak.

During this search, John Dykstra's then-still-functioning Apogee organization (which had previously done the special effects for *Firefox* and *Star Trek: The Motion Picture,* among others) was considered, but ultimately rejected. So was Industrial Light and Magic, the George Lucas-owned special effects company which had developed the F/X for *Star Wars* and many other productions. Eventually, the final choice centered, as previously noted, on Douglas Trumbull's newly formed Entertainment Effects Group (EEG).

Trumbull was a well-regarded F/X supervisor who'd started his career as the illusions ace behind the "slitscan" effects (moving, geometric patterns of lights and shapes) featured in the climactic "Stargate" sequence of *2001: A Space Odyssey.* Trumbull also supervised the F/X for the mystical flying saucers of *Close Encounters of the Third Kind* and supplied various tricks for *The Andromeda Strain* and *Star Trek: The Motion Picture* (a project on which he split the effects load with Apogee). Moreover, by early 1981, Trumbull had also become a full-fledged movie director, with his 1971 ecological SF film *Silent Running.*

Therefore, Douglas Trumbull's reputation as an innovative and talented special effects supervisor was well established by the time he hired onto *Blade Runner*. However, his EEG company (based in Marina Del Rey, California, on Maxella Street; "Maxella," would become a substitute name for the effects facility) was then relatively new. EEG had been cofounded with longtime Trumbull associate Richard Yuricich; Yuricich and Trumbull had first worked together on *2001* and would continue their association through *Silent Running, Close Encounters of the Third Kind,* and *Star Trek: The Motion Picture.*

Speaking to this writer in 1981, Trumbull said of EEG, "We have the largest, most complete special effects facility in the world, bar none. We absorbed most of Paramount's special effects operation when we moved into the Maxella facility, and now we're geared up with the total effects equipment spectrum; optical printers, our own 70mm cameras, multiplane and motion control systems, everything. I think I can safely say that what we have is significantly larger and more complete than either ILM or Apogee."

Primarily concerned with "trying to attain the gritty, highly realistic, almost documentary-like quality of *Alien*, which I admired very much," Trumbull had enlisted the aid of his key EEG effects chiefs to bring those same traits to *Blade Runner*. Dick Yuricich would, with Trumbull, cosupervise the entire operation; Robert Hall, who had done similar work on *Close Encounters*, would head the EEG optical photography group. Dave Stewart was picked as director of miniature photography, Greg Jein would steer the miniatures department, while electronics and motion control systems design would be supervised by Evans Wetmore. Other key EEG/*Blade Runner* personnel would include miniature technician Bob Spurlock as well as Matthew Yuricich, who would be responsible for the film's extensive use of matte paintings (hand-painted scenes incorporated into a scene to realize sets or vistas otherwise too expensive to build).

"Generally, my job on *Blade Runner* was a supervisory one," Trumbull explains. "Dick and I would conceive of the technique, design a general approach to any effects problem, and then direct the entire crew towards the end product of creating believable illusions. This included supervising lighting, perspective, and the decisions as to what photographic processes would be used when. I just put it all together."

Trumbull then went on to explain why he accepted the *Blade Runner* assignment in the first place. "First, I was sick unto death of doing effects movies where all the action took place in outer space and involved pristine spacecraft. I also liked the underlying concept of Ridley's film. The original script that I read needed a lot of work, but the production chiefs knew that, too. Eventually, an enormous amount of script revision occurred, to the point where *Blade Runner* really does represent what Philip K. Dick was getting at in his original novel. Namely, that once an android evolves to where it's indistinguishable from a human being, what's the point in making the distinction?"

Although now staffed and eager to go, the *BR* effects team immediately ran into two problems. One was the fact that Trumbull had been preparing to direct his second feature film when approached to do the *Blade Runner* special effects (an elaborate MGM-financed science fiction film named *Brainstorm*). "But Ridley knew my own movie was still a few months down the road," Trumbull explains. "So we made an arrangement where Dick Yuricich and I would start up the *Blade Runner* work, and then once I became more fully involved with *Brainstorm*, I'd hand over the *BR* supervisory reins to someone else I'd handpick for the job."

The second problem facing the *BR* F/X crew, however, was a larger obstacle, and one that had already dogged Scott's film since inception: money. When *Blade Runner*'s proposed special effects sequences were first broken down by EEG during preproduction in order to determine an F/X budget, $5.5 million was the resultant figure. The problem was that by the time the actual time to begin shooting those effects had arrived, only $2 million was available.

"That was a firm figure," Trumbull told this writer in 1982. "We had absolutely no headroom there. Unfortunately, two million dollars was an almost minuscule amount for the number of effects we were first presented with doing for Ridley's picture."

At this point Trumbull, Yuricich, and Ivor Powell (who had met and worked with both men on *2001*), sat down and came up with a potential solution. Instead of hiring EEG as an independent contractor, the *Blade Runner* production company would in effect lease the entire Maxella facility and put EEG directly on the *BR* payroll, thereby sidestepping any additional costs for the F/X firm's overhead. This strategy still did not pull down the cost of *Blade Runner*'s special effects to the necessary $2 million mark, however. Therefore, one additional cost-cutting measure was implemented: dropping some of the proposed F/X shots altogether.

"That was the point where all the original opening effects scenes that had been storyboarded by Sherman Labbey or painted by Mentor Huebner—the replicants' escape from the furnace asteroid, the scene of Deckard landing on a farm at the beginning of the show—were cut from the film," Trumbull relates. "One sequence I was particularly sorry to see go had Deckard arriving in Los Angeles from the desert on this futuristic train. He got out at Union Station in downtown L.A. and then got into his car, which sort of flowed out onto this auto-mated freeway which could control a vehicle's speed and direction independently of its operator. But then Deckard got caught in this horrendous traffic jam. So he set his car on autopilot, got out, and walked over to this huge tower that looked something like a concrete mushroom. There he entered an elevator and exited on top of the tower and waited on a ramp, where a police Spinner flew down and picked him up to carry him to police headquarters."

Following this cost-cutting procedure, Scott and the EEG Group finally arrived at a tentative F/X budget of $2 million—even though the special effects schedule still indicated that at least thirty-eight F/X shots would have to be executed for the film.

SCOTT F/X

Most special effects units begin filming their own sequences following the end of principal photography. However, Scott had made the deci-sion of starting *BR*'s F/X while the film's live-action shoot was still underway. "I was confident that, with careful planning and clear lines of communication between the set and EEG, we could lock in our effects ideas and begin implementing them in advance of the usual postproduction process," the director points out.

To achieve this careful integration, great care was taken to story-board and plan as many F/X shots as possible before the *BR* shoot even began. In fact, Scott and Michael Deeley had had the EEG group begin preliminary work on the film's special effects as early as August 1980. Then, once principal photography started, Scott and Trumbull also agreed that an EEG F/X supervisor should always be present on the *Blade Runner* set during the filming of any sequence which would require the later addition of special effects (a job which often fell on the shoulders of Richard Yuricich).

The F/X crew at EEG now began to experience the same degree of personal involvement that Scott had demonstrated to *Blade Runner*'s writers, production designers, and filming crew. One EEG staffer who experienced the director's dedication firsthand was *Blade Runner*'s chief modelmaker, Mark Stetson, who had stepped in as a substitute for Greg Jein when the latter was unable to work on *BR* due to a prior commitment.

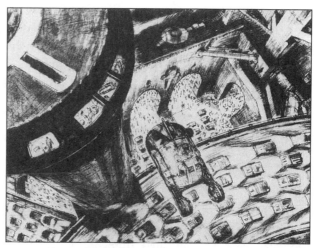

Preproduction art by Mentor Huebner shows a proposed but unfilmed opening to Blade Runner, *in which Deckard was to be caught in a huge (land-based) traffic jam before being flown by Spinner to Police HQ.*

"Ridley was fairly amazing," Stetson recalls. "Incredibly energetic. He came to us as often as he could during principal. Once production wrapped, Scott was also spending a lot of time at EEG, even though he was constantly traveling back and forth between L.A. and London, where he was engaged in other postproduction work. In fact, I'd go so far as to say that Ridley Scott was more involved with this film than practically any director I've worked with," Stetson concludes. "He was most interested in the design of *BR* because of his background in art direction. So he had plenty to say about the development of the miniatures even before they were moved to a shooting stage. Then, when they got to the stage, Ridley's eye was often in the camera. Not for every shot, but many."

One last (and important) addition to the EEG crew was a late arrival. This person was hired in April 1981, roughly four weeks after Entertainment Effects had begun shooting the completed model of the Tyrell Pyramid (the first major effects sequence to be filmed for *BR*). This new team member's name was David Dryer—who, along with Douglas Trumbull and Richard Yuricich, is credited with supervising *Blade Runner*'s special effects.

Tall, lean, and invariably well-dressed, David Dryer broke into filmmaking as a teenager by cutting the original negatives of the religious films his father was directing at the time. Born March 5, 1943, Dryer graduated from USC Film School in 1965 and numbered among his classmates such future directors as George Lucas and Hal Barwood. For thirteen years Dryer directed and designed television commercials (many of them filled with special effects) for a division of Columbia Pictures. Among these works were TV spots for Disneyland and numerous automobile shoots, a specialization that culminated in Dryer's designing the Datsun logo in 1976 and extensive other assignments from that same company.

During this period Dryer also found himself engaged in and experimenting with the full gamut of special effects. "In the past Doug Trumbull, Richard Yuricich, and I had all worked together," Dryer commented. "Richard had once been a camera assistant on a commercial I directed and, in the process of doing a lot of logos and other commercials, I had even worked with Jimmy Dickson, the slitscan cameraman on *2001*."

But *Blade Runner* was Dryer's first feature film assignment. How had he been assigned to such a formidable feature his first time out of the gate? And how, in particular, had Dryer found himself taking over such a complex effects film from one of the most gifted cinematic illusionists of all time?

"Well," Dryer explained, "because of Doug Trumbull. As you'll see on the final credit crawl I share a contractually stipulated credit, along with Doug and Dick, for supervising *Blade Runner*'s effects work. Actually, it was Trumbull who got me the job."

As has been previously noted, Douglas Trumbull had known that his time and energies would eventually reach a state where they would become consumed with his upcoming *Brainstorm* project. That state was reached in February 1981; therefore, after considering a number of possible successors, Trumbull settled on Dryer, due to the former's understanding of the latter's intricate grasp of effects procedures. Trumbull then approached Scott, Deeley, and Powell with a suggestion that Dryer replace him. Dryer was called in for an interview that same month (February), and by April he was hired for the job.

Dryer recalls, however, that the transition was not without its price. "When I first came on Ridley was not all that sure of my credentials or capabilities. He was constantly double-checking with Richard or Doug on my ideas. I can't say that I blame him, because, really, Scott didn't know me from Adam. But as time went on," Dryer says with a

From left to right: Director Ridley Scott, Designer Syd Mead, and Special Effects Supervisor David Dryer study an F/X schedule at EEG.

smile, "Ridley got to understand that I was delivering the goods he was expecting from me."

Trumbull had been involved with *Blade Runner*'s miniature effects shooting for about a month when Dryer signed on to the project (Dryer stayed on until the end of the *BR* effects shoot, which officially wrapped near the end of 1981). "Doug and I overlapped each other for about a week," Dryer explained. "At that time he had shot a few straight, nonbackground takes of the Tyrell Pyramid. It then became clear that Doug's commitment to *Brainstorm* precluded any more of his day-by-day involvement with *Blade Runner*. However, during the entire *BR* effects shoot Doug would occasionally drop in when and if he had the time. He showed up one day, for example, when we were shooting some of the interior Spinner mock-ups live on the EEG stage, mainly because I had to go back to another stage that day to film some miniatures. So over the entire *Blade Runner* effects period, Doug and I would bounce back and forth occasionally to cover one another, when we had the chance.

"The fact that I was so heavily involved is certainly not meant to downgrade either Trumbull's, Yuricich's, or Scott's contributions,"

Dryer adds. "Their input and invention was great. Once the principal photography was over, for instance, Ridley was at EEG quite often and very much involved in what went on. Incidentally, Scott doesn't ever consider how difficult something is if he wants it. He was always very challenging and demanding, and I respected that. If you made Ridley happy, then you'd really done something to be proud of."

Future Noir now turns to an intricate (and technical) examination of *Blade Runner*'s special effects. Those uninterested in such "hardware data" are recommended to jump ahead to the next chapter ("Postproduction and the Music"). But for those who *are* interested, yet feel that the specialized terminology used by F/X artists is too daunting to understand, I have two words for you: don't worry. This author will supply plain definitions for every important effects term used in what follows. One last word of encouragement: the nice thing about the special effects tribe is that the more you read their language, the more you understand it.

However, first I must describe the common practices of the EEG group from 1980 to 1982 and their Maxella facility itself.

As was a usual Trumbull effects-oriented practice in 1982, all of *Blade Runner*'s EEG effects were duped (duplicated), composited (sandwiched together), and matted (ditto) onto 65mm film, whose frame is twice as big as the standard 35mm film used in motion pictures. Trumbull had chosen 65mm stock because it gave a richer and more convincing look to his special effects (generally speaking, the larger the negative, the sharper the image and the clearer the final composite). These finished 65mm shots were then reduced to a 35mm anamorphic (widescreen) negative.

As for the Entertainment Effects Group's physical plant, three EEG stages were primarily used for filming *BR*'s F/X. These were the "smoke" room, where the opening "Hades" landscape was shot; Stage 2, where the smaller motion-controlled Spinner traffic was photographed on a seventy-five-foot-long track; and the "Compsey stage," where the majority of flatwork art, multiplane clouds, and interior Spinner video imagery was filmed. Additional EEG effects work concerning the Hero Spinner, mock-up Spinner, and Hades landscape was also done at the 22,000-square-foot Maxella facility.

But what was this "Hades landscape?"

Merely the first, and most awe-inspiring, shot in the film.

HADES

The opening shot of *Blade Runner* shows a vast industrial landscape, with cracking towers belching huge fireballs of gaseous petroleum waste while numerous Spinners fly overhead. In the background can be seen two Tyrell Pyramids, their air-travel warning lights blasting upward from the tips of these structures into the sky (a photograph of this scene appears on the front cover of this book at the lower right).

This mammoth industrial wasteland, which the EEG crew came to nickname either "the Hades landscape" or "Ridley's Inferno," was intended to represent the industrialized suburbs which now surrounded the city of L.A. in 2019.

The staggering Hades Landscape miniature as seen in the film. Model work by EEG.

"The Hades landscape was supposed to be this incredible sort of New Jersey or Long Beach-type of industrial wasteland gone berserk," Trumbull comments. "It had thousands of light sources, the Tyrell Pyramids, and gouting flames burning off toxic gases from smokestacks. To obtain these effects necessitated a rigorously controlled combination of miniatures, motion control passes, and front projection."

Front projection (an effects procedure in which an image or background is "front projected" onto a highly reflective screen), was used to produce the sulfurous flames writhing and spewing from the landscape's industrial towers. But the actual flame footage that *was* front-projected here had been obtained through the efforts of a small crew under the direction of Bob Spurlock.

Spurlock first shot a number of high-speed 35mm gasoline explosions in the EEG parking lot and in the desert just outside of L.A. The resulting flames were then front-projected onto white foam cards slotted into the top of the Hades towers during a second pass from Trumbull's motion-controlled, computer-operated camera, dubbed the "Icebox" system. (Motion-control cameras are a critical effects tool. The

Icebox system itself will be explained in a few pages, but generally speaking, motion-control systems are computer-controlled cameras with the ability to precisely and automatically pan, tilt, track, etc. Such electronic precision allows them to exactly repeat the same camera move for every take required to add a different F/X element to the "same-frame" strip of film.)

"We'd go back and expose those fire explosions in registration to the entire Hades set," Dryer further explained. "All you'd see on the negative was the fire. This was later optically added with what's called a cover matte to give the flames some density, so that you wouldn't see too many of the other light sources through the flames."

But what of the Hades miniature itself? Designed by Tom Cranham (and based on Trumbull's verbal descriptions), the forced-perspective Hades model was one of the largest miniatures used in the film. Yet though this landscape looks miles across in *Blade Runner*, the total dimensions of the Hades model measured only thirteen feet deep by eighteen feet wide. Furthermore, it was erected on three separate tables measuring six feet by thirteen feet each, which could either be joined together or filmed separately as each shot required.

The model Hades set was first built up from a Plexiglas sheet/cast-foam foundation. Miniature foam molds of the many small sub-buildings were then carefully applied to this Plexiglas/foam base. Only the front quarter of the miniature was detailed, mostly in etched brass. The remaining three-quarters of the model was primarily brass silhouettes hot-glued down to the table. Also included were a number of individual foreground towers from eighteen inches to three feet high. Many of these and the other large, model Hades buildings were based on a number of prior photographs taken of El Segundo, California, and Torrance, California, refining plants. Certain towers in these installations were then reproduced and worked out in miniature to make them appear to be ten times their original size.

"We also slapped an enormous number of extrusions on those miniature towers," said Dryer. "We called them 'RidleyTubes.' After awhile they began to look like intestines growing out of these structures. The whole process of retrofitting became an important consideration to our miniature work, too."

Then there were the Tyrell Pyramids seen in the background of the Hades landscape. Most of the major pyramid scenes (which also involved large-scale miniatures and will be explained shortly) were shot separately and then "matted in" (laying one element of a shot onto another in the same frame of film) after repeated computer-controlled camera moves had filmed the tabletop Hades model. For certain extreme long shots of the Hades landscape, however, large transparencies were made from still photographs of the Tyrell Pyramid model and physically mounted into the miniature set. These transparencies were then backlit.

The color Pyramid transparencies were actually thin sandwiches of bent neon tubing inserted within slim Plexiglas boxes built expressly to backlight each particular pyramid transparency. Dryer explains, "When you see those extreme-long-shot pyramids, chances are that they're the transparencies. Since we shot those scenes in the correct angle of approach, and since the perspective of an object that big that far away is almost flat anyhow, there's nothing to give away the fact that they're really only still photographs."

Dryer goes on to explain that nearly *seven miles* of fiber-optic strands and 2000 light points were threaded into the final Hades miniature in order to illuminate it. "Every night as I was driving home I would come to the top of Sepulveda Pass and look out over the San Fernando Valley, and I was struck by the fact that so many of the lights were varicolored; consequently, we used a number of different colored lights to shade our Hades lighting."

To provide the tabletop model's illumination, photofloods were first shone through the underside of the Hades landscape model's Plexiglas foundation. This provided a strong source of light from beneath the miniature. Next, a number of very small "grain of wheat" lightbulbs (so-called because they are the size of a grain of wheat) were inserted at various points throughout the Hades miniature. Finally, the ends of many ultrathin fiber-optic strands were threaded into either a building or some other area where a light source was felt necessary (such as the red "bulbs" seen on the landscape's smokestacks).

Now the tips of these nearly invisible strands were individually hand-colored with different dyes (red, orange, and yellow), to suggest multicolored points of light. Next, each fiber-optic strand was bundled up and fed into one of twenty small boxes, all of which had been equipped with several small interior projection bulbs. These bulbs would in turn be turned on, the fiber-optic strands would carry the illumination from the light boxes to the tips of the strands embedded in the Hades landscape, and—*voilà!*—instant illumination.

The brightness of the light boxes themselves was controlled by Trumbull's computer-controlled "Icebox" camera system, which had been programmed to not only suggest steady illuminations but a number of flickering flame sources onto which the front-projected fire explosions were applied.

"There's a funny story involving the lighting of Hades," recalls Mark Stetson. "I have this very clear memory of Doug Trumbull and Ridley coming over to the model shop early on to review the work in progress on that miniature. They stood in front of it for about five minutes with their arms crossed and their brows furrowed. Then they glanced at each other and Doug finally said, 'This looks like shit!' [laughs].

"What had happened was that, at the time, we were going to solely light that model from the bottom. But it just didn't work—none of the etched brass silhouettes were showing up. You can also imagine how that miniature looked in the shop when Doug and Ridley first saw it; it was being toplit by all those ghastly fluorescent lamps on the ceiling that most workshops have.

"Anyway, all you could see were these black silhouettes with nothing else going on. Now, not long after Doug's comment, I was flying back into L.A. from San Francisco, at night, and I happened to glance out the plane's window. What I saw were these endless streams of multicolored, individuated lights passing below us. That experience and Doug's comment made me realize that we'd been initially after the wrong image in only using bottom light for that model.

"So what we wound up doing was lacing the whole Hades set with miles of fiber-optic cables and using those along with the bottom light to illuminate it. Doug's criticism also led us to adding all those illuminated foreground spires onto the Hades landscape. Now, Trumbull's criticism may have hurt, but he'd been right—it made all the difference in the world to the Hades miniature once those fiber-optics and grain-of-wheat bulbs were switched on."

According to Trumbull, another element that helped "save" the Hades model—and many other miniatures seen in the film—was his previously mentioned Icebox camera system (so named because of its bulky appearance).

"We'd drive everything we could on the Icebox," Trumbull said. "In some city shots, though, where we had so many lights flashing and up to ten in-camera passes going on, we simply couldn't feed all the information into the available computer channels. So we actually had guys sitting around with manual electric switches to hit these light sources off and on at certain cue points."

Developed for *Close Encounters* (and also used in *Star Trek: The Motion Picture*), the Icebox was an eight-channel, rack-mounted computer-controlled camera system that had the honor of being the first motion-control device ever used on location (during the filming of *Close Encounters,* when Steven Spielberg and his crew were shooting many scenes inside a Mobile, Alabama, airplane hangar). It was fed its information by tapes (not floppy disks) and had a solid core, self-checking memory.

The Icebox's major benefit, however, was the fact that it could endlessly repeat the same "move" or pass" on a model. "All that means is that you could switch on the lights on the Hades model, for instance, and program the Icebox to move the camera a certain way for one shot. Then you could switch off the lights and bring the camera back to its original start position. Then we'd insert the small white cards into the Hades landscape onto which we would project the fireball footage. The Icebox would then rewind the film that had just been shot and make a second pass exactly like the first one, recording the fireballs onto the same piece of film which had just exposed the Hades lights. In this way we were able to build up layer after layer of various effects on the same piece of negative. All in all," Trumbull concluded, "the Icebox was a real workhorse."

However, simply building, lighting, and photographing the Hades miniature was not enough. A close scan of *Blade Runner's* opening sequence shows that Ridley's Inferno (and almost every other miniature or optical effect in the film) is also cloaked in a suffocating petrochemical haze. This mist had actually been added on by the effects crew to suggest a choking, omnipresent smog. The question is, how does one create *miniature* smog?

The solution was the fact that nearly all of *Blade Runner's* miniatures were shot in a separate room filled with vaporized mineral oil. This diffusion added a tremendous sense of depth and aerial perspective to the *BR* miniatures and helped to leave the forced-perspective background of the Hades model a vague blur.

All *Blade Runner* smog effects were shot in this same, self-contained area, which was forty feet wide and sixty-five feet deep; EEG called it their "Smoke Room." This self-enclosed stage could hold tabletop miniatures, model Spinners, or any other reduced-scale artifact; furthermore, to monitor the models being filmed in this area, EEG had installed specially designed infrared sensors in the Smoke Room to constantly scan the miniature shooting stage, sensors that could measure the mineral oil vapor's density and precisely control that density for long periods of time.

However, mineral oil vapor is exceptionally irritating to humans; consequently, no one was usually allowed to enter the Smoke Room during a shot. Instead, Smoke Room operators were housed in separate booths equipped with remote-control Icebox and lighting operating rigs.

One final touch was applied to the opening Hades shots: lightning bolts streaking down from the sky. These "bolts" were actually a series of hand-painted lightning strikes separately rendered on large, black pieces of artboard (with between five to seven individual paintings used to illustrate each strike). The paintings were then optically composited into each shot by means of a venerable piece of F/X equipment called "a triple-headed printer," which is essentially a film projector/film recorder housed within the same unit.

TYRELL'S PYRAMID

Although the Hades landscape is the first miniature seen in *Blade Runner*, the first *job* undertaken by the EEG model crew had been to build foamcore mock-ups of both the Spinner and Tyrell Pyramid, which are key visual icons in the film. These prototypes then served as guides for the construction of the actual Spinner/Pyramid models, two of *BR*'s most important miniatures.

"The Tyrell Pyramid was designed by Tom Cranham, EEG's effects designer for *BR*," Stetson explains, "under Doug's input. That was a project that went very well. Trumbull was explicit in what he wanted, and at the time Cranham was working right with us there at EEG—Tom left before the effects wrapped, though. But we still had a very interesting time of it.

"Since the actual size of the Tyrell Pyramid was supposed to be well over a mile high—anywhere from 600 to 900 stories tall, depending on who you talked to—we guesstimated our scale on the single Pyramid model at about 1/750; one foot on the model equaled 750 feet in reality. In constructing this miniature, we used acid-etched brass plates extensively, layering them in, particularly on the flying buttresses that rise up on each side of the building. The middle section of the pyramid was composed of styrene and plastic patterns that were rubber-molded and cast in clear polyester, backed with acrylic sheets that were cut exactly to size. This way any shrinkage that occurred during the molding process wouldn't change the geometry of the assembly. Then we filled it with fiber-optics.

"The finished full Pyramid model—and again there was only one; we used optical sleight of hand to duplicate it in the film—was actually much lower than it looks. About two and a half feet high, with a nine-foot base."

As the camera moves progressively closer to the Tyrell Pyramids at the beginning of *Blade Runner*, this sequence concludes with a cut and a push-in shot that reveals eight narrow windows (two rows of four stacked one upon the other) on the face of the Pyramid itself. Through the second window from the right on the bottom stack of four can be glimpsed tiny, turning ceiling fans, plus the dwarfed figure of a man standing before this window. Actually, what viewers are witnessing is a miniature "Interrogation Room," a scale-model representation of the live-action set where Holden conducts his near-fatal interview with Leon. And just as we take in the movement of those miniature fans, *BR* cuts to the beginning of the scene of Leon's V-K test in the full-scale Interrogation Room set itself.

Blade Runner *Special Effects Supervisor Douglas Trumbull (right, hand raised) with EEG's Tyrell Pyramid miniature, which was 2½ feet high with a nine-foot base.*

The miniature Interrogation Room was part of a large, separate, four foot high by five foot wide model built by EEG in order to allow their camera crew to photograph detailed close-ups of the elevators and offices on the face of the Tyrell Building. Called the "Pyramid insert model," it was elaborately detailed and equipped with a flat top section standing in for the roof of the Tyrell Building. This insert model also included working, motorized, three-inch-high miniature elevator cars running on separate tracks (photographed with motion control), a miniaturized representation of Tyrell's office and bedroom, and the aforementioned small-scale Interrogation Room.

The miniature Interrogation Room was primarily built by EEG modelmaker William George. George equipped this model with tiny, electrically driven, rotating ceiling fans, hand-crafted miniature furniture, and a one-inch-high human figure to represent Holden. Although this miniature room was itself only three inches high, it proved to be a perfect visual match with the full-sized Interrogation Room set built on the Burbank Studios lot (which featured life-sized rotating fans).

"That cut at the beginning of *Blade Runner* between the model Interrogation Room and the full-sized set is extremely effective," notes Mark Stetson. "In fact, it's one of the best lead-ins between a miniature and a live-action set I've ever seen."

LEON'S V-K TEST

"What's interesting effects-wise about Leon's interrogation scene is the number of things that were planned for it but never developed," David Dryer now notes. "For instance, at first we'd intended to cut back and forth between Brion James and Morgan Paull as Leon's interview wore on, getting closer and closer to each man until you could see them reflected in each other's eyeballs. And we indeed did do some close-up work of eyeballs for that—I think this was even reported in a magazine—but we never composited all the elements together, so that never made it into the sequence."[3]

Another dropped effect which would have first appeared during

---

[3]The magazine article Dryer is referring to here is Don Shay's 1982 *Cinefex/BR* piece "2020 Foresight."

Leon's V-K test was an unusual firearms idea from Ridley Scott—a "Black Hole" gun.

"What I particularly wanted to avoid in *Blade Runner*'s weaponry was any indication of the common laser pistol," Scott said. "We all felt that a bright streak of light coming out of a barrel had become a horrible cliché, and we were sick to death of it. Then David Dryer came up with the idea that our pistols discharged a high intensity, particle-beam-type material that imploded on contact, drawing in so much light on the way that it became a black beam instead of a light streak. And whatever section of the body it hit would collapse in on itself. That would lead to a rather elegant demise—very little blood or gore.

"I thought this was an interesting concept," Scott concludes. "A black beam would have been the diametric opposite of the expected laser ray. So we intended to later animate this dark effect and dub our weapons Black Hole Guns."

Unfortunately, this effect—which would have made its first appearance when Leon ventilates Holden—never fully materialized. This despite Douglas Trumbull's entreaties to the *BR* prop department to build him a large-scale version of a "Wham-o Air Blaster," which Trumbull planned to use on-set during principal photography to discharge a large blast of air at an actor and suggest the desired implosive effect. "We would have then optically superimposed the black beam over that invisible air gust," notes Dryer. "Unfortunately, like a lot of other things on this show, the Black Hole Gun idea got left by the wayside."

However, an aborted optical attempt at portraying the Black Hole Gun's ebony ray *does* survive in the film—but you'll need a laser disc player and a sharp pair of eyes to spot it. When Leon fires his (otherwise conventional) gun at Holden from underneath the table, a black streak of light *can* be briefly seen racing along the bullet's trajectory.[4]

"We did some animation tests and created a black streak," confirms

---

[4]Try looking on Warner's Director's Cut laser disc, Disc I, Side I, "Chapter 3: Leon's Emotional Response," frames 11937–11941. A purplish streak starts on the same frame as the flash and explosion of Leon's bullet going through the table. This ray then appears as a blue-black rod of light for the next four frames, moving screen right from the bottom-middle of the frame until it exits on the bottom-right of the frame. Apparently, this blink-of-an-eye effect was left in the film because the filmmakers either forgot about it or assumed viewers wouldn't notice it. And we probably wouldn't—without the advent of videotape and laser discs.

Dryer, "making up a very short, subtle effect and compositing it into the moment when Leon first fires his gun. It's almost imperceptible. We never developed that idea any further, however, because of a basic visual problem. If you shoot a black ray—nothing happens. It's just a dark streak. That's not very dramatic."

AN ASIAN BILLBOARD

Following the wounding of Holden, *Blade Runner* now cuts to a series of breathtaking (miniature) nighttime cityscapes of Los Angeles, 2019 A.D.

Our first glimpse of the city proper reveals an imposing skyscraper to screen right; in the distance can be seen many other (model) buildings, some with blinking neon signs (one for the now-defunct Pan Am airline). In the extreme background are moving points of light, which were optically inserted to suggest three levels of airborne traffic winging their way through the night. These were not model cars, however, but simple animated light effects, provided by *BR/EEG*'s chief animation and graphics supplier, John Wash.

Now a miniature police Spinner flies in from the middle background before making a graceful curve around the foreground skyscraper on screen right—an arresting structure itself. Running down one side of this building is an enormous "media screen" on which is projected the smiling face of a traditional geisha girl.[5]

This giant woman now holds up a pill. She swallows it. Her image is then replaced with a series of graphics created by John Wash (showing a snow-covered mountain with blue skies above and Japanese ideograms to its right), before returning to a close-up of the same geisha swallowing her pill a second time. Obviously, the L.A. of 2019 has not lost its fondness for advertising. (Viewers are never told what the twenty-first-century Los Angeles' film and television industries would be like, however. This is a most curious *Blade Runner* omission, considering its director's advertising background.)

---

[5]"You've heard the expression, 'Everything but the kitchen sink?'" Dryer asks. "Well, for that 'Asian Billboard' scene, we actually *did* throw in a kitchen sink. A real one. It's way in the background of that shot, pretending to be another building, a dark piece of an old sink that we threw some lights on."

A model Spinner flies past a miniature billboard in this gorgeous EEG composite shot.

"One futuristic notion I am absolutely sure of is that, in 2019, everywhere you look you'll be assaulted by media," says director Scott. "A visually appealing offshoot of this concept which then occurred to me was the idea of gigantic advertising screens, something similar to the DiamondVision screens you see at most of the major stadiums in the United States today. But for *Blade Runner*, I posited that each single tube of these futuristic screens would at least by ten feet by ten feet, and that each tube would produce a single aspect of a total picture, whether that screen was only ten or as much as a hundred stories high."

David Dryer adds that, "We then hypothesized that the whole sides of certain *Blade Runner* buildings would be information-oriented video screens, lighting up only at night. During the daytime you might actually see that there were visible windows on the other sides of the screens, but at night, the only apparent thing would be these gigantic, electronically generated images.

"So first we shot a lot of hard-sell, oriental-looking commercials in 35mm at EEG," Dryer continues. "The *Blade Runner* casting department had pulled out two Oriental women and sent them down to Maxella for us to photograph. I filmed them giving the camera alluring looks, or blowing smoke and popping pills and other things that were not particularly healthy.

"We then created fifteen *faux* commercials from fifteen to forty-five seconds long, which could either be used by the live-action unit as background videos, or by EEG to project onto the various miniaturized advertising screens. For the screens themselves, we took a silver-painted, plastic mold-form material that looked like a series of tiny nubby lightbulbs and projected our commercials onto that. We actually blanked out some of these little nubs with black paint to make it appear as if some of the bulbs had burned out."

"Actually," Mark Stetson adds, laughing, "the material we used for that screen on the side of the skyscraper came from Toys R Us! We'd pillaged it from a game called 'Doodle Ball,' and applied it to the side of the model building, making a screen about fifteen by twenty-four inches.[6]

"The reason we chose Doodle Ball was because it was composed of this vacuum-formed material that had a thin styrene sheet with a series of regular little domes on it. We bought a ton of those games and threw away everything but the trays; it was cheaper to do that than vacuform our own."

Ten "commercial screens" in all were either manufactured or scavenged by EEG, in a variety of sizes. These ranged from eight inches by ten inches to ones six feet high and four feet wide. The EEG *BR* commercials (providentially directed by Dryer, a man not unused to such assignments) were subsequently thrown by 35mm projectors onto EEG's Doodle Ball screens, which had been physically slotted into the miniature cityscapes themselves.

At which point David Dryer suddenly interrupts any further information about *Blade Runner*'s special effects to make this personal statement:

"You know, there's something I'd like to clarify about that pill the geisha is swallowing in those advertisements. Because I have a copy of the Criterion laser disc of *BR*, and toward the end of that there's a supplement claiming that what the woman is swallowing is some kind of digestive aid. That is not correct. In fact, I remember seeing that and thinking, 'Where do these people come up with these things?'

"What happened," Dryer continues, "was that Ridley and I had a meeting where he told me, 'I want a bunch of phony oriental commercials where geisha girls are doing unhealthy things. Smoking, taking drugs or whatever. To kind of continue with the oppressive feeling

---

[6] According to Dryer, this building wasn't a model after all. "The building with the Asian billboard on the side of it was actually just a plain old black box. I had the model department guys run some fiber-optic lights through to jazz it up," *BR*'s cosupervisor of F/X points out. "We'd run out of the time and money to build any more miniature buildings at that point."

throughout the landscape.' So I made a quick conceptual decision that what the geishas were swallowing were birth control pills. This was strictly my idea—it seemed to make sense that birth control would be heavily advertised in such an overpopulated future."

Having gotten that particular burden off his chest, Dryer was next asked by this author if the EEG effects crew had ever come up with a pet name for all the various advertising screens cluttering up *Blade Runner*. "Well," Dryer says, laughing, "after Ridleyville, RidleyTubes, and Ridley's Inferno, why not RidleyVision?"

SPINNER TO POLICE HQ

Rick Deckard is now introduced to the audience while leaning against a display window, behind which numerous television sets portray images intentionally scrambled by Ridley Scott.[7] Next Deckard glances up toward the film's bizarre (four-foot-long, two-foot-high EEG-built model) "advertising blimp;" its RidleyVision screens flash such John Wash-designed graphics as "Best Future," "Breathe Easy," "All New," catchphrases used to advertise the Off-world colonies.

All of these sights are witnessed through *BR*'s ubiquitous curtain of rain and smoke. Yet rain and smoke have traditionally generated monumental obstacles for effects technicians, because their full-scale qualities are almost impossible to miniaturize. How were these problems avoided?

To begin, Dryer first decided *not* to employ the traditional method (simple double exposures) of layering rain into *BR* special effects shots. "Double exposures, just photographing rain against black and then laying it in on top of a scene, usually results in an all too obvious foreground 'curtain' between the viewer and the actors," Dryer says. "Therefore, Robert Hall, Dave Stewart, and I worked out formulas for double exposures and cover mattes that had never been done before, plus photographic tricks to make *BR*'s rain effects shots look more real.

---

[7]Two different video images were fed via off-camera three-quarter-inch tapedecks into the TV sets behind Ford. One was a "generic advertisement" created by David Dryer during his *BR* geisha girl shoot. The other was a clip from an older but genuine commercial Dryer had once worked on, showing a woman's hand holding a sunball.

Because we immediately realized that we had an enormous problem here, due to the fact that we had to photograph individual layers of rain and raindrops at different distances and specific angles for every rain shot we were dealing with in the film.

"So first Hall and I reasoned that the only way you can see rain at night is if it's backlit. To get this backlit effect, we'd do a partial composite of most of the elements in a scene—and with all the miniatures and mattes, there'd sometimes be thirty elements to a shot—and then pull a low-contrast black-and-white print off that composite. Then we'd take that low-contrast print, combine it with a low-contrast print of backlit rain effects we'd shot against black, and run both through the optical camera at the same time, to reexpose them as a single element on the optical composite negative.

"So now if there was an area in the background of a scene that was lighter, you could see rain in front of it. If it was a darker background, you wouldn't see as much rain. Almost every shot used this technique. Using a fine-grain black-and-white stock for the rain shots also helped, because we could then, by filtration, add whatever colors we might need to the rain to match the backlit colors of a particular scene. As soon as we did this the rain just dropped right back into the shot."

The black-and-white EEG rain shots themselves were filmed at two locations. One was at the Burbank Studios, in front of a darkened, isolated building, which was backlit with arcs and other bright lights. Rain machines were then suspended at a height of forty feet and dumped the water for the cameras. The majority of the rain effects, however, were shot in the EEG parking lot. One layer of rain was shot at a time, although as many as four layers of precipitation (including fore-, mid-, and background rain shots) wound up being composited in some shots.

As for *Blade Runner*'s special smoke effects, the solution for this technique sprang from a discarded rain idea. Dryer explains, "We were thinking of doing some actual water projections on little miniature screens to get the feeling of rain pattering down in an alleyway as you passed it. We never really did that, but we did end up shooting miniature smoke effects that way. Quite often, in fact. We'd fix up a little four-inch by five-inch screen into an area within a miniature set and make a pass to expose slow motion smoke effects on that card."

Following Deckard's arrest at the Noodle Bar by Gaff, both men take a journey above the L.A. streets in a flying police Spinner. Not only is this one of the most mesmerizing moments in the film, it was also one of *BR*'s longest and most complicated F/X sequences.

The scene begins in a full-scale Spinner occupied by Ford and Olmos, filmed on Warner Brothers' New York Street set. Then this sequence cuts back and forth between a miniature Spinner rising up from a model city set and live-action shots of Harrison Ford and James Olmos sitting within a full-scale Spinner cockpit mock-up.

Gaff's Spinner rises up from the street in a special-effects shot which incorporates miniature flying vehicles with model buildings.

As had already happened with the art department and the later full-scale, operational vehicles built by Gene Winfield, the star of EEG's miniatures department quickly became the police Spinner. Four different kinds of model police Spinners of varying sizes and capabilities were constructed for *Blade Runner*. One was a fifteen-inch version (used for many of the flybys over Hades and through the city), another was a three-and-a-half-inch version (used as one of the vehicles buzzing the precinct station), and the third-size model Spinner incorporated a number of tiny, one-inch miniatures that were placed on both the large-scale Pyramid enlargement section and the police headquarters roof.

But the most arresting model Spinner built for the film—the one seen lazily spiraling down to land atop the (miniature) police headquarters—was also *Blade Runner*'s largest and most complex miniature flying auto. Appropriately enough, this impressive construct was dubbed the "Hero" Spinner.

"'Hero' is miniature maker's jargon referring to any select model out of a group of models," Stetson said. "The 'beauty' model, in other words, the one that gets closest to the camera." At forty-five inches long and sixty-five pounds heavy, with a total construction cost of $50,000, the Hero Spinner incorporated a sophisticated variety of functions to become one of the most dazzlingly detailed miniatures ever built for a film.

"The original Syd Mead Spinner design indicated a number of capabilities and aerodynamic detailings, so we reproduced those on the model," Stetson goes on to say. "This included two lifting, winglike, fin-appearing side panels, plus two articulated rear panels that opened up like an insect rubbing its wings together. Also two wheel covers that rotated up or down, which happens when you see that shot of the Hero model flying down toward the Precinct Station. The Hero Spinner also had a dash that lit up just like the full-sized one, and included two large eighteen-inch-tall puppets representing the driver and passenger. These puppets' heads could move, and the driver puppet's arm moved to rotate the steering wheel. In fact, the Hero Spinner did almost everything the real one could."

The Hero Spinner was mostly the work of Tom Phak, whom Stetson called "one of the best modelmakers in Hollywood," and of Bob Johnston. "Tom did most of the sculpting and pattern work," Stetson pointed out. "Sean Casey, who did the mold work on the whole show, actually cast the body. Johnston was responsible for all the mechanism work in the car, including seven axes of controlled motion and all the main motors, which ran through a series of gear boxes. Bill George was responsible for a lot of the interior detailing on the Hero Spinner, as was Tom Phak. George sculpted the passenger and driver figures, while Tom did most of the work on the exterior. The graphics were worked up as sort of a press-on tech kit—high-quality decals, if you will."

Although the final Hero Spinner was indeed impressive, it is really only seen in the film for one brief touchdown scene atop police HQ. "But a sequence like that landing is enough of a payoff to justify building a model that you really only notice for one shot," Stetson concludes.

Additionally, other model airborne cars were constructed for *Blade Runner*. "The miniature department also built some flying cars that weren't police cruisers," Stetson explains. "These vehicles were only used as background detailing for the introductory Hades sequence and Deckard's flight to the Tyrell Pyramid.

"Three background vehicles were made," Stetson continues, "all by Bill George, in a week and a half. Billy worked with Chris Ross on the look of those. But since there was nothing crucial about them, very little design work was done; George started out with some vacuform patterns, made shells, and then the vehicles themselves. They were eighteen inches long."

Yet it was the fifteen-inch police Spinner that was used for the shot of Gaff and Deckard lifting off from the city street near the Noodle Bar. A high overhead shot next reveals a number of model buildings surrounding it. One, at upper screen right, was a structure which had been cast from the same mold used for the police headquarters building miniature (which will be explained in a moment), but was put into this scene without the intricate detailing applied to that latter structure. Another, in lower screen right, was the same building used to represent Leon's "Yukon" Hotel later in the film—the EEG modelmakers simply switched around the small letters on the miniature electric sign atop the hotel to read "Nuyok" instead.

Which leads to a discussion of the miniature *BR* city buildings, a major effects project in itself.

"Way back when Greg Jein first pulled out of the project," commented Mark Stetson, "the construction of the model city began. It was an assignment that stretched well into the same time period as the live-action shoot on the Burbank lot."

Blade Runner's miniature buildings started with a series of designs by *BR* special projects consultant Wayne Smith. "Wayne cruised down Wilshire Boulevard in Los Angeles and shot some buildings that caught his fancy, in terms of ease of construction and interesting detail," Stetson said. "Wayne really created the miniature buildings on his own, although he did get some ideas from a series of renderings by Larry Paull and David Snyder on the mood of the thing."

Smith then hired Jerry Allen to foreman the construction of buildings, which had been planned from the beginning as crucial factors in the "Spinner Ride to Police Headquarters" sequence (whose general design concept had originally come from Ridley Scott). With a crew of six, Allen built a dozen buildings ranging in scale from one-half inch to one-quarter inch to the foot. A few other miniature buildings were also bought from local L.A. modelmaker Rick Price, structures that had been originally built for television commercials.

The largest of this first set of *BR* buildings topped eight feet. Stetson and his crew also retrofitted the structures by covering their surfaces with a variety of "nurnies," an old modelmaker's term for "meaningless details."

However, after spending months building these miniature build-ings, there was an abrupt and major change in direction. "The shot we're all proud of is the initial flight through the city and over the precinct station," Dryer says. "But that changed considerably in scale and conception as it evolved. Our miniature buildings were originally done on a much larger scale, and the original miniature set was a forced-perspective street with a building at the far end to cut off the horizon. But around April of 1981, all that went out the window."

Stetson elaborates: "When Ridley came down to see the first setup we'd made of the miniature buildings, he didn't like it. Period. He'd changed his mind on the overall concept. Instead of the depths of the city, which is essentially what we'd been asked to produce and is what he already had on the Burbank New York Street set, Ridley wanted to go into megastructures. Huge buildings that had been erected on pre-existing structures. It all would have been more organized if this approach had been planned from the beginning. But Ridley literally came in and decided on this new direction after the city was complete, on the stage, and set up for a shot. We were really caught with our pants down. It was pretty depressing."

After Scott's bombshell, Stetson and his modelmaking crew "went bananas. We had to move very fast. We literally grabbed any shape or large leftover or bit of cylindrical tubing we could get our hands on and turned it into a building." Compared to the first set of buildings, these miniatures were drastically reduced in size, yet still imparted a larger megastructure feeling and invoked a greater sense of vastness in the shots. For example, what was supposed to be a 500-story build-ing was actually a miniature only four feet high.

Thirty of these smaller structures were then constructed. Some of the "buildings," however, were only preformed grid patterns backed with paper, through which holes had been punched. Backlighting then transformed these flat surfaces into windows and other building light sources.

The EEG Smoke Room was then filled with these "second genera-tion" buildings in a sort of free-form, building-block set (most of these cityscape sequences were directed by David Dryer and David Jordan, with Bob Spurlock a key member of the stage crew). For certain angles and aerial perspectives buildings were set on their sides, mak-ing them appear vertical to the camera's eye (as in the POV shot of Gaff's Spinner landing on top of police HQ). The EEG Icebox system was then used to shoot all of these sequences.

All of the preceding effects elements—motion-controlled Spinners, miniature buildings, and RidleyVision, came together in what was known on the EEG stages as "FX Shot 19." It is that shot that has the camera looking directly between Ford and Olmos and out of the Spinner's windshield as they fly through the city.

The resulting image contained a full block of twenty miniature buildings (whose perspective had been matched to a eight-by-ten-inch slide of projected Syd Mead landscape art). On top of this image were laid RidleyVision screens, random city lights, strobes, searchlights, and a number of other flying vehicles coming both toward and away from the camera. All told, FX Shot 19 utilized thirty-five separate elements in a single shot. It also required the use of a full-scale Spinner cockpit mock-up.

"The difficulty with that Spinner mock-up," Dryer explains, "was that we were forced by a scheduling problem to go in and shoot the mock-up interiors with Ford and Olmos and *then* provide the background views for what was going on outside the windows. It would have been much easier for us to have shot those using rear or front projection with the actors during principal photography."

To solve this problem, the EEG Spinner interiors were first shot onstage with the actors and a 65mm camera, incorporating live interactive lighting coming in through the windows and playing over the faces of Ford and Olmos to suggest they were passing outside light sources. The mock-up Spinner's panel lights were also turned on, but, interestingly, it was decided not to channel video imagery into the full-scale cockpit's monitors during the shoot; this was because the cockpit was so confined that it was physically impossible to pipe the video in. Rather than fight the lack of space, Dryer decided to later matte in the cockpit monitor imagery.

This matted-in, full-sized Spinner dashboard monitor imagery was later shot separately on EEG's Compsey machine. A large, horizontal animation stand (a backlit device on which artwork is photographed one frame at a time), the Compsey (short for Computer Operated Motion Picture System) had been built by Douglas Trumbull for use in *Star Trek: The Motion Picture*. It utilized a twelve-channel motion-control system, with both a joystick and manual control, and featured numerous extras (many specialized photographic tools, plus yaw, pan, tilt, etc.). The Compsey motion-control system could also make the artwork panels inserted on it move horizontally or vertically for rear and front projection, provide top- and backlighting facilities and, in general, supply anything needed to enhance the composited, animated art seen on the Spinner's interior monitors.

After shooting the live-action Spinner cockpit interiors and compositing the art for its monitors, EEG now sat down to plan how to show the scenery passing outside the cockpit. By this time the various miniature components of the city's landscape had been photographed and composited. But how would audiences be convinced that they were seeing real rain and megastructures passing by the Spinner's windshield?

David Dryer explains. "First we did a number of optical tricks whereby we could reference the live-action footage of Harrison and Olmos in the cockpit to the special effects that were going to be seen outside the windshield. We then simply set up, on stage, a full-size Spinner windshield, which was steadied by metal stands and set into the exact camera registration which had been established during the live-action shoot. In front of this Plexiglas shield we erected a very large rear projection screen on which we ran the composite opticals of the flight over and through the city. The camera simply shot through the windshield and saw the large composites on the screen. For further verisimilitude I tried to correctly time the miniature searchlights on the screen with the interactive lighting we'd done during the live shoot. And we also used little air-guns to splatter water on the windshield and suggest that ever-present acid rain. All of this was later matted into the live-action shot."

Now came the capper to Deckard and Gaff's effects-laden flight through the night skies of 2019 Los Angeles: their Spinner's beautiful descent onto police HQ's roof.

"Some people think we used real air-traffic control patterns on that touchdown, but we didn't. We did try to make it look interesting, though," says David Dryer. "Basically, we filmed the Hero Spinner as a stand-alone shot on the Icebox system and added everything we could think of in terms of motion-control pitch and yaw and roll. Then we composited that footage over previously shot film of the precinct station model and model buildings around it."

"A fellow named Chris Ross did the original pattern for the shape of the police headquarters building, which scaled out at one-quarter inch to the foot," says Stetson. "One pattern repeated seven times gave us most of the shape for the main structure. The rooftop, though, was a different story. That was made from a mold I had originally done for *Close Encounters: The Special Edition*, which is seen in that movie as this saucerlike ceiling Richard Dreyfuss stands under after he enters the Mothership. So what we basically had there was an available, on-the-shelf round mold, which made it easy for us to design the precinct station roof. We pushed a lot of fiber-optics through that to light its top, and then added a motorized Spinner landing ramp, which you can see sinking into the top of the roof as Gaff's Spinner comes in."

Amusingly, another very distinctive spacecraft also found its way into this part of the cityscape. "Bill George had been making a replica of the *Millennium Falcon*, Han Solo's ship from the *Star Wars* movies, for his own amusement," Stetson explained. "It was about five feet tall. At the time we were so frantic to get more buildings into the cityscape that we grabbed Bill's ship, bristled it with etched brass, and plopped it into different shots. Instant building.

"If you want to pick out the *Falcon* in that Hero Spinner landing sequence, look at the first of the two separate model shots making up that scene," Stetson concludes. "The *Millennium Falcon* is right in the mid-foreground of the frame. In fact, the camera flies right over it during the beginning of that first shot. Just look for this little flashing blue Pan Am sign in the upper left of the frame at the start of that first shot, before the Hero Spinner starts coming in for a landing. The big, dark pointy building dead center in the foreground is the *Millennium Falcon*." *(A* Dark Star *model spaceship was also used as a building behind the Asain billboard.)*

SUNRISE AT TYRELL'S

Inside Tyrell's Office, a cloudy morning sky reveals a slowly rising sun outside the room's immense picture window (a sun which has climbed a little higher into the sky every time the camera cuts back to any of the five shots showing the window). Also revealed are the tops of the Tyrell Pyramids, dwarfing the three human inhabitants—Rachael, Tyrell, and Deckard—going about their business within the office.

This "Sunrise at Tyrell's" sequence signals the appearance of the first impressive special effects sequences provided by Matthew Yuricich, *Blade Runner*'s chief matte artist—for more than half of the upper areas of the frame seen during the wide shots in Tyrell's office are actually paintings executed by Yuricich.

A longtime Douglas Trumbull associate, Matthew Yuricich (brother to Richard) has had a long and multicredited matte painting career. As early as 1956, Yuricich was painting mattes for the likes of *Forbidden Planet*; two decades later he provided the stunning matte work for *Close Encounters* (over 100 paintings!) as well as mattes for *Star Trek: The Motion Picture*. And in 1976, Yuricich won a Visual Effects/Special Achievement Academy Award for his work on *Logan's Run*.

For *Blade Runner*, however, Yuricich found his usual approach to matte paintings relegated to the production's backseat.

"I don't look on the *Blade Runner* paintings as real matte shots," Yuricich said to this writer in 1982. "Certain parties associated with the production would probably cut my throat for saying that, but I considered most of my *BR* paintings as an excuse to provide backgrounds for flying toys. Those mattes were necessary, granted, but not *primary*. When I ordinarily do a matte, like those in *Close Encounters*, it's because they *have* to be there. But what I did on *Blade Runner* was to really just lay out a background for the effects work going on in front of it."

Be that as it may, certain key *Blade Runner* scenes would not have been possible without Yuricich's contributions. Beginning in March 1981, Yuricich worked eight months on the project, providing twenty full mattes "and a lot of partial ones" for the project.

Yuricich was assisted on his *BR* labors by Rocco Gioffre, a talented young matte painter whose own credits include such films as *Gremlins, Buckaroo Banzai, National Lampoon's Vacation* (for which he provided the "Wally World" mattes), *RoboCop, Cliffhanger,* and *Hook*. In Gioffre's own words, he had been hired as a *Blade Runner* "swing shift artist, after the production team went back and started to change some mattes that supposedly were already in the can. Rather than have Matthew stall out and proceed with the same shots all over again, I was hired to do this replacement work."

Gioffre's working hours were from 4 P.M. till midnight; among the *BR* matte paintings on which both he and Yuricich labored was the famous shot of Deckard dangling by one hand from a rooftop girder above a deserted city street.

"A young woman named Michele Moen was also very helpful in making the matte paintings come alive," Gioffre adds. "She was the artist who came up with all the interesting little details that were inserted into the paintings, like sparkling lights or water reflections and glowing neon signs. Michele worked closely with matte cameramen Robert Bailey and Tama Takahashi to add all those bells and whistles. They really helped sell those mattes."

As for the matte work seen in Deckard's initial meeting with Rachael in Tyrell's office, this scene had originally been visualized as a front-projected sequence set up on the Burbank soundstage while live-action photography was taking place. A plate of the miniature pyramid was to have been thrown forward and seen behind the actors, making it look as if the top of the building was looming over them outside (to simulate sunlight streaming in the window, a number of yellow-gelled arc lights were simultaneously hung over the set).

But the final result was deemed unsatisfactory. "It was decided right from the start that I'd have to put a painting in there," Yuricich recalled, "to mask out all the lights they had hanging up near the top of the set. But then the front projection didn't turn out the way Doug or Ridley wanted, and they weren't happy with that. So in I went with my paintbrush. Very little of that scene is now a set. I ended up having to repaint most everything just above the actors' heads, including most of the columns in Tyrell's office, the ceiling, the sky, and the right wall."

The rising sun seen through Tyrell's office window was a (John Wash) animated effect, also done at EEG. But since Yuricich had already been notified that this animated sun would be laid in over his painting, the matte artist had previously composed colorations around the area where the sun would be inserted, giving this portion of his matte painting subtle butterscotch-tinted gradations that were later married to Wash's animated artwork.

Which leads to a basic question: how did Yuricich do his *Blade Runner* mattes?

Interestingly, all the *BR* matte paintings had first been designed by Syd Mead, who laid transparent paper over photographs of the live-action sequences needing matte paintings and then painted watercolored

The interior of Tyrell's Office during filming . The painted backdrop outside the window will later be used as a guide for the insertion of a Matthew Yuricich special effects painting.

scenes around them as guides for Yuricich's actual mattes. "As for my paintings themselves, those were rendered on pieces of masonite board seven feet long and three feet high," Yuricich explained. "And one of the ways I determined where the painting was going to be inserted in a shot was to request a live-action frame-clip from the scene. I then projected that clip like a slide onto a white board and drew a line over the projected image where the matte itself would be inserted."

Final detailing on the Tyrell office window shots included some multilevel clouds that were seen outside the window, painted by Yuricich and then photographed on the EEG Compsey system. At one point Tyrell also "lowers a blind" on the window by polarizing the photosensitive glass to darken and cut down on the incoming light; this effect was achieved during postproduction at EEG, through the use of animation F/X (to show the shade coming down).

"There was also supposed to be a fairly arresting miniature special effect seen through that window in Tyrell's office," adds Ivor Powell. "That was going to be a front-projected model of a large Spinner, landing on a pad outside the window as Rachael walked across the room toward Deckard. But EEG never completed that shot, because there already was a big rush going on for other effects material. Ridley was very disappointed by this exclusion; he now felt the scene didn't have the visual detailing he thought it should. To compensate, he put in all those water reflections you see shimmering on the walls and furniture of Tyrell's office and on the actors' faces."

DECKARD'S APARTMENT

After finding Zhora's snake scale in Leon's tub, Deckard drives his sedan back home for some well-deserved rest. His car pulls out of L.A.'s 2nd Street tunnel and then into the Ennis-Brown House's driveway. Only the first story and overhanging balcony of this structure are genuine; everything above the building's lower story is a Matthew Yuricich matte painting, which shows Deckard's apartment building towering up into the sky and huge megastructures looming behind it in the distance.

Yuricich's painting was further augmented by a number of other special effects tricks. Miniature rain and smoke F/X were composited in after principal photography, for instance, and a sweeping spotlight seen in the upper right of the frame as Deckard enters the driveway was separately photographed in EEG's Smoke Room and optically added to the shot. Finally, another "geisha billboard" commercial was also composited into this matte, to appear in the far distance in the upper middle of the frame.

After Deckard is in his apartment and Rachael storms out, leaving behind her childhood photograph, Deckard picks up the picture. A close-up of this photo then reveals Rachael as a youngster sitting next to her "mother" on a shadow-dappled porch—and demonstrates once again Scott's obsessive use of "layering." Suddenly, the shadows on the porch begin *moving*, as the viewer hears the dim sound of laughing children on the soundtrack.

This startling effect was easily acquired, according to Ridley Scott and Terry Rawlings. "That still photograph was actually part of some motion footage shot on the Warner back lot using a chosen pair of extras to represent Sean and her mum," says Ridley Scott. "As for the way the photograph moved," continues Terry Rawlings, "first we shot those extras sitting on a porch as a live-action scene. Then, one frame of that footage was chosen to be blown up as a still photograph. That's the snapshot you see Harrison and Sean carrying around.

"But you'll also notice that when Ridley cuts to a close-up of that photo, just before it moves, the angle is so tight you can't see the borders of the snapshot. That's because it *isn't* a snapshot you're looking at then. What we'd done was cut to a freeze-frame close-up of the same bit of live-action footage chosen for the photograph. Ridley then allowed that freeze-frame to naturally roll forward into the live-action, which is where the 'photograph' comes alive. The shadows you see waving across the porch are the same shadows that were cast on the extras during the Burbank shoot.

"Those freeze-frames were done during postproduction in London," Rawlings concludes, "by a man named Peter Govey, who, I think, also worked with Ridley on *Legend*."

After watching Rachael's photograph move, Deckard now walks out onto the balcony of his apartment to idly regard a canyonlike, urban vista far below. The live-action part of this shot was filmed on a "balcony set" located within a soundstage at the Burbank Studios. During live-action filming, an off-camera spotlight was swept across the set and later carefully matched to a cel-animated searchlight which plays across the balcony of Deckard's apartment as he leans out to look over the city.

Much of the left side of this shot was further augmented by a detailed Syd Mead-designed/Matthew Yuricich-executed matte painting. But, as Douglas Trumbull explains, there was also much more here in the way of special effects.

"Throughout *Blade Runner* there are a number of what I call 'enhanced matte paintings,' which means that not only the live-action footage and matte painting are there, there are also miniatures plus special lighting effects plus miniature rear projection," Trumbull says. "The shot of Deckard going out on the balcony of his apartment at night is a good example of that; you have not only the live-action plate, but a shot of the street below, flying vehicles, and movement on the street itself. That's definitely an enhanced matte painting."

Some of the enhancements which EEG added to this shot were the optical compositing of a small Spinner model seen flying above the street and a number of animated effects rendered on the Compsey animation stand. Yet David Dryer was still not satisfied with the final result. "I always had problems with that shot," Dryer says. "What I'd wanted was this incredible feeling of depth, from foreground to background. But that shot kept looking two-dimensional, and still does today."

THE BRADBURY

More enhanced matte paintings are on display during the scene where Pris approaches Sebastian's decrepit apartment building. These are seen when Daryl Hannah walks down the street toward the Bradbury Building and a wide shot reveals a vast futuristic cityscape beside and behind this structure.

Like the master shots seen in Tyrell's office, only part of Pris' scene here incorporated live-action footage; specifically, the street-level action, the first two stories of the Bradbury, and the building to the right of it (which, in a clever move, had its genuine neon sign reading "Canada" retouched in Yuricich's matte to read "Nada" instead). But while these elements are real, everything else is either a miniature or another Yuricich matte painting.

A closer examination of this scene reveals the following: Pris crosses the street as a (real) truck lumbers past her. At the same moment, a miniature/composited Spinner glides close by overhead, its searchlight casting interactive illumination on the right side of the frame (animated lighting effects). Michele Moen also added extra illumination here by painting in a stronger glow around the two Trafficators seen on the left and right sides of the frame.

"There was also supposed to be another elaborate matte painting seen in that sequence where Pris is walking toward the Bradbury," explains Rocco Gioffre. "That never made it to the final cut. Originally there was going to be this high-angled matte shot looking down on Pris passing by the Million Dollar Movie Marquee. Then you'd realize that the street she was walking on was really only the top layer of this incredibly deep, multilayered freeway system. Because you were going to see big vents in the street revealing this dense stack of high-speed freeway ramps beneath her.

"Now, some work was done on that. What the live-action crew had done while they were on location in downtown L.A. was to get up on a roof across from the Bradbury and shoot some footage looking straight down at Pris walking below. Then Matthew had painted a detailed matte of the area surrounding her—the vents and freeway ramps—and a guy named Glen Campbell, who was one of the EEG cameramen, had added in some straight-animation-type cars driving along those ramps. But that shot was never used. Part of the reason was because it was too dark, even though Matt Yuricich had painted in this little pool of light from a street lamp that Pris passed under so you could see her better. Matthew did the same trick on *Forbidden Planet*, by the way, when the spacemen are getting a tour of all this gigantic Krel machinery, and a spotlight blinks down on them so you can pick their bodies out from this mass of giant mechanisms."

One F/X shot which *did* survive the final cut is when Pris pauses before the Bradbury, looks up, and sees the blimp passing lazily overhead (as they had already done with the Spinners, most of the actual model blimp photography was accomplished by EEG cameramen Don Baker and Tim McHugh). A few minutes later, however, when Pris enters the Bradbury with Sebastian, the replicant again looks up—this time while standing in the Bradbury's atrium—to see the blimp eerily passing behind the (real) multipaned window set high on the atrium's roof.

In order to pull off this brief F/X shot, EEG still lab member Virgil

Morano came up with a comparatively simple solution. Morano first visited the Bradbury Building and took a large-format still photograph of the atrium window. A positive print of this shot was then affixed to a thick piece of glass, and all the spaces between the many atrium panes on the photograph were carefully cut away from the print. Next, this glass pane and photograph were attached to the front of EEG's motion-controlled camera rig, so that they moved as the camera did. The end result was that, although the blimp model itself remained stationary, the resulting footage from the moving camera shot through the glass pane suggested that the blimp was drifting behind the areas cut out from the photograph.

THE ESPER

Meanwhile, back in Deckard's apartment, Ford is subjecting Leon's photograph to a digital scan through his Esper machine (a prop built under the supervision of EEG employee Mike Fink).

The many flash-and-fade stills which comprise this segment had originally been shot by Trumbull's EEG team. "Doug had this little stage built right off the side of the Tyrell office set," recalls David Dryer, "which was supposed to represent the area seen in Leon's photograph: two and a half small, interconnecting hotel rooms. The far room had a mirror reflecting its other side, the side you couldn't see. Which had another mirror reflecting this little alcove that couldn't be seen from the first room, either. That whole setup was lit by Ridley to look like the paintings of Vermeer and Edward Hopper.

"Then we sat Rutger down in a chair at a table with his back to the camera. The original idea was that Batty had been turning his head when Leon took his snapshot, so his face would be blurred. Since we were shooting that sequence with a still camera, we set the shutter for a five-second exposure for that particular shot to make sure Rutger's movements would look appropriately blurry."

Utilizing a motorized Nikon still camera which had been attached to a platform, which in turn rested on a camera dolly, the EEG technicians then pushed the Nikon through the "Leon's Photograph" set. As they moved the EEG cameramen panned and tilted and shot from a number of different angles, while always making sure that they still-photographed the all-important mirror reflections that would ultimately reveal a hidden Zhora and her sequined dress. For those parts of the set seen in extreme close-up (a whiskey bottle, two glasses, a fan), a separate series of large 8x10 still transparencies were shot.

All these stills were then rephotographed, in sequence, on motion picture film, and tied together by Don Baker on the Compsey animation stand, with John Wash adding the numerous coordinate points, crosshairs, zooming rectangles, and blue flashes that are seen throughout the Esper sequence. The resulting footage was transferred to videotape and fed into the Esper monitor which Ford watches during the Esper scene itself.

However, once principal photography shut down in Los Angeles and Ridley Scott moved to England to complete *Blade Runner's* post-production phase, the director decided he wasn't satisfied with certain aspects of EEG's Esper scene and ordered a selective reshoot. These were done by the London-based Filmfex and Lodge/Cheesman. Among the changes were a rethinking of Batty's head blur (the first photograph now shows the replicant simply sitting still at a table, with his back to the camera), and the various reshooting of certain close-ups.

"What people don't realize about that Esper scene is that when Deckard's computer reveals Zhora, the Zhora they see isn't Joanna Cassidy!" says Michael Deeley, laughing. "Neither are some of the shots of what's supposed to be Rutger Hauer. We used stand-ins there, both during the original filming and the reshoot in London. I can't remember which shots aren't of Hauer *[neither can the actor himself—this author asked],* but I can definitely tell you that the woman you see lounging in bed with that snake tattoo isn't Joanna, in any shot *[Joanna Cassidy confirms this].*[8]

"But that whole Esper scene was very difficult to do. We never really had the proper money to go high-tech with it. Of course, today you could probably do it on a home computer."

One final tidbit here: as stated elsewhere in this book, the "hardcopy" photograph which Deckard receives from the Esper of Zhora's face and snake tattoo does not match the angle seen on the Esper monitor. "You know something?" says Terry Rawlings. "We never noticed that at the time we did the shot—not until all the *Blade Runner* fans called our attention to it. Chalk that up to another 'technical error'!"

---

[8]This author has also been unable to ascertain the names of the two doubles who stood in for Cassidy and Hauer.

ELEVATOR TO HELL ―――――――――――――――――――

After Batty, Sebastian, and Pris share their tense breakfast in J. F.'s apartment, Roy persuades the prematurely aging genetic designer to take him to Tyrell. The pair begin their journey up the side of an elevator on the Tyrell Pyramid.

The miniature, motorized elevator seen here had been constructed on the "Pyramid enlargement model," which also held the Interrogation Room and Tyrell's office (when the elevator stops at the top of the structure, Tyrell's miniature office and bedroom can be glimpsed at screen left, represented by a long narrow window illuminated by four lights). According to Mark Stetson, "If you could examine the bracing on those model elevator cars, you'd find they were in the shape of two Ms. 'MM' for Michael McMillian, the miniature maker who constructed them."

Of course, not all of *Blade Runner*'s special effects were limited to the arcane province of EEG's miniature department or Smoke Room; some were accomplished live, on set, utilizing traditional and time-tested techniques. One such effect dealt with the death of Eldon Tyrell.

Before explaining this effect, however, one first must understand that Ridley Scott had been well aware of the criticism leveled against

The EEG special effects camera crew shoots a miniature elevator climbing up the side of the Tyrell Pyramid. This elevator was located on a separate, larger-scale section of the Pyramid built by EEG's model crew, under the supervision of Mark Stetson.

what some saw as *Alien*'s overuse of gory shock effects (a criticism which does not hold water when one realizes how much of *Alien*'s violence was actually only *suggested* and not shown). Also, there had been a critical (mis)perception that *Alien* was populated with two-dimensional characters (proving that the subtle complexity of that film's performances had been lost on many reviewers).

Therefore, Scott had doggedly imbued *Blade Runner*'s characters with a conscious examination of their *human* qualities—an effort which, ironically, was later undercut by Ford's laconic and unnecessary on-screen narration. Even more interesting was Scott's ambiguous handling of *Blade Runner*'s one ultraviolent touch: Tyrell's murder.

"For the moment when Tyrell's head is crushed between Batty's hands," Scott said, "we had originally thought of solely focusing on the full-scale prosthetic Tyrell head manufactured by Michael Westmore, which had been packed with foam and latex brains. We indeed shot that, but then mostly cut it out of the American release. Instead, Joe Turkel was provided with a number of tubes filled with studio blood running through his hair, and after Batty started to put his thumbs into the latex head's eyes, we cut to a two-shot of Rutger and Joe where you could see the blood running off the real actor's head. This floor effect was quite convincing. As it turned out, we even had to cut back on the live-action shot a bit, because audience reaction during the sneak previews was a bit negative."

In order to replicate a lifelike *duplicate* of Joe Turkel's head, Michael Westmore first "did a total life cast off of him. What that means is that when Joe came over to the shop I had in Studio City then, we sat him down in a chair and packed soft dental-alginate all around his head. Turkel breathed through two straws we had in his nose sticking through this substance.

"Now, you might think having his head encased in warm plastic would've freaked Turkel out, but it didn't. In fact, very few men or women who have this procedure done for them for a movie—and there've been a lot of them—do get upset. Most of the ones who freak out, strangely enough, are the macho-type guys, who all of a sudden get very scared and concerned.

"Anyway, this whole casting procedure only took about an hour. Then, once the alginate hardened, we split it in half," Westmore continues. "In effect, we now had a positive impression of Turkel's head. A mold, in two pieces. We'd only cast him down to his collar area, because Ridley had told us he'd have his camera in much tighter than that.

"We now joined together those two alginate pieces and filled them with a silicon substance, which hardens up as a tough solid, to act as this head's understructure. Next, around this silicon 'skull,' we applied a fleshlike, latex liquid rubber to suggest Tyrell's facial skin. We then painted that to match Joe's own skin coloration, and added a proper wig and eyebrows—hair by hair. The final touch was a pair of glass eyes. Which you really can't see in the film, because Rutger's thumbs are in there!"

Westmore's final touch was hollowing out the brain-pan of Turkel's unnervingly realistic artificial head and inserting thin-walled blood bags behind the dummy's eyes, which Rutger Hauer could puncture with his thumbs. David Dryer notes, "Michael Westmore's artificial Tyrell head was full of all kinds of goodies. It was very realistic. In fact, it sat on my desk at EEG for a month. Every morning when I'd come in to work, there it would be, staring at me."

After killing Tyrell as well as Sebastian (offscreen), Batty then descends in the pyramid's elevator, glancing up at the stars which can be seen through the elevator's glass-topped roof. Stars which, through the shocked and angry replicant's eyes, seem to be swimming in his gaze. "EEG did an old Hitchcockian-type trick there," says David Dryer. "We executed a motion-control dolly pull-back on a field of stars painted by John Wash and simultaneously zoomed in. That push-pull type of thing, which Hitchcock did so well in *Vertigo,* to suggest James Stewart's fear of heights. I had a gut feeling Ridley would like that type of effect; after all, Batty's looking up at the heavens where he came from—presumably his assignments were Off-world—and he's so emotional at that moment that he feels the stars closing around him as the elevator descends.

"In fact, that descent was the whole reason I got assigned to this picture in the first place. During my first meeting with Ridley, after Doug Trumbull had nominated me as an effects supervisor, Scott was talking about this Batty elevator sequence and I said, 'Oh, I get it. It's Orpheus, descending into Hell.' Ridley stopped for second, turned around and looked up at me, and said, 'We're going to get along just fine.'"

THE SHOWDOWN ─────────────────────────────

It is during the final Deckard/Batty chase that EEG's matte painting department was given its widest exposure, for no less than nine different paintings were used starting from the moment when Deckard first bursts through the window of Sebastian's apartment and scampers onto the Bradbury's ledge.

Most of these vertiginous matte shots are either of the street in front of the Bradbury as seen from a great height, or wide cityscapes of the surrounding metropolis and Bradbury Building. The majority were painted by Matthew Yuricich; however, two mattes (including the dizzying view seen when Deckard cautiously inches around the outer corner of the Bradbury near a flutelike stone projection) were solely executed by Rocco Gioffre.

Another of these Gioffre mattes has an interesting history. The painting proper is seen after Deckard has climbed up the outer wall of the building and reached the momentary safety of the Bradbury's roof; to the left of the detective is a dark, claustrophobic shot of the city's ancient buildings hulking in the night. "The way Syd Mead originally designed that shot, however," Gioffre explains, "didn't look anything like the final matte. Syd had initially come up with the idea that when Harrison Ford picks himself up from that puddle he's crawled into on the roof, the audience would see this bright, broad expanse of the city that went on for miles and miles beside him, with two huge, pillarlike buildings in the middle framing an even bigger structure on the horizon. But that design was rejected by Ridley as looking too open—he wanted the viewer to feel like Harrison was really trapped at that point. There were also some concerns that these futuristic buildings in the background made too sharp a contrast with the antiquated one Ford was crawling on. So I painted a darker shot with all these old buildings hemming him in."

As previously mentioned, the matte-painting shot of Harrison Ford holding onto a girder and dangling above a far-below street was jointly painted by Yuricich and Gioffre. However, this painting posed certain technical problems for the EEG crew during the live-action shoot.

"We had to get a matte of the street below Ford's dangling feet," Dryer says, "but the live action set was not prepared to give us the materials we needed to draw that matte. So we simply laid a white foam core beneath Harrison hanging from that three-story rooftop set on the Warner lot, then got a careful photographic exposure of the difference between the white foam core and the exposure on Harrison's pants legs. Later, through a combination of high-contrast printing, some cleaning up, and a little bit of rotoscoping, we were able to get a pretty clean matte off that shot.[9]

"Another difficult aspect of this shot concerned the 65mm camera we were using," Dryer continues. "It was the Mitchell number three, the third one old man Mitchell *[inventor of the Mitchell camera, one of the mainstays of the film industry]* ever made, and it weighed about seventy-five pounds. So there was an engineering problem involved in getting that camera to look straight down on Ford and not pose a safety hazard to the actor. With that kind of weight cantilevered out over Harrison, there was always a risk that the camera would break a casting and come right down on him. Which Michael Deeley was just a little bit concerned about. So we rigged a special plate and support to get that camera actually looking back down over itself more than ninety degrees to parallel. Then we took that footage and composited it into a Matt Yuricich matte painting, which covered up the fact that Harrison was only twenty feet off the ground instead of over a hundred."

Yet with all these impressive cityscapes and vertiginous shots of wet city streets, Rocco Gioffre feels that the best *Blade Runner* matte painting shots are the ones that its viewers don't notice. "The mattes that really work are the subtle ones," Gioffre concluded. "For example, there's a low-angle shot of Rutger Hauer leaping across the two roofs during that final chase, and in the upper distance, where you're looking up behind him, Matthew added some buildings. That was done because the original photography looked too black. But I also think it's a nice matte touch—hardly anyone notices that that painting is there. It lends a lot of feeling to that shot."

END OF THE F/X

By the time *Blade Runner* wrapped, the originally proposed thirty-eight F/X shots had risen to a total of ninety. These were cut down in

---

[9]A rotoscope is a device that projects single frames to be rephotographed or to be traced by hand in the production of artwork or animation details.

Harrison Ford dangles high above an L.A. street at Blade Runner's *climax; the street below is a matte painting done by Matthew Yuricich and Rocco Gioffre.*

editing, however, to approximately sixty-five. "Though our price tag for all those shots rose a bit during production, to about $3.5 million," explained David Dryer, "every overage had been prerequested and approved before we spent any additional money.[10] And we ultimately came within $5000 of our final budget. That's pretty remarkable, given the size of the picture and everything that went into it. Not to mention that astronomical F/X budget overruns are far too common in this business."

"I feel that the whole process of making a movie is a special effect," said Douglas Trumbull, when asked for his definition of the F/X term. "Because the basic concept of motion pictures—a series of still photographs projected in rapid succession—*is* a special effect.

"The kind of work that I find most challenging, however, is what we call photographic effects. That's really pushing the art form to its ultimate leading edge. Given the circumstances, I think we partially achieved that on *Blade Runner*. But I look forward to further challenges. To really be able to create illusions that are significantly advanced from anything anybody's ever done is something I find very exciting."

Ironically, *Blade Runner* was Douglas Trumbull's second-to-last theatrical motion picture assignment. While the director/effects ace

---

[10]Part of *Blade Runner*'s effects budget went to the then new but now well-established Dream Quest, Inc., a special effects company which supplied some of the animated readouts seen on the film's many video screens and monitors.

next went on to direct and supply the special effects for 1983's *Brainstorm,* this project was fraught with such internal political bickering—not to mention the tragic passing of its female lead, Natalie Wood, who accidentally drowned during a hiatus in the production—Trumbull decided to quit the motion picture business and concentrate instead on supplying theme parks and hotels with amusements and special visual presentations. One of these attractions was the Trumbull-designed "Back to the Future" ride at Universal Studios; his latest achievement is a multimedia thrill ride installed in the Las Vegas-based Luxor Pyramid.

And what are David Dryer's feelings concerning the *Blade Runner* effects? "Making them was heaven and hell," *BR*'s F/X supervisor recalls. "We took everything we did very seriously, worked incredible hours and, I think, produced some lasting work. It was also an excruciatingly painful experience; there was a lot of tension going on behind the scenes the general public wasn't aware of.

"But all in all, I'm very happy with the final film."

POSTPRODUCTION
AND THE MUSIC

The music in Blade Runner *is so devastatingly beautiful. Yet at the same time it is many other things. Tacky, ominous, haunting, sad. Vangelis did an extraordinary job; his score became a major character.*

—RUTGER HAUER

PRINCIPAL WRAPS—POST BEGINS

Work on *Blade Runner*'s special effects wrapped on December 19, 1981. Yet the film was far from finished; Scott and company now had to focus on postproduction.

Strictly speaking, postproduction means any work done on a film after shooting is completed. In reality, post is that period during which a motion picture's more technical elements—its sound effects, dubbing, special effects, color timing, music, and so forth—are created, manipulated, and added to the film.

Blade Runner's postproduction schedule was originally slated to begin on Monday, July 6, 1981, and last thirty-four weeks. During this time, everything from editing the picture, mixing its sound, redubbing dialogue, and shooting inserts (a close-up, short scene, or other shot which can be filmed after principal photography and "inserted" into a picture during its editing process) would be completed. However, *Blade Runner* was already sixteen days behind schedule because of the two-week reshoot which had spanned late March/early April. But since postproduction is a somewhat more flexible phase of filmmaking than principal photography, *Blade Run-*

ner's postwork began on July 13, only one week later than originally planned.[1]

Scott now found himself shuttling between back and forth between England and Los Angeles as he labored to finish his picture. Although the director made frequent visits to Trumbull's Marina Del Rey effects facility during this period, much of his time was spent in London. Here Scott concentrated on supervising *Blade Runner's* insert photography (begun during the first two weeks of October 1981, at both Pinewood and Elstree Studios, but sporadically returned to up until January of 1982), mixing the film's sound, and completing its editing (which was also done at Pinewood).

It's been said many times that a motion picture is made or broken in the editing room. *Blade Runner* was no exception. From July 13 through mid-September of 1981, Scott and editor Terry Rawlings laboriously pieced together a first assembly, a director's first cut, and a director's fine cut of *BR*.

But before any of this fine-tuning could take place, *Blade Runner's* director and editor first had to determine just what it was they were dealing with. And as Rawlings relates, the first screening of fully assembled *BR* footage was an unnerving one.

"After I'd finished my first assembly of the whole film, which at this point was simply a string of sequences cut into their proper order with whatever dialogue was usable, Ridley and I went into a screening room at Warner Brothers and ran the picture for ourselves," Rawlings recalls. "There were just the two of us.

"The entire time, we never said a word. Then, when the film finished and the lights came up, Ridley turned to me and said, 'God, it's marvelous. What the fuck does it all mean?'

"We knew then we had a lot of work to do to really get the audience to understand what was going on. Because this was a very difficult story to translate. Obviously, lots of decisions were going to have to be made in the editing room."

These decisions would include tightening, switching around, or completely restructuring entire sequences to make the film more

---

[1] The *completion* of postproduction would not end as originally scheduled, however. *Blade Runner's* post period was originally set to wrap March 8, 1982; instead, various problems kept Scott working on the picture for an additional two months. *BR*'s postproduction was finally completed near the end of May.

accessible to the general viewing public. Some of these edits were substantial (Scott's decision to drop the Holden Hospital scene, for instance), but some were more subtle.

For example, the scene where Roy Batty pushes a nail through his hand had originally been intended (and filmed) to occur *after* Batty slams his head through the flooded bathroom's wall. But Scott and Rawlings now decided it made more sense to suggest that Batty's nail-impalement had been the stimulus needed for the dying replicant to be able to smash his head through the wall in the first place.[2]

By late September 1981, Scott and Rawlings were satisfied that they had put together a much clearer rough cut of the picture. However, now the filmmakers faced a crucial deadline: the first screening of *Blade Runner* for Tandem Productions was only a few days away, but Rawlings and Scott hadn't yet found the time to do a temporary sound mix on the picture. This was an absolutely essential procedure; it would sweeten the dialogue, add a temporary music track, and generally make Tandem's first exposure to the assembled film that much more comprehensible.

"That temporary mix was the most whirlwind sound job I've ever done," remembers Terry Rawlings. "It really was amazing. Ridley and I went into a mixing theater owned by EMI at Elstree Studios on a Saturday, where we spent the whole day mixing two or three reels. Yet we had a total of about twelve reels to do!

"So I said to Ridley, 'Look, if you're going to maintain this sort of pace, we're never going to have anything to take back to the States with us.' Ridley said, 'All right.' The next day—Sunday—we finished *nine or ten reels* of temp tracks!

---

[2]Reediting this bit resulted in a continuity error, though. As originally filmed, Batty pulled his head out of the lavatory wall, entered the decaying bathroom, and taunted Deckard. Ford responded by smashing Hauer across the face with a lead pipe. The replicant then stumbled backward and accidentally broke a curtained window behind him with his elbow, at which point Deckard ran away and Batty pushed that nail through his hand.

Sharp-eyed viewers will now note, however, that when Batty does his nail-push in the final film, he's standing next to a broken, curtained window. And when Hauer looks down at the nail protruding through the back of his hand a moment later, one can clearly see the bathroom's yellow-and-black tiled wall at screen right. Yet Batty isn't *in* the bathroom! Finally, when Hauer then does enter the flooded lavatory, the same curtained window is intact—until he reels back and smashes it, of course.

"That was the most *exciting* experience. The boys in the sound effects department had cassettes and tapes streaming in from everywhere, and ultimately the whole mix was done on the fly. Yet it stood up very well, I think. In fact, some of those temp tracks were used on what you've been calling The Workprint, the one that was shown at the Nuart and Castro Theaters in California in 1991. And I honestly think that parts of that temp mix sounded better than what was done for the final film.

"That session also became one of those fantastic, exhilarating events one remembers the rest of their career," Rawlings concludes. "The sound boys who run that stage, in fact, still talk about that weekend to this very day."

Yet Rawlings and Scott's victory must have felt a hollow one, given the subsequent reaction to the picture at the first Tandem screening.

"It was a disaster," recalls Michael Deeley. "Bud and Jerry clearly loathed what they were seeing. I still have a comment sheet recording their reactions; some of the kinder remarks were 'Dull. Pointless. Confusing.' Matters didn't improve as we went along, either. On January 21, 1982, we ran the picture a second time for them. By this time an initial version of the voice-over had been laid in—which Ridley and I hadn't wanted on the picture anyway—but even this concession didn't work.

"Here's one Tandem comment—'Why is this voice-over track so terrible? He sounds drugged. Were they all on drugs when they did this?' And here's another, which is my favorite—'This movie gets worse every screening.' That's just the sort of thing one wants to hear after a year's work."

Although the Tandem relationship was now plainly deteriorating, Ridley Scott, according to Deeley, "didn't let the situation deter him. He just pulled his horns in and kept moving. Forward."

Another key contributor was about to move on. After watching his illustrational style help set the overall look of the film, Syd Mead left the *BR* team in September of 1981. "*Blade Runner* was an excellent experience," Mead said. "It was personally fulfilling, a genuine jolt, to see one of my designs constructed on the Burbank lot. Making movies is the way to showcase futuristic imagery. But, really, at the time I was just too close to my first full-scale filmic encounter to really appreciate its significance. Although I must say, I certainly enjoyed it."

Yet nature abhors a vacuum. So when one significant *Blade Runner* contributor left the project, another stepped forward to take his place.

VANGELIS

Evangelos O. Papathanassiou, better known to music and soundtrack aficionados by the name Vangelis (pronounced, incidentally, with a hard "g," as in "get"), was born March 29, 1943, in Volos, Greece. He was raised in Athens. A self-taught musician unable to read music, Vangelis composed his first piece, for piano, at the age of four. The musician quickly became adept at all types of keyboards and, at eighteen, joined the Greek rock band Formynx, in which he played a Hammond organ. Formynx quickly became Greece's first popular early-sixties rock group. But when a military dictatorship assumed power in his homeland in 1968, Vangelis moved to Paris.

Here he formed another band called Aphrodite's Child, a group that featured singer Demis Roussos, a popular European performer. (There is an interesting footnote here: Aphrodite's Child's first major hit was titled "Rain and Tears." If the order of those words is reversed, we're suddenly confronted with something very close to a famous utterance by Roy Batty: "Tears in rain.")

By now, Vangelis was gaining a reputation as a first-rate composer of electronic music, one whose mastery of the synthesizer went well beyond the primitive noodlings usually produced on that instrument during this period. This reputation served him in good stead when the Greek musician next began composing a number of scores for French TV and films in the 1970s. One such collaboration was with French "nature film" director Frederic Roussif, for whom Vangelis did the music for *Apocalypse Des Animaux* and *Opera Sauvage*. (*Sauvage*, in particular, remains one of Vangelis' most haunting and durable achievements.)

In the mid-seventies, Vangelis left Aphrodite's Child and moved to London. Here Vangelis both signed a recording contract with RCA and fulfilled a longtime ambition by building a self-contained twenty-four-track music studio (or "laboratory," as he calls it), Nemo Studios. Located near London's Marble Arch, Nemo was the location where Vangelis composed his music for *Blade Runner*; this same studio also witnessed the birth of some of the talented musician's most popular solo albums, which included *Heaven and Hell, China,* and *See You Later.*

At roughly the same time, Vangelis was recording albums with Jon Anderson, lead singer of the popular supergroup Yes. The composer subsequently stunned the rock world when he was offered—and turned down—the opportunity to replace Yes keyboardist Rick Wakeman, when Wakeman decided to leave that high-profile band.

Since then, Vangelis has contributed distinctive, highly melodic scores to well-received TV series like *Cosmos* and created over two dozen soundtracks for such film directors as Costa-Gavras (*Missing*), Roman Polanski (*Bitter Moon*), and Ridley Scott (*Blade Runner* and *1492: Conquest of Paradise*).

However, despite the amount of biographical information currently available on this man, Vangelis is actually an extremely private and serious musician who shuns the public limelight—which immediately presented a problem regarding this book.

Although Vangelis was certainly aware of *Future Noir* (and seemed to support it), he is also notoriously interview-shy, preferring to express himself through his music. Therefore, beyond some comments passed on through longtime associate Andrew Hoy (a British musician/Polydor Music employee who began working with the Greek composer in 1979, was present throughout the entire *BR* scoring process, and still spends virtually every day with the man), Vangelis declined to be questioned for this book.

However, numerous telephone calls and faxes to the musician's current home base in Athens *did* result in a wealth of information regarding *Blade Runner*'s soundtrack, much of which is now presented for the first time.

THE SCORE

"I never thought that we were going to use Vangelis to start with," recalls Terry Rawlings. "We tried different things at first . . . funnily enough, I initially listened to a lot of Jerry Goldsmith music while I was cutting *BR*. But I didn't realize what we were going to get from this picture, what Ridley was going to try and make. But, you know, when Ridley's visuals start coming out, everything changes. It always does."

Blade Runner's in-house musical expert had first met Vangelis while Rawlings was editing and Vangelis was composing his Oscar-winning score for 1981's *Chariots of Fire*. Their paths would professionally cross once again after Scott, who had been mulling over the choice of a suitable *BR* composer himself, invited Vangelis to watch a rough assembly of *Blade Runner* with the musician's manager, Jiannis Zographos.

According to sources, Vangelis was "thrilled and terrified" by what he saw at this screening. "Thrilled" because of the film's beauty, "terrified" because *BR* forecast what Vangelis thought to be a chillingly plausible future. Despite this visceral reaction, however, the Greek composer still had to decide whether he was actually going to accept the assignment of scoring Ridley Scott's new picture.

"Vangelis is very interested in film, but he is not a man who takes his scores or other work at all lightly," explains Andrew Hoy. "The first thing he always likes to do is to screen footage and put his nose in it, to try and get some sense of the film. What does it look like? What's it feel like? What stimulation is he getting from the images? After this, Vangelis' next requirement is a discussion with the director; it's important for him to see if he's able to get into the same areas his director's looking for.

"*Blade Runner* obviously met those criteria," Hoy adds. "My definite impression of why Vangelis decided to score the film was because *of* the film. Even in its unfinished state, Vangelis was immediately impressed with *Blade Runner*."

Having now emotionally committed himself to the project, the composer next began deciding which tonalities would best suit *Blade Runner*'s score. Ultimately, Vangelis settled on an overall mood which this author likes to think of as "futuristic nostalgia": a dizzying melange of unabashed romanticism, ominous electronic rumblings, gutter-level blues, delicate celestial shadings, and heartbreaking melancholy. In short, a groundbreaking, potent effort which still stands as one of the finest (and *saddest*) musical scores to ever envelop, uplift, and energize a science fiction film.

But through what methods were these moods arrived?

"At this stage of his musical development, which was from around 1978 through 1982, Vangelis was fascinated with percussion instruments," continues Andrew Hoy. "He was experimenting with mixing these with various synthesizers to achieve an acoustic-electronic effect. Gongs and bells lay everywhere; Vangelis used to collect them like a magpie."

Therefore, such percussion instruments as chimes became an integral part of *Blade Runner*'s music. Yet unlike his previous film, *Chariots of Fire,* which Vangelis had felt would benefit from a more traditional, orchestral-sounding score, *Blade Runner* posed completely different challenges. "*Chariots of Fire* had been small-scale, intimate, human. But now Vangelis was dealing with a huge, open-space adventure story," Hoy says. "A very different kind of adventure story. What Ridley had done was mix the past with the future. You saw the strangest things—flying cars rolling by Hare Krishnas, that sort of thing. It was a world where the new and startling rubbed shoulders with the leftovers, the leftovers meaning the nostalgic essence of what had once been popular on Earth. I'm sure Vangelis recognized this theme and responded to it."

Yet even if they now had a supremely talented musician on their team, Vangelis did pose a potentially bothersome complication for the rest of the *Blade Runner* staff. The problem was this: most big-budget Hollywood film scores are the very last element to be added to a picture, usually demand the services of numerous musicians, and are completed in as little as a few days. Or, at maximum, in a few weeks.

Yet Vangelis is the most literal of hands-on artists; he not only composes, arranges, and produces his own music, Vangelis *performs* it as well. Meaning that the *Blade Runner* score would be produced through the labors of essentially *one man*.

"Vangelis makes handmade music for movies," says Hoy. "In the same way, I imagine, that the old Disney artists used to make their cartoons. And that takes time. I'm not flattering him by using this comparison; honestly, given the rapid-fire demands of today's music marketplace, it could be the wrong way to do things. But in my opinion, it surely is his way."

Within the movie business, however, time is money. Therefore, Vangelis' time-consuming, Old World methods could conceivably strain *Blade Runner*'s already overburdened schedule. Nevertheless, in late December 1981, contracts were signed and the composer began the process of creating his *Blade Runner* score.

Vangelis' working methods closely mirrored Ridley Scott's own technique of "layering." The musician would first improvise the basic melody of each track, lay down that melody onto magnetic tape, and then refine it by piling other sounds and/or textures on top the foundation track, working and reworking the resulting mass of music much like the way a sculptor kneads a lump of clay.

During this process, Vangelis would usually work alone. His long days and nights in the Nemo Studios were, however, punctuated by occasional visits from Ridley Scott or Terry Rawlings, who would keep the composer informed of the latest breaking news on the *Blade*

Runner postproduction front. "Ridley certainly wasn't hanging around the studio every day," notes Andrew Hoy. "But my impression is that he would always be close enough to what anybody was doing for one of his films, certainly musically, to keep in touch. Vangelis respected this, because he respects Ridley. Vangelis also knows that when you work on a picture you are actually working for the director. I'm not saying he never argues or fights for certain things, but at the end of the day, Vangelis always wants his music to be acceptable to the director and right for the film."

THE ALBUM(S)

The great controversy surrounding Vangelis' official *Blade Runner* soundtrack has always been why it took so long to appear. After all, in 1982, *BR*'s final credits promised that this effort would be available on Polydor Records. Yet the "official soundtrack" did not see light of day until 1994, twelve years after the film's release!

During this dozen-year period, endless speculation arose as to the cause of this delay. Was Vangelis angry about something? Were there business problems? Had a falling out occurred between director and composer?

Yet while this debate raged on, a *Blade Runner* soundtrack *did* appear. It didn't feature Vangelis, however. To make matters even more confusing, at least three *other* recordings sporting various versions of Vangelis' *BR* score were released before the 1994 debut of the official soundtrack. Unfortunately, the first of these efforts was a soulless copy of the original—a replicant soundtrack, if you will. The others were either incomplete or illegal (a 1995 "bootleg" appeared too late for this book).

Turn to appendix E for a quick rundown of the various imitations, compilations, and pirate recordings of *Blade Runner*'s soundtrack, all of which appeared between 1982 and 1994.

Blade Runner: Vangelis. As previously noted, June 1994 was the moment that finally saw the release of the long-delayed Official Soundtrack. Titled *Blade Runner: Vangelis*, this Atlantic/Warner Music UK release (the Polydor deal referred to in the film's closing credits had, by now, gone the way of the dodo), features twelve separate tracks, some of which are overlaid with snippets of dialogue heard in the film.

BR: Vangelis includes much of the picture's most popular music. Among these selections are the "Love Theme," "Tales of the Future," "Memories of Green," and the "*Blade Runner* End Title." Yet much was missing, too. One could understand why Gail Laughton's "Harps of Ancient Temples" or the blimp's "Ogi no Mato" had not been included—these weren't Vangelis compositions. But where, for instance, was the breathy, sinister, two-note synthesizer riff Vangelis had created to run under Tyrell's death scene (a cue which the 1993 bootleg had called "The Prodigal Son Brings Death")?

As Andrew Hoy explains, these exclusions were not the result of any oversight on Vangelis' part—during the intervening years between the film and soundtrack's release, the musician had merely rethought the score's concept.

"If you listen to the *1492: Conquest of America* soundtrack album, which is the last movie Vangelis scored," Hoy begins, by way of explanation, "it's made up of cues directly taken from the film. But it is also filled out with other pieces Vangelis was working on at the time he was preparing the soundtrack for release.

"Vangelis has always mixed the old and new on his soundtrack albums. The only way I can explain his approach is to point out that many, many soundtrack albums simply repackage every bit of music that appears in a film. Every note, every theme, every motif. That's fine, if you're a movie buff. But Vangelis has never taken that route. He's an artist who very much believes in the responsibilities an artist should assume today.

"For instance, if you go out and buy a CD, it costs you ten pounds. And Vangelis has always been quite concerned that the consumer get full value for their money, that a record should be the best a record can be. But by its very nature, there are many bits and pieces on movie soundtracks that most people *don't* want to sit and listen to. Who wants to put up with a reprise of the same theme every ten minutes? So what Vangelis always tries to do is combine original soundtrack elements with fresher material. To reinvent his scores in order to come up with a new listening experience, one that forms an integrated whole."

But to return to one of the original questions posed at the beginning of this section: Why did it take so long for Vangelis to authorize the release of his soundtrack? The most widely held theory—one espoused by Katy Haber, Ivor Powell, and Ridley Scott—is that Vangelis was so peeved at the director's constant recutting of the film during the soundtrack's preparation, continual alterations which forced the musician to constantly change his music as well, that Vangelis suppressed the soundtrack.

Andrew Hoy, however, disputes this commonly held belief: "I don't believe Vangelis would ever get to the point of feeling that he couldn't put a soundtrack album together just because a director kept changing things. That's the nature of the game. Vangelis is a professional, and he understands these sort of things going in. I'm not saying he didn't get frustrated with the fiddling on *Blade Runner,* but from what I've been able to pick up, everyone was frustrated by the fiddling."

Whatever the fundamental reasons behind Vangelis' late release of the *Blade Runner* soundtrack (and after a year's research, I'm afraid this author must still file this subject under the heading "Topic for Further Research"), one point is certain—the *BR* score was also delayed during the time of its initial conception.

As Michael Deeley points out, "We had considerable difficulties with the music at the time it was supposed to be turned in. In fact, we didn't receive a final score until April of 1982. Somehow I got the feeling Vangelis wasn't as keen to do the music as he had been originally, and was holding back. Perhaps we can chalk that up to an 'excessive artistic conscience.' Or perhaps he felt that the deal that he made wasn't as good as the one he might have made.

"Another problem was that he couldn't seem to find the time to *do* the score. Vangelis wanted to do absolutely everything himself, yet I got the impression that he was very scattered at the time. Then again, Vangelis is not a dreary and steady person. And he produced an astonishing soundtrack."

When asked why that soundtrack wasn't immediately released, Deeley replies, "There was a colossal amount of excusing going on about that, but you've heard all of it already, I'm sure. All I know was that Vangelis was quite a handful towards the end of our association process—and that he wouldn't sign his contract, because times had changed or some damn thing. It may well be that he was distressed by other circumstances. But at the end of the day, the important thing was the music he contributed to the film. Which was breathtaking."

This author must concur. For, as Deeley states, it really *doesn't* matter why the "Official" *Blade Runner* soundtrack took so long to appear, because, at long last, it is finally available.

And like the film it supports, it is beautiful.

XII

SNEAKS AND
PANIC

A detective thriller set in the near future, Blade Runner *has been directed by Ridley Scott, the distinguished British filmmaker responsible for* Alien, *one of the fifty top-grossing movies of all time.*

—*BLADE RUNNER* PRODUCTION NOTES
ORIGINAL *BLADE RUNNER* PRESS KIT
JUNE 1982

MORE POSTPRODUCTION ────────────────

While Vangelis was composing his music score, Scott, Deeley, Powell, and Rawlings were concentrating on tying off the remaining aspects of *Blade Runner*'s postproduction work. Much of this labor concerned various pickup shots, close-ups, and other odds and ends that Scott felt were either necessary for or would add spice to the final product.

For example, in a letter by Michael Deeley dated September 18, 1981 addressed to Charles Weber of Tandem Productions (Weber was a Tandem executive who'd been assigned by that company to monitor *Blade Runner*'s progress), Deeley outlined the cost of a number of additional postproduction shots for which *BR*'s producer needed Tandem's budget approval. Among these were:

1) A close-up effects shot, to be done by England's Oxford Scientific Company, of Pris seeing a miniature world through Sebastian's microscope.

2) A request to "shoot something dramatic" for the Batty Incept Tape which Bryant shows Deckard at the beginning of the picture. Ridley Scott had suggested that a sequence portraying Batty in a sort of futuristic prison camp while displaying his replicant powers would be a good audience-grabber.

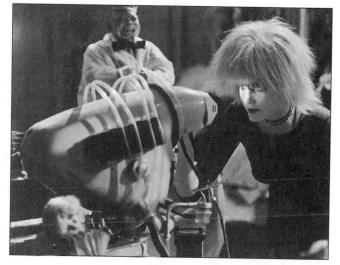

Pris (Daryl Hannah) peers through Sebastian's bulbous microscope. A miniature landscape was actually inserted within this prop, but said landscape was never filmed for BR audiences to share Hannah's view.

3) A point-of-view shot of Deckard looking down from the roof of Sebastian's building at the nighttime street far below just before he makes his leap between the buildings (the letter suggested doing this shot live, from a real skyscraper in New York).
4) A close-up view of Rachael's bullet going through Leon's forehead at the climax of the alley fight.
5) A full-scale dance sequence in the Snake Pit showing Zhora's nightclub act. This was by far the costliest addition, with an estimated price tag of £166,000, or over $200,000.

This September 18 letter from Deeley was then followed by a missive from Katy Haber to Weber dated September 24, 1981. Again, this second letter requested more postproduction additions; this time the filmmakers felt *Blade Runner* needed:

6) To reshoot the giant staring eye seen at the beginning of the film in order to make it move, as the reflections of the giant flames superimposed on the eyeball moved with it.
7) A reshoot of the "stars through the roof of the elevator" shot, which Batty sees after killing Tyrell. Scott had felt that the original

did not work. Instead, a miniature elevator interior and a motion-control shot asked for as a substitute.

8) A point-of-view shot of a sprawling cityscape that would be seen by Deckard as he crashes out of the window in Sebastian's apartment while trying to escape from Batty near the end of the film.

However, despite these requests, virtually every one of these additional segments was officially vetoed by Tandem in a letter of reply sent by that company on September 29, 1981. Interestingly, this letter also referred to the fact that Tandem was concerned with the ending of the picture, and that the company further felt there should be no reference at *Blade Runner*'s climax of Deckard being a replicant (a plot point that was to become a major source of debate throughout 1981, 1982, and for years to come, as we shall see).

One other area of postproduction disagreement between Tandem and the *BR* production team involved the film's opening credits. By early January 1982, Scott and Deeley had decided that each major actor would receive a single-card credit before the start of the film. Tandem, however, did not, and countered with a number of their own ideas for the opening credits. Two were:

- Showing a black background, in front of which slow raindrops would splash down, forming a trough on the bottom of the screen as the credits flashed on and off.
- No written credits at all. Instead, Harrison Ford would *read* the front credits, which would then be repeated as written credits at the end of the picture.

Unlike the eight proposed shots/segments previously discussed in this chapter, however, Scott won the *Blade Runner* credits skirmish, for the finished film did indeed open with single-card credits for the primary cast and crew.

THE PUBLICITY MACHINE GEARS UP ───────────

Although the *BR* filmmaking apparatus was still hip-deep in postproduction at this time, by January 1982, the Warner Brothers/*Blade Runner* publicity department was acting as if the film was already completed.

Warner now began a full-fledged campaign to spread *BR* fever across the land. Virtually every film, general interest, or genre magazine was peppered with requests from Warner's publicity department as to these publications' interest in printing extensive coverage of the film. Books on the screenplay and preproduction art were also being put together. Then, on January 12, 1982, the first *Blade Runner* trailer was released (which prominently featured the Ink Spots singing "If I Didn't Care"). This first trailer ran one minute and forty-two seconds: a second *BR* trailer was then released June 7, 1982, and ran three minutes and nineteen seconds.

Furthermore, a Los Angeles-based company named M. K. Productions assembled a sixteen-minute promotional film featuring interviews with Scott, Ford, and Mead talking about *BR*. This 16mm featurette had been specifically designed to circulate through the country's various horror, fantasy, and science fiction conventions, and ended with a smiling Scott saying, "Enjoy the convention."

Such specialized venues were also being treated to slide shows regarding the picture. Jeff Walker, a special promotional consultant working for Warner Brothers, traveled from city to city showing selected shots from the film and answering audience questions regarding the project. Walker had also arranged for the science fiction conventions to see something special: a full-scale Spinner used during production, which was put on display in the various hotels/and or convention halls where these "cons," as they are called by fans, took place (the first such Spinner appearance was at the 1981 World Science Fiction Convention, held in Denver, Colorado, over Labor Day weekend).[1]

Many of the other *Blade Runner* cars, however, had been intentionally destroyed after the shoot had wrapped. "The cars were destroyed so that they wouldn't show up in any other movies or TV shows before the film they'd been built for opened," Gene Winfield explained. "The production did keep two Spinners, two Deckard sedans and one police sedan, though, for later promotional tours."

Other publicity items prepared at this time included the *Blade Runner* press book, which included over a dozen black-and-white stills

---

[1] In 1983, the World Science Fiction convention voted *Blade Runner* Best Dramatic Presentation of 1982, for which it won a Hugo Award (beating out *E.T.* for the same honor). In 1992, *Blade Runner* was named the Third Most Favorite Science Fiction Film of All Time at that year's World Science Fiction Convention. *Star Wars* came in first, *2001* second.

and a thick sheaf of textual material (separated into different categories like "The Genetic Engineering Revolution"). The design for a *Blade Runner* one-sheet (poster), featuring comic-booklike depictions of Ford, Young, and a Spinner landing on police headquarters (painted by an artist named "Alvin"), was likewise submitted and approved. Also set in place during this period was a promotional tour which Ridley Scott and Harrison Ford would make together in the week before the film actually opened.[2]

THE AUTHOR RESURFACES—AND DIES

In the midst of this promotional activity, however, a key figure surfaced once again.

By this time, Philip K. Dick had publicly endorsed the *Blade Runner* script which he'd previously rejected. But now the author was chafing under another irritant: the novelization of the film.

"I was offered a great deal of money and a cut of the merchandising rights if I would do a novelization of the *Blade Runner* screenplay," Dick said to this author in early 1982. "Or I could have let someone like Alan Dean Foster [*who'd previously novelized Scott's* Alien] come in and do it. My agent figured that I would make about $400,000 from the deal if the film was a hit and I had a slice of the various spin-offs.

"*But*—part of this package required the suppression of my original novel," Dick continued. "So I said no. And they got nasty again. They began to threaten to withdraw the logo rights. To say that we wouldn't be able to say that *Sheep* was the novel on which *Blade Runner* was based. That we'd be unable to use any stills from the film. We remained adamant, though, and stuck to our guns. They eventually caved in. In rereleasing the original novel I only made about $12,500. But I kept my integrity. And my book."

In addition to Dick's unhappiness with the treatment of his source novel, there was another aspect of *Electric Sheep* which became problematic for both Ridley Scott *and* the book's author.

---

[2]During this junket, Ford made an appearance on *The David Letterman Show* on June 22, 1982. When asked by the host of that television program to describe what *Blade Runner* was like, Ford said, "It's not a musical comedy, David."

Earlier in *Future Noir*, Scott was quoted as saying that , "I'm afraid I never fully read *Do Androids Dream of Electric Sheep*. I couldn't get through it. It was too difficult. I tried, though."But when Dick subsequently heard about Scott's comment, Dick bristled at it. In the subsequent articles which began to proliferate on the film, Dick was more than happy to underline what he felt was one more Hollywood aggravation.

However, the ongoing Dick/*Blade Runner* feud was finally laid to rest shortly before Christmas of 1981. At that time (much to the author's surprise), Scott extended an invitation to Dick for a personal meeting; the director also invited the author to a private showing of twenty minutes of completed *BR* special effects footage, which was to be held at the screening room of the EEG facility in Marina Del Rey.

Present at that screening was David Dryer. "I got a call from one of the ladies at the *BR* production department saying that Philip K. Dick was coming down at three in the afternoon for a screening," Dryer recalls. "She told me to assemble an effects reel showing the best of the best. So I did. I planned on showing it to Dick in EEG's screening room, which was pretty remarkable. Doug Trumbull had one of the best screening rooms I've ever seen. The image on that screen was spectacular—it was in 70mm—and a great sound system had been installed that made the floor rumble.

"Now, Vangelis hadn't supplied any music yet, but Matthew Yuricich had been painting some of his mattes to old Vangelis albums— Matt likes to paint to music. Since we were already familiar with that, we decided to also play Vangelis music while we showed our reel to Dick.

"Then the production rented out a chauffeured limousine to pick Philip Dick up in Santa Ana," continues Dryer. "They were really giving him the deluxe treatment. That limo drove him all the way up to Maxella, and when he arrived at EEG, I noticed Dick had brought a woman along with him *[Mary Wilson]*. I could also tell right away that Dick was unhappy; he acted like somebody with a burr up their ass. First he started kind of grilling me in this grouchy tone about all kinds of things—he wanted to know what was going on, told me that he'd been very unhappy with the script, and so on and so forth.

"So first we gave him a quick tour of the EEG shop, which I thought might settle him down. But Dick didn't seem impressed, even when we showed him all the preproduction art and the actual models we'd used for certain effects shots. Then we went into the screening room."

Moments before the screening proper, Ridley Scott slipped into the small theater and introduced himself to Dick. "Dick was a bit guarded at first," recalls Scott. "Until we doused the lights, turned up the music, and ran the reel for him," adds Dryer.

The author, however, according to *Blade Runner*'s coeffects supervisor, "didn't say a word at first. He sat there for twenty minutes like a statue. Then the lights came up, and Dick turned around to me. He said in this gruff voice, 'Can you run that again?' So the projectionist rethreaded and ran it again.

"Now the lights come up a second time. Dick looks me straight in the eye and says, 'How is this possible? How can this be? Those are not the exact images, but the texture and tone of the images I saw in my head when I was writing the original book! The environment is exactly as how I'd imagined it! How'd you guys do that? How did you know what I was feeling and thinking?!'

"Let me tell you, that was one of the most successful moments of my career," Dryer concludes. "Dick went away dazed."

The author next was personally escorted by Scott on another tour around the EEG facility, where the director took special pains to show the author of *Do Androids Dream of Electric Sheep* a number of *Blade Runner* production stills, which prompted Dick to later tell this writer that "Rutger Hauer looks like the perfect Batty—cold, Aryan, flawless." Then Philip K. Dick at last sat down to talk with the director who was adapting his novel.

"When I finally met Ridley," Dick said to me in late January 1982, "I kept thinking of how I had continuously sniped at *Alien* and how I knew he must have seen those statements. As he looked at me and I looked at him, I knew he had to be thinking about this. I thought, 'It may well be that Ridley will pop me one for this right here.'

"But Ridley surprised me. He was very cordial, awfully nice to both me and my friend Mary. It was very fine treatment. During the twenty-minute showing, Ridley even sat behind us to explain the continuity of each sequence he ran up on the projector."

Dick and Scott now had their first face-to-face discussion regarding *Blade Runner* itself. "It was very frank," Dick said, "certainly not the clichéd formality of mutual compliments. I expressed certain ideas that I hoped would be in the film, and then Ridley said they would not be in the film," Dick said, laughing. "Yet he was very friendly, very honest, very open in what he said. Even though we openly disagreed on a number of points, the air of cordiality was always maintained."

According to Dick, the main source of contention between the two men was a primary one: that of the basic difference between "what Ridley and I saw *Sheep*—and, by inference, *Blade Runner*—as being all about.

"To me, the replicants are deplorable. They are cruel, they are cold, they are heartless. They have no empathy, which is how the Voight-Kampff test catches them out, and don't care about what happens to other creatures. They are essentially less-than-human entities.

"Ridley, on the other hand, said he regarded them as supermen who couldn't fly. He said they were smarter, stronger, and had faster reflexes than humans. 'Golly!' That's all I could think of to reply to that one. I mean, Ridley's attitude was quite a divergence from my original point of view, since the theme of my book is that Deckard is dehumanized through tracking down the androids. When I mentioned this, Ridley said that he considered it an intellectual idea, and that he was not interested in making an esoteric film.

"But I think Harrison Ford will realize the ambiguities of Deckard's character," Dick concluded during his 1982 discussion. "He's an intelligent actor. I'm sure Ford will show just how distasteful his job is for him. I have faith in that."

Despite their essential difference of opinion, Scott and Dick parted on friendly terms. The hatchet had been officially buried; the author of *Do Androids Dream of Electric Sheep* now completely reversed his previous negative attitude and became a wholehearted *Blade Runner* supporter.

Yet the greatest of all possible misfortunes lay only a few months ahead—for the man who had been primarily responsible for the film having been made in the first place would never see the final print.

On March 2, 1982, Philip Kindred Dick died. His passing was sudden and unexpected. The author had been recuperating from a stroke which had hospitalized him in late February. He had then been diagnosed as having every chance of recovering when a second stroke and subsequent heart attack took his life.

Ironically, just before his death Dick had also been (according to a quote attributed to the author's agent, Russell Galen, in Kenneth Turan's "Blade Runner 2" article) eagerly anticipating the release of *Blade Runner* "like a kid on Christmas Eve." This author can attest to Galen's statement, for I myself had telephoned Dick just a few days before his first stroke. And although our conversation was brief, Dick had signed off with this line: "I can't *wait* to see *Blade Runner!*"

Even more ironic was the fact that the author died less than four months before the release of the finished film.

Philip Kindred Dick's body was cremated, and on March 5, 1982, a small memorial service was held for the author in Santa Ana, California—Dick's final hometown.

THE DENVER AND DALLAS SNEAKS——————————— (A DIFFERENT VERSION #1)

Despite the author's passing, however, it was business as usual on the *Blade Runner* front. And the latest hurdle which the production had to overcome involved the first public screenings of the film.

Although other screenings of *BR* had already been held in late February 1982 for a small group of industry workers at the GoMillion Sound Studios in Los Angeles (and for an unsuspecting audience in Van Nuys, California, an event on which little information is available), Warner Brothers' official "sneak previews" were chosen for two different cities entirely: Denver, Colorado, and Dallas, Texas.

The Denver Sneak was held on the night of March 5, 1982 at the Continental Theater. The Dallas preview was scheduled for the following evening, March 6, at the Northpark Cinema. As for the print shown at these two locations, it was, in Scott's words, "a workprint. Something that was pretty rough, but close enough to what I was after to let a preview audience see." The roughness of this print included not yet being thoroughly color corrected or mixed; also, the final two reels were missing the last part of Vangelis' soundtrack, which the musician was still completing in his London-based recording studio.

Attending both previews were Scott, Deeley, and Haber. Initially, these *BR* functionaries must have been primed for exhilarating evenings. The previews had not only sold out in both cities, but wild applause reportedly greeted the beginning of each screening of the newest Harrison Ford/Ridley Scott opus.

Within minutes, however, it quickly became clear that something was seriously wrong.

In late 1993, this author wrote a *Blade Runner*-oriented piece for a magazine called *Video Watchdog*. Following its publication, I received a number of letters from readers who wished to further discuss my piece. One of these missives came from a Mr. David DeHay of Brownwood, Texas. DeHay actually attended the March 6 Dallas preview, and the portion of his letter describing the events of that fateful evening are worth relating in full.

"I attended the Dallas Sneak as a member of the press," DeHay wrote, "using my status as a reporter for an east Texas daily in a purely self-serving manner. When I called ahead for my press clearance, I was told that there would be a small press conference after the screening.

"The preview was held at the Northpark Cinema's main auditorium, which is a magnificent modern theater. I stood in line for a good couple of hours with a crowd composed largely of youngsters obviously attracted by Harrison Ford's name in [a local] newspaper ad [advertising the sneak]. Many stood in line clutching bags bearing the logo of the local comic & SF [science fiction] store. There was a buzz of real excitement in the air. Everybody knew Douglas Trumbull had done the effects. *Starlog* had said there was going to be the big climactic chase through the skyscrapers in the flying cars.[3]

"When the film actually rolled, I was transfixed," DeHay continues. "The level of detail in the look and atmosphere of this created world combined with the existential themes of the story to produce the closest thing to virtual reality that existed at that time. This film did not lead the viewer by the hand with needless expository dialogue, instead opting for a 'total immersion' approach. All the clues are there, you just have to pay attention. I appreciated not being taken for an idiot.

"Well, evidently I was in the minority.

"Almost dead silence greeted the end of the film. As the lights came up, the audience filed out as quietly as if they were leaving a funeral service. Many were confused and depressed by the film's atmosphere and ambiguous climax. Outside the theater, response cards were distributed and filled out. During that process I spoke to several audience members who complained about various problems understanding the story.

---

[3] A version of the final Fancher/Peoples shooting script had included a climactic scene with Deckard and Rachael driving a car away from the city while being pursued by Gaff's flying Spinner—this is the scene *Starlog* had become privy to, although it was never shot.

"Such a pall hung over the theater that the VIPs were hustled quietly out to their cars and the 'press conference' canceled. There hadn't been a great deal of press attention anyway."

"That was one of those evenings which does tend to linger in the memory," Michael Deeley dryly commented, recalling the Dallas sneak in 1995.

But why had an audience composed of at least a small number of SF fans reacted so poorly to one of the only truly *science fictional* films ever released by Hollywood?

One theory is that these viewers were apparently Harrison Ford fans, eager for the streamlined action heroics of a *Raiders of the Lost Ark* or *The Empire Strikes Back* and unprepared to accept the downbeat, noirish aspects of *Blade Runner* on its own terms. The fact that the same negative reaction had been observed at the Denver Sneak seems to add weight to this supposition. Even more troubling, however, was the number of walkouts which transpired in both cities during these screenings. Furthermore, those viewers remaining had voiced feelings of confusion regarding Scott's thoughtful, Marlowe in Metropolis-type thriller.

"The Denver and Dallas audiences were definitely thrown by *Blade Runner*," notes Katy Haber. "It was obvious that they'd had real difficulty understanding the story, never mind whether they liked it or not."

Considering all the creative disagreements which had preceded *BR*'s first previews, it's not surprising that the disastrous reception given the film in Denver and Dallas would soon have the figurative result of tossing a five-gallon gasoline can onto a smoldering campfire, particularly since the follow-up analysis which the Warner Brothers market research department now conducted on the Denver/Dallas previews did little to calm that panic.

Part of the preview process had included handing out audience reaction cards to the viewers, which would allow them to both rate and comment on the picture. According to two lengthy interoffice memos distributed to Deeley and Alan Ladd, Jr. on March 8 and March 10 by Warner's market research group (which had tallied up the results of these audience reaction cards and also performed a number of "call-back" telephone interviews with selected viewers who'd filled them out), the *Blade Runner* sneak preview crowds had found far more to fault the film with than mere plot incomprehension.

Basically, the March 8 and March 10 memos reported that the Denver/ Dallas reaction cards revealed five troubling areas of criticism:

- "That the film was hard to follow or hard to understand." (Some cards expressed puzzlement over what a Blade Runner was!)
- "That the film went too far in its graphic portrayal of violence" [particularly during the scenes of Tyrell's eye-gouging and Batty breaking Deckard's fingers].

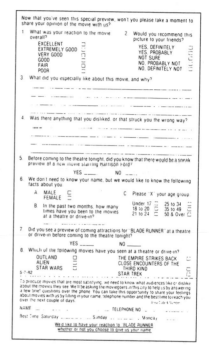

The audience reaction card passed out to viewers of the various Blade Runner *sneak previews.*

- "That it was too slow or 'draggy' in places."
- That the audiences had had "problems with the grimness of the movie or lack of character warmth and feeling." (Some cards "wanted to know why it was raining and why it was always so dark and gloomy," while others "found *Blade Runner* unrelentingly oppressive.")
- A significant number of the negative comments also centered around the film's ending, which at this point climaxed with Ford stepping into his apartment building's elevator toward a waiting Sean Young as the elevator doors closed behind them. Specific objections found this culmination "too abrupt," "unsatisfying," or "difficult to understand" (Gaff's tinfoil unicorn proved confusing as well).

However, despite this wash of negatives, it's important to note that even a cursory review of these collective comments reveals that the picture had *not* tested out as a failure. Instead, reactions from the two crowds had been more mixed than condemnatory. Much praise was lavished on the picture's visual, technical, and special effects aspects, for instance, and many viewers had termed *Blade Runner* "unique." Additionally, the "Overall Satisfaction Ratings" showed that of the 635 viewers who had seen the film in Denver, 22% of the audience had rated the picture "Excellent," while another 22% found it "Extremely Good." In Dallas, 749 viewers saw the film; of these, 21% rated the picture "Excellent," and another 21% judged it "Extremely Good."

Still, the Warner memos concluded that these positive figures were not strong enough to ensure a hit, and that the volume of negative responses on the reaction cards indicated a deeply divided audience. Part of which had been apparently too distracted by the film's elaborate production design and/or narrative subtlety to recommend the picture to their friends.

For a $28 million production like *Blade Runner,* this was ominous news indeed.

XIII

VOICE-OVERS, SAN DIEGO, AND A NEW HAPPY ENDING

Saturday, May 8, 1982, I had experienced what is perhaps the greatest movie of all time. Blade Runner *is a fantastic movie. The sneak preview of this magical spectacle here in San Diego, to top it off, also had Harrison Ford in person . . .* Blade Runner *is certainly Ford's best movie thus far. All his past movies pale in comparison to this masterpiece.*

—LETTER FROM RUEL HERNANDEZ TO.
STARLOG #64
NOVEMBER 1982

THE VOICE-OVERS

At this juncture in the making of *BR*, one of the most controversial aspects of the production emerged—Harrison Ford's voice-over.

Blade Runner's narration has given rise to its own folk history. Yet like most popular legends, only some of this history is truth—the rest has either been misunderstood or distorted. This author now begs his readers' indulgence throughout the following pages as he attempts to unravel the misperceptions which have accumulated around the interior monologues that accompanied Harrison Ford during his travels through the Los Angeles of 2019.

One common fallacy is that Deckard's voice-over is universally despised. Surprisingly (at least to this author, who also dislikes *BR*'s narration), this viewpoint is not as widely held as most might think. During the writing of this book I conducted an admittedly unscientific polling of about 200 friends, strangers, and acquaintances on the matter of *BR*'s narration. What I discovered was a significant number of viewers (about 30% of these 200) who actually *liked* the voice-over. The reasons for this acceptance were twofold: some viewers felt

Deckard's voice-over gave them important plot information they otherwise would have been unable to gain by simply watching the film (indicating that at least part of the Warner Brothers' screening reports had been correct), while others enjoyed what they saw as the narration's echoes of the hard-boiled narrations found in old films noir and forties' mystery thrillers.

However, it is equally true that the majority of viewers find *BR*'s narration grating and intrusive (Philip K. Dick certainly did, as witnessed by his comments concerning Fancher's script in chapter V). *Blade Runner* editor Terry Rawlings sums up the general attitude toward the voice-over when he says, "Throughout production, I kept saying that the angle they were taking with the voice-over was completely wrong. If you're going to do a voice-over, I'd say, you don't want it to say, 'Look at this! I have found a pen!' while you're showing a character holding a pen. That is moronic. In fact, Ridley had a rather scornful term for this sort of redundancy—he called it 'Irving the Explainer.'

"But the narration on the original theatrical cut of *Blade Runner* certainly sounded like Irving had written it. Which was annoying, because I'd been insisting that what the voice-over needed to reflect was those old Humphrey Bogart movies, whose commentaries were fantastic. Because there the characters weren't talking about what they were seeing, they were talking about what affected them. I kept repeating, 'Why don't we work this sort of angle into *BR*'s commentary? For instance, Deckard finds something. Then he tells us how he feels about what he's found, and how it affects him.' But nobody ever did that. The commentary that was released talked down to the audience. And I think that's sort of what offended everybody about it."

As Rawlings has pointed out, the use of a weary voice-over for a cynical *film noir* is indeed a time-honored cinematic device. And since *Blade Runner* is nothing if not a futuristic noir, it's not surprising to learn that the film had long been conceived as having the same type of ironic narration found on those early films.

Which explodes myth number two: that Ridley Scott never *wanted* a voice-over. Because it was Scott who pressed for the narration in *Blade Runner* in the first place.

Says Hampton Fancher, "Ridley was the one who initially pushed the voice-over idea. That's why it's on so many of my drafts. Scott was after the feel of a forties' detective thriller, so he liked the idea of using this *film noir* device."

Ample documentation exists to support Fancher's statement. For example, in the Fancher/*Dangerous Days* script dated January 7, 1980 (written six weeks before Scott accepted the project, and a patchwork scenario which also included large chunks of the writer's earlier *Do Androids Dream of Electric Sheep, Android,* and *Mechanismo* screenplays), Deckard has absolutely no narration. Yet on page five of Fancher's *Blade Runner* draft marked July 24, 1980—five months *after* Scott signed onto the film—the reader is introduced to Deckard through dialogue which is indicated by the abbreviation "(V.O.)", film industry shorthand for "voice-over":

> DECKARD (V.O.)
> It was 97 degrees in the city and no hope of improvement. Not bad if you're a lizard. But two hours earlier I was drinking Aquavit with an Eskimo lady in North East Alaska. That's a tough change to make. It was so good, I didn't want to leave, so I left a day early.

It was not only Hampton Fancher who wrote Scott-requested narrations, however: David Peoples also included voice-overs once he began working on the screenplay. For instance, on page six of Peoples' December 15, 1980 draft, Deckard's first lines are indicated—again—by "V.O.":

> DECKARD (V.O.)
> I've always been suspicious. Of everything. You tell me something . . . I don't believe it.

And on page five of the Fancher/Peoples/production team's "cobbled together" script (December 22, 1980), Deckard tells us that:

> DECKARD (V.O.)
> I look at the signs for emigration to the Colonies . . . If it's really so great Off-world, how come they gotta advertise? If you've got something really good, you keep it a secret. It's only the junk you push.

Obviously, then, the desire to initiate the stylistic device of narration had been a very early decision of the *BR* team, one with the full participation of Ridley Scott. (For the director's own thoughts on *BR's* voice-over, turn to appendix A.)

Now we come to the third most popular misconception regarding *Blade Runner*'s voice-over: that it was forced upon *BR*'s director following the disastrous Denver/Dallas sneaks. This issue is not quite as cut and dried as the two preceding it, however, for, as we have already seen, the Denver/Dallas showings *did* include a brief snatch of voice-over. Although the *amount* of Deckard's narration had significantly grown by the time of *Blade Runner*'s theatrical release, that expansion had been supported by none other than Ridley Scott himself (although hindsight indicates that the director was cajoled into doing so).

One *BR* participant who was very close to the voice-over controversy was co-*Blade Runner* screenplay writer David Peoples, who, when asked to help clear away the thicket of confusion surrounding the film's narration, eagerly jumped at the chance.

"The biggest misunderstanding involving *Blade Runner* is, I think, the whole history of the voice-over," Peoples relates. "That's really rankled me over the years. I'm happy to set the record straight.

"What happened was this: after I first came onto the picture, Hampton's script, at least the one I saw, had a voice-over on it. Now, I made a lot of changes to that screenplay but held, I hope, to the spirit and tone of the thing. Because it was already really good.

"Of course, part of this faithfulness meant keeping in the narration. But as we got closer to production, sometime around February of 1981, I think, both Ridley and I decided that it would be better for the shooting script if we stripped *out* most of the voice-overs. We came to this decision for two very practical reasons.

"First, we wanted to make sure that the storyline wasn't dependent on the narration. A good way to judge that would have been to remove most of the voice-overs from the script before principal photography, shoot the film without them, and then see how well the story was working without narration. Which is exactly what we did.

"That's not to suggest that we weren't going to put any voice-overs in afterwards, though. Because we were, and we did. It was never my understanding that we were *not* going to have a narration. Nobody ever said, 'Let's not have it.' That's my memory of the situation, anyway.

"That attitude sort of explains the second reason why we shot the film without voice-overs. You see, the script was changing throughout much of *Blade Runner*'s principal photography period, constantly changing this scene or that. So by the time we wrapped production, many, many changes had been made to the original shooting script.

A gorgeous still of a shot only seen at the San Diego Sneak Preview: Batty in the VidPhon booth.

Which of course would have thrown off the timing or content or placement of the original voice-overs that had been written before the shoot. If we'd kept them in, we would have had to move narration A to point Z, for instance. Or come up with a whole new speech for a sequence that had been reshuffled or rethought.

"But we'd anticipated that. We knew these changes would be coming before we got into them. So it had always been assumed that there'd be some kind of fine-tuning of the narration *after* the picture had been shot. Little did I know that I'd still be fine-tuning it six months after production wrapped!" Peoples concludes.

Work on the *Blade Runner* voice-overs did indeed last well into postproduction. In fact, Harrison Ford's narration was recorded not once but *three* times.

Ridley Scott supervised the first two sessions. The first took place in Los Angeles, at Goldwyn Sound, on November 5, 1981. Interestingly, this version had not been written by Fancher or Peoples but by Daryl Ponicsan, a novelist/screenwriter who'd scored a critical hit for the 1973 film *Cinderella Liberty*. "Daryl's a good writer," Deeley recalls, "but he was also a crony of Yorkin's. And Daryl was paid good money to write *very* light words, which only added to the cost of an already overburdened picture."

However, Ridley Scott was not happy with Ponicsan's attempt.

David Peoples was now flown to Pinewood Studios (where *BR*'s director was attending to various postproduction chores) in early January 1982, where Peoples himself drafted a new narration composed of both his own material and previous Fancher-created commentaries.

"I was having a really hard time with the voice-over at this stage because there was a different requirement for it," Peoples recalls. "The original plan had been to just fine-tune the narration during postproduction. But now there was not only the fine-tuning to consider, but some additional story problems that had come out of the shoot. Things weren't as clear in some cases as they needed to be. Which meant the voice-over had to explain certain things now.

"So the battle was to make the narration really oblique and poetic and to inject some information into it at the same time. That was awkward. First I'd come up with something that sounded prosaic and explanatory, and the next time the narration would sound terrific but wouldn't quite solve everybody's problems with the story. That voice-over became a real struggle."

Nevertheless, Harrison Ford was now flown to England, and the second *BR* narration was recorded at Pinewood on January 12, 1982.

But *Blade Runner*'s star was not particularly happy with the results. As Harrison Ford told writer Lance Loud for his 1992 *BR/Details* magazine article, "It was in my contract that I do the voice-overs, but I hated them. Ridley hated them as well, but when the film went over budget, they made me do it. I went kicking and screaming to the studio to record it."

"In fact, Harrison disliked the entire idea of a voice-over from the start," adds Katy Haber. "He thought it was overkill, that it was too overemphatic and disruptive. Ridley wasn't exactly committed to the idea, either—he kept waffling on the narration, partially because he wasn't sure that what had been written was strong enough to support the demands placed on it."

In any event, it was this second, Pinewood-based voice-over which was screened for the Tandem executives on January 21 with such negative results. At this point Scott decided to scrap the voice-over almost entirely. Instead, the director retained only a short piece of narration, the one near the end of the film, with Deckard watching Batty die on the roof. This was an old commentary to boot—Peoples' had written Deckard's rooftop voice-over on March 9, 1981 (before principal photography began), for his "narrationless" shooting script.

It was this short Peoples' voice-over, then, which preview audiences heard at the Denver/Dallas Sneaks, leading us back to the third misconception: that Scott had been forced to place narration on the film.

"Ah, the famous narration," Michael Deeley wryly recalls. "That's a fascinating story. What happened was that after the sneaks in Denver and Dallas, some of the preview cards came back expressing bafflement over the film's storyline. Although this confusion had not been expressed by the majority of the viewers, I must say.

"Still, when those cards came back, everybody panicked. And by everybody I mean everybody. Ridley was upset, I was upset, Tandem was upset. . . . It was alarming because we were sitting on an expensive picture that had gone over budget. That was a fragile position; nobody, particularly Warner Brothers or The Ladd Company, which at that point was pretty much on the financial skids, had enough ready cash to insure covering their losses if the film was released as was.

"So we were all jumpy as to how this picture was going to end up. And we all thought we had to do something about it. That's when the idea of a new narration came up."

At this time, however, Deeley and Scott were still at Pinewood Studios supervising *BR*'s dubbing. Furthermore, relations between them and Tandem Productions had so deteriorated that the pair were considered *personas non gratas* at this third recording session.

"Bud Yorkin wrote Ridley a very curt letter around that point that said, 'I've had enough,' states Katy Haber. "So now I was stuck in the middle of this very weird situation. Ridley and Michael had both been told to not be around, but I had been told to stay to follow through. So I was physically working with Bud Yorkin in Los Angeles on the one hand, and with Michael and Ridley in London by telephone with the other."

In any event, shortly after the Denver and Dallas sneaks, Harrison Ford, Bud Yorkin, and Katy Haber gathered together in a small Beverly Hills studio to record the third attempt at a *Blade Runner* narration. Joining the trio was Roland Kibbee (since deceased), a television writer and friend of Yorkin's who was primarily responsible for writing this third attempt. Kibbee created his version of the voice-over by stitching together his own input with selections from previous narrations written by those who'd gone before him.

"Bud Yorkin supervised that session," Haber continues, "and Harrison hated it. He hadn't wanted to do voice-overs in the first place, and by now I think he was sick of the whole movie anyway. Harrison also didn't like what Kibbee had come up with. So he purposefully, I think, recited that narration badly. I think he was hoping they wouldn't be able to use it. And of course they did—that third narration was the one they released with the finished film."

Unfortunately, neither Peoples nor Hampton Fancher had been privy to the details surrounding Ponicsan's, and Kibbee's involvement with the voice-overs, a situation which would later cause both writers acute embarrassment.

"Months after I'd finished working on the picture, right around the time it was released, in fact, Hampton and I attended a screening of *Blade Runner* at the Academy Theater," David Peoples explains. "This was the first time I'd seen it finished, with the music and effects and that stuff. And I've told this anecdote many times before, but as Hampton and I watched the film together that night, I assumed that he'd rewritten my narration and come up with this voice-over himself.

"I was a little upset by that, because I'd thought my voice-overs included some of the best writing I'd ever done. Plus there were a lot of sentences and phrases of mine in there and sentences and phrases that I recognized from Hampton. But there was a lot of new material, too. My overall impression of this voice-over—the way it sounded, the way it worked—was that it was horrible and embarrassing. The picture was great, but the narration was sort of like a piece of awful music laid on top of beautiful images and being played badly out of tune.

"I consoled myself with the thought that Hampton had had to rewrite this thing under duress," Peoples continues. "Since Hampton is a professional, I thought he'd just done the best job possible under the circumstances. That he'd just given the producers what they'd wanted.

"It wasn't until a long time after that night, though, that we both finally talked about that narration. And then I found out that Hampton had had nothing to do with it! In fact, he'd been sitting there in the theater thinking the same things about me! We were much relieved and had a good laugh about that, because neither of us was to blame for this stuff. I don't know that you could blame any writer for it, frankly, since they were all just doing their job under pretty bad circumstances.

"However, Hampton and I did feel tremendous frustration," Peoples concludes. "We agreed that the movie hadn't been totally ruined by this voice-over. On the other hand, we also both knew that we'd written more effective narrations than the one that was used. Stuff that would've worked better, and wouldn't have been as jarring as some of the overly informative and flat voice-overs that were ultimately put into the movie."

Michael Deeley, however, sees a different—and positive—facet of *Blade Runner*'s much-maligned narration.

"It's important to remember when talking about this issue," Deeley explains, "that when the 'Director's Cut'—quote unquote—came out ten years later, everybody said, 'My God, it's so much better!' But that opinion was expressed by people who had *already* seen the picture *with* the narration. I'm not defending that voice-over, God knows. But one of the good things about it is how the narration made *Blade Runner* more accessible to a general audience. Excepting the cultists, of course. Who already know more about the picture than I can remember."

RIDE INTO THE SUNSET

The confusion generated by the Dallas and Denver Sneaks also resulted in yet another last-minute and much-maligned element being inserted into *Blade Runner*'s original theatrical release—its so-called "happy ending" (or "Ride Into the Sunset"). This climactic scene showed Rachael and Deckard driving in Deckard's sedan outside the city limits in a beautiful, verdant landscape. Meanwhile, Deckard muses (in voice-over) that "Gaff had been there [Deckard's apartment], and let her [Rachael] live. Four years, he figured. He was wrong. Tyrell had told me Rachael was special. No termination date. I didn't know how long we'd have together . . . who does."[1]

Like the voice-over before it, *Blade Runner*'s happy ending has been the cause of much speculation and innuendo. And as has happened in the case of Deckard's narration, the rumors surrounding the

---

[1]According to Michael Deeley, this last bit of narration was not written by any of the screenwriters previously associated with the project. "That final narration was actually a—well, calling it a 'collaborative effort' is a bit much, because Ridley and Ivor and Katy and I just sat down in a bar one night and came up with those words ourselves. They never evolved from something as elaborate as a screenwriter working them up in a script; Ridley, I and the others just invented them. Hell, if you can't do something like that, you shouldn't be making movies."

origins of the "Ride Into the Sunset" contain more than their fair share of distortions and mistruths, incorrect assumptions which have been accepted as gospel by fans of the film.

The primary rumor behind the genesis of the happy ending has always been that Ridley Scott was forced to append it to his film following the negative responses of the Denver/Dallas sneaks. Well—yes and no. For, as Ivor Powell now relates, a form of this bittersweet ending had *always* been planned for the film. In fact, the sequence had even been assigned scene numbers and shooting days before *BR's* principal photography began.

"Scenes 137 through 139," Powell affirms. "We had originally scheduled to shoot them during the last two days of production, which were initially planned to fall on June 22 and June 23, 1981. Those would have translated to day seventy-four and seventy-five of the shoot."

But if such a happy ending had been planned all along, why didn't it surface during the Denver and Dallas Sneaks?

"Because the happy ending was totally generated *by* those sneaks," explains Michael Deeley. "Although it had actually been scripted and planned before we started filming, we ultimately ran out of time and money during principal photography and didn't have the resources to shoot that ending. Ridley later also changed his mind concerning the scripted climax during the editing of the picture. He now felt that it would be much better to visually end the film on a harder, more ambiguous note—the elevator doors closing on Deckard and Rachael—and to aurally climax *Blade Runner* with that line of Gaff's: 'It's too bad she won't live. But then again, who does?' We all liked that. We felt it left a lingering, enigmatic impression of the film.

"Once again, however, I must point out that Ridley went willingly along with the idea of filming the happy ending after Denver and Dallas," Deeley concludes. "So did I. Especially after the sneak preview cards came back and so many people expressed reservations about the original downbeat climax. The slight possibility that this ending might leave the door open for a sequel was also a factor for us shooting it."

Scott confirmed Deeley's statements in Kenneth Turan's "Blade Runner 2" piece. "It was the first time I'd experienced the heavy-duty preview process," the director recalled, "and I was so daunted by the negative or puzzled reaction, I didn't fight it. I thought, 'My God, maybe I've gone too far. Maybe I ought to clarify it.' I got sucked into the process of thinking, 'Let's explain it all.'"

However, as earlier indicated, the happy ending which was ultimately filmed was a *variant* of the originally scripted scene. Which leads to a question: what was that originally scripted ending supposed to be?

"First you were going to see this expansive matte painting of Deckard's sedan driving out of the city, with all of Los Angeles spread out behind it," picks up Ivor Powell. "But that got slashed because of budgetary reasons while they were still doing the effects. Then there'd be a dissolve, and you'd see Deckard's car coming out of a tunnel into this sparsely wooded area. At that point, while Rachael and Deckard were talking, they'd spot a unicorn galloping through the woods. Somehow this was supposed to tie in with Deckard's earlier dream of a unicorn—I never did quite understand how.[2]

"This unicorn appearance is mentioned in a late copy of the screenplay, if you're interested," Powell continues."[3] "However, the rest of that scripted ending was changed a little during production. The new plan had been to show Deckard putting the tinfoil unicorn Gaff had left at his apartment on the dashboard of his car. Then the camera would pull back up off the road where the car was driving, you'd see this thin forest, the camera would pull farther back, and now you'd see that that forest ended in a desert area of sorts, with all these interesting rock formations. Then the pullback would stop and Deckard's car would drive out into the desert, and that would be that. The end."

Blade Runner effects supervisor David Dryer also recalls this never-shot climax. "A number of different endings were on the drawing board, but we were never allowed to proceed with them because Deeley said stop. The one that sticks in my mind that I thought would be good was a move over the monolithic buildings in the city that did a match dissolve to the buttes in Monument Valley. Which would pick up an angle where there's very little vegetation or growth, just a long dusty road. And there would be the ground vehicle, with Harrison and Sean going off to die in the wasteland. That would have been a lot more fulfilling than outtakes from *The Shining*."

The Shining outtakes Dryer just referred to have become another much-discussed piece of *Blade Runner* legend. Footage from Stanley Kubrick's 1980 adaptation of Stephen King's best-selling novel did

---

[2]All unicorn information will be found in chapter XVII: The Director's Cut.

[3]The script Powell is referring to was dated February 23, 1981.

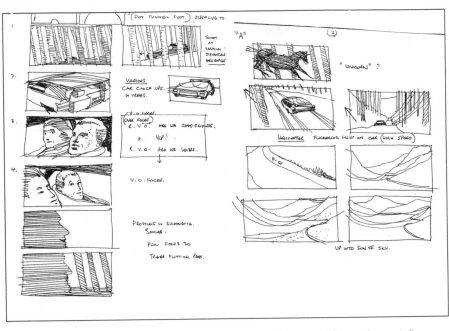

A storyboard drawn by Ridley Scott for Blade Runner's *original (but only partially filmed) ending. Note unicorn at top panel, third column from left.*

indeed find themselves in *BR*, in the new happy ending Ridley Scott was about to shoot. But first one must understand the nature of the new ending Scott had created.

What the director now envisioned was a pared-down revision of the original scenes 137 through 139. The new climax would first show Deckard's sedan racing through the woods, as seen from an aerial shot filmed by a helicopter. Next would come quick shots of Rachael and Deckard inside his car, with Ford thinking about Young's lack of a termination date. Finally, another cut would show mountainous (desert) terrain, suggesting the couple had escaped into some unknown wilderness.

The fact that this short new ending would, in effect, completely negate the pessimistic themes so carefully set forth in the film's preceding two hours did not deter the production from sending Katy Haber and a small crew to Moab, Utah, in March 1982 to film the landscapes needed as background for this sequence. "I was directing those shots," Haber now recalls. "Ridley was still in London working on post. So I was up in Moab for five days with a helicopter, the second unit cameraman, Deckard's car, and two doubles to drive it. We then spent those five days shooting at Monument Valley, with a long shot of the car driving down this road. But none of that footage came out. The whole time we were there it was either snowing or overcast or very dark."

After Scott was informed that the Moab footage was unusable, Ivor Powell, who had previously worked with Stanley Kubrick on *2001*, remembered the wide mountain vistas which had opened that director's adaptation of *The Shining*. "So I suggested Ridley get in touch with Stanley regarding those shots," Powell notes. Although *The Shining* footage had shown verdant landscapes as opposed to barren ones, Scott contacted Kubrick anyway, and the *2001* director obliged by giving the *BR* team free access to *The Shining*'s wilderness shots (which had been filmed from a helicopter for Kubrick by noted "surfing film" producers Macgillivray-Freeman Films). Kubrick's sole proviso was that Scott not utilize any footage which had already appeared in the 1980 film.

However, as Terry Rawlings goes on to say, no one had recalled Kubrick's legendary penchant for shooting many takes.

"I remember quite clearly those cans of film arriving from Stanley Kubrick's house. All we'd asked him for were shots of Jack Nicholson's yellow Volkswagen driving up into the mountains at the beginning of *The Shining*. Suddenly, we had something like 30,000 feet of film turn up to look at. We had all his outtakes. They were endless."

"We also had to be careful with the shots we finally chose," Rawlings concludes, "because they actually did show that Volkswagen down at the bottom of the frame. Thankfully, *The Shining* had been shot at 1.85:1, a more squarish format than the Panavision one in which *Blade Runner* had been shot. We were able to optically change that footage a slight bit, sort of letterbox it out, to stretch it into more of a rectangle. A good thing, too—if you projected the *Shining* outtakes we used in *Blade Runner* at their normal ratio, the audience would have seen this little yellow Volkswagen driving along in the year 2019!"

Ridley Scott now had only to shoot the live-action footage of Rachael and Deckard in his sedan to make *BR*'s new ending complete. Therefore, in late March 1982, Scott returned to the United States, and with Harrison Ford, Sean Young, a small crew, and Ivor Powell, the director traveled approximately two hours northeast of Los Angeles to film these shots near Cedar Lake, in Big Bear, California.

At this location, Deckard's sedan (which had also been brought along) was mounted on a flatbed truck. Ford and Young were then filmed in its interior as the truck traveled down a mountain road. A helicopter had also been secured to shoot the high downward angle of Deckard's land-bound car driving through the forest; this time, however, the flatbed was abandoned, and two doubles were used in Ford's, and Young's place for an aerial shot of the sedan traveling through the forest at high speed.

"I clearly remember the day we shot that live-action footage," says Ivor Powell. "Ridley and Sean and I all drove up together to the location. The trip was quite relaxing. It was a beautiful morning, Sean was listening to her Walkman and singing along to the music, everyone else was in a good mood . . . all in all, it was just a thoroughly pleasant day. Probably because we all knew that we were finally coming to the end of a monumental production."

THE SAN DIEGO SNEAK (A DIFFERENT VERSION #2)

If Powell and the other *Blade Runner* production members were pleased at the atmosphere surrounding their "happy ending" shoot, then they must have been ecstatic during the film's next preview. The ambiance embracing the third official *BR* Sneak—which was held in San Diego, California, at the Cinema 21 Theater on May 8, 1982 (a screening which this author attended)—was resolutely upbeat.

Like the Denver and Dallas previews beforehand, the San Diego *Blade Runner* screening played to a standing-room-only crowd. This author well remembers the mood in the Cinema 21 as being festive and electric. He also remembers the many Harrison Ford fans in attendance that evening; some were giggling pubescent girls, some were serious film buffs, some were science fiction fans wearing *Revenge of the Jedi* T-shirts (a *Star Wars* film also starring Ford that was then shooting near San Diego in Yuma, Arizona, and would soon undergo a title change to *Return of the Jedi*). All were ecstatic when Ford put in a surprise appearance at the screening, and the actor received a standing ovation from the entire audience when he walked into the theater five minutes before the showing began.

Also in attendance that night were Joanna Cassidy, Michael Deeley, Ridley Scott, Alan Ladd, Jr., Douglas Trumbull, and a visiting John Hurt (who'd suffered a bloody demise in Scott's previous *Alien*). The key sector of this crowd, however, was little noticed by the production team. Yet this same group would have a strong influence on the mostly positive reaction cards passed back to the Warner Brothers representatives at the end of the show. The composition of this group? The same science fiction fans noted earlier.

One member of this crowd was Cherie Buchheim, an intelligent, articulate young woman who was then in her early twenties. Buchheim's recollections of that May 1982 sneak are especially fascinating, and not only because she offers an amusing critique of the film's happy ending. Buchheim's observations also allow a rare glimpse into the science fiction mindset that would ultimately do so much to support *Blade Runner* through its lean years ahead. Not that Buchheim was particularly impressed with *Blade Runner* that evening, however, or wanted to attend the *BR* Sneak in the first place.

"Actually, I had no real interest in seeing *Blade Runner* that night," Buchheim recalls. "I might have been in one of my moods, though, because I kind of liked Harrison Ford . . .

"Anyway, I went with some friends who were also science fiction fans—one was a publisher of a *Star Wars* fanzine called *Empire Review*. I remember standing in line for hours waiting to get in. I also remember I'd dressed up for the occasion; I had on a trench coat and a snap-brim hat and a pair of black pants and boots and a silver sweater made of this shiny metallic knit. I was also wearing a pair of earrings that my father had given me for Christmas two years before, which had a battery pack that you could clip into your hair and would make the earrings light up.

"Once we got inside, I happened to notice Douglas Trumbull standing in this little recessed area with Harrison Ford at the back of the theater. I knew who Doug was because, at the time, I had some friends who worked at EEG with him.

"I'm not exactly shy, so I walked up to them and stuck out my hand. Toward Harrison. He took it, sort of gingerly. So I pulled him toward me and said, 'Look, I'm not going to hurt you. I just wanted to say that I'm sorry for every rude thing every woman has done to you since *Star Wars* came out. I also wanted to say thank you. Because I've had a lot of fun in the dark with you the past eight years.'

"Well, Harrison just gave me this blank look for a second, and then he and everybody else broke up. I didn't get it at first. Then I realized that what I'd just said hadn't sounded anything like what I'd really meant. It *was* pretty funny, though, so I laughed, too. After that Harrison totally loosened up. He even grinned and told me he liked my earrings."

However, two hours later, Buchheim "trashed" *Blade Runner* in her audience reaction card. "Some of the people I went with to that screening loved the picture. But I didn't," Buchheim recalls. "I really objected to the happy ending—I thought that was so stupid. Here you had this dark, brooding, rainy film where if the characters had enough money or their health was okay, they could go live somewhere else that was nice. But Deckard and the others had to live in horrible old Los Angeles, because they had nowhere else to go. And then, suddenly, Rick Deckard and his girlfriend are out motoring around in this gorgeous countryside in his open coupe. I mean, eh?

"In fact," Buchheim concludes, "for the longest time I used to maintain that they should have made *Blade Runner* with only music and images and no dialogue. And I wasn't the only one—I met a lot of women in fandom who didn't like *Blade Runner* for all kinds of reasons. From the serious objection of it being too downbeat and equipped with an unhappy ending, to the silly one of not liking the picture because they hadn't liked Harrison Ford's haircut.

"Still, I liked Harrison's performance—I thought that was excellent. And as I get older, I've begun to like *Blade Runner* more. I now realize I wasn't sophisticated enough at the time to appreciate everything that was going on in it."

What *was* going on in the version of *Blade Runner* screened at the San Diego Sneak? In essence, this print was totally unlike the previews seen two months earlier (Scott had made extensive changes since Denver and Dallas), and very much like the version which would be released seven weeks later as the official domestic cut.

There were a few differences, however, in the San Diego print which would be seen in no other version. These were:

1) A shot of Roy Batty in the VidPhon booth at the beginning of the film talking to someone. An earlier version of the script indicated that the replicant was calling Chew's Lab to see if the eye-maker was in. As seen in the San Diego version, however, the audience could only see Batty's lips moving, as if he was engaged in an unheard conversation.
2) A shot of Harrison Ford painfully trying to reload his gun after Batty has broken his fingers.
3) The aerial helicopter shot of Deckard's sedan racing along a road through the woods at the beginning of the new happy ending.

These differences, though minor, were enough to constitute the San Diego Sneak as the second version of *Blade Runner* seen by the public. And, of course, the San Diego preview was also the first time audiences had seen either the "Ride Into the Sunset" or the wall-to-wall narration which would also appear in the theatrical release.[4]

As for this author's assessment of the reaction to *Blade Runner's* new climax, I felt it had been mixed. Speaking to selected viewers after the screening, I learned that some in the crowd had felt that Deckard's voice-over explanation of Rachael being a new model replicant with no implanted termination date was too contradictory, or worse, a dramatic cop-out. Others found the concluding vistas of virginal timberland visually exhilarating, particularly after spending nearly two hours in the dank, cramped confines of 2019 L.A.

Despite this varied response to the new happy ending, however, the third *Blade Runner* sneak preview was—judging by the overall audience reaction—definitely more successful than the first two. There were, for example, no walkouts from this sold-out crowd. The director was also in high spirits after this screening. Smiling, accessible, answering questions from the crowd in the lobby, Ridley Scott eventually stated, "This has been our best response yet."

Toward the end of the evening, when the only people left in the Cinema 21 auditorium were the theater employees, the Warner Brother reps, the *Blade Runner* filmmakers, and myself, I stopped Scott in the lobby for a moment, produced my trusty tape recorder, and asked the director to briefly reflect on the differences between the Denver/Dallas Sneaks and this one.

"To begin, "Scott said, "a sneak preview is usually never the final print of a film. It is a rough cut, a workprint, an assemblage used to gauge audience reaction and to reorient the filmmaker towards a popular perception of his product. In this respect, I think the Denver/Dallas *Blade Runner* Sneaks served their purpose.

"Besides," Scott continued, "I think that the only true sneak audience problems concerned the climax of the film. We had originally ended *Blade Runner* with what we apprehended as an ambiguous finale; European, if you will. The Dallas and Denver Sneak Preview

---

[4]Another change between the San Diego Sneak and the Denver/Dallas previews was that a new bit of narration had been added to the scene of Deckard watching Batty die on the roof, replacing the only voice-over heard in Denver/Dallas.

versions climaxed with an elevator door closing on Rachael and Deckard's faces, leaving the nature of their plight unresolved. It was fairly apparent that the crowds didn't care for that. Which then forced us to shoot an alternative ending, one with Deckard and Rachael in Deckard's car cruising through the countryside, heading north, showing that they had escaped from the city. I think that this should be better accepted than our first choice of climaxes."

The generally "up" mood at the San Diego Sneak was later mirrored in the reactions culled from the audience response cards, which, on the whole, were far more positive than those collected after the Denver/Dallas Sneaks (although certainly not homogenous; a quick perusal of the San Diego card results shows a significant portion of the audience still bewildered, irritated, or depressed).

Warner Brothers was obviously heartened by the overall response, however. For the second paragraph of an interoffice Warner market research memo dated May 10, 1982 reads, "Moviegoer responses at this preview were significantly better than those from earlier sneaks in Denver and Dallas, and indicate that the major problems that were identified at the earlier sneaks have been either solved or substantially lessened."

In other words, Warner felt that the San Diego audience had liked Deckard's overexplanatory narration and the new happy ending.

There were still some problematic areas, however. The Warner memo cautioned that some San Diego viewers had had difficulties with "the perceived gloominess of the film" and its "slow and draggy" pace, particularly during the scenes in Deckard's apartment. Finally, the memo warned that "the presence of Harrison Ford in the theater was mentioned fairly often in the comment cards, and probably had some inflating effect on film ratings. This, combined with the fact that the audience included many hard-core science fiction buffs, should be kept in mind while reading the following report."

Such cautions seemed minor, though, in relation to the festive atmosphere in San Diego that night.

So, buoyed by the first audience which had enthusiastically embraced *Blade Runner* to its collective bosom, Scott, Deeley, Ford, and the rest of the *BR* family eagerly turned to the upcoming culmination of their labors: *Blade Runner*'s theatrical release.

THE THEATRICAL RELEASE

The scope and brilliance of Blade Runner's *vision is the good news. The bad news is that* Blade Runner's *story is absolutely hopeless, a confusing tower of babble that has great gaps of logic, abysmal structure and cardboard characters . . . In an attempt to explain things, a voice-over narration by Deckard, à la Sam Spade, has been added, but Ford reads it as if he had just been handed the lines; he sounds flat, unconvincing. And while the explanation helps on a few items, it still cannot fill the many holes.*

—REVIEW OF *BLADE RUNNER* UPON ITS ORIGINAL RELEASE
"RUNNER DOESN'T LIVE UP TO VISION," BY PHIL KLOER
FLORIDA TIMES-UNION, JUNE 29, 1982

A DIFFERENT VERSION (#3)

Seven years after Hampton Fancher first tried to option the film rights to *Do Androids Dream of Electric Sheep*, the cinematic adaptation of that novel opened nationwide, in 1,290 theaters, on June 25, 1982. The date had been specifically chosen by Alan Ladd, Jr., because two of the producer's highest-grossing previous efforts (*Star Wars* and *Alien*) had opened on the same date in 1977 and 1979; Ladd considered this particular date his "lucky day."

Interestingly, audiences who filed into theaters to view the latest Harrison Ford/Ridley Scott opus were actually seeing the *third* publicly screened version of the film. Following the San Diego Sneak, Ridley Scott had tightened up the picture's narrative and made five changes. Three were outright deletions, and two were last-minute "patches."

The trio of cut shots were Ford reloading his gun after Hauer had broken Deckard's fingers, an overhead helicopter shot of Deckard's

Harrison Ford poses beside a Blade Runner *poster during the star's 1982 tour to promote the original theatrical release of the film.*

sedan driving down a leafy road during the new "happy ending," and Rutger Hauer's introductory shot, which had shown Roy Batty standing in a VidPhon booth and talking. It was cutting this phone booth shot that caused a hasty rethinking of the entire VidPhon sequence, because now Scott and editor Terry Rawlings realized other footage was needed to take its place. But they had no time or money to shoot any further inserts.

Their solution? Duplicate two shots which *already* existed in the picture, toward the end of the film, insert these duplicates into the early VidPhon sequence, and hope that audiences wouldn't notice.

One of these "stolen" shots was a close-up of Hauer's clenching hand, which also appears in *Blade Runner*'s last act, just before Batty pierces his palm with a nail. "Besides filling in the necessary editorial gap," said Ridley Scott, "I also felt it better to let audiences know, at least subconsciously, that Batty's batteries were running down as soon as they were introduced to the character."

The second duplicated insert for the VidPhon scene also reappears much later in the film. "Once we'd duped and inserted that hand close-up into the VidPhon booth," observes Rawlings, "we then needed something to cut away to. So we stole another shot from near the end of the picture, when Batty is sitting on Tyrell's bed. It's a close-up of Hauer looking down, then looking up and smiling. We duplicated that, printed it in reverse, and then cut it in after the close-up of Roy's hand. So now it looks as if Batty is looking at his hand in the VidPhon, and then looking up and turning towards the sound of Leon tapping on the glass telephone booth."

The rank and file of the nation's moviegoers, of course, neither knew nor cared about such subtle alterations. All they were interested in was the overall effectiveness of this new motion picture.

Was it something they could recommend to their friends?

THE CREW'S REACTION

That question was initially answered by moviegoers who were anything but rank and file. The first audience to react to the original theatrical version of *Blade Runner* (a variant which, for simplicity's sake, I've been calling the Domestic Cut), were the actors and technicians who'd actually worked on the film.

Their opportunity to see the picture came through the traditional "cast and crew screening," which, in *Blade Runner*'s case, was held in mid-May 1982 at the Hollywood Theater. In attendance were most of the production's performers and crew. And although it had been almost a year since principal photography wrapped, it's not difficult to theorize that, for some members of this audience, memories of personality conflicts, budget cuts, and the T-Shirt War were still painfully fresh.

But then the lights went down, and the one-of-a-kind motion picture they'd labored so hard to bring to life flickered across the screen. Two hours later, the house lights came back up. And the resulting reactions seemed . . . complicated.

"I'd been really curious as to what the final film would look like," recalls M. Emmet Walsh, "because *Blade Runner* was one of the toughest pictures I ever did. And the crew! They'd put an enormous amount of work into this thing—you'd go down to that set, and most of the crew looked like coal miners. They'd have masks on and dirty, sweaty clothes, because of all that smoke and rain and shit. That was going on all the time. But a lot of the *Blade Runner* crew had never read the script. They'd just worked on it. And worked on it, and worked on it.

"Anyway, the cast and crew screening was first time most of us saw this picture. We watch it, it ends—and there's total silence. I mean, maybe there's a smattering of applause, but basically everyone was just stunned. No one knew what in the hell it was all about! They didn't know if it was good or bad or what. There was no feel to the crowd at all that night that they'd just seen something special."

Other *Blade Runner* cast members, however, remember seeing a much different film. "The first and only time I saw *Blade Runner* in a theater was at that cast and crew screening," recalls Daryl Hannah. "During the time of its original theatrical release, I was out of the country, shooting another picture on location. So I can still remember how excited I was when I saw *BR*. One reason was because it was the first film I'd ever had a substantial role in that actually came out!" Hannah says, laughing.

"But *Blade Runner* looked amazing," the actress continues. "And I was thrilled by it—by the storyline, the characters, the mood, everything. I was taken away by that movie, which is the main point of making a film. And I wasn't picking it apart like you usually do when you're a part of it. I experienced *Blade Runner* as a moviegoer, which was nice."

The disparity between Walsh's and Hannah's reactions was not an isolated case—*Blade Runner* seemed to encourage a diversity of opinions between its cast and crew, not a solidarity.

For example, two *BR* participants solidly *for* the film were Edward James Olmos, who said it was "unbelievable," and Joanna Cassidy, who called it "Powerful—I've seen it seven times in theaters since 1982." Yet Marvin Westmore thought the picture "beautiful, but cold." Ivor Powell, on the other hand, had mixed feelings: "It's a personal favorite of mine and I'm still proud of it, but *Blade Runner* is slightly disjointed—you don't feel for the replicants like you ought to." Terry Frazee was "amazed, but confused."

Perplexity, in fact, seemed the one common denominator running through this jumble of reactions, even among those who'd genuinely liked the film. As *Blade Runner* stunt coordinator Gary Combs recalls, "Now, I'd read the script and worked on this picture, but what I most remember during the shoot was talking with other folks on the crew and saying, 'I really don't understand this movie. I don't know what this movie is all about. And I never really did put it all together until I eventually saw it. *Then* I knew what it was all about! But I have to tell you, *Blade Runner* was one tough picture to figure out. A lot of the crew still doesn't understand it."

William Sanderson echoed this sentiment—but only to a point.

"Even now I'm not sure I get all of *Blade Runner*, all the things going on," Sanderson says. "And that cast and crew screening—whew! It was a little quiet after the movie was over, yeah. But I think a big part of that was because a lot of us were just blown away. I mean, I couldn't *believe* that motion picture!

"But then, right after the film came out, I remember picking up a newspaper and reading a review where a critic called *Blade Runner* a 'fascinating failure.' That stuck in my craw. I wish I could find that fellow right up to this day, because, to put it tritely, I'd tell him, '*Au contraire*, baby. *Au contraire*. *Blade Runner* is *not* a fascinating failure.'

"It did take a long time to catch on, though," Sanderson concludes.

THE CRITICS ATTACK ——————————————————

When the first *BR* reviews started coming in following the film's June 25 release, it rapidly became apparent that the ambiguity which had marked the cast and crew screening was being repeated in the national press. Yet within a few days, even the middle ground represented by Ivor Powell's response began falling away (just as it eventually would with the public). Critical reaction to the picture now became sharply polarized.

Unfortunately, the pole that drew the most attention was the negative one. It's easy to see why; for some reason, unfavorable *Blade Runner* reviews were particularly vitriolic, as if many of the nation's critics had somehow been personally offended by the subtlety and care that had gone into this picture. How else to explain such hostile reactions as that of Pat Berman, who, in writing for a Southern newspaper, slammed *BR* for being "like science fiction pornography—all sensation and no heart" (*State and Columbia Record*, Columbia, South Carolina, July 2, 1982)?

Perhaps this strongly negative response was generated by the same sort of confusion many of the picture's cast and crew had felt. If that was the case, then this would seem to indicate an inability of many critics to get past the (admittedly overwhelming) surface of the film in order to piece together its elliptical narrative and complex thematics.

Whatever the cause, the negative reviews kept pouring in.

For instance, Sheila Benson, in the *Los Angeles Times*, warned audiences to not ". . . let the words blade runner confuse you into expecting a super-high-speed chase film. Blade crawler might be more like it . . . "("Los Angeles in a Future Tense," *Los Angeles Times*, Los Angeles, California, June 25, 1982).

Janet Maslin, writing for the *New York Times*, called *Blade Runner*: "muddled . . . gruesome . . . a mess" ("Futuristic *Blade Runner*," *New York Times*, June 25, 1982).

The film was even condemned within some science fiction circles, the one area where it could be expected to be embraced. Respected British SF author Brian Aldiss, for example, in his 1988 book *Trillion Year Spree: The History of Science Fiction,* described *Blade Runner* as "an overheated farrago of SF crossed with private eye machismo and dragged down by pretentious sets" (*Trillion Year Spree: The History of Science Fiction,* Avon Books, 1988).

Yet all this critical sniping was as nothing compared to the heavy artillery the nation's leading film critics were about to unleash on the picture. Take the case of Roger Ebert (who, with his partner Gene Siskel, had become a major film reviewing force via the popular *At the Movies* television program). Ebert discharged what would become *the* chief criticism leveled against the film when he wrote: "The movie's weakness . . . is that it allows the special-effects technology to overwhelm its story" ("*Blade Runner* Runs on its Stunning Visuals," *Chicago Sun-Times*, September 11, 1992).

An even deadlier blow was struck by America's then leading film critic, Pauline Kael, who, in a long, penetrating but ultimately negative *BR* essay for the July 12 issue of the *New Yorker* (entitled "Baby, the Rain Must Fall"), sarcastically remarked, "If anybody comes around with a test to detect humanoids, maybe Ridley Scott and his associates should hide."

A few bad reviews won't kill a picture, of course. But as *Blade Runner* continued its run through July 1982, the negative ink began to swell and accumulate to such a point that the film is now remembered as generating nothing *but* bad press at the time of its original release.

That is not accurate history. A careful examination of the *Blade Runner* critiques published in 1982 does indeed reveal many positive voices, such as "New Wave" science fiction author Norman Spinrad's, who rebutted Brian Aldiss' dismissal of the film when Spinrad enthused that *Blade Runner* was "truer to what science fiction is all about than just about any 'SF movie' yet made (*Starlog* #64, November 1982).

Another positive *BR* critique came from *Christianity Today* reviewer Hiawatha Bray, who maintained that the film was "a surprisingly serious science-fiction release . . . of all the summer's releases, only *Blade Runner* is truly adult in its thoughtfulness and complexity" (*Christianity Today,* Volume 26 #14, September 3, 1982).

However, the most prophetic of the pro-*Blade Runner* reviews surely came from John Bloom who, in writing for the *Dallas Times Herald* ("Republican Pod People, Circa 1982," *Dallas Times Herald,* Dallas, Texas, June 25, 1982), noted that *"Blade Runner* is a well-crafted film, even despite occasional lapses and its occasional reliance on heavy-handed, graphic violence. I suspect history will be kinder to it than the critics."

Score one for Mr. Bloom. But as this nation's media has proven time and again, it's hard to say something positive about a topic when you're being drowned out by hysterically negative screeching.

Among all the naysaying and sarcasm which greeted *Blade Runner* upon its initial release, however, lurked a certain delicious irony. The two things reviewers hated most about this picture were the two very same eleventh-hour add-ons that Tandem Productions had so hoped would make the film more palatable to the general public: the voice-over and the happy ending.

Pauline Kael summarized the critical displeasure at Ford's narration in her "Baby, the Rain Must Fall" piece: "This voice-over, which is said to have been a late addition, sounds ludicrous, and it breaks the visual hold of the material."

Terry Kelleher, in the *Miami Herald* (Miami, Florida, June 26, 1982) then nailed the lid on *BR*'s "Ride into the Sunset" coffin by reporting that "what really irked me about *Blade Runner* was its seemingly tacked-on, totally superfluous, 'Feel Good' ending. After a depressing couple of hours at the movies, it's even more depressing to see the director succumb to a last minute fear of being too depressing."

A good point—but one that also proves how little some critics know about the harsh realities lying beneath the glamorous face of filmmaking.

AN INDIFFERENT PUBLIC ─────────────────────

Although *Blade Runner* did well enough during its opening weekend (grossing $6,150,000), that figure was deceiving. If one divides that $6 million dollars by the 1,290 theaters where the film was being run, the resultant sum clearly indicates something less than a box-office smash. And as June rolled into July of 1982, *BR*'s receipts kept steadily dropping at the box office.

What was happening? One theory came from syndicated columnist Marilyn Beck:

"I predicted weeks ago," Beck wrote, "that the glut of pictures being dumped on the market place this summer would result in many movies not finding audiences. Now that prediction seems to be coming true, with a situation Alan Ladd Jr. (whose company produced *Blade Runner*) refers to as 'a head-on collision course'" ("Big Summer at the Box Office Appears to Fizzle," *Democrat and Chronicle*, Rochester, New York, July 1, 1982).

Blade Runner had indeed had the bad luck to be released at a time when big-budget science fiction/fantasy films glutted the market. *Star Trek II: The Wrath of Khan, Conan the Barbarian,* John Carpenter's remake of *The Thing*—all of these mainstream genre films invaded multiplexes the same summer of 1982.

Or maybe *Blade Runner*'s lackluster box office could simply be laid at the feet of audiences unwilling to embrace a downbeat, morally ambiguous film featuring a dour performance from a leading action hero, one whose previous triumphs had been in upbeat entertainments like *Star Wars* and *Raiders of the Lost Ark.* In which case the callback reports produced by the Warner publicity department following the Denver/Dallas Sneak Previews had again been right. Yet the most probable factor behind the increasingly dismal financial showing of Ridley Scott's darkly visioned film can be summed up in two letters: *E.T.*

Blade Runner had been unveiled shortly after the release of *E.T.,* a Spielbergian bonbon which was not only in direct box-office competition with *BR,* but was also the sentimental antithesis of *Runner*'s gritty pessimism. And as profits continued to mount for this manipulative and saccharine tale of a friendly alien stranded on Earth, it became apparent to everyone—critics, audiences, filmmakers—that 1982 clearly was going to become the feel-good summer of *E.T.*

Yet, as Michael Deeley explains, he had not only known in advance that *E.T.* would be sharing *BR*'s time slot, he'd not been worried about it.

Not at first, at any rate.

"Although we knew in advance that *Blade Runner* would be coming out the same summer as *E.T.*, none of us were particularly distraught over the situation. The feeling we'd had was that by the time six weeks had passed—which was how long after Spielberg's film debuted that *Blade Runner* appeared in theaters—the slushy sentimentality of *E.T.* would have palled, and people would be ready for something a bit harder. That was what I genuinely believed.

"*E.T.* was quite charming," Deeley continues, "but I thought it was relatively lightweight. Which made me doubly sure that people would become bored with it quite quickly and be even more ready for us. The truth was, *E.T.* so dominated the atmosphere of what you might call 'space fiction' for that summer that nothing else was going to be considered. It took over the sensibility of audiences, which left no room for a different view.

"So I was very optimistic about *Blade Runner*'s chances, until it was demonstrated that I shouldn't have been. But I think history has borne out that optimism on my part. *E.T.* isn't very interesting nowadays, even though it made a lot of money for its director. While, on the other hand, the respect that *Blade Runner* has since earned tells the tale."

E.T., a complex storyline, a glutted market, an audience expecting one type of picture and getting another—all of these factors seem plausible reasons for the film's initially poor performance. However, there is one other theory to be explored, one that hardly ever comes up in discussions of this sort but seems (to this author, at least) to be just as plausible as any of the other rationales regarding *BR*'s box-office breakdown.

That theory involves a dangerous emotion that a film can sometimes generate in an audience, one which can critically influence any movie's failure or success. This emotion, and its resultant negative effect, was best described by Jeff Simon in *The Buffalo News* (July 18, 1982) when he cautioned that "if you demand narrative interest, pace and human feelings, [then] *Blade Runner* is, as my daughter succinctly put it, 'boring.'"

And boredom has yet to win over any mainstream audience.

SHOCK IN THE TRENCHES ━━━━━━━━━━━━

As *BR*'s financial returns in the summer of 1982 progressively plunged week after dismal week, the writing on the wall began appearing in ten-foot-high capital letters: *BLADE RUNNER* IS A FLOP. The realization hurt.

"On the personal level, I was very disappointed with *Blade Runner*'s performance," Michael Deeley recalls. "We all were. It had been such a hard thing to, a) get it made, and b) to keep it being made. But I've done a lot of controversial pictures. Some have come off, and some haven't. So at least to that extent, you sort of get used to failure."

Rutger Hauer, however, was less sanguine concerning the film's poor performance. "I had a number of problems with *Blade Runner* when I first saw it," the Dutch actor explains. "But most of these had to do with matters of interpretation or performance or technique. Basically, I'd been blown away by this film. So I could not believe it when moviegoers expressed this 'love it or hate it' attitude towards the picture. It was as if the audience had been split with a razor."

This split, the negative reviews, and all other mitigating factors eventually insured that *Blade Runner* would only gross a paltry $14 million during its initial theatrical run. Considering that the film's production floor had been over $28 million, it is not exaggerating to describe *BR*'s maiden appearance as a resounding financial flop, a situation which, under normal circumstances, would have ended the *Blade Runner* story right there.

GONE . . . BUT NOT QUITE FORGOTTEN ━━━━━━━━

Yet even in the midst of the gloom settling down upon the picture's first theatrical run, certain parties clung to stubborn thoughts of optimism concerning the film's eventual fate.

One of them was Hampton Fancher.

"I'd stayed away from almost every aspect of the production once I'd stopped writing *Blade Runner*'s script," Fancher told me in 1995. "The little I had seen of the finished product, dailies and rough assemblies and whatnot, made me angry, because it certainly wasn't the *Blade Runner* I wanted to see released. In fact, when I finally did go to see it at an Academy screening just before *Blade Runner* was released,

I knew a lot of the cast and crew members were going to show up, too. So I went hoping not to see any of the people involved, because I didn't want to boldfacedly hate them.

"But after I saw the completed picture, I was astounded. Some of that reaction came from purely selfish places. For example, I'd been hard up for an image one day when I'd been writing the screenplay, so I'd asked Barbara Hershey to give me something. And she'd started to tell me about this dream she'd had as a little girl, about these little baby spiders being hatched and eating up their mother. I then transferred that dream verbatim into the scene where Deckard tells Rachael that he knows her memories.

"Now, Barbara was in the audience at the screening that night, and I was just so thrilled that she was seeing her memory up there on the screen. That moment was like a little homage to Barbara's encouragement, because she'd helped me through the whole writing process."

However, Fancher was not only pleased by his personal associations with the picture—he also felt *Blade Runner* had much to recommend it for all audiences.

"Man, when that first Vangelis music cue went *ka-BOOM!* and you saw that industrial landscape, people just sucked the breath out of that room," Fancher recalls. "I was riveted by the rest of the picture, too. Discounting the voice-over and happy ending, which I hated, I thought Ridley had pulled off an incredible accomplishment. I was so thrilled at his genius.

"In fact, after the lights came up, I saw Ridley standing in an aisle and I rushed up to give him a hug. At first he kind of shrunk back; later on Ridley told me he was surprised to get a hug out of me, because he'd thought it was going to be a hit. But I said, 'No, no. I'm impressed! I had no idea you were going to mount the picture like this! I've never seen anything like it!'"

Fancher's enthusiasm might seem misplaced, given *Blade Runner*'s subsequent box-office brush-off. Yet within a relatively short period of time his excitement would be justified. For like *BR's* coscreenwriter and executive producer, not everyone had found the film to be a failure.

Indeed, a core cadre of original viewers had also been overwhelmed—in the most positive of sense of the word—by Scott and company's massive *future noir*. The experience had been so profound, in fact, that these viewers became born-again *Blade Runner* boosters, recommending or debating or writing about the picture at every opportunity. Before too long, these enthusiasts began meeting and linking up with one another.

Whereupon there suddenly existed a small but ferociously loyal network of *Blade Runner* aficionados, fans who would remain excited by the film long after its theatrical release. They would swap arcane information regarding the motion picture, rabidly follow the film's subsequent incarnations on videotape, collect various *Blade Runner* laser discs.

All the while, others kept joining the network.

THE CULT

Your review of Blade Runner *was unfair to both the director and the actors. Harrison Ford gave his character depth and intelligence, two qualities your reviewer missed.* Blade Runner *will no doubt end up as a cult movie. Its one error was to present too much for the average viewer. I'm not the only one in this town who saw the movie six times and noticed new things each time. It was rich in detail and excitement and long on drama and message.*

—LETTER FROM READER J. P. BYRD TO *PEOPLE* MAGAZINE
"MAIL: PEOPLE PICKS & PANS"
PEOPLE WEEKLY 18, NO. 8 (AUGUST 22, 1982)

If the pithy, prescient letter that begins this chapter had been written in 1992, its insights would be unremarkable. After all, by then *People* reader J. P. Byrd would have had a full decade to rewatch *Blade Runner* on video, and a good ten years to examine the many *BR*—related articles and essays which have been published since the film's 1982 release.

The fact that Byrd's missive was printed less than eight weeks after *Blade Runner's* original theatrical premiere, however, is nothing short of astonishing—not so much because of its early perceptiveness, but because of its *precision*.

In a few well-chosen words, J. P. Byrd's rebuttal of *People's* negative review had managed to neatly encapsulate the very essence of *Blade Runner's* widespread, and still growing, appeal.[1]

---

[1] Whoever and wherever you are, Mr. Byrd, I salute you.

A GROWING POPULARITY ━━━━━━━━━━━━━━━━━━

After its initial release and financial failure, it could be expected that *Blade Runner* would quietly fade from public consciousness. In fact, exactly the opposite occurred: the film rapidly *built* on the relatively small core audience which had originally embraced it, and this popularity continued to grow until the motion picture attained its current status as a cultural icon.

But besides the "depth, intelligence and detail" which J. P. Byrd pointed out, could there have been other causes behind *BR*'s remarkable metamorphosis from theatrical flop to cult film par excellence?

Most assuredly. And like a metaphoric chain reaction, each new cause unleashed an even greater effect, until the resulting explosion of interest simply became too *noisy* to ignore.

One of the first (and major) catalysts behind *BR*'s resurgence was the sudden, near-simultaneous expansion of the cable television and home video markets, both of which experienced a surge of consumer interest at the time of the film's release. Although videotapes and cable TV were still in their relative infancy in 1982, like all infants, they were hungry. Hungry for product, in this case. And one of the first providers who stepped forward to satisfy that growing appetite was Warner Brothers, *Blade Runner*'s parent company.

Following *Blade Runner*'s financial failure in 1982, Warners hurriedly initiated a then new distribution strategy designed to maximize profits from films whose initial box-office reception had been mediocre. The studio's plan involved pulling *BR* from its theatrical engagements and rereleasing the motion picture through Warner Brothers' own Warner-Amex Satellite Entertainment Network in late 1982, resulting in *Blade Runner* being quickly telecast on such premium cable television outlets as the (now defunct) Spotlight TV Channel. Now the picture was suddenly being pumped into the living rooms of millions of viewers who normally wouldn't have taken the trouble to see a science fiction film in a theater. Even more encouraging was the fact that many of those same viewers liked what they saw.

At the same time, Embassy Entertainment released *Blade Runner* on home video and laser disc in 1983. Once again the film proved popular in a new format; not only were the ever-loyal cadres of science fiction fans renting, rerenting, and buying the picture on tape and disc, the much-larger group of viewers who'd missed the film during its theatrical release were now trooping to their neighborhood video stores to see if the increasingly positive *Blade Runner* buzz was justified.

Yet another sector of the home video market for which *Blade Runner* held new appeal was those who'd initially loved the picture—or been puzzled by it. Putting *BR* on tape meant that any viewer who'd either already embraced the film or been confused by its narrative subtlety/visual overload could now rewatch *BR* a second, third, or even fourth time.

All of these factors eventually coalesced to make *Blade Runner* one of the most rented tapes on the home video market, to which numerous trade journals continue to attest. As for the retail end of the video business, *BR* producer Michael Deeley has informed this author that, according to a financial statement the producer received in late 1994, *Blade Runner* had sold almost a *half-million* cassettes!

Not all of the renewed attention given to *Blade Runner* can be ascribed to only home video or cable TV, however. For as interest in the film continued to build throughout the 1980s, things were also hopping on the literary front. Appreciative *Blade Runner* articles now began appearing in such influential cinema magazines as *Film Comment, American Film, Premiere,* and *Sight and Sound,* all trumpeting the same virtues which J. P. Byrd had pointed out in 1982. Meanwhile, things were also stirring on the print world's grassroots level. In December 1982, for instance, a young woman named Sara Campbell (based in Madison, Wisconsin), published the first *Blade Runner* fanzine.

This homegrown publication was titled *Cityspeak.* It contained articles, essays, short stories, poems, and letters of comment, all exclusively devoted to *Blade Runner. Cityspeak* was eagerly snapped up by core members of the nascent *Blade Runner* cult, and the first *BR* 'zine would continue to appear for two more issues until *Cityspeak* editor Sara Campbell's untimely death, at age twenty-six, in 1985.

The surest sign that *Blade Runner* had been embraced by the nation's literati, however, came in 1991, when the Bowling Green State University Popular Press published an entire book devoted to the film. Titled *Retrofitting* Blade Runner: *Issues in Ridley Scott's* Blade Runner *and Philip K. Dick's* Do Androids Dream of Electric Sheep, this impressive academic volume was edited by Judith B. Kerman and looked at "the multitude of texts and influences which converge in Ridley Scott's film." Among the book's nineteen well-written, scholarly essays were such thoughtful contributions as Kerman's own

"Technology and Politics in the *Blade Runner* Dystopia," Gregg Rickman's "Philip K. Dick on *Blade Runner:* They Did Sight Stimulation on my Brain," William M. Kolb's *"Blade Runner* Film Notes," and David Desser's "Race, Space and Class: The Politics of the SF Film from *Metropolis* to *Blade Runner." Retrofitting* Blade Runner then concluded with an exhaustive bibliography, also written by William Kolb, which catalogued every magazine, newspaper or book reference to the film. (An abridged version of this bibliography appears in appendix G: A Short *BR* Bibliography.)

The nineties saw the growing interest in *Blade Runner* then leapfrog onto an entirely new media: the home computer network. Such popular entities as Usenet newsgroups on the Internet and home pages on the World Wide Web now began featuring such popular *Blade Runner* "homes" as Murray Chapman's *Blade Runner FAQ* (Frequently Asked Questions) and Jon Van Oast's *2019: Off-World Page.* Both became easily accessible to computer users equipped with so-called "browser" software for the Web like Netscape Navigator. Users who logged on to these sites found them chockfull of digitized pictures, sound clips, trivia questions, and hard data, all specifically pertaining to Ridley Scott's classic. (For more information on how to connect with these and the many other *BR* sites, please turn to Appendix D: *Blade Runner* Online.)

Yet perhaps the greatest confirmation of the fact that *Blade Runner* had risen phoenix-like and triumphant from the ashes of its failure was expressed by Hollywood's most sincere form of flattery: it imitated the hell out of it.

The *BR* "look" began spilling over into literally dozens of television series, music videos, and motion pictures, all of which shamelessly copied the original's striking production and lighting designs. This wholesale pilfering was apparent in everything from medium-budget productions such as *Brazil* to low-budget action pictures such as *Cyborg II,* from short-lived television series such as *Mann and Machine* to more enduring entries such as the *Max Headroom* TV show. Even Asian animators and rock musicians got into the act; the Rolling Stones' 1989 "Steel Wheels" tour featured a *Blade Runner*-ish stage set, while the apocalyptic 1988 Japanese animated feature *Akira* was set against the Far East equivalent of Scott's 2019 Los Angeles. And this cinematic "borrowing" has continued unabated into the nineties; *Strange Days, Judge Dredd,* and *Johnny Mnemonic* (this last ironically designed by Syd Mead), were all released in 1995, and are only three of the most recent big-budget examples of *BR*'s all-pervading cinematic influence.

Obviously, then, the quality, design, and ideation which so typified *Blade Runner* had, like some invasive yet benign virus, been increasingly spread throughout its pop-culture host via the media's bloodstream. So ubiquitous was the film's artistic infestation, in fact, that *Blade Runner* became the touchstone for a ˚new literary movement, one which closely mirrored the motion picture's techno/sociological concerns.

The name of that movement? Cyberpunk.

THE BIRTH OF CYBERPUNK ——————————

A subbranch of literary science fiction, cyberpunk, like *Blade Runner*, was a clearcut product of the 1980s; both embraced the diversity of the increasingly complex social, cultural, and scientific landscapes that decade produced, while simultaneously questioning the value system of the Reagan-era power structure.

Cyberpunk also utilized many of the same narrative devices as *Blade Runner*; cyberpunk fiction was typically set in a sprawling megalopolis of the near, dark, and decadent future, pitted hard-edged, street-level outlaws against omniscient (and corrupt) corporations, and viewed emerging hypertechnologies with equal portions of fascination and distrust. And despite its air of superficial diffidence, cyberpunk—also very much like *Blade Runner*—was, at heart, essentially *moral* art, deeply concerned with all the flaws, compromises, and ethical choices that will always haunt humanity no matter how exotic or futuristic the background against which human dramas are played out.

Yet the most striking similarity between *Blade Runner* and cyberpunk is the most noticeable one: style. As editor Bruce Sterling, himself a noted cyberpunk author, wrote in the introduction to his 1988 paperback *Mirrorshades* anthology (Berkley/Ace), "Cyberpunk is known for its telling use of detail, its carefully constructed intricacy, its willingness to carry extrapolation into the fabric of daily life. It favors 'crammed' prose: rapid, dizzying bursts of novel information, sensory overload that submerges the reader in the literary equivalent of the hard-rock 'wall of sound.'"

And doesn't *that* all sound familiar?

THE INTERNATIONAL CUT (A DIFFERENT VERSION #4)————

In one sense, the eighties, growing interest with all things *Blade Runner*-ian peaked in 1987 with the release of The Criterion Collection's deluxe, letterboxed laser disc presentation of the film. For the first time, fans could enjoy *Blade Runner* in their homes in all its wide-screen glory, at a resolution sixty percent sharper than that possible on regular videotape.

The deluxe Criterion *BR* disc had been put together with the cooperation of Ridley Scott, who stressed that he preferred the wide-screen Panavision process in which the film had been originally shot. The deluxe Criterion disc was then pressed in the CAV format, which meant that such interactive functions as freeze-frame, slow motion, random access, and fast motion could be accessed through properly equipped laser disc players (a wide-screen CLV Criterion disc was also issued, but without these special functions, or the added supplements which I will discuss later).

In addition to the elements stated above, The Criterion Collection's CAV version of *Blade Runner* is notable for a number of other reasons. First, for many years it was Criterion's number one selling laser disc, indicating that the public was willing to pay a premium price (around $100) for a letterboxed version of a film obviously gaining in popularity. The second distinguishing characteristic of this disc was that it *didn't* contain the same version of the motion picture American audiences had seen during *Blade Runner*'s original theatrical release.

Instead, a somewhat longer, slightly more violent "International Cut" had been transferred onto the Criterion disc, a print that had previously played only outside the United States. This International Cut added approximately fifteen seconds of graphic footage which had been removed from the film following the Denver/Dallas Sneak previews, whose audiences had rejected the intensity of these moments.

In any event, these extra fifteen seconds of footage can be found in three sequences of the International Cut:

1) *Batty's Murder of Tyrell.* The International Cut added a close-up of Roy sticking his thumbs into Tyrell's eyes, which then bleed copiously. Another close-up showed Batty removing his thumbs from Tyrell's bloody sockets.

2) *Deckard's Fight With/Killing of Pris.* Two extra shots were inserted while Pris is beating Deckard up. After Deckard has fallen on his back to the ground, the International Cut showed Pris inserting two of her fingers into Deckard's nose and pulling it up. Another shot, from a different angle, then showed Deckard's head between Pris' legs, with her fingers pulling Deckard's nose even farther back.

After Pris has been shot once by Deckard and bounces off the wall onto Sebastian's apartment floor, all other versions of the film show Ford getting up and firing at her one more time (a total of two shots) to finish her off. However, the International Cut shows Deckard getting up and shooting her *twice more*, making Deckard shoot Pris *three* times. The International Cut also included a little extra footage of Pris thrashing around on the floor; it has *four* separate shots of Pris wailing and pounding her hands and fists on the floor, while all other versions contain only *three* shots of Pris doing this.

3) *Final Confrontation Between Deckard and Batty.* During Batty's murderous chase of Deckard through Sebastian's apartment, the replicant pauses to jam a nail through his hand. The International Cut added two extra shots here: one shows the nail popping out of the back of Batty's hand (in close-up), and the other (also a close-up) showed that protruding nail sticking out of the back of his bleeding hand.

TAPES AND DISCS

As has already been noted in this chapter, one of the major forces behind *Blade Runner*'s growing popularity throughout the eighties and early nineties was the fact that it was readily available on tape and laser disc. What follows is a brief rundown of the specific videotapes and discs that helped build that cult.

Blade Runner's tape and disc rights were first bought by Embassy Home Entertainment, an offshoot of producer Joseph E. Levine's now-defunct Avco-Embassy group. Little did Embassy know, however, that they would enter the *BR* trivia books when, in 1983, the company released two different versions of the same film.

The 1983 Embassy *BR* videotape (marketed in both the VHS and

Beta formats) was actually a copy of the same International Cut. However, the CLV format, pan-and-scan laser disc which Embassy released in 1983 (and re-pressed in 1987) was actually what this author calls a "Domestic Cut" of the film—exact "R-rated" copies of *Blade Runner* as it first appeared during its 1982 American theatrical run.[2]

Sadly, these two long-out-of-print discs became instant collector's items, since they are the *only* American laser discs (or tapes, for that matter) that showcase *BR* as it originally appeared in U.S. theaters. Indeed, for the next ten years (up until the 1993 release of video/laser disc copies of the Director's Cut), every single *BR* tape or disc released in this country was mastered with the unrated International Cut version.

Companies that released the International Cut usually didn't try to disguise the fact, however. For instance, an early Embassy *BR* video box displayed this amusingly hyperbolic caveat:

"WARNING: THIS FILM CONTAINS NEVER BEFORE RELEASED SCENES OF GRAPHIC VIOLENCE WHICH WERE EDITED OUT OF THE THEATRICAL RELEASE IN AN ATTEMPT TO SOFTEN THE VERY ADULT TONE OF THE PICTURE. SEE MORE OF THE FUTURE IN THE YEAR 2019 . . . IF YOU DARE!"

In 1986, Embassy again released the International Cut on videocassette, this time with CX encoding. In 1987 the third Embassy *BR* cassette was released, again sporting the International Cut; that same year heralded the arrival of the Nelson Entertainment *Blade Runner* International Cut tape, which was the first to feature Surround Sound (Nelson had bought the *BR* video rights from an out-of-business Embassy). And of course 1987 also marked the debut of Criterion's CAV/CLV International Cut discs.

For the next five years, the Nelson tape became the standard by which most people judged the film. But then, in 1992, New Line Home Video (Columbia TriStar Home Video) bought the *BR* video rights from Nelson Entertainment. The same year, New Line released its own *BR* tape in a new video box, one which proudly claimed that this version was a "Tenth Anniversary Edition" of the film. But all hopes of perhaps discovering yet another variant of the picture (the Workprint? the Director's Cut? something else?) were immediately

---

[2]The 1987 Embassy Domestic Cut disc also displayed an error on its dust jacket by displaying a "NR" (Not Rated) warning, suggesting that this same jacket was wrapped around the more violent International Cut. It wasn't—what lay within was the Domestic Cut.

dashed when viewers realized that New Line had simply repackaged the same old pan-and-scan International Cut that all other companies had been selling for the past decade, although this particular version was remastered, resulting in slightly better audio/video quality. The New Line tape even had the gall to open with the original Embassy logo! "10th Anniversary Edition," indeed.

But this International Cut glut was about to be swept away by a whole new phenomenon in the *Blade Runner* story: the discovery, reconstruction, and release of both the Workprint and the Director's Cut.

THE WORKPRINT

Fans of Ridley Scott's science fiction adventure "Blade Runner," starring Harrison Ford, flocked to the NuArt Theater on the Westside over the weekend to see a new 112-minute "Director's Cut" version not previously seen in theaters. The movie set a weekend box-office record at the revival house, taking in $31,496 for the Friday, Saturday and Sunday showings, according to Landmark Theaters. At the moment, there is only one print of the director's version in release.[1]

—"MORNING REPORT" (UNCREDITED)
LOS ANGELES TIMES, OCTOBER 1, 1991

The remarkable attention devoted to *Blade Runner* between 1982 and 1991 eventually resulted in what some may now see as a foregone conclusion: the theatrical rerelease of the picture.

However, such a move is actually an unusual one, especially by film industry standards. Conventional Hollywood wisdom has always maintained that once a film dies at the box office (as *BR* most assuredly did), it's gone for good. "We could cut our losses by unloading this product on cable or video," goes traditional studio thinking. "But rebook a ten-year-old picture—and a loser, at that—into multiplexes around America? Forget it." Which makes the fact of *Blade Runner*'s theatrical resurrection a most unusual occurrence.

When you realize that this rerelease happened not once, but *twice*—and in two consecutive years, with two completely different versions of the film—then "unusual" changes to "astonishing."

---

[1] Contrary to what the inestimable *L.A. Times* called it here, the version of *Blade Runner* shown at the NuArt Theater was *not* the Director's Cut. It was the *Workprint*, as we shall see later in this chapter.

EVERYTHING OLD IS NEW AGAIN————————————————

In 1989, a stereo-film preservationist named Michael Arick was performing his routine duties as asset manager for the Corporate Film and Video Services division of Warner Brothers Pictures when he made a most unusual discovery.

Arick had begun his singular career a few years earlier, after writing an influential feature article for the British Film Institute's house magazine, *Sight and Sound*. "That was an unusual piece," Arick now recalls, "because it touched on an area not many studios were familiar with—sound reconstruction. But it was a subject that very much interested me; in fact, I had already been specializing in the study and retrieval of stereo soundtracks from motion pictures produced during the early years of stereo sound. And the article itself explained how stereo sound elements from films made during the early 'scope period—wide-screen pictures of the fifties and early sixties—were almost uniformly missing from many studio prints. Because the studios had destroyed the original masters, not thinking they would use them again."

While researching his *Sight and Sound* piece, Arick had stumbled across "what were possibly the last one or two stereo prints of *East of Eden* and *Rebel Without a Cause*." Encouraged by his find and by the interest his article had generated among certain Hollywood studios, Arick then began hiring himself out as a sound reconstruction consultant, one employed by a number of different film companies (such as Fox) in order to catalog and recover whatever stereo prints he could find for each studio.

By the late eighties, Arick was working for Warner Brothers in this capacity. He'd been involved in the long process of tracking down and restoring that studio's stereo print library when, one day in September 1989, Arick found himself at the TODD-AO film vaults on Seward Street in Hollywood. This was where Warner Brothers stored many of their early stereo prints; at the time, Arick was searching for a large-format (wide-screen 70mm) print of the 1962 Natalie Wood musical, *Gypsy*.

What he found instead would alter film history.

"Whenever you're working on a restoration or retrieval project," Arick explains, "you don't just keep your eyes open for the particular title you're searching for—you're always on the lookout for anything else that looks promising. That's why, as I was walking up and down the aisles of the TODD-AO vault searching for a 70mm Technorama striped-stereo print of *Gypsy*, I was also keeping an eye out for any other interesting large-format prints I might find.

"Suddenly, I came across these Goldbergs *[metal film cans used to transport film reels back and forth to theaters]* that were marked with these words: "Technicolor. London. *Blade Runner*. 70mm print." I was immediately interested in that, because I knew a little bit about *Blade Runner*'s history. I knew that it had been cut in London, and that Technicolor London had probably done the processing for what I'd heard were only two or three 70mm *Blade Runner* prints ever made.[2] I also knew that if this was the case, then this London print was probably what you're calling the International Cut. The one with the extra violence shown in Europe.

"But I had to be sure those film cans really held *Blade Runner*," Arick continues. "A lot of these older Goldbergs have been freighted back and forth around the country for many years, and sometimes projectionists put the wrong film in the wrong can. So I pulled the reels out, gave them a quick visual check, and verified that they did indeed hold a 70mm version of *Blade Runner*."

Arick, however, did not screen the print—"There really was no reason to at that point"—so he was unaware of just what exactly he had found. Instead, the sound preservationist then spent the next few months in a "frustrating" attempt to reclaim the 70mm *Blade Runner* for Warner Brothers' own archives.

"There's always talk about 'lost' films and negatives," Arick explains of his efforts to secure this print. "But a lot of times, what's really happened is that this 'lost' material has somehow found its way into the hands of private collectors, which then makes tracking it down again that much more difficult. I didn't want that to happen to a rarity like a large-format *Blade Runner*. So I kept trying to obtain that print from TODD-AO before it suddenly 'disappeared.'"

Recovering the print, however, was no easy task. "The first time I asked for it was in September, but it wasn't delivered until December,"

---

[2]Although he admits his memory is cloudy on this point, producer Michael Deeley now says he thinks these 70mm prints had been struck for *BR*'s original theatrical release and were to be shown in two select movie houses, one on the East Coast, one on the West. "But due to certain circumstances, I don't think those prints were ever really placed in any U.S. theater during the film's initial playdates."

Arick recalls. "I couldn't really push the issue without rustling some feathers, because at the time there was some question as to whether this particular print actually belonged to Twentieth Century Fox. It was said they had distribution rights to the picture in England."

Eventually, however, the 70mm *Blade Runner* print—still unscreened—was delivered to Warner Brothers and Arick, who immediately placed the print in storage in an off-inventory vault, where it probably would have gathered dust as a low-priority item, if not for a certain telephone call Arick received a few months later.

THE FAIRFAX AND UCLA SCREENINGS

"In early 1990," writes William Kolb in his definitive article on the finding and reconstruction of *BR's* Workprint and the Director's Cut[3]:

A shot seen only in the Workprint: dancers in hockey masks and Geisha wigs undulate in plastic bubbles outside the Snake Pit Club.

[3]"*Blade Runner:* The Director's Cut That Nearly Wasn't," *The Perfect Vision*, Vol. 6, #23, October 1994.

"Rob Bartha, manager of the Los Angeles Fairfax Theater, requested a 70mm [Warner Brothers] print for their spring classic-film festival. The Warner theatrical exchange in Encino did not have a copy so Bartha requested they contact Arick at the studio. Bartha had heard about Arick's discovery and had gotten assistance from the studio in the past. Arick responded to the request and made arrangements for the exchange courier to pick up the [print] prior to the showing; in return, Bartha would clean the 70mm print for the studio."

The "1990 spring festival" to which Kolb refers was a short series of 70mm-only films which the Los Angeles Cineplex-Odeon Fairfax Theater was running in May of that year. And once the Fairfax had received the large-format print from Warner, they immediately scheduled a special 70mm *Blade Runner* screening at 10 A.M. on Sunday, May 6.

No one expected the strong audience response to this showing, however, especially the patrons who arrived Sunday morning only to discover that all tickets to the screening were already sold out.

Michael Arick, of course, hadn't needed a ticket to attend. But imagine Arick's surprise when what he'd expected to see—the International version of *Blade Runner*—was not in the least bit like what was unspooling across the Fairfax's screen.

"It only took me a couple of minutes to realize that what I was watching was a version of *Blade Runner* I was completely unfamiliar with," Arick recalls. "Right up front, instead of the usual expository crawl I'd come to expect, was a whole new definition for the word replicant, which supposedly had been quoted from a twenty-first-century dictionary. Another difference concerned this print's main titles: a white line zoomed in from offscreen, bisected the frame, and then the words 'Harrison Ford' and 'Blade Runner' sprouted up or down from that line to the sound of knife-blades scraping against each other. For a moment I was kind of confused by all this. Needless to say, I then became very excited."

So was the rest of the Fairfax's upscale, mostly film-buff audience, for the print they were watching was definitely *not* the International Cut. It was not even the domestic version, which had been originally released in American theaters.

Instead, what Arick had inadvertently salvaged was a 70mm print of the *Blade Runner* first screened at those long-ago, now-fabled Dallas and Denver Sneak Preview shows.

"There were so many differences between this version of the picture and any other I'd seen that I couldn't keep track of all of them," Arick continues. "The main dissimilarities, however, seemed to address themselves to two points. This Fairfax print *didn't* have any of Harrison Ford's narration on it, for example, except for a few words Ford says when Rutger Hauer is dying on the roof. This version also didn't have the original happy ending, where Ford and Sean Young drive off into the mountains together. Instead, the 70mm version climaxed with Ford walking into an elevator where Sean Young was waiting for him, as the doors closed on both of them."

When the Fairfax's lights finally came up, "the excitement in the auditorium was palpable," Arick recalls. "I and everyone else in that theater knew we'd seen something special. People were even hanging around in the lobby after the show holding little discussion groups, trying to figure out what the heck it was they'd just seen."

However, Arick knew that the best way to discover whatever *BR* variant this remarkable print represented was to get in touch with the film's director. Therefore, on June 27, 1990, Ridley Scott was invited to a private showing of the Fairfax print on the Warner Brothers studio lot, in Screening Room 5.

Arick approached this screening, however, with some degree of reservation.

"I'd heard that Ridley loses interest pretty quickly in his past work because he's always so focused on whatever job is currently at hand. And, in fact, about midway through this Warners screening, Ridley kind of fell asleep. He was in the middle of making *Thelma and Louise* then, though, so he was probably pretty tired.

"But then the weirdest thing happened," Arick continues. "After the screening, Ridley thought he'd seen the unicorn in this print. He hadn't. It wasn't there. He was a little insistent about that, though. So we all sort of went, 'Yeah, yeah . . .'⁴

"Anyway, Ridley told us what we'd shown at the Fairfax was actually a 70mm version of a Workprint he'd used for test screenings in Denver and Dallas in 1982. He seemed pretty pleased about seeing it again, in fact, Ridley more or less intimated that, since this version of the film was closer to what he'd originally intended than the one which had been originally released to theaters, maybe there might be

---

⁴The now-considered-to-be-lost original unicorn shot is discussed at greater length in chapter XVII: The Director's Cut.

some value in cleaning the Workprint up or restoring it and releasing it as a Director's Cut."

This "cleaning up" process referred to the fact that the Dallas/ Denver print had not yet been fine-tuned before showing it to those cities' audiences. Some of the editing was patchy, for instance. And the temporary sound mix done by Scott and Rawlings back in September 1981 for the first Tandem screening, which was still on this print, was loud and distorted. Additionally, instead of Vangelis compositions throughout, a temp music track (assembled by Terry Rawlings) was still on the last two reels of the Workprint during the Batty/Deckard fight.

"Despite those flaws, I still thought Ridley had come up with a terrific idea," explains Arick. "I briefly talked with him to see if he'd be interested in supervising the restoration of this print. But he was too busy with *Thelma and Louise*."

Arick, however, did not give up on the idea. He now kept suggesting that Warner Brothers begin some sort of process that would result in a restored *Blade Runner*. "My feeling was that since we had a sort of blueprint of Ridley's original version, we could go back and restore this print *and* insert certain other key elements into it as well. Like the unicorn scene, for instance, or the sequence of Ford visiting Morgan Paull in the hospital, or the violent moments that had shown up in the European prints. We'd also lose the narration and keep in Ridley's original ending, of course."

Warner Brothers, however, perhaps due to their knowledge that Ridley Scott was too involved with his latest film to personally supervise a *Blade Runner* reconstruction, showed little interest in Arick's proposal. So the 70mm *BR* variant was promptly returned to the studio's vault.

Yet by now, word-of-mouth concerning the Fairfax screening had spread throughout Los Angeles. Arick found himself besieged by "many" appeals from various revival houses to screen the 70mm Workprint. Arick politely declined all such requests, however, explaining that the solitary example of this version was far too precious to let out of Warner's vault.

Months passed. Early in 1991, Arick received another call. This time, it was Ridley Scott.

The director was nearing completion of *Thelma and Louise* and expressed an interest in buying the Workprint for himself (sales of theatrical-quality films to their directors are not uncommon in Hollywood). But, as Arick explained to Scott, "I couldn't do that. The print was so rare it would be like giving away the negative. Ridley understood that, so I made him a counterproposal. What I'd do is research how much a 35mm reduction dupe *[a process of duplicating the 70mm print back down to its original, 35mm Panavision format]* would cost. He thought that was a good idea. So I did a little homework and drew up a memo explaining that a 35mm reduction print would cost a minimum of $50,000. Ridley didn't want to pay that much, obviously, so he let the issue slide. We did talk about whether we could still interest Warners in somehow restoring this print, though."

What seemed like a golden opportunity for this reconstruction arrived in April 1991, when Scott agreed to allow a screening of the 70mm Workprint at the Academy of Motion Picture Arts and Sciences theater. The occasion? An event called the UCLA Los Angeles Perspectives Multimedia Festival.

"I made an exception of letting the 70mm print go out to this venue because the Academy really is careful with rare material," notes Arick. "And Ridley and I both felt the studio might become a little more excited over the Workprint if Warners could see how many people were still willing to turn out for this picture."

Subsequently, and as had happened at the Fairfax, the 70mm Workprint/Multimedia Fest screening sold out. But this time, all the tickets were gone a full *week* before the showing. Whereupon Barry Reardon, Warner Brothers' President of Theatrical Domestic Distribution, stepped in; Reardon scheduled a *second* festival Workprint screening, so that those viewers who'd been unable to secure tickets the first time around would have a second chance to see the film.

According to Arick, Reardon's intervention seemed a clear signal that Warner Brothers was becoming "a little more interested" in the Workprint. Equally clear was the overwhelmingly positive reaction the Multimedia Fest audiences gave to this "new" *Blade Runner,* a response written up a short time later by *American Film* magazine contributor Shawn Levy in his article "Ridley Scissorhands" (August 1991).

But Ridley Scott had been unable to attend this event; the director was still tied up with his ongoing *Thelma and Louise* commitments. Syd Mead, however, did visit a festival screening, and stayed after the show to conduct a lively *Blade Runner* question and answer session.[5]

---

[5]At the conclusion of one of these programs, a telegram from Ridley Scott was read to the Multimedia Fest audience. This message expressed the

By now, fascination with the 70mm Workprint had had two years to percolate throughout Los Angeles. It was time for corporate action.

Warner Brothers responded to the growing *BR* excitement by becoming actively involved in showcasing the Workprint at other theaters. First, however, the studio released copies of the original Domestic Cut to selected cities throughout the United States, in August 1991. This test run was used to verify whether the interest generated by the Workprint hadn't been a localized fluke and could sustain itself on the national level.

It did. These Domestic Cut screenings attracted sizable audiences in, among other cities, Houston, Dallas, and Washington, D.C. Encouraged by the results, Warner Brothers finally committed to manufacturing at least one 35-mm duplicate print of the 70mm Workprint, which would be leased on a theater-to-theater basis as a must-see special event.

Unfortunately, by the time a 35mm dupe *was* made, Michael Arick was no longer working at Warner Brothers, and Ridley Scott wasn't even aware that a copy had been made in the first place. Just as the director was unaware of the fact that a long-running, Los Angeles–based presentation of the Workprint would soon generate a whole new wave of *Blade Runner* mania.

THE NUART AND CASTRO SCREENINGS

"Not too long after I'd left Warners," Michael Arick continues, "I was surprised to hear that the studio had made a 35mm reduction dupe of the 70mm Workprint. My reaction was one of concern, not

---

director's pleasure at viewers finally being able to see a version of *Blade Runner* that was so much closer to its creator's original intent.

However, Scott's telegram also mentioned that same audience's rare opportunity to witness the director's beloved "unicorn shot." One can only imagine the embarrassment of the poor sod who had to read this telegram in front of the assembled Multimedia Fest attendees—although Scott was obviously still under the impression that his unicorn galloped through this *BR* variant, the 70mm Workprint actually displayed no unicorn at all!

One final note: a *third* showing of the 70mm Workprint transpired two days after the UCLA Perspectives venue. This special screening was strictly limited to AMPAAS staff members and industry insiders, however, and attendance was by invitation only.

satisfaction, because I'd heard that this copy had been struck off the original 70mm print with no attempt at any of the cleanup or restoration which Ridley and I had felt was necessary. Also, since the 70mm version had just been a blowup from the 35mm format the film had originally been shot in, this meant audiences were now going to see a print that was at least three generations away from its original negative. You can't do that sort of multigenerational copying without losing a lot of picture quality, as anyone who's made three or four successive duplicates of the same videotape will tell you."

Unknown to Arick, the 35mm print had not only been made, it was about to be shown to paying audiences. Warners had contacted Gary Meyer, executive vice-president of the Landmark Theater chain (which owned the NuArt and a number of other art houses around the country), to see if Meyer was interested in screening the Denver/Dallas Cut. Meyer was, and the new 35mm Workprint was scheduled for a two-week run at the NuArt. A further deal allowed Landmark to book the film into fourteen other theaters in its chain, including San Francisco's gorgeous Art Deco Castro Theater, which would be the second house to receive the Workprint immediately upon the completion of the NuArt run.

So, on Friday, September 27, 1991, a new 35mm reduction dupe of the 70mm Workprint printed off a 35mm internegative—hot soundtrack, grease-pencil marks, visible splices and all—made its premiere at the NuArt. In order to drum up local interest in the release, Warners took out print ads in L.A.-area newspapers featuring a copy of the original 1982 *BR* one-sheet (poster). A new white banner was laid diagonally upon the upper right corner of this ad; inside it were the words, "The Original Director's Version of the Movie That Was LightYears Ahead of Its Time!"

Shows were scheduled five times a day, with a midnight screening on Fridays. And from day one, the NuArt repeated the same pattern that had been set by the Fairfax and Multimedia Fest screenings: every show sold out. Lines began to form around the block hours before each performance, and suddenly this nearly ten-year-old film was the hottest ticket in town.

So hot, in fact, that some of the actual people who'd helped make the picture couldn't get in. "I'd always really wanted to watch the picture again in a real movie house," says Darryl Hannah. "So when that version of *Blade Runner* showed up at the NuArt, I did try to see it. But the line was so long I couldn't get in." Hampton Fancher, who by now was living in Manhattan but happened to be visiting Los Angeles during the Workprint's NuArt run, also had little initial luck in his own attempt.

"When I got to the NuArt, the first thing I saw was this incredible line stretching around the block," Fancher recalls. "That fascinated me. And as I was standing there, waiting to buy my ticket like everyone else, I kept looking around and seeing all these fucking kids dressed like up Deckard. I mean, they were wearing overcoats and smoking *Boyards*. It was really amazing. All of a sudden it struck me that some of them were really young. So young that they probably hadn't been born when I wrote the first draft. That was so odd."

However, by the time Fancher reached the ticket booth, the show he'd been waiting for had sold out. "So I pulled out the passport I always carry and waved it around and said, 'Hey, look. I'm the guy who helped write this movie. I'm willing to buy a ticket, but can't you squeeze me in somehow?' But they wouldn't do it. I was told there was no more room to squeeze anyone in."

The Workprint had received little publicity beyond the occasional print ad and NuArt flyer referring to the film, yet attendance figures broke all house records during the first week's run. Then, the second week topped the first week.

Warners and Landmark now realized they had an unexpected blockbuster on their hands. The Workprint's original two-week booking was hurriedly extended to four. Yet instead of decreasing, business kept steadily building. And at the end of its twenty-seven-day run, this preview version of a decade-old film had grossed *$230,059*, making the NuArt one of the top-grossing theaters in the country for that period.[6]

When the Workprint then opened on October 18, 1991, at the Castro Theater in San Francisco, lightning struck once again: during its thirteen-day run, this early version of *Blade Runner* shattered all Castro box-office records, ran to full houses every night, and because it made $94,000 during one week of its two-week run, made the Castro the top-grossing theater in America for that seven-day period.[7]

---

[6]Kirk Honeycutt, "Classics Pay Their Way in Pre-Vid Theatrical Runs," *The Hollywood Reporter*, Tuesday, June 4, 1992.

[7]According to William Kolb's "The Director's Cut That Nearly Wasn't," (*The Perfect Vision*, Vol. 6, #23, October 1994), a copy of the Workprint arrived at the Castro several days before October 18, while the film was still playing at the NuArt. This suggests that Warner made at least two 35mm reduction copies of the 70mm version—rumor has it that there may even be three.

A DIFFERENT VERSION (#1 AGAIN) ———————————

But what was it that these sell-out crowds were paying to see? On the technical level, this author can confirm that the NuArt Workprint was a fairly rough piece of work. For example, looking over the notes I jotted down during my second screening of the picture on October 10, 1991, I came across these words:

"Print doesn't seem properly color-corrected. Images are darker, grainier than theatrical print. Flesh-tones are off in some scenes (towards the red). Jumpy edits. Scratches. Dirt marks. Sound too high/distorted in some scenes. Image seems clipped off each side of frame—loss because of blow up/reduction?"

Despite its uneven technical quality, however, watching this "NuArt cut" was a mesmerizing experience. Because the Workprint was the most radically *different* of all versions of *Blade Runner*—no less than *seventy* different audio and visual dissimilarities exist between it and the Domestic Cut, the International Cut, and the Director's Cut (of course, the Workprint is the same as the Denver/Dallas Cut, so those sneaks don't count).

Obviously, this chapter hasn't the space to list each and every one of these differences—but we can touch on the high points.

BR WORKPRINT: THE DIFFERENCES

- Of all the many variations between the Workprint (which, we must keep in mind once again, is really the Denver/Dallas Sneak Preview Cut) and other versions of *Blade Runner* seen before 1991, only two will be of significant importance to most audiences.

  First, Harrison Ford's deadpan narration was completely absent from the Workprint (excepting one brief voice-over, which we'll examine later).

  Secondly, the Workprint concluded with Ridley Scott's preferred original ending—the elevator doors closing on Rachael and Deckard. There is no happy ending in the Workprint.

- Unlike the opening credit sequence which introduces all other versions of the film, the first Workprint credit consisted of a simple, white horizontal line streaking across the screen from right to left. The word "Harrison" (colored red) then shot up from this line at the same time the word "Ford" (also red) shot down from it. This action was accompanied by the harsh metallic sound of two knife blades being scraped together. This actor's credit then disappeared back into the line before the words "Blade Runner" (also in red, also to the sound of clashing steel) shot upward/downward in the same manner.

No other opening credits in the Workprint (WP) were shown.

- Immediately following these "white line credits," the WP showed not the postcredits expository crawl seen on other prints but an excerpt from a "2016" edition of the New American Dictionary, defining the word "replicant." That definition was:

    REPLICANT\rep'-li-cant\n. See also ROBOT (antique): ANDROID (obsolete): NEXUS (generic): Synthetic human, with paraphysical capabilities, having skin/flesh culture. Also: Rep, skin job (slang): Off-world use: Combat, high risk industrial deepspace probe. On-world use prohibited. Specifications and quantities—information classified. New American Dictionary. Copyright (C) 2016.

    This "dictionary definition" was then followed by a card bearing the words "Los Angeles, November 2019."

    When asked why the dictionary definition was changed for the first-reel crawl that now opens the film, producer Michael Deeley replied that, "The dictionary one was the one that Ridley did, and the other one was done, with ninety-nine percent certainty, by Bud Yorkin. Apparently there was some concern that audiences wouldn't understand our version after the Denver and the Dallas sneaks, so another was substituted. Compared to the original, I don't think the final one's literary attributes are that great."

- The Workprint also included a heretofore unseen shot of Deckard's meal at the Noodle Bar; a close-up of what appeared to be two large shrimp, noodles, and a mound of rice.

- In the WP, after Deckard has been arrested and taken for a ride in Gaff's spinner, Edward James Olmos can be heard talking to Ford in Cityspeak as Gaff flies toward police headquarters.

- Throughout the *Blade Runner* Workprint there was a much more visceral "feel" to the omnipresent rain which pervades the film. This was probably the result of the audio rain effects-track not yet being "sweetened," and the overall image of the WP picture being grainier than that seen on released versions.

- The third most significant WP alteration (after its lack of narration and happy ending) occurred during Deckard's meeting with Captain Bryant—M. Emmet Walsh informed Ford that not one, but *two* replicants "got fried in an electrical field" at the Tyrell Corporation. Which explained that missing sixth replicant. Interestingly, Ridley Scott had had Walsh loop his "two" line over a closeup of Bryant saying "one" during *BR*'s postproduction. The director then intended to insert this closeup (not seen in the WP: there, Bryant's "two" line is a voice-over) into the final film. But the actor's lip movements now noticeably did not match his new dialogue. So Bryant's closeup/"two" dialogue was dropped, and the original "one" line retained instead.

- As Deckard plays a desultory one-fingered tune on his piano before subjecting Leon's photograph to the Esper, all you can hear is the piano itself—otherwise there is no music. This means that the marvelously moody "Love Theme" saxophone riff heard here in all other versions was absent from the Workprint.

- After the Cambodian lady (mis)reads the number on the snake scale (in exactly the same manner as all other versions), the WP included a beautiful, rising, eighteen-second-long crane shot of Deckard winding his way through the crowds at Animoid Row. This teeming master shot is in no other version of the film.

- The dialogue between Abdul Ben-Hassan (the snake dealer) and Deckard is different in the WP. It also matches the pair's lip movements better than any other versions.

    The WP dialogue in this scene was:

    Deckard: Abdul Hassan? I'm a police officer, Abdul. I've got a couple of questions I wanted to ask you.

    Abdul: (speaks in his native tongue, waves his arms)

    Deckard: You made a snake, XB7 1. I want to know who you sold it to.

    Abdul: My work? Not too many could afford such quality.

    Deckard: How few?

    Abdul: Very few.

    Deckard: How FEW?

    Abdul: Perhaps less than I thought but still more than I can remember.

    Deckard: (grabbing Abdul's collar) Abdul, my friend . . . (*Animoid Row noise drowns Deckard out*) . . . about two seconds I'm gonna . . . (*noise drowns Deckard out again*).

    Abdul: Snake pit!.

    Abdul never mentions Taffey Lewis' name in the Workprint.

Also, Deckard holds onto Abdul's collar longer in the WP.

- Immediately following the scene with Abdul Ben-Hassan, the WP cut to a busy street outside the Snake Pit Club, and the camera then craned upward for a twelve-second wide-angle shot of this street not seen in any other version.

  Next the Workprint cut to a six-second shot of two women wearing hockey masks and writhing in a plastic, capsulelike extrusion hanging over the street on the second story of a curbside building.[8]

  The WP next cut to a six-second-long shot of a futuristic policeman standing on the street and silently pointing Deckard toward The Snake Pit.

- After Deckard "retires" Zhora and buys his bottle of Tsing-Tao in the WP, in the background could be heard the 1939 Ink Spots song "If I Didn't Care" (instead of "One More Kiss, Dear," which appears on all other versions). The WP's audio mix also boosted the amplification of "If I Didn't Care" so that it was much louder than "One More Kiss."

- In the Workprint, when Batty first meets Tyrell and Eldon asks Roy what he wants, Rutger Hauer replies, "I want more life, Father." This is very different from the "fucker" that ends Batty's line in all other versions. Yet the substitution of "father" does give the dialogue an extra note of complexity.

  This variant line, says R. Scott, "was filmed for cover, so the scene could play uncensored on network TV."

- Tyrell's death is not as violent in the WP as it is in the International Cut. This entire scene was also slightly reedited in the WP, with the cutting order of shots somewhat dissimilar to that found in the International Cut and the Director's Cut.

  The WP scene of Tyrell's meeting with and death at the hands of Roy was also about seven seconds *shorter* than other versions.

  However, the Workprint held onto the first shot of Roy's thumbs gouging into Tyrell's eye sockets about two seconds

---

[8]The shot of the two nearly nude women gyrating in the clear plastic capsule attached above the club's entrance was obviously intended as a form of living advertisement. But this "barker shot" was just as obviously dropped for technical reasons; clumsily framed and harshly overlit, it appears to have been hurriedly filmed, and would have been jarringly out of place with Jordan Cronenweth's otherwise impeccable cinematography.

Another shot seen only in the Workprint: a street cop enclosed in a protective plastic tube.

longer (cutting away just as the blood started to trickle down Roy's hands) than the same shot seen in the Director's Cut.

Also in the Workprint, when Batty begins to move toward a terrified Sebastian after Roy has murdered Tyrell, the Workprint has Hauer soothingly saying, "Sorry, Sebastian. Come. Come." These lines aren't in any other version of the film. The Workprint version of Tyrell's death then ended with an *audibly whimpering* Sebastian turning to run from Tyrell's apartment.

- At the point where Deckard enters the Bradbury Building to battle Pris and Roy, Vangelis' score was dropped altogether from this version of the film. Instead, various Jerry Goldsmith music cues from *Planet of the Apes, Freud,* and *Alien* were inserted on the WP soundtrack by editor Terry Rawlings; these different cues then ran on until almost the very end of the Workprint.

  Incidentally, this temporary musical score was occasionally annoying—composed of generic suspense music, loud and grating, with blaring horns and skirling violins.
- Pris' death scene in the Workprint demonstrated some curious

inconsistencies. While the shots of her breaking Deckard's nose á la the International Cut were included in the Workprint—with the sound of Deckard's crunching cartilage brought up loud on the Workprint soundtrack—Deckard himself only fired two shots to kill Pris, not the three seen in the International Cut. Yet Pris' screams as she thrashes around on Sebastian's floor were much louder in the Workprint, giving the moment an unnerving intensity absent from any other version of the film.

- When Batty pulls Deckard's hand through the wall and breaks his fingers, the WP's shot structure here is slightly different from that of all other versions: the WP does not show Deckard being pulled up against the wall before the camera cuts to Batty on the other side of that wall.

  Also, when Deckard straightens out his broken fingers and screams in agony, the WP presented a completely different shot of this moment, showing Ford's left profile, facing screen left.

- The two gory close-ups of the nail pushing through Batty's palm were omitted from the Workprint.

- The entire chase scene between Deckard and Batty is twenty seconds longer in the WP.

- After the fading Batty murmurs "Time to die" and releases his dove, the Workprint cut to Deckard's watching face as Ford delivered the only narration heard in this version of *Blade Runner*:

"I watched him die all night. It was a long, slow thing and he fought it all the way. He never whimpered and he never quit. He took all the time he had as though he loved life very much. Every second of it . . . even the pain. Then he was dead."

According to co-*BR* screenwriter David Peoples, "I think I wrote most of that final Workprint speech, but I can't be sure. Its history is interwoven between Hampton and me; we both remember contributing to it, although now our memories as to who did what are very unclear.

"Yet that particular speech is still a favorite thing of mine. It's one of the pieces I am most proud of writing for the film. No matter how much of it is ultimately mine or Hampton's."

According to Michael Deeley, this WP voice-over was dropped

when it was decided to impose a whole new, feature-length narration over the film following the Denver/Dallas Sneaks.

- The final scene of Deckard entering his apartment and finding a sleeping Rachael is approximately fifty seconds shorter in the WP than in other versions.

  Among the deleted material was the suspenseful buildup of Deckard discovering Rachael asleep before the endlessly rotating monitor screens; the WP cuts directly from Deckard entering his apartment to standing over Rachael, who is asleep on the bed.

  Also deleted was Deckard's third worried query of "Rachael?" Instead, the WP's last lines of dialogue (unlike the Domestic Cut, which includes Deckard's narration during the tacked-on ending) are Gaff's. The final words we hear in the WP are Deckard's memory of Edward James Olmos saying, "It's too bad she won't live. But then again who does?" as he fingers Gaff's tinfoil unicorn.

- After Rachael tells Deckard she loves him, the WP cut to Ford opening the elevator door and motioning for Sean Young to come forward. Missing in the WP were two shots normally seen here: Deckard checking the hall and walking toward the elevator, plus Rachael waiting in Deckard's doorway before he motions for her to come forward.

  The elevator doors then closed noiselessly after the couple, and the same music heard when the Spinner takes Deckard to the police station now played on the WP's soundtrack.

- The Workprint did not include the bogus "happy ending."

- Finally, after the elevator doors close, a title card bearing the words "The End" was seen on the WP. There is no "The End" title on the International or the Domestic Cut (or the Director's Cut, for that matter).

- Vangelis' *"Blade Runner* (End Titles)" music then began about ninety seconds into the WP's closing credits.

- The final line in the WP's end credits was a new one added specifically by Warner Brothers for the proposed Workprint/Landmark Theater chain run.

  It read, "This version copyright 1991 The Blade Runner Partnership."

So what were the final impressions left by the Workprint?

First, that Harrison Ford's fine, subtle acting had been immeasurably improved by the deletion of his deadpan narration, which had previously flattened Ford's excellent performance. Allowed to watch the actor more closely without being told exactly what Deckard thought or was going to do by a bullying voice-over, the viewer was made more aware of the low-key but complex shadings Ford had brought to his characterization.

Despite the problems he might have had during the making the film, or the reservations he'd harbored about being asked to portray a replicant, Harrison Ford has no need to dismiss his acting here—*Blade Runner* showcases one of the actor's most intelligent and fascinating performances.

Secondly, although it was grainy, roughly mixed. and unfinished, the *Blade Runner* Workprint afforded viewers a rare opportunity to assess a film's evolutionary progress. Serious *cineastes* were now given a unique opportunity to study what could be called, in literary terms, a rough draft of the film.

Finally—and perversely—the Workprint's very raggedness worked to its advantage. *Blade Runner's* theatrical release was slick and seamless, its various components smoothed out by tight editing, moody music, and perfectly color-balanced prints. Yet although the *BR* Workprint bristles with such technical imperfections as inappropriate library music, contrasting lighting, and awkward edits, these blemishes did not throw the viewer out of the frame.

On the contrary, they somehow made Ridley Scott's sullen, depressive mood piece that much more quirkily *alive*.

THE DIRECTOR'S CUT

Even in its diluted form Blade Runner *was a recognizable masterpiece—amusing to note the many critics who originally vilified it pretending they didn't in the light of it clearly being one of the most directional movies of the eighties. Now [with the release of the Director's Cut] it's even more of a masterwork than ever before. . . .*

—"PREVIEW: *BLADE RUNNER: THE DIRECTOR'S CUT*" BY ALAN JONES
STARBURST MAGAZINE
ISSUE #172, SEPTEMBER 1992

BUILDING A BETTER DIRECTOR'S CUT

As already noted in chapter XVI, by late September of 1991 the *BR Workprint* was selling out at its NuArt Theater engagement. Yet Ridley Scott, back in London and now casting for his upcoming *1492: Conquest of Paradise,* hadn't been notified that this version of *Blade Runner* was even in circulation. Word of the NuArt screenings finally did reach the director, however, while the engagement was still in progress. At this point Scott temporarily put his *1492* labors on hold to fly to Los Angeles and discuss the situation with Warner Brothers.

"Ridley had a number of concerns with this Workprint," recalls Michael Arick. "First, he didn't seem to appreciate the fact that the Workprint was being advertised as a Director's Cut, when it wasn't. Also, he felt very strongly that the Workprint itself wasn't up to the technical standards required for a broad theatrical release.[1] Ridley still felt there was an opportunity for him to restructure the film *as* a Director's Cut, particularly in the sense of being able to reinsert his unicorn footage."

Therefore, in early October 1991, Arick, Scott, and Mimi Polk (Scott's then-producer) held a meeting with both Barry Reardon (President of Domestic Distribution at Warner Brothers) and Peter Gardiner (Vice President of Operations and Corporate Film Video Services) to discuss the situation. According to Scott and Arick, the meeting was cordial but divided. The Warners contingent pushed for the release of the Workprint as a Director's Cut, especially since the studio had already invested so much time and effort in making duplicate prints of the WP; Scott, on the other hand, stressed that he could not support the Workprint as a Director's Cut because he was not satisfied with either its content or appearance. Warners countered by noting that the Workprint was doing such good business that it seemed more sensible just to let the issue ride.

"Ridley said this wasn't an issue of business," adds Arick. "It was art. His final film had been visually polished, and he'd done a lot of work to make it that way. But what was being shown at the NuArt was only an unrefined version of that final product. He didn't have a problem with letting people know that what they were seeing was a rough draft of *Blade Runner*, but calling it a restored Director's Cut was another thing."

Scott then proposed using the Workprint as a blueprint to help construct an all-new *Blade Runner,* one that would be assembled from the best available negatives of the original shoot. Reardon, who had always been a fan of the film, agreed. Now a new deal was struck—the Workprint would be allowed to play out its runs at the NuArt and Castro, but not at the fourteen other theaters into which the WP had been booked to appear following its Castro engagement. Instead, the original theatrical version of the film would be shipped to these other sites, while Scott worked on a new *BR* Director's Cut (hereafter occasionally referred to as the *BRDC).*

As for who would be in charge of the *BRDC* project, the overall

---

[1]Hampton Fancher rejects the Workprint on more aesthetic grounds. "Of all the versions, I prefer the Director's Cut," the screenwriter said. "After I finally saw the Workprint, I felt it was self-indulgent—too slow, too much music, too many extended scenes where nothing was really happening. The Workprint didn't have enough punch for me."

restoration itself would, on Warner's side, be supervised by Peter Gardiner. Arick was put in charge of Scott's end of the operation by Mimi Polk, who felt that the preservationist had both a firm grasp of the film and an insider's knowledge of Warner's workings, since Arick had recently been an employee of that studio. The final detail of this arrangement stated that no further distribution of the Workprint would take place until March 1992, at which date Scott was bound to deliver his newly restored cut.

Speaking to this author by telephone in 1993, Scott summed up his feelings and experiences regarding the origins of the Director's Cut this way:

"I came to Los Angeles to meet with Michael Arick and to see the 70mm print screened at the Fairfax. It had been some years, frankly, since I'd given thought to the film, and I wanted to refresh my memory. And after I saw it, I notified Arick and Warners that this was not the final cut of my film, pointing out the lack of my unicorn scene and the fact that the final fight between Deckard and Batty was using a temporary music track. Warners then agreed to pay for a sort of post-postproduction process where we could go back to the editing room and put the picture into the shape I'd originally wanted it."

"Following our meeting at Warners, I flew to London to attend a film festival," continues Michael Arick. "I then stayed on in England after that event—at my own expense—throughout November and December of 1991, in an attempt to catalog a written outline of the version of *Blade Runner* that Ridley had always wanted."

Arick was assisted in this task by Les Healey, who had worked on the original film under Terry Rawlings as *BR*'s first assistant editor. But what version of *Blade Runner* did Ridley Scott have in mind for his Director's Cut? After all, the Workprint had featured over seventy differences between it and the theatrical print, and there were also those additional shots seen in the San Diego sneak. What would stay, and what would be cut out?

The first decision was to completely remove any voice-over from the film. "But that wasn't a situation where Ridley had had ten years to think about it and then decided to strip out the narration," says Michael Deeley. "He'd actually expressed reservations about releasing the film with a voice-over right after the Dallas and Denver previews. I'd had even stronger objections. In fact, in March of 1982, I wrote an open memo to Warners, Tandem, and The Ladd Company stating a number of reasons why I felt *Blade Runner* shouldn't go out with a narration. I'd mentioned how I'd thought we'd cleared up some of the storyline confusion through recutting after the Texas and Colorado sneaks, for example. I'd also noted that a voice-over would seriously interfere with both the flow of the story and Deckard's character. But my reservations weren't acted upon, obviously."

Besides releasing the Director's Cut *sans* narration, Scott passed on a number of other suggestions to Arick which he felt would help improve his *BRDC*. These included: inserting the extra fifteen seconds of violence seen in the International Cut; removing the tacked-on happy ending; climaxing the film with the elevator doors closing on Rachael/Deckard; putting back in the two close-ups of the giant eye which had been missing from the Workprint; reinserting the scene showing Deckard visiting Holden in the hospital; and cleaning up various audio flubs. These last proposed improvements (which included eliminating the lip-flap seen between Deckard and Abdul Ben-Hassan at Animoid Row, and making sure that the snake scale ID number the Cambodian saleslady speaks aloud matched the number seen under her electron microscope), would be accomplished by assembling certain key actors and having them reloop their dialogue.

Scott also very much wanted to reinstate his beloved "unicorn shot." This (soon to be controversial) scene was filmed during postproduction in 1982 and had been originally intended to take place while Deckard was in his apartment playing his piano—suddenly, Deckard daydreams about a horned horse. Scott intended this reverie to have chilling relevance at film's end, with Gaff leaving behind a tinfoil origami unicorn to signify his knowledge of Deckard's innermost thoughts.

"Interestingly enough," Arick adds, "we weren't going to do anything to change Bryant's line about only one replicant being killed breaking into the Tyrell Corporation. I asked Ridley if he wanted to have me change that and substitute the Workprint's line about two replicants being killed. He said, 'Leave it alone.'"

One of the first originally trimmed sequences which Arick now attempted to track down for the *BRDC* was the Holden in the hospital scene. Twenty separate dailies of this sequence were subsequently unearthed but, according to Arick, "there was no soundtrack available. It hadn't been preserved, so what we essentially had was a silent sequence. We could have looped in some dialogue later on. But we never had the chance to do that."

The reasons? Time and misunderstandings. For while Arick and

Healey were in London laboriously attempting to ferret out the varying pieces of film Scott wanted to include in his Director's Cut, things had taken an entirely different turn back in Los Angeles. Some sources close to the process claim that Peter Gardiner did not know that a new version of the film was being attempted in London; instead, Gardiner had assumed that Scott merely wanted to add the unicorn shot and Vangelis' missing music to the already existing Workprint. This "Enhanced Workprint," Gardiner assumed, would then be released as the official *Blade Runner* Director's Cut.

Whatever the reasons behind Gardiner's thinking, the fact of the matter was that there now were *two* separate restorations taking place on two different continents regarding two dissimilar versions of the film. And looming over everything was the shadow of the clock: Arick and Warner Brothers, by contract, had only a few months to conclude the painstaking restoration process needed to deliver a completed version of the Director's Cut by its specified March 1992 due date.

Arick, meanwhile, unaware that a second variant of the *BRDC* was being assembled in Los Angeles, had compiled a list of the various changes Scott wanted for his own version and sent this list on to the studio. Feeling he had done everything he could in London, Arick then returned to America in early January 1992, confident that Warners would carry on in the manner Arick had laid out. He then moved on to other concerns, keeping what he calls "occasional surveillance" over the Director's Cut project.

However, Gardiner continued to move ahead with his own, Enhanced Workprint version of the reconstruction. By now the WP had had the temporary music tracks which Terry Rawlings had laid over the Workprint's final two reels replaced by Vangelis' original score for these reels; Warner had also redone the end credits which had been added to the Workprint for its NuArt/Castro runs, and added these new end credits (which displayed a slight but noticeable wobble) to Gardiner's Enhanced WP.

Surprisingly, all of these changes were then approved by Ridley Scott. Why? Gardiner's version of the Director's Cut, after all, was not the reconstruction Scott had originally envisioned, but one based on what the director had objected to as only a rough draft of his film. One answer to this seeming contradiction could be that Scott was simply too distracted by *1492* to notice that Gardiner's version of the Director's Cut was not the one Arick had been working on. Or perhaps Scott simply chose to avoid controversy, just as long as his unicorn appeared in whatever Director's Cut was ultimately completed.

That unicorn shot, however, soon became problematic as well; Warners now discovered that the original negative of this scene was *not* in Los Angeles. Instead, it seemingly had disappeared off the face of the earth.

"In fact, we couldn't find the original negatives for any of *Blade Runner's* trims," Arick recalls. "Nothing was there. Les and I had already searched high and low for these elements in London, and all we came up with were the positives of the trims and dailies that had been stored in the Pinewood and the Rank vaults in England since 1982. That meant that any new material we inserted into the Director's Cut wasn't going to look as good as the footage surrounding it, because the new stuff was going to have to be duped off negatives made from positives."

What caused this awkward situation? The primary reason seems to be that, although Ridley Scott had originally cut *Blade Runner* in London, the camera negative of the finished product had then been shipped back to Los Angeles in order for prints to be struck in the United States in 1982. *BR's* trim negatives had also been shipped back to the States at the same time; however, some time in the 1980s, these had been moved off the Warner Brothers lot for storage somewhere else. And by 1991, the exact location of this "somewhere else" had, according to Arick, "become confused. No one seemed to know where they'd been stored."[2]

Since the original negative of the unicorn scene could not be found, Warner now pushed the delivery date of the Director's Cut back from March to September 1992 in the hopes that this footage would eventually materialize. Meanwhile, Gardiner continued to restore the "Enhanced Workprint" by carefully cleaning up both the image and audio imperfections which had been so apparent during the WP's NuArt run. The result was, according to sources close to the process, a high-quality 35mm Workprint with new end credits and a nicely remixed Vangelis soundtrack, a remix which Scott himself had supervised.

Months had now passed. Then, in August 1992, film journalist

---

[2]Although some journalists have reported that the *entire* negative to *Blade Runner* has been lost, this is not the case—the original camera negative to the film today sits in storage at the Technicolor vault in Hollywood.

Kenneth Turan of the *Los Angeles Times* (who was preparing an article for that newspaper relating to the September release of the Director's Cut, one which would be published September 13, 1992 with the title "Blade Runner 2"), called Michael Arick to see how the *BRDC* project was progressing. Arick himself called Warner Brothers for further information—and was "very surprised to finally discover that they were planning on releasing a cleaned-up version of the Workprint. I was even more surprised to find out that this version *wasn't* going to have the unicorn in it."

Apparently, the studio had not found the missing unicorn negative, and a decision had been made to simply release the Enhanced Workprint without it. But Ridley Scott had no intention of this happening—once informed of the studio's plans, the director's agent notified Warner Brothers that Scott planned to publicly disown this version through full-page advertisements in the Hollywood trade papers if the Workprint was released as a Director's Cut.

Matters surrounding the Director's Cut were now quickly beginning to take on the same strained atmosphere that had accompanied the making of the original film. Therefore, in order to calm this controversy—and as they had already done almost a year previously—Scott, Polk, Arick, Reardon, and Gardiner met once again to discuss the problem.

DO ANDROIDS DREAM OF UNICORNS?

What was it about Scott's treasured "unicorn shot" that had raised such strong feelings in the director? And what were its origins?

For Scott's own insights into this scene, please turn to the unicorn section at the beginning of appendix A, But for more information on the unusual background of *Blade Runner*'s mythical beast, read on.

"That unicorn was Ridley's sole and personal obsession," recalls Michael Deeley. "No one ever quite got it."

"I always rejected Deckard's dream of the live unicorn," echoes Hampton Fancher. "That was purely a Ridley concept."

"The live unicorn definitely was Ridley's idea," agrees David Peoples. "Even though I was fortunate enough to have seen the original footage of that shot when I was in Pinewood reworking Deckard's narration back in 1982, I can't say I ever understood it. I certainly didn't write it."

Blade Runner's *fabled unicorn segment, restored for the Director's Cut, was one of the final live-action sequences shot for the film.*

Such were the reactions of the majority of *Blade Runner*'s cast and crew to that moment when Deckard dreams of a unicorn (a shot only seen in the Director's Cut), yet the scene itself is a fairly straightforward one.

Deckard is shown playing a desultory tune on his piano. This image dissolves to one of a unicorn running through woods. The beast gallops toward the camera, turns, and runs screen right. Then it tosses its head. A dissolve reveals Deckard back at his piano. End of unicorn scene.

Despite its brevity, the *meaning* of this shot continues to confound a great many viewers. For explanations, perhaps it's best to turn to those few members of the *BR* team who understood both the meaning and genesis of this much-debated shot.

"Deckard's unicorn dream," remembers Ivor Powell. "That was always a puzzle to some people. Actually, it was an idea Ridley had come up with during filming—it was never really scripted. Well, except for one brief reference in the climax of one of David Peoples' final drafts, where Rachael and Deckard are driving away from the city at the end of the film and spot a unicorn by the side of the road. Which was somehow supposed to tie in with Deckard's previous dream.

"The way this all came about was, originally Ridley wanted

Deckard to have an unusual daydream while he was sitting at his piano. Something like a very private thought. One that Gaff would later know without being told. Which was meant to suggest that Deckard had had a memory implant Gaff had been privy to, and that Deckard was a replicant. Which in turn explains the significance of Gaff leaving a tinfoil unicorn for Deckard to find at the end of the picture—Gaff was letting Deckard know that Eddie Olmos knew Ford's private thoughts.

"But this all came later. At first, Ridley couldn't figure out what he wanted this daydream to look like. He kept thinking and rethinking the basic concept until, finally, he hit on a unicorn. But this decision had come late in the day, so Ridley wasn't able to film that unicorn until we'd returned to England for postproduction."

Indeed, Scott's unicorn was almost the final shot to be filmed for *Blade Runner*—only the picture's eleventh-hour "happy ending" was photographed at a later date. But once Scott had decided on a unicorn, a unicorn it would be.

Therefore, *Blade Runner*'s mythical beast was filmed the first week of January 1982 at Black Park, England, a small wooded area (complete with lake) situated very close to Pinewood Studios. A white stallion was secured through a British film animal rental service to serve as the unicorn itself. Then, according to Ridley Scott, "Its horn was constructed out of a virtually weightless material—polystyrene—and applied to the horse's forehead with cosmetic glue. That horn and application were done by Nick Allder, an English [floor] effects man with whom I'd worked on *Alien*." Filming the unicorn (which was shot with an overcranked camera, resulting in slow-motion), "went very quickly and cheaply," recalls Scott. "We wrapped out on that in little more than a day."

Once Scott had selected which takes of the unicorn he was happiest with, the resulting footage was then cut together by Terry Rawlings, who temporarily scored the unicorn sequence by inserting cues from Vangelis' music for *Chariots of Fire*. "But the original unicorn sequence I edited into the film was nothing like the footage seen in the Director's Cut," Rawlings points out. "The negative for that original unicorn scene had been lost by the time they restored *Blade Runner* in 1992, and they couldn't find the positives either. *[A fact which will be explored in greater depth a few pages from now.]*

"Anyway, the original unicorn sequence went like this," Rawlings continues. "It was essentially a series of various intercuts. These began when Deckard picks up some photographs off the piano, swivels around on the piano bench, and then leans back against the piano itself. Then Ford began looking at a picture, and—flash!—you had a quick cut of this unicorn running through a forest. Then that went away and Deckard carried on looking at this snapshot. Next came another shot of the unicorn, coming right up to the camera. It then shook its head, and as it shook its head, I cut back to Ford shaking *his* head. Like he was shaking this thought out of his mind. Then Harrison laid down those pictures and the scene continued as you see it now, with Deckard picking up and taking Leon's photo over to the Esper.

"So basically, the substance of the original unicorn sequence displayed Deckard going through photographs and saying to himself, 'Memories,' you know? As if memories of his own were coming back. That was sort of the idea. Deckard's own thoughts were being triggered by these photos. He mulled those images over and then shook the memories out of his head."

According to Rawlings, both he and Scott were "quite pleased" with the way the original unicorn sequence turned out. Others, however, were not quite as happy.

A rare still of a sequence cut from all versions of the film—Deckard studies Leon's photos before drifting off into his (original version) dream of a unicorn.

"Tandem was uneasy with the unicorn sequence because it had been unscripted but Ridley shot it anyway," explains Ivor Powell. "I also don't think they quite understood it."

"That's an understatement," adds Terry Rawlings. "The money people kept pestering Ridley with questions like, 'What's with this unicorn?' 'What does it mean?' Ridley would reply, 'If you don't get it, what's the point in me explaining it?'

"That was frustrating, because virtually the last shot in the film—the one of Harrison finding the tinfoil origami—was an all-important connection between Gaff knowing Deckard's memories of unicorns. Tandem never got this connection at all, though. They said, 'Cut it out. It's too vague.' So the original unicorn sequence was indeed cut out very early on."

Today, disagreement still exists between the *Blade Runner* filmmakers as to whether the original unicorn sequence was ever shown to the public. Some *BR* participants say no—others insist it was seen during the Denver and Dallas sneak previews. As this author was not present at those sneaks and has been unable to verify whether this shot was indeed shown in Texas or Colorado, perhaps some kind reader who did attend the Denver/Dallas screenings will be able to contact me through my publisher and lay this uncertainty to rest.

However, the matter of the original unicorn sequence was actually only part of a larger controversy, one which revolved around the very nature of Rick Deckard himself.

DECKARD A REPLICANT?

If the abrupt inclusion of a galloping unicorn into *Blade Runner* was puzzling to some viewers, then the idea that Deckard might be a replicant—a notion the climax of the Director's Cut underlines more forcefully than any other version of *Blade Runner*—was even more difficult for people to accept. Indeed, this twist ending seems to engender more passionate debate than any other aspect of the film. And it's not only casual viewers who reject the Director's Cut's insistence that Deckard is a replicant; many of the film's *makers* also shy away from the concept.

But why? A simplistic explanation would be that audiences don't like their movie heroes being revealed as something less than human—no identification value, you see. Yet *Blade Runner*'s audience, in the main, is anything but simplistic. Consequently, *BR* fans who don't like the idea of Deckard being a replicant usually choose to state their objection in moral terms: what's the point of Deckard's spiritual awakening, they will ask, if *Blade Runner*'s android hunter turns out to be an android himself?

Ridley Scott has some interesting responses to that question, as evidenced near the end of his interview in appendix A. Before the *Future Noir* reader incorrectly assumes that Scott alone was responsible for the Deckard-as-replicant concept, however, it should be noted that author Philip K. Dick had already toyed with this idea in *Do Androids Dream of Electric Sheep* (when the novelistic Deckard suddenly finds himself under arrest in a strange police station, where he's confronted by a bogus investigator who suspects Deckard is an android). Furthermore, the *cinematic* notion of Deckard as a replicant originated with screenwriter Hampton Fancher.

"The idea of Deckard really being an android sort of invented itself," Fancher recalls. "In the final version of the screenplay I wrote before David Peoples stepped in—which I'm not sure he ever saw—I'd ended the film with Deckard coming back home and sitting down at his piano. There was a close-up of Deckard's hand going down towards the keys . . . and suddenly his hand cramped up, just like Batty's did. You weren't quite sure it was the same thing, but it looked an awful lot like a replicant clench. Then that image froze, the music came up, and that was it. The end. The last shot in the picture.

"I wanted the audience to walk away thinking, 'Is Deckard like Batty?' That was my whole point in creating this ending in the first place. The idea was supposed to be, take your own empathy test. Constantly monitor your emotional temperature. See how human you really are, because we can always be better at being human. It was a philosophical challenge, really. That's all the notion of Deckard being a replicant originally meant to me."

After David Peoples began his *BR* writing chores, however, Fancher's initial concept concerning Deckard's true humanity underwent a mutation—and a misunderstanding.

"In the ending I wrote for my first draft of December 15, 1980," Peoples himself explains, "Deckard kills Gaff because Gaff tried to terminate Rachael. Then Deckard takes Rachael to the beach—and he kills her, too. Next he returns to his apartment. Now he's sitting in his bedroom laying out ammunition for his gun, because Deckard knows that someone from the police department is going to come to his apartment and try and shoot him for murdering Gaff.

"At this point I invented a kind of contemplative voice-over for Deckard. Here, let me read it to you *[Peoples now quotes from his December 15 script]*:

"'I wonder who designs the ones like me . . . and what choices we really have, and which ones we just think we have. I wondered if I had really loved her. I wondered which of my memories were real and which belonged to someone else. The great Tyrell hadn't designed me, but whoever had hadn't done so much better. "You're programmed, too," she told me, and she was right. In my own modest way, I was a combat model. Roy Batty was my late brother.'

"Now, what I'd intended with this voice-over was mostly metaphysical," Peoples continues. "Deckard was supposed to be philosophically questioning himself about what it was that made him so different from Rachael and the other replicants. He was supposed to be realizing that, on the human level, they weren't so different. That Deckard wanted the same things the replicants did. The 'maker' he was referring to wasn't literally Tyrell, either. It was supposed to be God. So basically, Deckard was just musing about what it meant to be human.

"But then Ridley—" Peoples says, laughing "—well, I think Ridley misinterpreted me. Because right about this period of time he started announcing, 'Ah-ha! Deckard's a replicant! What brilliance! How *Heavy Metal!*' I was sort of confused by this response, because Ridley kept giving me all this praise and credit for this terrific idea. It wasn't until many years later, when I happened to be browsing through this draft, that I suddenly realized the metaphysical material I had written could just as easily have been read to imply that Deckard was a replicant. Even though it wasn't what I meant at all. What I *had* meant was, we all have a maker, and we all have an incept date. We just can't address them. That's one of the similarities we had to the replicants. We couldn't go find Tyrell, but Tyrell was up there somewhere. For all of us.

"So what I had intended as kind of a metaphysical speculation, Ridley had read differently, but I now realize there was nothing wrong with his reading. That confusion was my own fault. I'd written this voice-over so ambiguously that it could indeed have meant exactly what Ridley took it to mean. And that, I think, is how the whole idea of Deckard being a replicant came about.

"On the other hand," Peoples concludes, "while I may have accidentally initiated or inherited this suggestion of Deckard's android nature, it quickly became Ridley's, because he's the one who picked up the idea and ran with it."

One manner in which Scott ran with Peoples' idea involved staging a scene where Harrison Ford's eyes are seen to glow, just like the replicants'. It is a moment, however, that still seems to annoy or puzzle some of the major *Blade Runner* participants.

"In my script, it was much more ambiguous whether Ford was a replicant or not," points out Hampton Fancher. "I wanted people to only think as an afterthought that *maybe* Deckard was an android. I fought very hard for that. But when I finally caught the film and saw how Ridley had made the replicants' eyes glow, and then you saw Ford's eyes glow, I thought, 'Aw, shit.' That device made explicit what I'd wanted to be ambivalent. I didn't like the glowing eye effect, either—it was too obvious. I found it vampiric, almost. Like a B-movie trick."

"I never understood why Ridley wanted Harrison to have those glowing eyes," Katy Haber adds. "I always thought that was a very weird red herring. Besides, Harrison definitely didn't want to be a replicant."

In point of fact, Ford actively resisted the idea—being revealed as a replicant at the end of the film was, in the actor's estimation, almost as wrong-headed a decision as Deckard's narration. "The biggest problem [I had with *Blade Runner*] was . . . at the end," Ford was quoted as saying in Lance Loud's October 1992 *BR/Details* magazine piece. "[Ridley] wanted the audience to find out that Deckard was a replicant. I fought that because I felt the audience needed somebody to cheer for."

"*I* never thought Deckard was a replicant, either," continues Michael Deeley. "That what just a bit of bullshit, a little extra layer Ridley put in. Also an obfuscation. Not only did I never believe Deckard was a replicant, I also thought it futile to try and make him one. Harrison resisted the idea, too. But that was Ridley's pet theory, even if it didn't make any sense. Why would you do that? Deckard would be the *first* replicant you'd knock off if you were getting rid of them. Anyway, just because you say, 'Wouldn't it be funny if Deckard was an android?' doesn't necessarily make it so."

Deeley has a most unexpected ally in his point of view: Bud Yorkin. "Is he or isn't he a replicant? You can't cheat an audience that way," Yorkin is quoted as saying in Kenneth Turan's 1992 *Los Angeles Times Magazine* "Blade Runner 2" article. "It's another confusing moment."

Confusing or not, the Director's Cut's revelation regarding Deckard's inhumanity was a story point Ridley Scott had been tinkering with long before 1992. "There was an ongoing conversation during the filming of *Blade Runner* about Deckard being a replicant," recalls Terry Rawlings. "And it's a concept I have no trouble with. It's only logical, really. For instance, why would Olmos leave this tinfoil unicorn in Deckard's apartment, unless it was a clue that he knew Deckard's memories had been implanted?

"Besides, Ridley and I had many concrete conversations during the editing of *BR* as to how to best suggest him being an android. One

Filming the sequence of Deckard discovering Gaff's tinfoil unicorn (note cameraman right foreground). Is Deckard a replicant?

nice way was the scene of Deckard's eyes glowing, when Harrison's at the doorway of his kitchen behind Sean Young. Ridley had blocked that out very carefully; he purposefully put Harrison in the background of that shot, and slightly out of focus, so that you'd only notice his eyes were glowing if you were paying attention. I love that—it's subtle. It was *meant* to be subtle. I don't think Ridley ever wanted to bring out a troupe of dancing bears holding up neon signs reading,

'Deckard is a replicant!' Instead, he was going for something more ambiguous. Ridley himself may have definitely felt that Deckard was a replicant, but still, by the end of the picture, he intended to leave it up to the viewer to decide whether Deckard was one."

Despite Rawlings' final assertion, however, knowing that Scott intentionally meant Deckard to be a replicant certainly casts new light on a number of *Blade Runner* sequences that previously may have seemed cut and dried. For example, with the *BRDC*'s exclusion of the theatrical version's happy ending and its emphasis that Deckard is a replicant, we can now only assume that both Young and Ford have been cursed with a replicant's limited four-year lifespan—meaning that their time together will be very short. Also, following Rachael's V-K test, Tyrell's amused reaction to Deckard's astonished realization that the replicants have been endowed with artificial memories gains added, sinister significance—if Tyrell is aware that Deckard is a replicant with false memories himself. And Gaff's line to Deckard on the rooftop at the end of the picture—"You've done a man's job, sir"— takes on an ironic double meaning in the *BRDC*.

Despite all the preceding evidence which this author has presented, however, there will always be those who resist the idea of Rick Deckard being a replicant. These naysayers will find such a concept illogical, or one that robs *Blade Runner* of its hero's affecting *human* dimension. In response, I can only say that that first objection ignores Ridley Scott's original intent, while the second misses the point. For the replicants are human too—"More human than human," in fact.

Besides, the question of whether Deckard is or is not an android really depends on which version of the film you watch.

For in all other variants of *Blade Runner*—the ones shorn of the unicorn sequence—Deckard only *may* be a replicant. Because Gaff's leaving behind a tinfoil unicorn at Deckard's apartment could simply mean that Olmos had already been there, seen the sleeping, fugitive Rachael, and let her live.

But couple Gaff's tinfoil origami with the very private vision Ford has of a live unicorn in the *BRDC* and ask yourself why Gaff chose that particular calling card. Then recall the scene where Deckard told Rachael he knew her private memory concerning the spider outside her window.

The only logical conclusion is an inescapable one: in the Director's Cut, Rick Deckard *is* a replicant.

RELEASING THE THEATRICAL VERSION ─────────

When we last left the history of *Blade Runner*'s Director's Cut, it was August 1992. Ridley Scott had threatened to denounce the Workprint if it was released without his unicorn, and all concerned parties were gathering to discuss how to best remedy this situation. Michael Arick now picks up the story.

"That second meeting at Warner Brothers was pretty interesting. By now, the pressure was really on—distribution contracts had been drawn up for the Director's Cut to be released to theaters around the country, but Ridley made it clear that he wasn't going to support any version without the unicorn in it. And the release date was only about a month away."

In some respects this second meeting was a replay of the first: Warners again suggested that Scott allow the release of the Workprint, while Mimi Polk repeated that the original deal had involved a cut approved by the director. Eventually, a compromise was reached; Warners would not release the Enhanced WP *if* Arick could deliver a version of the film sanctioned by Scott before the September 1992 deadline.

On the face of it, such a deal placed Arick in a very delicate position. Not only was he now obligated to deliver a new cut of *Blade Runner* within a ridiculously short time period, but if he failed to meet this deadline, the responsibility of a botched *BRDC* would fall directly onto the preservationist's shoulders. "I still thought we could make it," Arick counters, "but only if we radically downsized our original restoration conception."

Scott agreed that the project was possible if less were attempted and now gave Arick a new set of instructions. For this latest version of the Director's Cut, gone would be such niceties as the reinsertion of the Holden-in-the-hospital scene; instead, Scott wanted Arick to remove Ford's narration, reinsert the giant staring eye at the beginning of the film, color-correct and otherwise technically adjust the final print, digitally remaster the *Blade Runner* soundtrack, and end the film with the elevator doors closing on Rachael and Deckard. Most crucially, Scott insisted that—somehow—his unicorn find its way back into the picture.

In effect, this second Warner Brothers *BRDC* meeting meant that both Arick's original vision for the restoration *and* the Enhanced Workprint had been set aside in favor of a *third* version of the Director's

Cut. The problem was, by the time all the necessary agreements and paperwork had been ratified, Arick had only twenty-one days in which to complete a seemingly hopeless task.

"That meant I had to resign myself to coming up with a Director's Cut that was only a slightly modified version of the original theatrical release," Arick recalls. "But it was better than nothing."

The preservationist now wholeheartedly threw himself into gear by first attending to the technical requirements. Working with some of the highest quality film laboratories and technicians in Hollywood, Arick was able to strike a brand-new 35mm *BR* negative, one which was produced from an interpositive of the original theatrical release.

Next, Arick digitally remixed the film's soundtrack, using both the film's original two-track mag tape dialogue master and four-track magnetic tape M&E (music and effects) master as audio guides. Careful frame-by-frame counting then had to be done to remove the approximately eighty words of Ford's narration heard on the original theatrical release.

"Actually," explained Scott, "I rather liked the delivery and content of the brief voice-over Harrison had done for the Workprint. But I figured since we were going to remove all the rest of the narration for the Director's Cut, I'd have to excise the Workprint voice-over, too, just to maintain some kind of uniformity."

Then fate stepped in in the form of good fortune: a positive piece of footage of Scott's original unicorn shoot was discovered in London's Rank film vault.

"This wasn't the same unicorn footage I'd originally cut into *Blade Runner*," notes Terry Rawlings, "but an outtake Ridley had discarded back in 1982. But it was the only unicorn shot they could find, positive or negative. I don't know what happened to the original material—at the time this restoration was going on, I was off on another picture, so I'd asked a man who works with me a lot on sound, Jimmy Shields, who did *Alien* and *Legend* and what have you, to search out things on my behalf.

"What was eventually discovered was this positive outtake, whose color had shifted towards the green, and was quite dirty besides. That was sent to Michael Arick in Los Angeles, who then had that film cleaned up and color-corrected. They also struck a new negative off it before cutting the result into the Director's Cut. That's the reason why if you look at a print of the *BRDC*, the unicorn shot doesn't match up, quality-wise, with the rest of the film. It's all rather sad, really. Not only is that sequence not the real thing—it's just a re-creation of the original unicorn scene—it also looks totally different from anything else in the picture."[3]

When asked why the negative of *Blade Runner*'s original unicorn sequence had disappeared, Rawlings replied, "I have no idea. But when a film has been sort of out there for ten years, or however long it was before Warners decided to do the Director's Cut, companies tend to say, 'Right. We've got all the things we need. We've got the video master and master neg and all that sort of stuff, so we don't need trims anymore.' And they throw that stuff away. Plus the film was recut, you see, before it was released. And those cut negs were put into these 'out' areas, which we call in England 'XNGs,' or 'deleted scenes.' So if the company was happy with what they had at that time, they may have dumped it. Companies do that occasionally. They do it too much, actually."

Meanwhile, Peter Gardiner had continued to work on restoring the Enhanced Workprint (which the studio had now officially renamed "*Blade Runner*: The Final Director's Cut Version"), as a contingency against Arick not being able to complete his own Director's Cut. But the preservationist's perseverance and dedication finally paid off. Despite not having the time to correct unadjusted sound levels or the slight wobble seen in the new end credits, and despite a last-minute processing error (which resulted in certain reels of the Director's Cut looking darker than other reels), Michael Arick delivered Ridley Scott's approved version of the *BRDC* to Warner Brothers on September 4, 1992—exactly one week before the film's locked-in national release date.

Yet even though Arick had accomplished the seemingly impossible, he was less than happy with the final results. "I was pleased that we were able to release something approximating Ridley's original vision of the film," the preservationist told this author in late 1995, "but I wish we'd had the time to do the job properly. Frankly, if the entire process had gone a bit more smoothly, I'm pretty sure we would have been able to track down the violence sections, lay some new dubbing over the hospital scene, and clean up the audio errors. At the very least, we would have had a release print that looked a hundred percent better than what went into theaters."

---

[3] The "re-created" unicorn shot can be found on disc 1, side 2, chapter 4 ("Deckard's dream") of Warner Home Video's Director's Cut laser disc, frames 19507–19868.

Scott agrees with Arick's reservations. "The so-called Director's Cut isn't, really. But it's close. And at least I got my unicorn."

The *Blade Runner* Director's Cut was released on September 11, 1992, to fifty-eight theaters around the United States. Audiences who knew nothing of this version's complicated and frustrating journey to the screen might have thought they were only seeing a tweaked variation of the theatrical release, one without Deckard's narration and the tacked-on "Ride into the Sunset," but with a brand-new unicorn. However, these differences were enough to promote positive box-office revenues; the *BRDC* opened with the highest per-screen grosses of that 1992 weekend. And business continued to grow. By mid-October, the Director's Cut was screening in ninety-five theaters, and the film hovered within the top-fifty grossing motion pictures in the United States for a ten-week period. Following its U.S. release, the *BRDC* was then booked for screenings throughout Europe, Japan, and Australia, where it met with similar success.

Not bad for a film that was already a decade old. Or which had previously gained such wide exposure on cable TV, laser disc, and home video.

THE CRITICS REACT

With the deletion of the voice-over and happy ending—two elements that had been roundly criticized during *BR*'s initial opening—one would think that the *BRDC* would have received strong critical support during its 1992 release, especially in light of the film's all-pervasive cult. Yet this was not the case.

Critical reaction to the Director's Cut was again strongly divided, with most of the negative reviews reflecting the *Houston Chronicle*'s Jeff Millar's complaint that its "virtues are undiminished, problems unsolved" (September 11, 1992). However, according to William Kolb's "*Blade Runner*: The Director's Cut That Nearly Wasn't," reviews of *BRDC* on the whole were actually slightly more *favorable* than they'd been during the film's original theatrical release. "The average among newspapers publishing quantitative ratings rose by half a 'star' from the 1982 version," Kolb tells us.

Among the favorable *BRDC* reviews was one published by Gary Arnold of the *Washington Times*. Arnold noted that, "Harrison Ford's performance and the mythic, elegiac aspirations in the story are decisively improved by silencing the hapless narration. . . . 'Blade Runner' achieves a coherent thematic vision when left to its original narrative devices" ("Harder Edge and Well-placed Cuts Make This 'Blade Runner' Much Sharper," *Washington Times*, September 11, 1992).

But perhaps the single most important difference between the reviews received by the film in 1982 and the 1992 *BRDC* was economic. Unlike the 1982 negative press, which had kept many potential fans of the picture away from those theaters in which it was playing, the anti-*BRDC* critiques seemed to have absolutely no financial impact on *Blade Runner*'s 1992 incarnation. Its box-office performance was respectable, its fan base already established.

Ultimately, the Director's Cut served as one more brick in the ever-growing wall of the *Blade Runner* legend.

A DIFFERENT VERSION (#5)

Thus far, *Future Noir* has pointed out that there were four different versions of *BR* seen by the general public—the Workprint, the San Diego Sneak, the Domestic Cut, and the International Cut—before 1992. Obviously, the release of the Director's Cut then supplied us with version #5. (And if Peter Gardiner's "*BR*: The Final Director's Cut" is ever shown, this will be Version #6!)

Those who have seen the *BRDC* may think, however, that the only differences between the Director's Cut and the DC/IC are its lack of narration and happy ending, and its inclusion of Scott's beloved unicorn. But that's not quite accurate. There are actually at least *seven* differences in the *BRDC*.

Here they are:

BRDC DIFFERENCES

    1) Deckard's narration has been completely eliminated.

    2) Some added dialogue from the blimp was inserted to fill the hole created by Deckard's missing voice-over, originally heard in the Domestic/International/San Diego Cuts while Deckard was waiting for a place at the Noodle Bar ("They don't advertise for killers in a newspaper . . . "). This added *BRDC* blimp line consists of a female voice saying, "This announcement has been

brought to you by the Shimata-Dominguez Corporation, helping America into the New World."

3) A twelve-second-long unicorn shot was added as Deckard plays his piano.

4) The music track during the unicorn scene was also changed. Originally, in the International/Domestic/San Diego Cuts, the beautiful saxophone solo from Vangelis' "Love Theme" was heard as Deckard plinks on his piano. But for the *BRDC*, a new twelve-second music cue by Vangelis (which had been composed back in 1982 and was retrieved by Arick and Scott especially for inclusion in the *BRDC)* is heard instead. This takes the form of an atonal chorus wailing over the shot of the unicorn running through the woods and concludes with the sound of an electronically generated "hunting horn" that's heard as the unicorn shot dissolves back into the image of Deckard at the piano.

5) The Director's Cut features no happy ending or "Ride Into the Sunset." Instead, the *BRDC* ends with the elevator doors closing on Deckard and Rachael, as did the Workprint.

6) The extra violence seen on videocassette and laser disc copies of the International Cut was deleted for the *BRDC*.

7) A newly remixed digital soundtrack was created for the *BRDC*.

MORE TAPES AND DISCS

At the same time the Director's Cut was being released to theaters in the United States, plans were also afoot for this version's eventual appearance on home video and laser disc. The first step occurred when it was announced that all prior video/laser versions of the film (with the exception of the Criterion Collection's International Cut) would be withdrawn from circulation after August 8, 1992 to make way for the *BRDC*'s September 1992 theatrical release. The *BRDC* would then become the only available authorized version of the film (again, with the exclusion of the International Cut laser disc) when the Director's Cut was shuttled to tape and laser disc in 1993.

The first home video version of the *BRDC* appeared in Japan on January 22, 1993, in a letterboxed tape priced at ¥3800. At roughly the same time, a wide screen single disc, subtitled CLV Director's Cut laser disc, was also released in Japan.

American audiences had to wait until May 19, 1993 for the *BRDC* to be released on tape by Warner Home Video. Happily, this video was also letterboxed—unhappily, it had been encoded with Macrovision, an anticopying system that softened and degraded the overall image. No such problem plagued Warner's subsequent two-disc, letterboxed, CAV laser disc of the Director's Cut, however. Generally speaking, the imagistic and audio qualities of this disc far surpassed those of the *BRDC* seen in motion picture theaters!

For instance, the *BRDC*'s digital soundtrack means that the Director's Cut laser disc can be turned up *very loud* without suffering the inevitable distortion that analog-only soundtracks produce. Furthermore, the CAV *BRDC* laser disc features warm colors and rich hues that faithfully reproduce the original *Blade Runner* theatrical viewing experience far better than prior video editions. The *BRDC* CAV disc also shows more visual information on the bottom and sides than the letterboxed Criterion CAV disc; in fact, both Warner's Director's Cut discs and letterboxed tapes have an extremely wide viewing area, one which reveals more picture details than theatrical prints.

One small but memorable example of this extra imagistic space can be observed on *BRDC* tapes and discs during the scene when Deckard tells Rachael that "somebody" will come after her if she tries to flee the city. For it is only on the Warner home video/disc versions of the Director's Cut that Deckard can be seen comfortably touching Rachael's right shoulder, as he gives her this bad news.

All in all, then, and despite the fact that this "Director's Cut" does not accurately represent the true intentions of its creator, the *BRDC* is a most satisfying home video experience. It may not be flawless—there are some awkward side breaks on the CAV Director's Cut laser disc, for instance, especially during Deckard's city street chase of Zhora—but all in all, these home editions are a vast improvement over the murky, pan-and-scanned *BR* products released to consumers in 1983.

To paraphrase Ridley Scott, the *BRDC* tapes and discs may not be perfect. But they're close.

And at least they have a unicorn.

FINAL SHOTS

Director [Ridley] Scott finds himself "progressively amazed" as interest in Blade
Runner *"gets bigger and bigger and bigger."*

"Everything on Blade Runner *was a little bigger, a little better," says Rutger
Hauer wistfully. "You can only be a genius so many times in your life."*

—FROM "BLADE RUNNER 2," BY KENNETH TURAN
LOS ANGELES TIMES MAGAZINE
SEPTEMBER 13, 1992

As I write these words, in late
1995, it's been over twenty years since a struggling screenwriter
named Hampton Fancher first read a novel titled *Do Androids Dream
of Electric Sheep* and decided to make a movie out of it.

Since then the words *Blade Runner* have permeated the global consciousness. It has influenced scores of other motion pictures, seen its
reputation reversed from big-budget bomb to revered classic, become
an object of obsessive fascination, and spawned a once-a-year film festival (held in Israel, where *BR* is the *only* film screened.) It's even
spawned a sequel.

In book form, anyway.

The year 1995 saw the publication of *Blade Runner 2: The Edge of
Human.* Published in hardcover by Bantam/Spectra Books, written by
K. W. Jeter (the same writer who'd been friendly with and influenced
by Philip K. Dick so many years ago), *BR 2* mixed characters from
both *Do Androids Dream of Electric Sheep* and *Blade Runner* to pick
up the *BR* story one year after the events depicted in the film.

The plot begins with Rick Deckard as a fugitive, since he's refused
to terminate Rachael. Now the couple have fled Los Angeles and live
in a remote wooded area. But this is no Eden like retreat—Rachael is

forced to spend most of her days in a suspended animation chamber, one that slows down her built-in termination date. However, Deckard occasionally reawakens her. The couple will then share a fleeting moment together—an afternoon, a night—before Rachael must enter hypersleep once again.

This strange relationship is suddenly shattered when Sarah Tyrell, Eldon's real niece—and the physical model for Rachael—kidnaps Deckard and brings him back to Los Angeles. Sarah's reason? Political enemies of the Tyrell Corporation are trying to shut down the company following Eldon Tyrell's death at the hands of one of his own products. Since Sarah has inherited her uncle's corporate empire, she now wants Deckard to track down and kill *BR*'s missing "sixth replicant" before her political enemies can use the fact of its continued existence against her.

While *Blade Runner 2* is well written and imaginative (the narrative takes place during a 2020 summer, for example, with Los Angeles baking under a blistering heat wave), it's also something of a disappointment. The plot seems attenuated, the characters overly familiar, and even a last-minute plot twist can't save the book from a sluggish feeling of dullness. In sum, *Blade Runner 2* seems aimed more at hard-core science fiction fans than discriminating readers. No matter—Jeter has also been contracted to write *Blade Runner 3*. Perhaps in that novel, this exceptionally gifted author will regain his footing and deliver the worthy *BR* successor his talents are capable of.

As for *film* sequels, Ridley Scott recently told this writer that he is tentatively slated to begin a science fiction project titled *Metropolis* in either 1996 or 1997. Alas, Scott also informs me that this will *not* be a *Blade Runner* sequel. Hollywood projects are never set in stone, however. So let's keep our fingers crossed.

Some final notes:

In the twenty years since this author first began writing about motion pictures, he has never attempted a project with the scope of this book. It's been a sometimes elative, sometimes horrifying experience; not too unlike the making of *Blade Runner* itself, come to think of it. But I do hope I have at least conveyed some of the enthusiasm and respect I feel for this most uncommon product of the Hollywood system.

This author further hopes that the next time you, the reader, watch

Blade Runner on video or in a theater, you will penetrate its beguiling surfaces to ponder over the many subtexts, social criticisms, and elegant structures hiding beneath—*Blade Runner*'s condemnation of the objectification of women, for example, or the film's quirky dialogue, which for the most part concisely conveys the day-to-day realities of the strange culture in which *BR* takes place without hitting you over the head with wearying exposition. I further hope that the next time you watch this film, you'll also remember a bit of this book and be able to impress your friends with some astounding bit of *BR* trivia they've never heard of.

Finally, this author most sincerely hopes that the next time you watch a film—*any* film—you'll come away with a tad more understanding of and compassion for the tremendous amount of blood, sweat, and tears that go into the making of all motion pictures.

Until next time, then.

In the immortal words of that anonymous Spinner cop:

"Have a better one."

APPENDIX A

INTERVIEW WITH
RIDLEY SCOTT
IN WHICH THE DIRECTOR
REMINISCES ON *BLADE*
RUNNER FOURTEEN YEARS
AFTER THE FACT AND
ANSWERS SOME OF THE
FILM'S MOST FREQUENTLY
ASKED QUESTIONS

An evident love of special effects, combined with a craftsmanlike determination to tell a good story with well-drawn characters, have been the main features of Scott's movies.

—*THE ILLUSTRATED WHO'S WHO OF THE CINEMA*
EDITED BY ANN LLOYD AND GRAHAM FULLER
MACMILLAN PUBLISHING CO., 1983

Ridley Scott was born November 30, 1937. His feature film credits (as of 1995, and as a director) are: *The Duellists* (1977), *Alien* (1979), *Blade Runner* (1982), *Legend* (1985), *Someone to Watch Over Me* (1987), *Black Rain* (1989), *Thelma & Louise* (1991), *1492: Conquest of Paradise* (1992), and *White Squall* (1996). He has also functioned as a producer, a capacity which actually began with *Blade Runner* (the end credits list the motion picture as "A Michael Deeley-Ridley Scott Production"). Scott also produced *Thelma & Louise* and *1492: Conquest of Paradise*. Other directors for whom Scott and his company Scott Free have produced films include 1994's *The Browning Version* (produced by Ridley Scott) and *Monkey Trouble* (1994, Executive Producer, Ridley Scott).

In 1993, Scott was set to direct an adaptation of the best-selling nonfiction work *Crisis in the Hot Zone* (based on a true story concerning a near-outbreak of the deadly Ebola virus in Washington, D.C.), but that deal blew apart. At the time of this writing, Ridley is preparing to direct *GI Jane*, the story of the first female Navy SEAL, which is to star Demi Moore.

The following interview is an edited composite of a series of formal conversations concerning *Blade Runner* which took place between Ridley Scott and this author on the following dates: September 10, 1980; May 15, 1981; June 12, 1982; February 17, 1994; September 22, 1994; September 13, 1995; and December 4, 1995.

PAUL M. SAMMON: I'd like to begin with a query regarding one of Blade Runner's *biggest question marks: the "Unicorn Scene" in the Director's Cut, that moment in the film when Harrison Ford is slumped at his piano and daydreaming about this mythical beast. Before we get into that shot's thematic meanings, I'd like to ask about its origins. Was it in any way influenced by* Legend, *the film you did after* Blade Runner, *which also featured unicorns?*

RIDLEY SCOTT: No. That unicorn was actually filmed prior to any thought of making *Legend*. In fact, it was specifically shot for *Blade Runner* during the post-production process. At that point in time I was editing the picture in England, at Pinewood Studios, and we were heading towards a mix. Yet I still, creatively speaking, had this blank space in my head in regards to what Deckard's dream at the piano was going to be all about.

That was distressing, because this was an important moment for me. I'd predetermined that that unicorn scene would be the strongest clue that Deckard, this hunter of replicants, might actually be an artificial human himself. I did feel that this dream had to be vague, indirect. I didn't mind if it remained a bit mysterious, either, so that you had to think about it. Because there is a clear thread throughout the film that would later explain it.

Anyway, I eventually realized I had to think of an image that was so personal it could only belong to an individual's inner thoughts. And eventually I hit on a unicorn.

You mentioned the word "dream," which is interesting. Because the way you staged that scene in Blade Runner, *it's almost as if Ford's drifting off into a reverie.*

Yeah. Well, actually, he's pissed. He's drunk. On a rather strange bottle of twenty-first-century Johnny Walker Red. Which he took with him, you may remember, when he went to get his hard copy from the Esper.

Unfortunately, I don't think I really played Deckard drunk enough in that scene. What I mean by that is the Deckard character was supposed to be somewhat Marlowesque, after the Raymond Chandler antihero, you know? And Marlowe was always a little tiddly. So I thought that that scene would be a good opportunity to see our own hero a bit drunk while he was trying to work, as he was puzzling over these old photographs.

Ah, Blade Runner's *infamous photographs. Why did you choose that particular device to associate with the film's replicants?*

Because photographs are essentially history. Which is what these replicants don't have.

One final question regarding the replicants' fascination with photographs— couldn't these snapshots also be interpreted as hard-copy analogs of the artificial memories implanted in the androids?

Definitely. Don't forget that just prior to the unicorn scene, Deckard has told Rachael that her memories are not hers. Then he gives her a couple of examples of these implants, like the spider giving birth outside her window. At which point Rachael basically breaks down and leaves Deckard's apartment. And he feels, I guess, guilty about that process.

We next find Deckard poring over the photographs and doodling at his piano. And of course what we then do is reveal an extremely private and innermost thought of his, which is triggered by the music Deckard is playing. Now, music, in my mind at least, is a very visual medium. It can provoke intense imagery. So when Deckard kind of drifts off at that moment, I thought that the image which came into his mind ought to be something which we would otherwise never see in the movie.

I must confess that when I first saw the completed film at the San Diego preview, I felt the exclusion of the unicorn scene seriously disrupted the connections you were trying to make. I picked up on the other clues that Deckard might be a replicant— his collection of photographs, the scene where Ford's eyes glow—but without that specific shot of the unicorn in the woods, I felt more inclined to accept Olmos' act of leaving behind the tinfoil unicorn as merely an indication that Gaff had come to Deckard's apartment and decided to let Sean Young live. But then, when I saw the Director's Cut, the inclusion of the live unicorn made a more emotional impact. Now I could see that that tinfoil origami was a sign Gaff knew Deckard's thoughts.

So it's almost as if there are two different movies there. In the original theatrical release, Deckard might be a replicant; in the Director's Cut, he is one.

They *are* two different movies. But the Director's Cut is closer to what I was originally after.

What I find interesting about that unicorn scene is that while so much has been made by the critics of the unicorn, they've actually missed the wider issue. It is not the unicorn itself which is important. It's the landscape around it—the green landscape—they should be noticing.

I understand what you're saying. But, to be fair, I can also understand the confusion. The original prints of Blade Runner *did, in fact, conclude with green landscapes. Even if they were tacked-on ones.*

Tacked on, as you say. By some of the producers, and by the studio. Which I'm sure we'll talk about later.

But before that happened, my original thought had been to never show a green landscape during *Blade Runner*. We would only see an urban world. But I subsequently figured, since this moment of Deckard noodling at the piano offered the pictorial opportunity of a dream, why not show a unicorn? In a forest? It's an image that's so out of place with the rest of the picture that even if I only run it for three seconds, the audience will clearly understand that they're witnessing some sort of reverie.

Given the confusion that that unicorn has raised in some circles, I'm not sure your faith in the audience was justified.

I know what you mean. Maybe I should amend that to say, I was sure that the part of the audience which was paying attention would understand it! [laughs]

Besides creative differences, I understand another reason the unicorn shot was deleted from the original theatrical prints had something to do with the fact that you'd filmed it relatively late in the game.

True. Besides the tacked-on ending, the unicorn scene was more or less the last thing I shot for the picture. By that time, the pressure had grown quite intense to just get the bloody film into theaters.

That raises another question. Over the years, you've been quoted as saying that you very much wanted that unicorn footage back in the film. Yet my own research indicates that when certain producers originally requested that you delete that shot, you didn't necessarily object. What's the real story here? Had the Blade Runner *pressures grown so great, the problems so numerous, that you finally just threw in the towel?*

No. You see, by then I'd been through the whole process of going to war. Which was making the movie, with all its attendant budgetary problems and "clashes with certain producers" and so on. Still, I really thought I'd got it with *Blade Runner*, you know? I genuinely felt I'd made an interesting movie.

Then came the confusion that followed the previews in Texas and Colorado. Which created—I guess the word is insecurity. A certain insecurity was going around at the time between myself and the Ladd Company and Michael Deeley and Yorkin and Perenchio, the film's other producers. It was that insecurity which led to the original deletion of the unicorn sequence.

Frankly, I'm not surprised. Blade Runner *is quite an unusual, stylized and, if I may say so, artistic product. Especially for the studios. That must have been difficult, particularly since you and I are both well aware of the fact that—at least in terms of the Hollywood commercial mindset—anything smacking of "art" automatically breeds insecurity.*

I never thought about it that way. My way of thinking was, hey, I just made the movie.

Moving on, why did you decide to primarily film Blade Runner *on the Warner Brothers back lot? That seems an unusual choice for you, given the penchant for location shooting I've noticed in your other pictures.*

Actually, Michael Deeley and I did quite a bit of location scouting on *Blade Runner*—Boston, Atlanta, New York, even London. Funnily enough, today I could probably shoot *Blade Runner* in the city of London, because of the way it's being developed. It's as spectacular as New York.

In any event, we had done all this location hunting before I finally realized I'd never be able to control the two or three real city blocks we'd need to dress as a set for the length and space of time I'd need them. Which would have been months. We never could have done that in a genuine city and kept a lid on the situation. Therefore, it became very apparent that my only alternative was a studio back lot. Which I was really scared to death of, because back lots always look like back lots.

You managed to make it not look like a back lot.

Well, the fact that we were shooting at night was certainly a helpful factor. But Warner's back lot isn't that big. So if we hadn't filmed *Blade Runner* at night, you would have been able to see beyond the margins of our sets to all those small hills which surround the Warner Brothers' studio. That's also the reason it's raining all the time in *Blade Runner*, you know. To disguise the fact that we were shooting on a back lot.

Were the constant rain and night-time exteriors purely pragmatic decisions? I mean, that ubiquitous damp and darkness certainly adds to Blade Runner's *atmosphere.*

It does help lend a realistic quality to the story, yes. But really, a lot of the reason we finally settled on all that rain and night shooting was to hide the sets. I was really paranoid that audiences would notice we were shooting on a back lot.

This is a basic question, but how did you latch onto the actual title for this film? I do know you bought the rights to the words 'Blade Runner' from Burroughs and Norton, but who initially discovered those words? And why did you choose them?

That's a good question, but a long answer.

We actually spent months, in early 1980, when I first came out here to Los Angeles—Hampton Fancher and I, and sometimes Michael Deeley—spending every day slogging through the *Dangerous Days* script. Now, Hampton had composed a clever screenplay about a man who falls in love with his quarry. But for budgetary reasons, he'd kept it very internal. So I said to him, "You know, Hampton, as soon as this Deckard character walks out a door, whatever he looks at must endorse the fact that his world has reached the point where it can create replicants. Otherwise this picture will not fly. It'll become an intellectual sci-fi."

This was the point where we began to create the architecture of the film. Not long after, we'd arrived at a screenplay which I think nicely integrated Hampton's original storyline, characterizations, and dialogue with what we'd managed to logically decide what *Blade Runner*'s outside world had to be like.

But then I finally said to Hampton, "You know, we can't keep calling Deckard a goddamn detective." And he said, "Why not?" I replied, "Because we're telling a story in 2019, for Christ's sake. The word 'detective' will probably still be around then, but this job Deckard does, killing androids, that requires something new. We've got to come up with a bloody name for his profession."

That was on a Friday. Hampton slunk in the next Monday. We had our meeting, and he said, "By the way, I've come up with a name." And I asked, "What is it?" But instead of telling me, he wrote it down. And as he handed the slip of paper Hampton said, "It's better that you read it than hear it."

Of course, it read "Blade Runner." I said, "That's great! It's wonderful!" But the more I enthused about it, the more Hampton looked guiltier and guiltier. So I asked, "Where'd it come from? Is it yours?" [laughs] Finally, he said, "Welll. . . no, not really. Actually, it's William Burroughs'. From a slim book he wrote in 1979 called *Blade Runner: A Movie*." And I said, "Well, we gotta buy it, we gotta buy it!"

Burroughs, who turned out to be a fan of Philip Dick's, then said "Sure!" when we approached him, and gave it to us for a nominal fee. So that's how the title was acquired. I thought the words "Blade Runner" very well-suited our needs. It was a nice, threatening name that neatly described a violent action.

It also neatly describes Deckard's character, which runs on the knife's edge between humanity and inhumanity.

Yes, it does. What's more, there are a lot of delivery services in Hollywood that now have exactly the same style of typeface. [laughs]

How did you get along with Hampton?

It used to vary a bit day by day, but basically I thought we got along extremely well. Incidentally, I think Hampton's definitely got a touch of genius. He'll be amused to hear me say that.

One thing I've always found amusing about the response to this picture is how it's perceived as being such a deadly serious work. Now, don't misunderstand me—I think you created a motion picture which is both thought-provoking and mature—but I also remember you telling me you were trying to create a live-action version of Heavy Metal. *A comic book, in other words. And* Blade Runner *is a comic book.*

It is indeed. I really made a film which is a comic book, and you've got to remember that. But people always misinterpret this aspect of the production.

They also underestimate the huge problem of taking a comic strip and adapting it to the screen. That's a difficult process, because comic strips work on a two-dimensional level. You're looking at one line here, one line there, some terrific artwork and dynamic layout, and your brain supplies the rest. But to duplicate that experience in a film requires enormous discipline and preplanning. This is one reason that I won't even touch a futuristic picture until I get its script into reasonable shape. Because everything else springs from that, including the picture's visual aspects. Which in turn creates the concrete environment of that future.

Therefore, if I do a science fiction, it's got to somehow not be wasted, if you know what I mean. Sci-fi presents a wonderful opportunity, because if you get it right, anything goes. But you'd better have drawn up your rule book for the world you've created first. Then you'd better stick to it.

What about the ethical problems regarding the replicants in Blade Runner? *More than once, they're compared to slaves.*

I always felt I'd been a bit fanciful with the underlying concept of the replicants, really. Because if a society decided to produce a second-class species, that society would also probably develop it with subhuman capabilities. You wouldn't want your twin objecting to your going to its cupboard to remove its kidney. The fact that the replicants in *Blade Runner* are indeed intelligent complicates the situation. You immediately have a huge morality problem. But I must say that I'm not comfortable with these issues. If I'd gone into them in *Blade Runner*, I would have had a totally different picture. So I didn't.

Why not?

Two absolutely essential considerations are critical to the success of any so-called Hollywood picture. The first is that the end result of any film is communication with its audience. And the second is, the larger the film, the larger your budget—which also means the larger the audience you have to consider. I think a lot of people actually don't realize that.

So what you've got to set in your mind, right up front, is what kind of audience you're hoping your subject will reach. Therefore, unless you're a fool, you construct your story and budget and the scope of your film accordingly. In other words, if you're going to end up in an art cinema, you should stay within the confines of a small budget movie, which will allow you to explore most any esoteric idea you wish. But if you're going to attempt to follow along the path of a Spielberg, then your choice of subject matter and the way you're going to explain and communicate your story to that larger audience is, of necessity, going to be on a slightly more simplified level. I wouldn't say on an any less intelligent level, just less esoteric.

Choosing to present your subject matter in this manner sounds like a delicate balancing act.

Well, it all gets down to instinct. If you apply pure logic to your choice of subject, that's dangerous. Potentially sterile. So to a certain extent you're drawn into a film by your own instincts. And I think that my instincts happen to be fairly commercial ones.

Moving on to a plot point, one that's constantly discussed, is the matter of how many replicants Deckard's supposed to be hunting. Specifically, I think you know what I mean—the confusion from Bryant saying that out of the six original escaped androids, one was already dead, leaving five. But Deckard only retires four. I already know the answer to this question, but could you officially put it on the record?

I assume you're speaking of Mary, the sixth replicant we had to drop. I'd actually cast that part. Given the role to an interesting young lady about the same age as Daryl Hannah, whose name I can't recall—

Stacey Nelkin?

That's it. Actually, we removed Mary's scenes because we couldn't afford to do them. We suddenly realized, about the third week into filming, that with the kind of detail I work with, we were going to have to build in a hedge against going over budget. In other words, we'd have to remove some scenes, remove some action. Mary's action, as it turned out.

So all this confusion resulted from a money issue.

Yep. Stacey was devastated, poor thing. I still feel a bit badly about that. I'm also sorry the character itself had to be written out; Mary was going to be the only replicant that the audience would have gotten to see naturally fade away. What we'd come up with was a situation that took place early on in the film. In a dark room, with the other replicants watching Mary die. That's how we were going to introduce the replicants.

That's interesting, because in the last draft of the script I have mentioning Mary, she survives up until the end of the film. At which point we see her hiding in a closet in Sebastian's apartment. Until Deckard shoots through the closet door, killing her.

We'd rewritten that. Mary's primary scene was now going to take place very early on. You'd witness all these replicants hovering over her deathbed before you even met Roy Batty. So it gave these replicants an instant sort of sympathy. I was sorry to see that go—it was rather a sad scene, actually.

Let's discuss an interesting visual motif that runs throughout Blade Runner. *It begins with that giant eye at the start of the film, the close-up of the blue iris which is intercut with the wide shots of the industrial landscape. Was that meant to be a symbolic or literal eye?*

I think it was intuitively going along with the root of an Orwellian idea. That the world is more of a controlled place now. It's really the eye of Big Brother.

Or Eldon Tyrell?
Or Tyrell. Tyrell, in fact, had he lived, would certainly have been Big Brother.

I ask this because Blade Runner's *special effects storyboards suggested that the eye belonged to Holden, the Blade Runner shot by Leon in the Interrogation Room.*
That was the early intent, yes. But I later realized that linking that eye with any specific character was far too literal a maneuver and removed the particular emotion I was trying to induce.

Inserting that gigantic, staring orb up front set up an interesting paranoid vibe, I thought. Because instead of the audience watching the film, the film is watching the audience. . . .
You hit it. *Blade Runner,* in a sense, actually is about paranoia. And that eye underscores Deckard's dilemma, because by the end of the film, he believes he may be a replicant himself.

Continuing with Blade Runner's *use of vision, there seems to also be a definite "eye motif" in the film. I mean, besides the giant eye in the first act, you have the Voight-Kampff machine that looks into eyes, Chew works at an eye lab, Batty holds up artificial eyes in front of his own, Tyrell's eyes are gouged out, the replicant's eyes glow . . . this sort of thing persists throughout the picture. Was this insistent repetition intentional on your part?*
Well, who was it that said that the eyes are the window to the soul? I believe that. Just as I believe that they are the windows in your head.

But the basic reason I started out the film on an eye and then continued to emphasize eyes through action or dialogue was because of the Voight-Kampff machine. It just sat there and focused on the windows in your head. Therefore, it was logical that I begin the film on this window and attempt to develop and sustain that imagery throughout the film.

Also, you know, when you think about it, the eye is the single most vulnerable aperture in your body. Without your eyes, man, you've got nothing. And sticking something through someone's eye is a very simple way of killing somebody. That feeds right back into the atmosphere of paranoia I was attempting to create.

So it all comes back to the Voigt-Kampff machine. Which was a stroke of collective genius. First came Philip K. Dick, who invented this totally believable instrumentality and term—"Voigt-Kampff" sounds like a real piece of equipment, like an Arriflex. Then Hampton Fancher brilliantly expanded and deepened Dick's concept. Finally, Syd Mead came up with a marvelous design for a working model of this imaginary thing. All of these accomplishments were quite extraordinary.

The use of the Voigt-Kampff instrument raises a basic question, though. If Blade Runners have photographs and videotapes of what replicants look like—and you establish both of these facts early in the film—why do they have to give them a Voigt-Kampff test to determine if they are indeed replicants?
If replicants have been replicated from human beings, then I guess a law would

have to be passed as a "fail-safe." One demanding that all replicants had to be tested in case you found the real thing. Either way, they would deny being replicants.

Obviously, the glowing eyes of the replicants were meant to be a dramatic and not a literal device, correct?

Yes. Because if you could walk into a room and see someone's eyes shining away at you, why take the trouble of testing them? You'd just blow them away where they stood. So that retinal kickback was primarily a cinematic technique, mainly used as a tip-off for the audience.

However, I'd also intended a couple of other, more subtle things with the replicants' glowing eyes. One was semihumorous and slightly ironic—the fact that, despite all their technology, the genetic designers of *Blade Runner's* world still hadn't quite perfected their product's eyeballs. So that kickback you saw from the replicants' retinas was a bit of a design flaw. I was also trying to say that the eye is really the most important organ in the human body. It's like a two-way mirror; the eye doesn't only see a lot, the eye gives away a lot. A glowing human retina seemed one way of stating that.

Your casting of Sean Young was an interesting choice—she's almost too beautiful to be true.

But that was the point, you see. If this patriarchal technology could create artificial women, then they'd surely design them to be young and sexually attractive. *Blade Runner* even obliquely comments on this, through Pris' designation as a "pleasure unit." That's a totally fascistic concept, by the way, and I don't agree with it. I don't even want to discuss it. But that would be the reality of this civilization.

Also [laughs], when Sean was made up in her forties outfit, she somewhat reminded me of Rita Hayworth. She had that look. And Hayworth had been my ideal of the sphinxlike femme fatale ever since I saw her in *Gilda [1946, and an important* film noir]. So I suppose you could say Rachael was my homage to *Gilda,* in a way.

I'm sure this has been brought up to you before, but the only people Deckard kills in the film are women. And the first one he kills, Zhora, he shoots in the back. Now, the film noir hero was always cynical, but Deckard's actions seem to carry things beyond that. What this further deconstruction of the film noir protagonist intentional on your part?

Yeah, but you know, I was going down this avenue of exploring Hollywood. The first real Hollywood movie I'd done was *Alien,* and *Alien* was pretty dark. So I decided to make *Blade Runner* a further inversion of Hollywood values.

What I was really dealing with in *BR* was an antihero, an almost soulless man who really didn't give a shit whether he shot these artificial humans in the front or shot them in the back. He's simply there to do the job. But what we learn at the beginning of the film through the voice-over, which is now gone, thank God, is that he's also begun to act with a certain amount of remorse. Deckard starts the picture realizing he's getting touched by his work. Which of course sets up the ensuing situations that turn his world upside-down.

The fact that Deckard eliminates only women in the film perversely feminizes him, then.

Yes.

Personally, I found those moments when Deckard kills Pris and Zhora to be a fairly savage commentary on male chauvinism.

Exactly. I would totally agree with that.

I also noticed there's a similarity between Harrison Ford finding a snake scale in a tub in Blade Runner *and Michael Douglas finding a sequin in a tub in* Black Rain. . .

That's very well spotted. But I have to tell you, I didn't like that. We needed a clue in *Black Rain*, and somebody on the crew who'd seen *Blade Runner* suggested the sequin. And I said, "No, we can't. I've already done this once." But we couldn't think of another goddamn clue! So in fact, it's absolutely a repeat. I hated doing it.

One touch which has caused endless speculation among hard-core fans of the film is the chess game that's played between Sebastian and Tyrell, the one which Batty uses as a ploy to finally meet his maker. The theory has been raised that the moves and pieces on the boards seen in Blade Runner *are an homage to an actual, classic chess match played in 1851, called "The Immortal Game." Is that correct?*

I've seen that speculation somewhere myself. The answer is no. What's that line you see at the end of film credits? "Any resemblance between this photoplay and actual events is purely coincidental?" [laughs] I'm afraid that's the case with *Blade Runner's* chess game—it's purely coincidental.

Could you talk a bit about the final night's shooting? I understand it was fairly brutal.

You could say that. Most of the final evening was taken up filming Ford and Hauer on this twenty-foot-high set we'd constructed on the back lot to stand in for the roof Deckard's hanging from at the end of the picture. And I had the completion bond people breathing down my neck—they were going to rip me off that roof. Yet we still managed to squeeze Rutger's "tears in rain" speech in.

Then I needed a shot of the dove Rutger releases flying away into the sky. We'd tried to grab that earlier, but the bird had become rather wet under the sprinklers we had going, and when it was time for it to fly off, it merely hopped out of Rutger's hand and walked away. So I later shot another bird during the day, as an insert, in London, next to the incinerator at Elstree Studios. Which of course didn't quite look right.

Tandem was pushing you that hard to wrap things up?

Yes. I did manage to grab another shot or two the last day by moving that rooftop set into a soundstage. But basically, the completion bond people were just saying "screw that" to anything else I wanted, so we closed down. In fact, you can notice in the last scene after Rutger has died that the sky behind him is going blue. That was dawn. A real dawn. That was literally it—it's a wrap, babe.

If all the other animals of Blade Runner's *world are artificial, why is that dove real? Were you sacrificing internal accuracy for symbolism? Using that bird to represent Hauer's departing soul, or as a "dove of peace"?*

I think the dove came from Rutger. Hauer was good to work with, and very much a contributor. He used to come in with lots of ideas. Rutger said, "Can I use the dove?" And I said, "It's a bit on the nose, don't you think?" But he was so intense about it I eventually said, "Go for it." I think he pulled it off. But it was a last-second idea—I mean, we photographed it that morning, so we had to run off and get some pigeons very quickly.

Of course, technically, in that particular world of 2019, there would be no live pigeons there. Everything would be dead.

Speaking of Hauer improvising, did he actually improvise that evocative final line, "Tears in rain?"

Yes. "Tears in rain" was Rutger. I was never going to get to shoot all those wonderful sights Rutger described, "c-beams glittering in the Tanhauser Gate," and so on, because we couldn't afford it. Yet somehow it worked better just staying on his face as he described what he had seen, and how we would never see that in our lifetimes.

Hauer's death is a moving moment.

Very. You know, I was up on the rooftop set about to shoot that, and I told an A.D. to go get Rutger. But the assistant director told me Hauer wanted to speak with me first. So I had to climb down a bloody ladder and walk across the lot to Rutger's trailer. And there he was, smiling, saying, "I've written some of this scene." Which was his "Tears in rain" line. I thought it was wonderful. As was Rutger's performance as Roy.

You ran up against the studio hierarchy for the first time on Blade Runner, *resulting in a reputation for being difficult and for going over budget. What's your side of this story? I'm sure your troubles with Tandem enter into this at some point.*

They do. But let me answer your budget question first.

By the time of *The Duellists,* I was a pretty successful commercial director, who ran his own company with other directors under its roof and made sure that their budgets didn't get out of hand. Now, I'd been able to function on *The Duellists* and in fact get it going by taking no fee and doing a completion bond. In other words, I could afford to do that. I'd also paid for the screenplay, chosen the writer, etc. Then *Alien* came to me as sort of an invitation to dance. With Hollywood. And the entire time I was filming that, I had my own line producer in there keeping a close watch on the budget, as well as a completion bond guarantor who always let me know where we were, spending-wise. I say all of this to illustrate the fact that I've always run my own stage.

Anyway, we were pretty well on budget on *Alien.* I do remember that I came to a point where they felt that we were going to go over a little. But the film was budgeted at $8.9 million and we went to $9.2, or $9.4. So I went about $500,000 over budget. Today if you did that you'd be a fucking hero. I mean, today there are guys who go $20 million over budget and move on to the next movie! Anyway, I went $500,000 over, by commission, mostly because of one scene. Because certain people didn't want to do the end capsule, "sleeping beauty" scene of *Alien.* I said, "Are you kidding? We must shoot this! That is the real last act!" And it was, when Sigourney Weaver gets into that capsule.

So I walked into *Blade Runner* from *Alien*, believe it or not, with a tiny reputation for being excessive. And I thought, "Well jeez, if that's all it takes to get this reputation, guys, I'll be excessive."

Anyway, it was some time before I decided to saddle up back onto science fiction. It took me almost two years to kick off with *Blade Runner,* and that was after a lot of hemming and hawing and trudging around looking at various locations. At which point I decided that the only way for me to do *BR* was to somehow fake it up on a studio back lot. So we budgeted it out and I think it came out at somewhere near $15 or $20 million.

Now, this figure was already well above what had been projected for the original *Dangerous Days* script. But Hampton had written a certain type of film, of a certain scale, and then *Blade Runner* grew. Really, I think, in terms of what I wanted to add to it.

Finding that initial $15 or $20 million, though, wasn't easy. First we had Filmways drop out, although they were actually quite nice about the way they handled that. Then we couldn't find the start funds we needed, because at this point in time it was about two years after *1941 [Steven Spielberg's costly WWII comedy],* and about one year after *Heaven's Gate.* Both of which had cost considerably more money than our estimated budget, and both of which had flopped. So there was some fiscal hesitation going on in the industry. Yet $15 or $20 million certainly wasn't inordinate, it was about medium high.

So Michael Deeley said to Filmways, "Okay, okay," and quickly bailed out and went and saw a few people, and then brought back in The Ladd Company and Tandem. Tandem basically came in with expenses money, which is the money that you are short of. With a view to also picking up any money we went overbudget on as well. Right?

Yes?

So I think that by the time Tandem signed on we'd finally budgeted the film out—and I'll get to the point in a moment—to about $22.5 million.

Which ultimately ended up costing a little over $28 million.

Yes. So I think Jerry Perenchio and Bud Yorkin were originally obliged to put in somewhere between $3 or $4 million for *Blade Runner,* which then rose by another $3 million or so. Which in those days was a lot of money. But for those guys, I think it was a drop in the ocean.

Anyway, eventually I was rightly beaten up because of our involvement with Tandem. And that was the crossover point for me. Because when I looked around—and this is not being superior in any form, and mustn't come out as being superior—I realized I was essentially with, for the most part, the wrong kind of people to make this movie. We'd started the process with people who, on the surface, felt pretty supportive. On reflection, however, and I discovered this fairly quickly, I found out that Tandem and I just didn't think on the same wavelength. They were people who were basically—well, let's call them sophisticated television people. People who weren't capable of visualizing the type of accurate film budget I required for a film. Tandem, I think, always felt that my asking for additional funds while we were shooting *Blade Runner* was, to some degree, some kind of indulgence. It wasn't. It was me, as the director of that film, having a certain vision. And I was sticking to that fucking vision!

You were simply being true to your project.

That's right. Something else Tandem didn't understand.

I know you also had problems with your crew while you were filming Blade Runner. *To what do you ascribe that?*

Well, I didn't have problems with everyone on the crew. But you know what? I think it might have been something as simple as certain people on the crew not understanding what I was trying to get.

I mean, Jim Cameron [*Terminator 2*], when he makes a film, nobody asks a fuckin' question. Because now the world is educated as to special effects and such. But in those days, they didn't know what the fuck I was doing! I was the only one saying, "We do this, we do that, we paint it gold, we paint it black . . ." And people around me were giving me blank stares and saying, "Gold? Black? Why?" Eventually, I would get really angry and say, "Just do it!" Which was frustrating, believe me.

In Future Noir, *I mention the tension that grew up between you and Harrison Ford while you were shooting the film. It's certainly not my main focus in the book, but I'm curious—what do you think caused this rift?*

I think it's honest to say that doing *Blade Runner* wasn't tremendously smooth in terms of a working relationship with Harrison. There's no point in pussyfooting around that.

Harrison's a very charming man. But during the filmmaking process I think we grew apart, mainly because of the logistics of the film I was trying to make. In concentrating on getting *Blade Runner*'s environment exactly the way I wanted it, I probably short-changed him.

By not giving him as much attention as the environment?

Yes. That was a failure on my part, I suppose.

But when a film is being made, nobody ever thinks about the director, you know. In fact, there were times when I could tell Harrison was displeased with me, and I'd think, "What about me?! I've got nineteen thousand other things to think about and deal with."

I actually said something like that to him once. I said, "Listen, this is my movie, I have my performance as well as you have yours. And, you know, both will be brought together. That's all I can promise." Because if I hadn't, a lot would have gone out the window. To put that kind of thing on screen requires enormous attention to detail. And it can finally only be accomplished through one pair of eyes.

You still sound conflicted about the experience.

Well, our rift was very draining. At the same time, our collaboration was an exciting one, because Harrison is so smart. He's a very intelligent, incisive, and articulate man. At the end of the day, though, as I say, I think I probably short-changed him.

Funny enough, we got along much better after the production was over and during the process when we were doing our *Blade Runner* press junkets. Even though those junkets varied between the film getting thrashed and people kind of eulogizing it. That was very confusing—when you get that sort of response, you don't believe anybody.

In any event, Harrison and I did get on better later. So it's not as if we parted mortal enemies. I was never really able to talk to him in depth to find out whether Harrison liked the film or not, however. Or liked what we had done.

Another controversial aspect of Blade Runner *was Ford's voice-over. Now, in almost all of the scripts I read, Deckard does narrate the story in one form or another. Which I always assumed was a nod toward the old Marlowesque, film noir convention of the hard-boiled private-eye narrating his story in a world-weary voice. But I understand you were never really comfortable with Deckard's voice-over.*

No. Nor was Harrison. *Apocalypse Now* was made—when?

It was released in 1979. Why?

Because I always felt that one of the main backbones of *Apocalypse* was its voice-over. Which actually gave another dimension to Martin Sheen's character, by letting you inside his head. That voice-over worked very well; it was somehow well written and somehow well delivered. But voice-over is extremely difficult to pull off, because in a way it has to be totally internal and reflective. If the tone of what you're saying is just a bit off, it's never working. And then you start to struggle with the performance—is it not functioning because it's tonally incorrect, or what?

The bottom line of Deckard's narration was that we just couldn't get it. We wrestled with it and wrestled with it. Which frustrated Harrison to no end, because he's clearly a talented and formidable actor. So neither he nor I were comfortable with it. The trouble is, the more you do it, the more you start to convince yourself that, well, it's going to be okay. You don't become pragmatic. That's unfortunate. It's only when you really view and hear these things years later that you think, "Oh my God! It's awful!" Because, A) *Blade Runner's* voice-over was overexplanation, and B), the narration, although admittedly influenced by Raymond Chandler, wasn't Chandleresque enough.

Do you see what I mean? I felt Deckard's narration could have been more lyrical. Because Marlowe, I always felt, was a little bit of a street poet. *Blade Runner's* narration wasn't really written that way. We struggled to have it written that way, but nobody could put that spin on it.

Were the weaker elements of the narration also influenced by the Denver/Dallas sneaks?

Actually, we dropped most of the voice-over at first, and then previewed that version without it in Denver and Dallas. But the studio felt there were certain areas of confusion within the storyline. People didn't know this and didn't know that. To which my initial response was, "Well, that's the whole point of watching the goddamn movie. To find out what *Blade Runner's* all about!"

But frankly, I then became puzzled myself by the preview audience's reactions. Because I'd felt that *Blade Runner* might have been subtle, yes, but also comprehensible. So I think I let myself be swayed by my own confusion.

Anyway, I was losing wicket at that point. So we ended up struggling to put the voice-over onto *Blade Runner* not for street poetry, which was our original intention, but to clarify things. Which I think became ridiculous. So did Harrison.

How did the idea for tacking on Blade Runner's *happy ending with helicopter footage from* The Shining *come about?*

By the time I agreed to add the happy ending, I was so beaten up, so on the ropes, that I was spittin' in the bucket. I was punchy, really. Because prior to this I'd been insisting that we had to end *Blade Runner* when Rachael and Deckard go into the elevator.

But Tandem said, "No, that's too depressing. And this is already the most depressing film we've ever seen. [laughs] We've got to end this on an up note! Something heroic, with them driving off together in the countryside." At first I fought that. I said, "But there is no countryside! It's all either industrial wasteland or factory farms!" And they replied, "Well, shit. There you go again!" *[laughs]*

So I eventually capitulated and said, "Look, I'll tell you what. I've got an idea. Since I don't want to go off reccy-ing for another four weeks *[looking for another location]* to try to find this perfect landscape—and we'd already tried to shoot some landscape footage in Monument Valley, and failed—let me talk to Stanley Kubrick. I know Stanley a little bit, and I'm going to have him help me solve this." And they said, "WHAT?!?" I just replied, "Leave it to me."

So with the help of Ivor Powell, who'd worked with Stanley on *2001*, I got Kubrick's number and called him up. Because I figured, if anybody's going to know where the best mountain scenery is, it's got to be Stanley!

Now, this was the first time I'd ever called Kubrick, but he was quite cordial. I explained the problem I was having getting hold of the proper landscape footage for this new ending on *Blade Runner*—which he'd heard about—and then said, "You know your opening footage of *The Shining*? I'm sure you must have shot hours of that . . . have you got anything I could use from that?" Stanley said, "Sure. I'll send you something. Go ahead and take a look and cut what you want. As long as you don't use anything that I used."

Within two hours I had seventeen 2000-foot rolls of helicopter footage. And that's how it happened.

By this point you had a new happy ending and a new voice-over on the film. So now you're at the San Diego sneak preview—and you cut a few scenes after that sneak as well, including a shot of Deckard reloading his firearm and a couple of other shots. Were these moments edited out after that preview because they were deemed unnecessary padding?

I think people felt generally that the film was a little slow after the San Diego preview, so I trimmed a bit here and there. *Blade Runner is* a bit slow, in a sense, since it has its own pace.

The overall critical reaction to Blade Runner *wasn't very kind during the film's initial release.*

God, no. You would have thought we were boiling babies or something.

Pauline Kael's review of the picture was particularly scathing.

You know, there are cases when I think that the taking up of valuable media space by critics, for destruction, seems pointless. Not to mention the fact that Ms. Kael wouldn't have had a job if we didn't have a film industry.

Why do you think the general public initially rejected the picture?

I think people were confused, because they expected another experience from the one they got. *Star Wars* had already happened twice by then, Harrison was an established star because of *Raiders of the Lost Ark*—

—A very particularized star, of a very particular type.

As you say. An action hero. And I had done a film without action, with visual density substituting action, with essentially an unsympathetic character. *Blade Runner* taught me that the American public tends to favor a high-fiber diet. Which infers that the American system is one containing a certain degree of optimism.

I, on the other hand, tend to be a bit darker. To look to the dark side. Not because I'm a manic-depressive, but because I find darkness interesting. Particularly in its more unusual aspects. I'm sure this has something to do with my own heritage. I am a Celt, after all. And the Celts are traditionally fascinated by melancholia.

Anyway, so what circa–1982 American audiences got from *Blade Runner* was not what they expected. It's funny. I remember going to the very first *BR* preview, and since Harrison was now a known face, he had to be snuck into the back of the theater. He came with his wife Melissa Mathison, a very sweet lady who's a good writer.

After the preview was over, Harrison and I were sitting in this little office in the cinema. And I was depressed. Because there had been a kind of a silence emanating off the people who were watching our movie. Harrison was a little confused and a little worried as well. But then Melissa came over—and I'll never forget this—and she said, "I just wanted to tell you how much I loved your movie." She said it very quietly, and she really meant it. That was great. It helped a lot.

Professionally speaking, how did you react to the initial failure of Blade Runner?

Relatively philosophically. Remember, not long before *Blade Runner* I had done *The Duellists*, to very good critical acclaim and virtually no box office. Then came *Alien*, which in one sense was almost the reverse situation. So I had already experienced both extremes in my professional life.

How did you take the film's failure on the personal level?

I think it's safe to say I was quite disappointed. Because I did think *Blade Runner* was quite unique.

We began this discussion with an examination of one of Blade Runner's *most controversial elements: the unicorn. I'd like to wind our talk up with its other most high-profile ingredient: the question of whether Deckard is or isn't a replicant.*

Well, in preparing the storyline, it always seemed logical to me that in the full turn of events, which pertained to a film of paranoia, that Deckard should find out he was a replicant. It seemed proper that a replicant detective might begin to wonder whether at some point the police department hadn't done precisely the same thing to him.

So I always felt the amusing irony about Harrison's character would be that he was, in fact, a synthetic human. A narrative detail which would always be hidden, except from those audience members who paid attention and got it. But Tandem felt this idea was corny. I said, "I don't think it's corny, I think it's logical. It's part of the full circle of the initial idea. Ties it off with a certain elegance, in fact." That's why, at the end of *Blade Runner,* Deckard picks up that teeny piece of foil—

—the tinfoil unicorn origami—

—right, the unicorn, which visually links up with his previous vision of seeing a unicorn. Which tells us that the Eddie Olmos character A) has been to Deckard's apartment, and B) is giving Deckard a full blast of his own paranoia. Gaff's message there is, "Listen, pal, I know your innermost thoughts. Therefore you're a replicant. How else would I know this?"

But how can Deckard be an android when he's physically outmatched by the replicants, whom you've previously established as being stronger than humans?

Deckard was the first android who was the equivalent of being human—with all our *vulnerabilities.* And who knows how long he would live? Maybe *longer* than us. Why build in the "aging" gland if you don't have to?

Now you're bringing immortality into the equation, which is a completely different factor—

—one I find fascinating—

—but I must say I better appreciate the more subtle suggestions that Deckard might be a replicant. Such as the fact that he collects photographs, which you see scattered over his piano. And of course the most significant visual clue is that over-the-shoulder, out-of-focus shot in Deckard's kitchen, when you see Ford's eyes briefly glowing. Was that setup intentional?

Totally intentional, sir. I was hoping there'd be those who'd pick up on that.

Since *Blade Runner* is a paranoid film, throughout there is this suggestion that Deckard may be a replicant himself. His glowing eyes were another allusion to that notion, another of the subtle little bits and pieces which were all leading up to that scene in the end where Deckard retrieves Gaff's tinfoil unicorn and realizes the man knows his secret thoughts.

Actually, though, my chief purpose in having Deckard's eyes glow was to prepare the audience for the moment when Ford *nods* after he picks up the unicorn. I had assumed that if I'd clued them in earlier, by showing Harrison's eyes glowing, some viewers might be thinking "Hey, maybe he's a replicant, too." Then when Deckard picked up the tinfoil unicorn and nodded—a signal that Ford is thinking, "Yes, I know why Gaff left this behind"—the same viewers would realize their suspicions had been confirmed.

The only problem I have with Deckard being a replicant is that if he's a replicant to begin with, it rather undercuts his moral evolution as a human being. Because when the film starts, Deckard's clearly on the cusp of a change—he's trying to get out of his profession. But he's still the macho jerk. Then, as the story progresses, he just as clearly gains insight into the wretchedness of his profession, not to mention the growing empathy he displays toward the replicants. Which, to me, are demonstrably human characteristics. But if Deckard's a replicant—well, it almost wipes out his spiritual rebirth.

Unless he's a more sophisticated replicant and has had a spiritual implant. And is a Nexus–7.

Interesting thought! What do you mean by that?
Well, it's not exactly an action-oriented idea. Because now we're getting into the notion of a world and a situation which at some point is going to fail us. But that's the value of science fiction, going into these interior philosophies.

Expand on this idea of Deckard being a "Nexus–7."
If Deckard was the "piece de resistance" of the replicant business—"more human than human," as Tyrell would say—with all the complexities suggested by that accomplishment, then a Nexus–7 would, by definition, have to be replication's perfection. Physically, this would mean that the Tyrell Corporation would be prudent in having Deckard be of normal human strength *but* extended lifespan—resistance to disease, etc. Then, to round off their creation, the perfect Nexus–7 would have to be endowed with a *conscience*. Which would in turn suggest some kind of need for a faith. Spiritual need. Or a spiritual implant, in other words.

That sounds like the perfect idea to pursue in a Blade Runner *sequel. A course I understand you're thinking of taking, because, in a* Newsday *article (dated October 6, 1992), you're quoted as saying: "I'd really like to do that. I think 'Blade Runner' made some very interesting suggestions to the origins of Harrison Ford's character, addressing the idea of immortality. I think it would be a very intelligent sequel." What are the sequel possibilities for* Blade Runner?
Well, that's partly a game. The Hollywood thing. It'll cost a lot of money to buy the title off the original producers, and the question remains, is the title worth it, or should I prepare another project that's along the lines of the same genre? Notwithstanding the question of using an actor named Harrison Ford. Because by the time you end up paying $2 million just for the bloody rights and another $15 to $20 million for Harrison, it's kind of crazy, you know? I don't know yet—it's something I'd certainly like to do, and science fiction is certainly something I want to get into again. Because as we all know, the arena of science fiction, if you attack it correctly, or whatever way you address it, is an area in which anything can happen.

Despite it's potential cost, the proper Blade Runner *sequel could, I think, be immensely profitable. You wouldn't have to fight the same battles in trying to get the audience to understand the picture, for instance—*Blade Runner's *now a well-known piece of entertainment history.*
Well, I definitely feel that if I went back to a sequel, any such project would have to further perpetuate and explore the idea that Harrison Ford was a replicant. And if he is a replicant, maybe we'd explore the idea that instead of a four-year lifespan, he has an indefinite lifespan.
There could also be the idea of a *Blade Runner* sequel which contains a situation where they've perfected the process of cryogenics to prolong lives—in a world that has a big population problem. Following that line of thought, the next thing you'd have to develop would be the Off-world angle—you certainly couldn't have hordes of people with extended lifespans living on an overcrowded Earth. So perhaps Off-

world in a *Blade Runner* sequel really means "the frontier." A place that maybe has become so perverse that the right to die a normal death becomes the thing to seek for.

What about this "Metropolis" picture you're planning on doing in a couple of years? Rumor has it that this is actually a Blade Runner *sequel.*
They will say that, won't they? That sort of talk'll get me into trouble.

All I can say at this point is that *Metropolis* is indeed a science fiction picture. We've got rather a good first-draft screenplay, which was better than I expected. But you know, like all these subjects, *Metropolis* requires a lot of preplanning. Big preplanning. We've got to go on one more draft, well, several more drafts. But this project actually looks more than promising.

I guess we'll have to wait and see. . . Two last questions. First, have you watched Blade Runner *lately?*
You know, it ran on the BBC in mid–1995, when I was home for a short time. And I thought, "I'm going to sit down and watch this thing, to see if I can last twenty minutes." Which is what usually happens after you've made a movie—you bail out. You think "Oh God, I've seen this." So when you hear that people never watch their movies again, there's a very good reason for that.

Anyway, I watched my so-called Director's Cut. And you know what? I was absolutely stunned by how clear it was in terms of story. The removal of the voice-over also makes a tremendous difference.

But my final impression was of how much of *Blade Runner* was Hampton Fancher's movie. I think you've got to lay it with Hampton, because the script is his. David Peoples did some colorful stuff with Hampton's blessing, and these two guys get on very well. But really, it's Fancher's motion picture.

Blade Runner works on a level which I haven't seen much—or ever—in a mainstream film. It works like a book. Like a very dark novel. Which I like. It's definitely a film that's designed *not* to have the usual *crush-wallop-bang!* impact.

Last question—what do you think is the film's most important quality?
I think *Blade Runner* is a good lesson for all serious film makers to "stand by your guns." Don't listen to acclaim or criticism. Simply carry on.

Hopefully, you'll do some worthwhile work which stands the test of time.

APPENDIX B

DIFFERENT FACES OF
BLADE RUNNER—
HOW MANY VERSIONS?

There are essentially five different theatrical/video/laser disc cuts of *Blade Runner* which have been seen by the general public, and one different American television broadcast version:

1) *The Workprint* (WP) (same as Denver/Dallas sneaks, Fairfax Cut, UCLA Cut, NuArt/Castro Cuts—shown 1982, 1990, and 1991)
2) *The San Diego Sneak Preview* (SDS) (shown May 1982, once only)
3) *The Domestic Cut* (DC) (original 1982 American Theatrical Release)
4) *The International Cut* (IC) (1982 version shown in Europe/Asia)
5) *The Director's Cut* (BRDC) (released theatrically 1992)
6) *The Broadcast Version* (TV) (version broadcast 1986 over U.S. network television)

The differences between both the various theatrical versions and the broadcast television version are:

A) THEATRICAL/VIDEO/LASER DISC VERSIONS ─────────

I) THE WORKPRINT (WP) (SAME AS DENVER/DALLAS SNEAKS, FAIRFAX CUT, UCLA CUT, NUART AND CASTRO CUTS) (NOT AVAILABLE ON TAPE OR LASER DISC)

The Workprint is the most radically different version of *Blade Runner*—at least seventy audio/visual dissimilarities exist between it and the Domestic Cut, the International Cut, and the Director's Cut.

Comparing the Workprint to the chapter marks found on the Warner Brothers Director's Cut laser disc, we discover some of these differences are:

DISC I, SIDE I, CHAPTER I: CREDITS AND FOREWORD
- Ladd Company Logo appears on a white screen (not a black one).
- Opening credits consist of a white horizontal line streaking across the screen from right to left. The word "HARRISON" (colored red) shoots up from this line at the same time the word "FORD" (also red) shoots down from it. This action is accompanied by a harsh metallic sound, like two knife-blades being scraped together. Ford's credit then disappears back into the line before the

words "BLADE RUNNER" (also in red, also to the sound of clashing steel) shoot upward/downward in the same manner. No other opening credits in the Workprint (WP) are seen.

- Immediately following these "white line credits," the WP shows a text card with this excerpt from a 2016 edition of the New American Dictionary, defining the word "replicant":

REPLICANT\rep'-li-cant\n. See also ROBOT (antique): ANDROID (obsolete): NEXUS (generic): Synthetic human, with paraphysical capabilities, having skin/flesh culture. Also: Rep, skin job (slang): Off-world uses: Combat, high risk industrial, deepspace probe. On-world use prohibited. Specifications and quantities—information classified. New American Dictionary. Copyright (C) 2016

This "dictionary definition" is followed by a card bearing the words "Los Angeles, November 2019."

DISC I, SIDE I, CHAPTER 2: EYE ON THE CITY
- Two full-screen shots of the giant staring eye are omitted from the WP.
- As camera pushes in toward Tyrell Pyramid, an (offscreen) air-traffic controller voice can be heard on the WP soundtrack, suggesting opening scene in WP is a POV shot seen from an approaching Spinner. Voice of air-traffic controller says, "Spinner niner-nine-Red-two, Tyrell Approach Control. Radar contact two-zero, miles west. Spec planning pad Red-two, spec Green sector automated approach."
  WP also omits two master shots of Holden standing in interrogation room during camera's approach to Tyrell Pyramid.

DISC I, SIDE I, CHAPTER 3: LEON'S EMOTIONAL RESPONSE
- After Leon shoots Holden and wounded policeman crashes through wall, WP includes longer shot of Holden slumped over computer, face resting on keyboard. A smoking hole is visible in Holden's back in the WP; also, the blades of a ceiling fan which have fallen down over him brush Holden's hair.

DISC I, SIDE I, CHAPTER 4: STREET SCENE; INTERRUPTED SUSHI
- No narration by Deckard in WP (until Batty death scene on rooftop).
- Editing is somewhat different in this scene.
- Announcer's voice coming from the blimp has more dialogue. WP adds these words: "Let's go to the colonies! This announcement has been brought to you by the Shimata *[Japanese for "I have made an error"]* Dominguez Corporation. Helping America into the new world."
- Throughout the Workprint there is a much more visceral "feel" to the omnipresent rain which pervades the film. Probably because the WP image is darker and grainier and the sound effects track is not as "sweet" as other versions.
- WP includes a close-up of Deckard's meal at the noodle bar: two large shrimp, noodles, and a mound of rice.
- Shot of Deckard cleaning his chopsticks is longer.

- When Gaff first speaks, WP stays on Ford (instead of Olmos), and shows Deckard poking at his noodles and having problems eating them.
- Flight to Police HQ includes dialogue of Gaff insulting Deckard in Cityspeak.

DISC I, SIDE I, CHAPTER 5: THE OLD *BLADE RUNNER* MAGIC
- The shot of Captain Bryant pouring Deckard a drink is missing from the WP (although we do see Ford setting down an empty glass).
- Bryant's lines, "I need the old Blade Runner. I need your magic" are also missing.

DISC I, SIDE I, CHAPTER 6: THE REPLICANTS IN QUESTION
- During Bryant's briefing to Deckard in The Blue Room, M. Emmet Walsh has an extra (offscreen) line while both men study the videotape of Leon's interrogation by Holden. Bryant says: "That's Leon, ammunition loader on intergalactic runs. He can lift four-hundred-pound atomic loads all day and night. The only way you can hurt him is to kill him."
- Captain Bryant also informs Deckard that not one but *two* replicants "got fried running through an electrical field" at the Tyrell Corporation. Which accounts for the missing sixth replicant.
- Total running time for Chapters 5 and 6 here in the police station is about eighteen seconds shorter in WP than in Director's Cut.

DISC I, SIDE I, CHAPTER 7: RACHAEL; THE VOIGT-KAMPFF TEST
- The WP includes a voice-over of the same air-traffic controller heard at the start of the WP (with a Chuck Yeager/NASA Mission Control-type/military Southern accent) guiding Gaff's Spinner at the beginning and end of its flight to Tyrell's Pyramid.

  The first set of directions is: "Police niner-niner-five, Tyrell Approach Control. The winds zero-nine-zero at six, and the altimeter two-niner-niner-two" ("995" is the number of Gaff's Spinner. It can be seen on the side of the vehicle).

  The second set of directions is: "Spinner niner-niner, Tyrell Approach Control. Radar contact two-zero miles west. Spec planning pad Red-two, spec Green sector automated approach" (the same directions heard at the start of the film). The WP also now features air-traffic control giving instructions to a second Spinner: "Pad two. The winds zero-niner-zero at six. Spinner two, Tyrell Approach Control. Spec planning Yellow."
- After Rachael asks Deckard, "May I ask you a personal question?", the WP gives Deckard an extra offscreen line: "What is it?"
- During Rachael's V-K test, the almost subliminal "spider line" heard on the Director's Cut ("Orange body, green legs") is much louder on the WP's (still rough) soundtrack.

DISC I, SIDE I, CHAPTER 8: LEON'S APARTMENT
- The old man with the strange breathing apparatus who opens the door to Leon's hotel room for Gaff and Deckard has a line in the WP as he does so. He says, "Kowalski."

DISC 1, SIDE 1, CHAPTER 9: CHEW'S VISITORS
No differences.

DISC 1, SIDE 2, CHAPTER 1: "IF ONLY YOU COULD SEE . . . "
- The WP is missing the shot and dialogue of the seated Batty leaning back and asking Chew, "Now, where would we find this J. F. Sebastian?"

DISC 1, SIDE 2, CHAPTER 2: A VISITOR WITH SOMEONE ELSE'S MEMORIES
- Sound of Rachael in the elevator whispering "Deckard" is louder on the WP soundtrack.
- Sound of laughing children is louder when Deckard examines Rachael's photograph.
- A loud humming sound can be heard while Deckard thumbs through Leon's snapshots.

DISC 1, SIDE 2, CHAPTER 3: PRIS MEETS SEBASTIAN
- Sound of Pris inhaling her last drag on cigarette is louder.
- The WP music score stops after Pris hides under trash (but continues on Director's Cut until Sebastian drops his keys).
- Sound of Pris breaking window in the side of Sebastian's van is louder.
- As Pris and Sebastian leave the Bradbury's elevator, the sound of chimes can be heard. These chimes (which are the same heard in the film as Pris prowls through the sleeping Sebastian's workroom) continue as the pair walk toward Sebastian's apartment.

DISC 1, SIDE 2, CHAPTER 4: DECKARD'S DREAM
- In the WP, Deckard's one-finger piano playing plinks out a slightly different version of the tune played by Harrison Ford in all other variants of *Blade Runner.*
- No unicorn shot in the WP.
- There is no music track here in the WP other than Deckard's piano playing—none of Vangelis' "Love Theme" (heard on the Domestic and International Cuts), none of Vangelis' "Unicorn Music" heard on the Director's Cut.

DISC 1, SIDE 2, CHAPTER 5: COMPUTER PHOTO SCAN
- A low "whirring" sound comes from the Esper here that's not audible on the Director's Cut. Vangelis' music during this scene is also somewhat different.
- WP has Deckard muttering, "Hello, Roy" when he scans Leon's photo and sees Batty seated at the table.
- After Deckard receives the hardcopy photo of Zhora in WP, his (offscreen) voice asks, "Zhora or Pris?"

DISC 1, SIDE 2, CHAPTER 6: MANUFACTURED SKIN
- An extra verse of Vangelis' Middle Eastern sounding "Tales of the Future" music is heard at the beginning and end of this scene.
- In the WP, when Deckard first gives the snake scale to the Cambodian lady, she has an extra line of dialogue: "It will take a moment."

- Cambodian lady's voice seems higher-pitched when she (mis)reads the snake scale ID number.
- After the Cambodian lady (mis)reads the identification number on the snake scale (in exactly the same manner as all other versions), she gestures in direction of Abdul Ben-Hassan's shop. The WP now includes eighteen-second-long crane shot of Deckard winding his way through the crowds at Animoid Row. Shot dissolves into same shot of Deckard approaching snake shop seen in Director's Cut.
- Although the sight of Deckard tapping on snake shop window is the same in both the Director's Cut and the Workprint, the *sound* of Deckard's tapping is extended for a slightly longer period in the WP.
- The dialogue between Abdul Ben-Hassan (the snake dealer) and Deckard is different in the WP. It also matches the pair's lip movements better than any other versions. WP dialogue in this scene is:

> *Deckard*: Abdul Hassan? I'm a police officer, Abdul. I've got a couple of questions I wanted to ask you.
> *Abdul*: (speaks in his native tongue, waves his arms)
> *Deckard*: You made a snake, XB7 1. I want to know who you sold it to.
> *Abdul*: My work? Not too many could afford such quality.
> *Deckard*: How few?
> *Abdul*: Very few.
> *Deckard*: How FEW?
> *Abdul*: Perhaps less than I thought but still more than I can remember.
> *Deckard*: (grabbing Abdul's collar) Abdul, my friend . . . (Animoid Row noise drowns Deckard out) . . . about two seconds I'm gonna . . . (noise drowns Deckard out again).
> *Abdul*: Snake Pit!

- Abdul never mentions Taffey Lewis' name to Deckard in the Workprint. Also, Deckard holds onto Abdul's collar a few seconds longer in the WP.

DISC I SIDE 2, CHAPTER 7: MISS SALOME'S DRESSING ROOM
- Immediately following the scene with Abdul Ben-Hassan, the WP cuts to a busy street outside the Snake Pit Club. Camera then cranes upward for a twelve-second wide-angle shot of this street not seen in any other version.
- WP now cuts to a six-second shot of two women wearing hockey masks and Geisha wigs writhing in a plastic, capsule-like extrusion hanging over the street on the second story of a curbside building. WP music here is different, more ominous and disco-like. Said music continues over next shot.
- WP now cuts to a six-second long shot of a futuristic policeman standing on the street and silently pointing Deckard toward The Snake Pit.
- Same disco music continues in the WP as Deckard enters the Snake Pit but is eventually replaced by Snake Pit Club music heard in the Director's Cut.
- The WP has the Snake Pit's (offscreen) master of ceremonies give a different introduction to Zhora's dance: "Ladies and gentlemen. We have for your delight and pleasure this evening a spectacular act. Before you, a

woman. And with her, a snake. Watch her take the pleasures from the serpent that once corrupted man."

- Bar scene is two seconds longer in WP.
- Shot of Deckard holding up sequin in Zhora's dressing room is about four seconds longer in the WP; in an added closeup, Deckard turns the sequin in his finger and camera sees it more clearly.
- After Zhora runs out of dressing room after nearly strangling Deckard, WP cuts back to Ford frantically loosening his tie and making gurgling noises, suggesting Zhora nearly beheaded him.

DISC 1, SIDE 2, CHAPTER 8: PURSUING ZHORA
No differences.

DISC 2, SIDE 3, CHAPTER 1: RETIREMENT . . . WITNESSED
The sound of the dying Zhora's heartbeat is much louder in the WP.

DISC 2, SIDE 3, CHAPTER 2: HOW MANY TO GO?
- After Deckard "retires" Zhora and buys his bottle of Tsing-Tao in the WP, in the background can be heard playing the 1939 Ink Spots song "If I Didn't Care" (instead of "One More Kiss, Dear," which appears on all other versions).
- The WP's audio mix also boosted the amplification of "If I Didn't Care" so that it was much louder than "One More Kiss."

DISC 2, SIDE 3, CHAPTER 3: "WAKE UP. TIME TO DIE. "
- Brion James's death scene was somewhat truncated here—the Workprint did not include the shot of Leon's lifeless body falling forward and knocking Deckard to the ground.
- Nor was the shot of Rachael stepping forward and holding Deckard's gun in her outstretched hand included. Instead, the WP cut directly to Deckard's apartment.
- The alley scene is about eight seconds shorter in the WP than in the Director's Cut.

DISC 2, SIDE 3, CHAPTER 4: "I AM THE BUSINESS"; "I OWE YOU ONE."
- No differences.

DISC 2, SIDE 3, CHAPTER 5: THE REAL THING?
- The WP does not include Vangelis' "Love Theme" while Rachael is standing and looking at the photographs on Deckard's piano—instead, a different, more eerie piece of Vangelis music is heard.
- WP includes a bit more of Rachael's performance at the piano. Also, although the piece is the same, the music Rachael plays here is given a somewhat different interpretation.
- WP cuts out a nearly thirty-second-long close-up profile shot of Rachael letting down her hair, a shot seen in the Director's Cut.
- A few moments later, as Deckard joins Rachael at his piano and says, "You

play beautifully," the Vangelis musical score changes for the rest of this scene and is quite different from that in any other version of the film (this different music is particularly noticeable during the shots when Ford tells Young to say, "Kiss me").

DISC 2, SIDE 3, CHAPTER 6: "THERE'S ONLY TWO OF US NOW"

No major differences, except a slight variation in Vangelis' music.

DISC 2, SIDE 3, CHAPTER 7: "WE NEED YOU, SEBASTIAN"

No major differences, although Vangelis' music is slightly louder here.

DISC 2, SIDE 3, CHAPTER 8: THE RIGHT MOVES

Just before this scene ends and cuts to Tyrell's Pyramid, the "whispering dolls" are loudly heard on WP soundtrack—and only on WP soundtrack..

DISC 2, SIDE 3, CHAPTER 9: THE PRODIGAL SON BRINGS DEATH

- The WP has Batty saying, "I want more life, Father" instead of, "I want more life, fucker" ("father" was an alternate take, intended for "TV coverage").
- A kettledrum is heard during Batty and Tyrell's conversation in the WP rather than the ominous synthesizer heard in all other versions.
- The WP holds on Batty's thumbs gouging into Tyrell's eyes about two seconds longer than the Director's Cut, until blood begins to trickle out.
- After thumb-gouging shot, Tyrell's death is also edited differently than the same sequence seen in the Director's/International Cut. Editing sequence here for the WP is as follows: close-up of Batty's thumbs gouging Tyrell's eyes until blood first starts to leak down the replicant's hands. Cut to Sebastian. Cut to Batty's face. Cut to Batty's thumb leaving Tyrell's eyes. Cut to Batty letting go of Tyrell's head. Cut to the replicant owl. Cut to Batty. Cut to Sebastian. Cut to Batty, who starts walking toward Sebastian (compare the cutting here to that found in the Domestic Cut related later in this appendix).
- The Workprint version of Tyrell's death then ended with an *audibly whimpering* Sebastian turning to run from Tyrell's apartment.
- WP has Batty saying an extra line of dialogue to Sebastian as he approaches the terrified toymaker: "Sorry, Sebastian. Come. Come."
- Tyrell's death scene is seven seconds shorter in the Workprint than in the Director's Cut.

DISC 2, SIDE 4, CHAPTER 1: "NO WAY TO TREAT A FRIEND"

- In the WP, as Deckard drives his car through the 2nd Street tunnel, he hears a radio dispatch from Bryant telling the Blade Runner to investigate one "J. F. Sebastian, age twenty-five," at the Bradbury building. A moment later in the WP, as Deckard sits parked on the side of a street, as Deckard sits parked on the side of a street, he hears nothing from his police radio. In all other cuts, Deckard hears police dispatchers while driving through the tunnel, and then hears Bryant after he's parked his car on the side of the street. Also, the "Deckard parked" shot is about eight seconds shorter in the WP.

DISC 2, SIDE 4, CHAPTER 2: DEATH AMONG THE MENAGERIE

- At the point where Deckard drives up to the Bradbury Building to battle Pris and Roy in the WP, Vangelis' score is dropped altogether from this version of the film. Instead, various Jerry-Goldsmith music cues from *Planet of the Apes, Freud,* and *Alien* were inserted on the WP soundtrack by editor Terry Rawlings; these different cues now run on as the film's musical score until almost the very end of the Workprint.
- The WP has Deckard startled by a loud whisper just before he enters J. F.'s apartment. Other versions show him hearing an unexplained buzzing sound.
- The WP shows Pris jamming her fingers up Deckard's nose (with the sound of Deckard's crunching cartilage brought up loud on the Workprint soundtrack), then letting his head drop back. This shot is in the International Cut, but not on the Domestic/Director's Cuts.
- The WP scene of Pris and Deckard's battle is about eight seconds longer than in the Domestic/Director's Cuts because of the addition of the nose-breaking shot.

DISC 2, SIDE 4, CHAPTER 3: "PROUD OF YOURSELF, LITTLE MAN?"

- The WP holds the shot of the elevator bringing Roy to Sebastian's apartment about two seconds longer.
- The WP includes the sound of a thunderclap when Batty turns Pris' dead head in Sebastian's apartment and looks at her face (this sound isn't on other versions).
- When Batty pulls Deckard's hand through the wall and breaks his fingers, the WP's shot structure here is slightly different from that of all other versions: the WP shows Deckard's gun being grabbed, a close-up of Deckard's face, gun pulled through the wall, a cut to Batty, another close-up of Deckard's face (other versions show gun being grabbed, close-up of Deckard, gun pulled through wall, Deckard being pulled against wall, medium shot of Batty).
- The WP inserts a close-up of Deckard's first finger being broken (seen in no other prints). This "finger" was part of a prosthetic hand made by Michael Westmore/John Chambers."
- The WP stays on Deckard running and stopping to set his first broken finger in a single shot after Batty paints his lips with Pris' blood; other versions show Batty painting his lips, a cut to Deckard running, cut back to Batty starting to howl, cut back to Deckard running and then setting his fingers.
- The WP presents a completely different shot of Deckard screaming after he's straightened his first broken finger. (WP shows Ford in profile facing screen left and screaming, other versions show Ford full-faced, filmed head-on and screaming.)
- The WP inserts an extra line for Hauer after Batty says, "Four, five, how to stay alive." Extra word is "Coming," delivered by Batty in a melodramatic voice—which gave this extra line an unintentionally comic spin.

DISC 2, SIDE 4, CHAPTER 4: WOUNDED ANIMALS

- The WP shows additional footage of Deckard both approaching and climbing the armoire, before sticking his head through the bathroom floor's hole.

- The WP has additional footage of a stripped-down Roy running through the abandoned rooms of Sebastian's apartment.
- The two gory close-ups of the nail pushing through Batty's palm were omitted from the Workprint.
- After Batty first butts his head through the hole in the bathroom wall, he has an additional line of dialogue in the WP: "You're not in pain are you? Are you in pain?"

DISC 2, SIDE 4, CHAPTER 5: THE BUILDING LEDGE
- Visually the same as all other versions, but when Deckard first steps on ledge, the Blimp music heard in other versions is missing from the WP.

DISC 2, SIDE 4, CHAPTER 6: THE ROOF
- The WP still continues to play temporary (non-Vangelis) temp music here.

DISC 2, SIDE 4, CHAPTER 7: TO LIVE IN FEAR
- Still more temp music, but otherwise no differences.

DISC 2, SIDE 4, CHAPTER 8: LIKE TEARS IN RAIN; "BUT THEN AGAIN, WHO DOES?"
- Temp music score ends as Batty and Deckard sit on the roof staring at each other.
- After the fading Batty murmurs, "Time to die," and releases his dove, the Workprint cut to Deckard's watching face as Ford delivered the only narration heard in this version of *Blade Runner*:

"I watched him die all night. It was a long, slow thing and he fought it all the way. He never whimpered and he never quit. He took all the time he had as though he loved life very much. Every second of it . . . even the pain. Then he was dead."

- In all other versions of the film, an out-of-focus police Spinner, facing head-on into the camera, is now seen rising in the background behind Batty's shoulder (Batty is sitting in the foreground in *close-up*). However, the Workprint substituted something totally different—a wide master shot showing a *complete* Spinner, rising up from the left background of the frame (the viewer's POV here is the same as when Batty first tossed Deckard onto the roof). Concurrently, one could also see the full-figure seated bodies of Batty and Deckard in this shot, occupying, respectively, screen center and screen right.

DISC 2, SIDE 4, CHAPTER 9: SOUVENIR OF DREAMS
- Temp music begins again as Deckard searches for Rachael in his apartment (WP temp music ends as Deckard uncovers the sleeping form of Rachael on his bed).
- The final scene of Deckard entering his apartment and finding a sleeping Rachael is approximately fifty seconds shorter in the WP than in other versions.
- Among the WP's deleted material here is the suspenseful buildup before

Deckard discovers Rachael asleep in front of the magnified, endlessly rotating video screens; the WP cuts directly from Deckard entering his apartment to him standing over Rachael on the bed.

- Deckard calls out "Rachael" twice in the WP here, three times in all other versions.
- The WP also deletes the master shot seen in other versions of Deckard entering the bedroom from left rear background to see the mass of sheets on the bed in the foreground; instead, the WP shows a close-up of Deckard's face mentioned above as he bends down and lifts the sheet from Rachael's face.
- After Rachael tells Deckard she trusts him, WP cuts to Ford opening elevator doors and waving Sean Young forward. (Missing in the WP were two shots normally seen of Deckard checking the hall and walking toward the elevator, plus Rachael waiting in Deckard's doorway before he motions for her to come forward.)
- The elevator doors then close noiselessly over the couple (no sound effects here in the WP), and the same music heard when the Spinner takes Deckard to the police station (on Disc 1, Side 1, Chapter 4 of the Director's Cut disc) now plays on the WP's soundtrack.

DISC 2, SIDE 4, CHAPTER 10: END CREDITS
- After the elevator doors close in WP, a title card bearing the words "The End" is seen on the WP. There is no "The End" title on the International or the Domestic Cut (or the Director's Cut, for that matter). This end title makes closing credits run about five seconds longer in the WP.
- The Workprint does not include the Domestic/International Cut's bogus "happy ending."
- Vangelis' "*Blade Runner* (End Titles)" music then begins about ninety seconds into the WP's closing credits.
- The final line in the WP's end credits is a new one, added specifically by Warner Brothers for the proposed Workprint/Landmark Theater chain run. It reads, "This version copyright 1991 The Blade Runner Partnership."

2) *THE SAN DIEGO SNEAK PREVIEW (SDS) (NOT AVAILABLE ON TAPE OR LASER DISC)*

The *Blade Runner* sneak preview shown in San Diego, California, in May 1982 was quite close in overall content to the final theatrical release of the film. However, three extra shots were seen in this version which were not in the Workprint or any other version. Two of these can be referenced against the Director's Cut laser disc—the third against Criterion's International Cut. They were:

DISC 1, SIDE 1, CHAPTER 9: CHEW'S VISITORS
(DIRECTOR'S CUT DISC)
- In the Director's Cut (and all other versions of the film), Roy Batty is first introduced through a close-up of his spasming hand, an indication that his artificially induced lifespan is nearing an end. A moment later Batty steps out of a VidPhon Booth to confer with fellow replicant Leon (Brion James) about the loss of some incriminating photographs.

The San Diego Sneak Preview (SDS), however, did not have this close-up of Batty's hand. Instead, Roy was introduced standing in the booth in a full shot, talking to someone on the telephone. One script indicates he was calling Chew's Eyeworks to determine if the eye designer was working at his facility at that moment.

DISC 2, SIDE 4, CHAPTER 4: WOUNDED ANIMALS (DIRECTOR'S CUT DISC)

- During the final showdown between Deckard and Batty in replicant designer J. F. Sebastian's (William Sanderson) apartment, after Batty breaks two of Deckard's fingers, the SDS included a shot of a fumbling Deckard reloading his handgun while huddled against a wall. This was a logical action since Deckard had just squeezed off a number of shots, ones that killed Pris and missed Batty in a doorway of Sebastian's decaying flat. This "reloading shot" was dropped to tighten the overall tension of the scene.

DISC 2, SIDE 4, CHAPTER 20: "SHE WON'T LIVE, BUT THEN AGAIN, WHO DOES?" (CRITERION INTERNATIONAL CUT DISC)

- The SDS also displayed extra footage at the beginning of Deckard and Rachael's "Ride into the Sunset"—a high-angled shot (taken from a helicopter) of Deckard's sedan driving along a road in a forest.

  Parenthetically, the San Diego Sneak was also the first time audiences were exposed to *Blade Runner*'s new happy ending and the extensive voiceovers through which Harrison Ford narrated the film.

3) THE DOMESTIC CUT (DC) (ORIGINAL AMERICAN THEATRICAL RELEASE) (AVAILABLE ON DISCONTINUED EMBASSY LASER DISC)

The version of *Blade Runner* seen during its original theatrical run was virtually identical to the San Diego Sneak, except:

- The three extra shots seen in the San Diego Sneak (Batty in the VidPhon Booth, Deckard reloading his gun, overhead view of Deckard's sedan at beginning of happy ending scene) had all been cut from the film.

DISC 1, SIDE 1, CHAPTER 9: CHEW'S VISITORS (DIRECTOR'S CUT)

- The Domestic Cut (DC) also inserted two shots which had not been seen in either the SDS or WP: the close-up of Batty's spasming hand in the VidPhon booth, and a close-up of Roy's head in the phone booth, supposedly looking down at his hand and then turning and smiling at Leon tapping on the booth's glass to snag Batty's attention. Both of these shots were not new material, however, but shots that had been "stolen" from later sequences in the film, duplicated (with the "Smiling Roy" shot reversed as well) and inserted into the VidPhon scene.
- The DC also includes Ford's wall-to-wall narration and the happy ending.

4) THE INTERNATIONAL CUT (IC) (EUROPEAN/ASIAN THEATRICAL RELEASE) (AVAILABLE ON CRITERION LASER DISCS AND DISCONTINUED TAPES)

This is the *Blade Runner* variant most people have seen, and the version most responsible for the film's growing reputation. Ironically, it is *not* the same version that was shown theatrically during *BR*'s original release in the United States.

This "International Cut" was shown at theaters outside the U.S. at the time of *BR*'s 1982 theatrical release. However, this print was also the one which was later almost exclusively offered on American home video, laser disc, and cable TV from 1983 to 1992, until the 1992 (theatrical) and 1993 (video/disc) release of the Director's Cut mostly supplanted it. Strange how a version which was never originally seen in America during the film's first release should be the one responsible for fueling *Blade Runner*'s cult following!

The International Cut (still available on the Criterion Collection's *BR* laser discs) is the somewhat more violent, unrated version (the SDS and the DC were both rated "R"); it adds about fifteen seconds of additional footage not seen in the Director's Cut, in three sequences. Those sequences can be found on the Criterion *BR* laser disc at:

DISC 2, SIDE 3, CHAPTER 17: ROY MEETS HIS MAKER (CRITERION DISC)

- Tyrell's death scene is more graphic in the International Cut (IC)—the IC has two additional shots of Batty's thumbs pulping Tyrell's eyes.

    In order to illustrate this fact, it should first be pointed out that, in all versions of *Blade Runner*, Roy Batty kisses brilliant corporate head Tyrell (Joe Turkel) before taking the man's head between his hands and literally squeezing the life out of him. However, both the Domestic/Director's Cut versions of this sequence are markedly less visceral than the one found on the International Cut.

    The Domestic/Director's Cut version of Tyrell's death (which can be found on Warner's Director's Cut, Disc 2, Side 3, "Chapter Nine: The Prodigal Son Brings Death," frames 40555 to 41205) is edited like this: Batty kisses Tyrell. Begins squeezing Tyrell's head. Cut to a close-up of Batty's thumbs just beginning to press into Tyrell's eye sockets. Cut to a long close-up shot of Batty's straining face, over which can be heard the sound of Tyrell's cracking skull. Cut to Sebastian's horrified reaction. Cut to a medium shot of Batty holding Tyrell's bloodied head and letting it drop out of frame.

    Now, compare this sequence to the events found in the International Cut (Criterion Disc 2, Side 3, "Chapter 17: Roy Meets His Maker," frames 37645 to 38284): Batty kisses Tyrell. Begins squeezing Tyrell's head. Cut to Batty's thumbs pushing into Tyrell's eyes. Cut to Batty's straining face. *Cut to Batty's thumbs gouging deep into Tyrell's eyes, with blood squirting from both sockets.* Cut to Batty, straining. Cut to a horrified reaction shot of Sebastian. Cut back to Batty's face. *Cut to a close-up of Batty's thumb pulling out of Tyrell's bloody sockets.* Cut to a two-shot of Batty releasing Tyrell's head, which drops out of frame.

    Not only are the Domestic/Director's Cut versions of Tyrell's death edited slightly differently from the IC's version, a quick comparison of the frame counts between these versions reveals that the international print is actually eleven frames *shorter* than the Domestic/Director's Cut, whose longer running time is taken up by the long take held on Batty's face.

DISC 2, SIDE 4, CHAPTER 18: DECKARD AND PRIS (CRITERION DISC)
- The IC has additional footage of the fight between Pris and Deckard.
- And additional footage of Pris' death:

For instance, the Director's/Domestic Cut (Disc 2, Side 4, "Chapter 2: Death Among the Menagerie," frames 7931–9177), begins with Pris kicking Deckard across the room after he has discovered her masquerading as a doll, and is edited thusly:

Deckard's head is pinned between Pris' thighs: Pris is riding Deckard's shoulders. The replicant turns Deckard's head around 180 degrees, giving the unnerving impression that she's broken his neck. Pris then slaps Deckard three times across the sides of his head with her open palms. Cut to a close-up of Pris' watching face. Cut to Deckard's head falling backward, to bounce off the floor. At this point the Domestic/Director's Cut includes a clearly heard audio effect of Deckard's nose breaking just before his head hits the floor—yet we have not seen Pris touch Deckard's nose!

Compare this moment to the Criterion *Blade Runner* (Disc 2, Side 4, "Chapter 18: Deckard and Pris," frames 5723–7226). (NOTE: The Criterion dust jacket incorrectly lists this chapter as occurring at the end of side three when it actually begins on side four): Deckard is kicked by Pris. Has his head turned around. *But now there are only two slaps to the side of his head.* Cut to Pris looking down. *Cut to a side shot of Deckard's head between Pris' legs, as she inserts two fingers into his nose and begins pulling it backward.* Cut to another shot of Pris' watching face. *Cut to a different angle of Deckard's head between Pris' legs, with her fingers pulling his nose even farther back.* Cut to a close-up of Pris' face straining with effort. Cut to the same last shot seen in the Warner's disc—Deckard's head falling back onto the ground and the same "nose-crunching" sound effect.

This time, however, the inclusion of this sound punctuates the fact that Pris has indeed broken Deckard's nose.

Another segment of Pris' death scene also plays differently between the International/other cuts. In the Domestic/Director's Cut, Pris begins to cartwheel toward Deckard; he shoots her, once. She crashes against the wall and falls to the floor. Cut to Deckard rolling over. Cut to Pris thrashing on the floor. Cut to Deckard getting to his feet. Cut to Pris, thrashing and screaming. Cut to Deckard, looking at her. Cut to Pris, still thrashing. Cut to Deckard, aiming his gun and firing for the second time. Cut to Pris' body, spasming upward in a slow-motion death throe.

The female replicant's death in the Criterion/International version, though, is more graphic:

Pris cartwheels toward Deckard. He shoots her, once. Pris hits the wall and floor. Cut to Deckard, looking. Cut to Pris, thrashing. Cut to Deckard, getting up. Cut to the thrashing Pris. Cut to Deckard, looking. Cut to Pris' third thrashing. So far, the International Cut's continuity is the same as the Domestic Cut's.

However, at this point in the IC, we see Deckard raise his gun (not shown before) and fire it for the second time. *Cut to a fourth shot of Pris thrashing and screaming. Cut to Deckard firing his gun a third time.* Cut to Pris' body rising up off the floor in slow motion.

All told, then, the International Cut includes three extra shots in this sequence: Deckard raising his gun, Pris thrashing a fourth time, and Deckard firing a third round into the female replicant.

DISC 2, SIDE 4, CHAPTER 19: BATTLE ON THE ROOF (CRITERION DISC)
- Additional shot on IC shows close-up of Batty pushing nail through palm of his hand.
- Additional IC footage shows that nail pushing through the back of Batty's hand (also in close-up).

    These two added close-ups of Batty nailing himself occur on the Criterion CAV laser disc *Blade Runner* on Disc 2, Side 4, "Chapter 19: Battle on the Roof," at frames 16530–16555 and 16611–16646.
- The IC also contains Ford's "long-form" voice-over.
- The IC includes the happy ending.

5) THE DIRECTOR'S CUT (BRDC) (AVAILABLE ON WARNER BROTHERS TAPES AND LASER DISCS)

The so-called *Blade Runner* "Director's Cut" (which really isn't) is essentially the same as the Domestic Cut, with three crucial exceptions:
- *Blade Runner* Director's Cut (BRDC) has no narration (at all).
- BRDC does not have additional violence seen in International Cut.
- BRDC does not have happy ending/"Ride Into the Sunset."

DISC 1, SIDE 2, CHAPTER 4: DECKARD'S DREAM
- BRDC also features Deckard's daydream of a unicorn, which shows this mythical beast galloping in slow motion toward the camera through a forest, turning right, and shaking its head and mane before the shot fades back to Deckard at the piano. This occurs while Ford is drunk in his apartment and plinking at his piano on Warner Brothers Director's Cut laser disc, Disc 1, Side 2, "Chapter 4: Deckard's Dream of the Unicorn," frames 19508–19872.

B) AMERICAN BROADCAST TELEVISION VERSION ——————————

6) THE BROADCAST VERSION (TV) (NOT AVAILABLE ON TAPE OR LASER DISC)

An edited, 114-minute 18-second version of *Blade Runner* was first aired on the CBS television network on Saturday, February 8, 1986. This version was the same as the Domestic Cut except the violence was cut back even more and the swearing was eliminated. The source print appears to have been taken from the 1983, pan-and-scan Embassy laser disc version of the film (which was the same version seen during the American theatrical release: refer to appendix F: Videography for further details on the 1983 Embassy disc), since there was negative damage that occurs at one place on this Embassy disc which also occurred exactly at the same point on the *BR* print aired by CBS.

Most of the edits on this CBS broadcast pertained to harsh language in general and Captain Bryant's dialogue in particular. For instance:

- Bryant's line "Don't be an asshole, Deckard" was changed to "Don't be an ass, Deckard"
- The "Christ" was cut from Bryant's line "Christ, Deckard, you almost look as bad as that skin job you left on the sidewalk."
- The "goddamn" was cut from Bryant's line, "He's a goddamn one-man slaughterhouse."
- Batty's line "I want more life, fucker," was changed to "I want more life."
- Zhora's nudity was eliminated by CBS slightly zooming in/cropping the image of her breasts in Zhora's dressing room.

BLADE RUNNER
BLUNDERS

THE MISTAKES

Making any motion picture is an endless series of compromises. Since there's never enough time or money, oftentimes a picture is released with certain mistakes the filmmakers may wince at but hope they can live (or get away) with.

Like any other film, *Blade Runner* has its fair share of bloopers and blunders: flubbed dialogue, continuity mistakes, mismatched shots. But unlike most motion pictures, *Blade Runner* has been subjected to an inordinate amount of scrutiny—which makes tracking down those blunders that much easier, and that much more fun.

Presented for edification and your amusement, then, is this catalog of classic *Blade Runner* blunders. Plus a few that even the filmmakers may not have caught.

- When Gaff's (full-size) Spinner first lifts off from the street by the Noodle Bar, two cables supporting the vehicle from an out-of-frame crane on which the Spinner was hung are clearly visible in the shot. One is attached to the front of the car, one at the rear. These can be spotted on the Warner Brothers Director's Cut laser disc on side one chapter four between frames 16332 to 16398.

     Both Ridley Scott and Terry Rawlings spotted this flub after the scene was shot; but Scott told the editor to leave it in anyway, because, despite the briefly visible cables, he still thought the shot "looked wonderful."

- During the miniature special-effects "liftoff" sequence portraying Gaff's Spinner rising up from the street near the Noodle Bar, two large model buildings can be seen on the right hand of the screen. The one on the upper right is the miniature police HQ building (with its landing lights turned off and rooftop Spinners removed)—but the Spinner hasn't reached police headquarters yet.

     The other miniature building sports a large neon sign, reading NUYOK. This is the same model and sign which was used for Leon's YUKON Hotel; the modelmakers merely scrambled the letters on the sign.

- Gaff's lips can be seen moving during his and Deckard's flight to Captain Bryant's office, but we don't hear what he's saying. Originally Edward James Olmos was heard insulting Deckard in Cityspeak during the flight. This dialogue track was removed, however, when it was decided to make the journey a voiceless "mood piece," instead.

- Captain Bryant tells Deckard that six replicants have escaped from an Off-world colony. One (identified as "Holden" or "the Burglar" in early versions of the script) was "fried" breaking into the Tyrell Corporation. This should leave five replicants. But Deckard only "retires" four during the film.

  This mistake was entirely due to the fact that scenes featuring a sixth replicant ("Mary") had been dropped early in production because of a budget shortage. Yet Bryant's "six replicants" dialogue had already been recorded. Ridley Scott later tried to correct this problem during a postproduction dub by having actor M. Emmet Walsh change Bryant's line to "two" replicants having been fried. But the director thought the result looked technically sloppy: "Too much lip-flap," Scott says. (The director had wanted to insert a close-up of Bryant saying "two.") So, after the Dallas/Denver sneaks, the original "one fried replicant" vocal track was put back in and released with the final film.

  Since then a great deal of misinformation and speculation has been generated by Bryant's gaffe. I hope that this (verified) explanation now officially "retires" the subject.

- More "lip-flap" is evident during Deckard's first meeting with Rachael in Tyrell's office. This occurs when Harrison Ford asks Sean Young if Tyrell's owl is artificial. "Of course it is," Rachael replies.

  Young's original recorded line, however, was, "Of course not," which makes sense when you realize that Tyrell was wealthy enough to afford a genuine owl. The reason Rachael's line was later changed through redubbing was that Ridley Scott subsequently realized that the owl's eyes are not only seen glowing, it is also the first animal shown in the film. Therefore, Scott felt it was better to immediately establish that Tyrell's artificial organisms looked exactly like real ones (except for their eyes, of course). So Young's dialogue was changed to alert the audience of this fact. (If you look closely enough, you can spot the discrepancy between Rachael's redubbed dialogue and her on-film lip movements on the Director's Cut laser disc on disc one, side one, chapter seven) "Rachael: The Voigt-Kampff Test," frames 26723 to 26874.

- The first shot of Roy Batty in *BR* is a close-up of his clenching hand in a telephone booth. This shot is actually a duplicate of one seen later in the film when, during Batty's chase of Deckard through Sebastian's apartment, Roy pauses for a moment to drive a nail through his hand. You can briefly glimpse the nail in Batty's hand in the "telephone booth" scene if you examine frames 38401 to 38402 on side one, chapter nine ("Chew's Visitors") of the Director's Cut laser disc.

  The second shot of Roy Batty in the final film is a close-up of his face looking down (supposedly at his hand), and then looking up, smiling, and turning screen left in response to Leon's (offscreen) tapping on the VidPhon booth. But even though Roy is supposed to be alone in the booth, the thumb and first finger of a second person's hand can be seen on the extreme left of the screen, resting on Roy's shoulder. (Try looking for this hand on the Director's Cut disc at side one, chapter nine ("Chew's Visitors") between frames 38423 to 38668).

  This shot is also a duplicated "steal" from a later shot in the film, which occurs when Rutger Hauer is sitting on Joe Turkel's bed and Tyrell lays his hand on Roy's shoulder. It was inserted for continuity's sake—to suggest Roy was looking "down" at his "clenched hand," and to use a reaction shot (of Roy looking up and smiling at Leon's offscreen tapping on the glass VidPhon booth). This duplicated shot was also "flopped" (reversed) so that Batty would appear to be turning left toward the direction of Leon's tapping; as seen in Tyrell's bedroom, Batty turns his head in the other direction.

- The titles on the Million Dollar Movie marquee, which can be seen across the street from Sebastian's apartment building, change between the shots when Pris hides herself under the trash and Sebastian drives up in his Armadillo van.

  This mismatch was the result of the *BR* production crew spending over a week on location in downtown Los Angeles at the Bradbury Building. During that period, the Million Dollar Movie, which then as now (1995) is a real and still operating movie theater, was showing Spanish-language films. And the theater had a program change between the night Daryl Hannah's solo scenes were shot and the night William Sanderson's scenes with her were shot. Contrary to rumor, the titles on the marquee are *not* some sort of Spanish-language in-joke inserted by Ridley Scott.

- When Daryl Hannah skids into Sebastian's Armadillo van's window and breaks it, it's not a stunt. The actress actually slipped on the wet pavement and shattered the (real) window with her (real) elbow, chipping the bone in eight places in the process.

- When Pris is standing outside the Bradbury talking to Sebastian, her hair is wet. Yet when she steps out of the elevator with William Sanderson in the Bradbury Building, it's dry. Once inside Sebastian's apartment, however, her hair is wet again. This is charitably called a "continuity error."

- When Deckard uses his Esper machine to examine Batty's photograph, the woman revealed lying on the daybed with a towel around her head is *not* Joanna Cassidy. Instead, it's an (unknown) female stand-in who was used to "replicate" Cassidy during the filming of "Zhora's" scene here. And when Deckard requests a "hard copy" of this woman, the close-up angle of the "Zhora" face seen on the resulting photograph does not match the close-up angle of the "Zhora" seen on the Esper screen.

  Finally, Rutger Hauer only appears sporadically during the Esper sequence, primarily on the actual photograph which Deckard inserts into his Esper terminal. Some of the other shots of "Hauer" revealed during the subsequent examination of the photo are actually carefully disguised close-ups of yet another (anonymous) stand-in, who also doubled for Hauer during the Esper reshoot in London.

- The female Cambodian vendor on Animoid Row reads the wrong serial number off the enlarged snake scale she examines under her electron microscope. This woman says the number is "990–6907XB71." But the image under the microscope (at least what's visible) shows no "990–69." It appears as if she at least got the "07XB71" part right, however.

  This mistake arose from the fact that the live-action portion of this scene was shot before the enlarged insert was done by David Scharf, who overlaid the snake scale with the wrong number.

  Also, the Cambodian woman does not remove the snake scale from its plastic bag before putting it under her microscope. At the very least, what should be revealed is the blurred image of a scale seen shot through plastic.

Finally, the snake scale enlargement is actually a (real) electron microscope photograph of a female marijuana plant. This photo (without the serial number) can be found in David Scharf's book *Magnifications: Photography with the Scanning Electron Microscope* (Schocken Books, 1977).

- During Deckard's conversation with Abdul Ben-Hassan (the artificial snake merchant), their lip movements do not match their dialogue. Said dialogue/ movement was correct at the Denver and Dallas Sneak Previews and in the Workprint, but certain producers on the *BR* team thought that this original exchange was confusing and did not give the audience enough verbal information during a key scene. New dialogue was written and dubbed in during postproduction, in the hope that it would clarify matters. Which, once again, resulted in noticeable "lip-flap" (one of *BR*'s most constant blunders).

- The "Zhora chase" and her subsequent death scene contain more errors than any other sequence in the film. This was because the filmmakers were forced to rush through this setup in a single take—the sun was coming up, and they had to get Joanna Cassidy's death down in one take. Or not at all.

  First, Zhora pulls on high-heeled boots in her dressing room. Yet when Joanna Cassidy is being chased by Deckard through the street, her boots are now flat-heeled.

  The second time Zhora is shot, you can clearly see the actress clutching something in her right hand; also, you can see a black tube running up from that hand into Cassidy's right sleeve. The actress was holding a triggering mechanism to fire off the hidden squib that would explode the blood bag taped beneath her costume on her right shoulder—the black tube housed the electrical wires running up to the squib (said black tube was not filled with blood, as others have claimed). You can clearly see this tube on side three, chapter one ("Retirement . . . Witnessed") of the Director's Cut laser disc, from frames 813 to 857.

  A stunt woman doubles for Joanna Cassidy as Zhora smashes through the plate-glass windows in the shopping arcade. This double is also wearing "flat" boots, and does not look very much like the real actress. Also, just after Joanna Cassidy is shot for the first time (in the shoulder) and the film cuts to a shot of her stunt double crashing through a window, no wound is visible on the stunt double's shoulder.

  When Zhora is shot a *second* time, it's on the same spot on the same shoulder. The reason behind this goof was that this sequence had been a "one take only" affair, simultaneously filmed by a number of different cameras placed at different angles. Both the first shoulder wound and the second one, therefore, are actually the same piece of footage, but shot from two different angles.

  However, even though Zhora is shot twice in the same place, when her body is later seen lying on its stomach on the street, the dead replicant now has *two* bullet holes, one in each shoulder. Was this the makeup department's way of trying to show us how Zhora's wounds were supposed to look in the first place?

- This isn't a blunder, but . . . suppositions have been printed which propose that the window of the car upon which Deckard is thrown during his fight with Leon is broken before Ford hits it, and that this "prematurely broken" window is a gaffe. Sorry—the art department had purposefully broken this window *before* the fight, because the car in question was supposed to be an old, abandoned derelict.

- During the sequence when Deckard buys a bottle of Tsing Tao after killing Zhora, a cut on his (right) cheekbone is clearly visible. (Sean Young is also visible in this shot, incidentally, but in the background and out of focus. She's wearing a white fur coat and leaning against a *Jovan* sign.) A few moments later, Captain Bryant tells Deckard that there are "four more replicants to go." The cut is still visible. Bryant leaves, Deckard spots Rachael in the crowd, and he follows her, but now his cut has disappeared. So has Deckard's bottle of Tsing Tao. Neither cut nor bottle is visible a moment later, either, when Leon pulls Deckard into the alley. The cut reappears on Deckard's cheekbone after Leon's death.

  What's the story behind Deckard's on-again, off-again wound? According to *BR* editor Terry Rawlings, this disappearing cut was the result of a post-production editorial decision. "The way that sequence was originally edited," Rawlings explains, "it ran like this:

  "Deckard kills Zhora. He spots Rachael in the crowd and follows her. Leon pulls him into the alley, where Deckard receives his cut. Then Rachael kills Leon, and Deckard and Rachael walk back to the bar. Deckard buys his bottle of liquor. Gaff and Bryant appear, and they talk while Rachael waits on the other side of the street. Then they leave and Rachael starts walking away. Deckard follows her on the other side of the street.

  "Now, we decided part of that didn't make sense. Because after Deckard gets his drink and after the other two policemen leave, here he is walking down one side of the street while she's walking down the opposite one. Why wasn't she with him? Gaff and Bryant had left, so she should have come over. After all, she'd just saved Deckard's life.

  "So all of that reshuffling was done because it seemed more logical for Rachael to save Deckard's life and for Deckard to take her home with him. Ridley and I also felt that for Deckard to go back and buy that bottle after Leon's death and to talk to the two policemen *and* to chase after Rachael again really stopped the story.* It played a little dull in the original cut, frankly."

- Right before Leon is shot in the head by Rachael, you can clearly see two monofilament (fishing) lines attached to the prosthetic makeup on Brion James' forehead. These lines were used by an off-camera Marvin Westmore as a down and dirty way of yanking open the hole in James' head.

---

*"Re-editing this scene also saved us an embarassing continuity error," Rawlings adds. "Because if we'd left Bryant saying there were four more replicants for Deckard to go, after he'd killed Leon, that wouldn't have made sense. Because there would have been only three to go—Batty, Pris, and Rachael. I think that 'four to go' line was a hold-over referring to Mary, whose part had already been written out by the time we shot the alley fight. But by having Bryant say 'four to go,' before he killed Leon, things made sense again. But none of us caught this error at the time—we were just lucky that we re-edited this scene for the reasons I've already stated."

Better look fast, though—these replicant fishing lines are only visible for one frame (they come slanting in from a diagonal at upper screen right). On the Director's Cut laser disc, they can be spotted on side three, chapter three ("Wake up! Time to Die") at frame 7532.

- When Deckard falls asleep on his bed after Rachael had rescued him, he's holding a shot glass on his chest. Yet when he awakes moments later, the shot glass is gone—it's the *bottle* of Tsing Tao he knocks over as he rises. Where did the shot glass go? Terry Rawlings: "Rachael was filmed removing the glass from Deckard's chest, but this shot was later edited out."

- Daryl Hannah's "raccoon mkeup" keeps slightly changing and looks different at least three times; when Pris first applies it, when she peers into Sebastian's microscope, and when Pris has breakfast with Roy and J. F. later that morning.

- When the camera approaches the Pyramid right before we see Roy and Sebastian riding up in the elevator for their fateful meeting with Tyrell, the sky above the Pyramid is clearly orange—the same orange seen when Deckard and Gaff fly to the Pyramid earlier in the film. This is an outtake from that earlier sequence. To compound the problem, when an exterior shot of the miniature elevator is shown a few moments later traveling to the top of the Tyrell Pyramid, the sky above the building is light *blue*.

- The position of the chess pieces on Sebastian's board does not match the position of the pieces on Tyrell's board—and they're supposed to be playing the same game.

- The cables holding up the full-sized Spinner which hovers in front of Deckard as he's parked in his car on the rainy street are (slightly) visible again when the Spinner takes off, after the policeman's saying, "Have a better one."

- During their battle to the death, Pris starts cartwheeling toward Deckard from across a room. But just *before* he shoots her for the first time, you can see a bloody squib go off (at frame 8763) in Pris' midsection. Then you can see a wound in Pris' midsection—once again, *before* Deckard shoots her.

  The "bloody squib" is only visible for one frame (8763 again) on side four, chapter two ("Death among the menagerie") of the Director's Cut laser disc. You can see the wound from frames 8764 to 8769 on the same chapter and disc.

- After Batty punches through the wall and grabs Deckard's gun hand, he pulls Deckard's arm back through the hole and Harrison Ford's body slams against the wall. If you look closely, you can see this (false) wall unnaturally shaking under the impact of Ford's body.

- During the final Deckard/Batty confrontation, after Batty has howled the first time, Deckard is seen scurrying through a room empty of all but a single mannequin wearing a dress and sunbonnet. He then enters a second, darkened room. If you look on side four, chapter four ("Wounded animals"), frames 15907–15939 of the Director's Cut disc, you can see the shadows of two other people on the wall behind Deckard, running along in front of him. These "mystery shadows" belonged to cinematographer Jordan Cronenweth and director Ridley Scott.

- Right after Batty pushes the nail through his hand and Roy looks at it protruding through his skin, glance over to the right side of the frame—you'll see the yellow-and-black tile wall that appears in the bathroom, the same tile wall that Batty butts his head through—but Batty hasn't entered the bathroom yet! This gaffe arose when this sequence was recut after filming to suggest that Batty had pushed the nail through his hand to give him the added strength needed to butt through the wall (see chapter XI: Postproduction and the Music for further information on this reedit).

- Midway through Deckard's frantic climb up the side of the Bradbury Building, there's a close-up shot of his two hands hanging on to the edge of a gray strip of stone. Look closely here—the shot is actually *upside down*! "We couldn't get that close-up to look right for some reason," explains Terry Rawlings. "So in order to make it appear as if Ford's fingers were hanging onto this thing, we turned it upside down."

  This "upside down close-up" appears on side four, chapter five ("The Building Ledge") of the Director's Cut disc, from frames 21504 to 21542. And if you look *really* closely, you'll notice that the raindrops are falling *up*!

- When Deckard finally makes it to the roof of Sebastian's apartment building, one moment it's raining, one moment it's not, and the next moment it's raining again. The "dry" moment of this "on and off" goof occurs on side four, chapter six ("The Roof") of the Director's Cut laser disc, from frames 22529 to 22730.

- After Deckard has been rescued from falling and thrown back down onto the roof by Batty, Harrison Ford's shirt is clearly untucked and riding up toward his chest. His naked stomach is bared. Cut. The next instant, as he backs up into a sitting position, that same shirt is discreetly back down again, covering Ford's famous abdomen.

- Here's one of the most famous *BR* blunders:

  When the dying Batty releases his dove and the camera looks upward, the bird is seen flying into a clear blue sky, which does not at all match the dark, rainy sky we should be seeing. That's because, during principal photography in Los Angeles, the original dove became too wet to fly and refused to take off as planned. Scott was forced to pick up this shot with another bird months later on another continent—outside England's Elstree Studios, at a different time of day.

APPENDIX D

BLADE RUNNER
ONLINE

One of the key sleuthing tools used by Rick Deckard in *Blade Runner* is the "Esper." This powerful computer allows him to examine a 2-D photograph in three dimensions . . . in the privacy of Deckard's own living room, no less.

Yet at the time of *BR*'s release, true home computers were still in their infancy; now-outdated models like the Apple II and Commodore 128 were just coming to the public consciousness. Now, fourteen years later, the most fanciful *Blade Runner* research sources—which most perfectly illustrate the film's prophetic value—are the numerous home pages, chat rooms, and Web sites located on the "Information Superhighway": the Internet, a cyberspace region that can be reached through such powerful, real-world home computers such as Pentium-based PCs, Macintosh 9500s, and Amiga 4000s.

Luckily, *Blade Runner* is a much talked-about motion picture on the Internet and World Wide Web. And the home computer user can spend literally hours (if not days) digging up all manner of information. What's available are *BR* stills, sound clips, digitized images, roundtable discussions, and more—even a complete copy of Hampton Fancher's July 24, 1980, script. The easiest way to access this treasure trove is by simply calling up such Web Browser software as Netscape Navigator on your PC, typing the words "Blade Runner" in Netscape's "Directory" requester, and hitting the return key. *Voilà!* You will be immediately transported to a listing of sites available in *Blade Runner* cyberspace.

But there are other ways to access *BR* on the Web/Net, as well. What follows is a detailed listing of all *BR*-oriented sites available to the general public as of October 1995. Both site names and uniform resource locators are noted; the latter must be entered on your computer *exactly* as shown, with all upper and lowercases, underscores, punctuation, question marks, etc. (The one thing you should *not* enter is the period mark—"."—at the end of each sentence containing the uniform resource locator).

As for where to start, this author considers Murray Chapman's *Blade Runner FAQ (Frequently Asked Questions)* page and Jon Van Oast's *2019: Off-World* page two of the most comprehensive sites. Plugged-in hackers, however, are urged to log on to whatever area strikes their fancy, in order to better uncover the latest news regarding their favorite *future noir*.

BR ON THE INTERNET AND WEB

1. *alt.fan.blade-runner*
   Usenet newsgroup with continuing dialogue on issues and questions in *Blade Runner.*

2. http://wc62.residence.gatech.edu/coop/gfx/brgfx.html
   Atkins, Brian (gt47722a@prism.gatech.edu). "Brian Atkins' *Blade Runner* Images." World Wide Web page with scanned images of the bootlegged soundtrack booklet.

3. http://www.cs.tufts.edu/~katwell/blade.runner
   Atwell, Kenneth E. (katwell@cs.tufts.edu). "*Blade Runner* Script." World Wide Web page with complete copy of Fancher's July, 24, 1980 script.

4. http://swerve.basilisk.com/A/A_Benjamin_BRunner_110.html
   Benjamin, Andrew. "At Home With the Replicants: The Architecture of *Blade Runner.*" World Wide Web page features an essay studying the interlocking relationships between *Blade Runner*'s architecture, its environment, and the replicants.

5. http://www.wsu.edu:8080/-brians/science_fiction/blade runner.html
   Brians, Paul (brians@wsu.edu). "Study Guide for Philip K. Dick: *Blade Runner.*" World Wide Web page includes a section breaking down *Do Androids Dream of Electric Sheep?* into each of its respective chapters while asking questions/making notes on same.

6. http://www.cm.cf.ac.uk/M/.LINK/title-exact?+Blade+Runner
   Cardiff Movie Database. *BR* cast, credits, filming locations. Links to digitized images, the "*Blade Runner* FAQ," and the "2019: Off-world" page.

7. Available via anonymous ftp from
   rtfm.mit.edu:/pub/usenet/news.answers/movies/bladerunner-faq
   Chapman, Murray (muzzle@cs.uq.oz.au). "*Blade Runner* Frequently Asked Questions," ver. 2.4. Usenet, July, 25, 1995: 42 pages. Chapman's *Blade Runner* FAQ (also known as the "*BR* FAQ") is a periodically updated compilation of sources, information, and answers to frequently asked questions about *Blade Runner.* This is one of the oldest and best *BR* sites.

8. http://www.uq.oz.au/~csmchapm/bladerunner/bladerunner.html
   Chapman, Murray (muzzle@cs.uq.oz.au). "*Blade Runner* FAQ Home Page." World Wide Web page with hypertext version of Chapman's *BR* FAQ containing cast and crew biographies, analysis, descriptions of different versions of the film, references, questions and answers, plus soundtrack information. Links to images, sounds, and video clips.

9. rec.arts.sf-lovers, alt.cult-movies, and rec.arts.movies.
   Gillogly, Jim, "*Blade Runner*: The Director's Cut." *Usenet,* September 30, 1991:
   Review of the Director's Cut.

10. http://www.rit.edu:80/~dbh6913/ blade/brindex.html
    Hentschel, Dan (dbh6913@grace.isc.rit.edu). "Dan Hentschel's *Blade Runner* Homepage." World Wide Web page with links to the "*Blade Runner* FAQ" and the "2019: Off-World" page.

11. rec.arts.sf.movies.
    Hobson, Darryll. *"Blade Runner—The Cut." Usenet,*
    April, 19, 1993: Criticism of the Director's Cut.
12. rec.arts.movies.reviews, and rec.arts.sf.movies.
    Johnson, Ken. *"Blade Runner: The Director's Cut." Usenet,*
    March, 16, 1993: Review of the Director's Cut.
13. rec.arts.movies and alt.cult-movies.
    Knight, David B. *"Blade Runner—The Director's Cut." Usenet,*
    May 9, 1991:Yet another Director's Cut review.
14. rec.arts.movies. Mahoney, Frank. *"Blade Runner: The Director's Cut."*
    Usenet, September, 12, 1992: Review of the Director's Cut.
15. http://www.corpcomm.net/-dnewland/dnrunner.html
    Newland, Dan (dnewland@corpcomm.net). "Christian Symbolism in
    Ridley Scott's *Blade Runner."* World Wide Web page with a *Blade Runner*
    essay examining its title subject, dated September 7, 1995.
16. http://bau2.uibk.ac.at/perki/films/brunner/br.html
    Perkhofer, Michael and Stephen Bowline (perki@bau2.uibk.ac.at, sbow-
    line@odo.elan.af.mil). An informative World Wide Web page on Vangelis. Also
    includes *Blade Runner* synopsis, cast info, credits, soundtrack information on the
    bootlegged and official releases, interviews with Vangelis, digitized soundtrack
    samples, pictures, and digitized film sequences.
17. http://farnsworth.mit.edu-reagle/Stuff/bladerunner.html
    Reagle, Joseph M., Jr. "The Parting of the Mist: Film History—*Blade*
    Runner." World Wide Web page looks at the nature of the replicants and
    their relationship with Deckard.
18. http://www.wit.com/~xtian/blade_runner.html
    Rohrmeier, Christian (xtian@freedom.wit.com). "The Official *Blade*
    Runner On-line Magazine." World Wide Web page with scanned and digi-
    tized text and images from the 1982 *Blade Runner Souvenir Magazine.*
19. http://dcs.umd.edu/~bri/blade_runner.html
    Silverman, Brian (bri@dcs.umd.edu). *"Blade Runner."* A complete tran-
    scription of the 1982 theatrical release; if you were ever curious about the
    exact wording of a certain line of *BR* dialogue, here's where you'll find it.
20. http://kzsu.stanford.edu/uwi/br/off-world.html
    Van Oast, Jon (jon@kzsu.stanford.edu). "2019: Off-World." An excellent
    World Wide Web page with *Blade Runner* news, the *"Blade Runner* FAQ," a
    compilation of network discussion, and references to publications, posters,
    and models. Links to the online magazine, scripts, soundtracks, film clips,
    and digitized images.
21. http://www.smartdocs.com:80/~migre.v/Bladerunner/
    Vayser, Mike (migre.v@smartdocs.com). "Mike Vayser's *Blade Runner*
    Pages." World Wide Web page with large, correct aspect-ratio stills from the
    Director's Cut, plus a hypertext version of the *"Blade Runner* FAQ."
22. http://www.voyagerco.com/CC/ph/p.bladerunner.html
    Voyager Company. *"Blade Runner."* World Wide Web page for the Crite-
    rion Collection concentrates on their *BR* laser disc. Includes film clips, digi-
    tized images, credits, and laser disc liner notes.

APPENDIX E

THE SCORE:
BLADE RUNNER
SOUNDTRACK CATALOG

1) THE FIRST BOOTLEG SOUNDTRACK

Blade Runner (Original Motion Picture Soundtrack). Performed by Vangelis. Bootleg: not licensed for public sale, 1982. No company or catalog number (audiocassette tape, stereo).

SIDE A
1. Los Angeles, November 2019 (1:46) Vangelis
2. Leon's Interrogation (1:12) Vangelis
3. Lift-Off (1:10) Vangelis
4. Deckard Meets Rachael (1:29) Vangelis
5. One More Kiss, Dear (4:00) Skelling and Vangelis
6. Blade Runner Blues (10:19) Vangelis
7. Love Theme (4:57) Vangelis
8. The Prodigal Son Brings Death (3:35) Vangelis

SIDE B
9. Tales of the Future (4.46)
10. Dangerous Days (1:02) Vangelis
11. Wounded Animals (10:58) Vangelis
12. Tears in Rain (2:41) Vangelis
13. End Titles (7:24) Vangelis

Total tape time: 55:19

In early June of 1982, mere weeks before the film's release, a bootlegged copy of the *Blade Runner* soundtrack began circulating through Los Angeles's film-community underground. Rumor had it that this unauthorized recording originated from an unknown sound engineer who'd recorded a dupe of Vangelis' score during the film's final mixing sessions. Whatever its genesis, this first bootleg was immediately a hot property, as then current rumors insisted Vangelis' original score would never be released.

The first bootleg took the form of a 60-minute audiocassette housed in a clear plastic case. Affixed to this tape's "A" side was a simple white label with the typed words "BLADE RUNNER." Although "listenable," overall sound quality was subpar, marred by hiss, harsh treble, and frequent bass distortion.

Nevertheless, as the first (and for some time only) release of Vangelis' music for Ridley Scott's film, the first bootlegged *Blade Runner* score was an essential collector's item—despite this tape's lack of the "Main Title and Prologue," "Deckard's

Dream," and "Dangerous Days" tracks, cues that would later and ironically first be compiled on the *second* bootlegged *Blade Runner* soundtrack.

2) THE NEW AMERICAN ORCHESTRA SOUNDTRACK

a) *Blade Runner: Orchestral Adaptation of Music Composed for the Motion Picture by Vangelis.* Performed by the New American Orchestra. Musical director, Jack Elliot. Burbank, California: Warner Brothers Records, Inc./Full Moon, 1982. Catalog Number 23748–1 (33 1/3 speed record album, stereo).

b) *Blade Runner: Orchestral Adaptation of Music Composed for the Motion Picture by Vangelis.* Performed by the New American Orchestra. Musical director, Jack Elliot. Burbank, California: Warner Brothers Records, Inc./Full Moon, 1982. Catalog Number 23748–4 (audiocassette tape, stereo).

c) *Blade Runner: Orchestral Adaptation of Music Composed for the Motion Picture by Vangelis.* Performed by the New American Orchestra. Musical director, Jack Elliot. Burbank, California: Warner Brothers Records, Inc./Full Moon, 1982. Catalog Number 23748–2 (compact disc, stereo).

1) Love Theme	(4:12)
2) Main Title	(5:01)
3) One More Kiss, Dear	(4:00)
4) Memories Of Green	(4:50)
5) End Title	(4:17)
6) Blade Runner Blues	(4:38)
7) Farewell	(3:10)
8) End Title Reprise	(3:08)

Total disc time: 33:16

For many years, this was the only official release of *Blade Runner*'s score, yet it does not contain any actual music from the film! Instead, what disappointed buyers realized they had purchased (and subsequently had to be content in purchasing, for over a decade), was an insipid orchestral arrangement of the soundtrack, one specially performed by the "New American Orchestra."

Imagine the surprise of Vangelis admirers when they discovered that neither the Greek composer nor his original performances were present on this recording; imagine their horror when they realized that all of Vangelis' moody, hypnotic synthesizer cues had been replaced by bland orchestral "cover" versions, played by faceless studio musicians noodling away on conventional instruments.

Listless, uninspired, and clocking in at only 33 minutes, the New American Orchestra's "score" is shamelessly incomplete (two of its eight meager tracks rehash the same "End Title" theme!). It's also a grave disappointment in the artistic sense; the lone positive comes from top-ranked L.A. session-player Tom Scott, who contributes a soulful saxophone to the NAO's version of Vangelis' "Love Theme."

Otherwise, this dismal, homogenized, rushed-into-production anomaly (which was dumped onto the market solely because of the difficulties then surrounding Vangelis' original contributions; see chapter XI: Postproduction and the Music), can only be recommended as Muzak for androids.

3) THE VANGELIS "THEMES" COLLECTION

Vangelis: Themes. Composed, arranged, produced and performed by Vangelis. New York, New York: Polygram Records Inc., 1989. Compilation copyright Deutsche Grammophon, 1989. Catalog Number 839 518–2 (compact disc).

1) End Titles from *Blade Runner* (4:57)
2) Love Theme from *Blade Runner* (4:55)
3) Memories of Green   (5:42)
Total tracks time: 15:34

In 1989, Vangelis released an album compiling selections from various scores he'd composed for his film work. Titled *Vangelis/Themes*, this compact disc included main title themes from *Missing, The Bounty,* and *Chariots of Fire.* Also included were key cuts from previous Vangelis albums such as *Opera Sauvage, China,* and *L'Apocalypse des Animaux.*

Blade Runner fans, however, were thrilled to learn that *Themes* represented the first official release of original music cues from their favorite motion picture—ones performed by Vangelis himself, as heard in the film. Three *Blade Runner* cuts are here: "End Titles from *Blade Runner*," "Love Theme from *Blade Runner*," and "Memories of Green." This last cut, incidentally, first appeared on Vangelis' earlier, *See You Later* (1980) album before later being reused by Ridley Scott in an orchestrated version for Scott's 1987 film, *Someone to Watch Over Me.*

Confusing? Perhaps. But no more so than the tangled history of *Blade Runner* itself. In the final analysis, *Vangelis/Themes* is an excellently compiled, marvelous sounding introduction to the general film work of this talented composer—not to mention a historically noteworthy "first appearance" of three powerful *Blade Runner* cues, (finally) performed by their original creator.

4) THE SECOND BOOTLEG SOUNDTRACK

Original Motion Picture Soundtrack: Blade Runner Bootleg. Limited Edition of 2,000 (not licensed for public sale). Off World Music, Ltd., 1993. Catalog Number OWM 9301 (compact disc).

1. Ladd Company Logo (0:24), John Williams
2. Main Titles and Prologue (4:03) Vangelis
3. Los Angeles, November 2019 (1:46) Vangelis
4. Deckard Meets Rachael (1:29) Vangelis
5. Bicycle Riders [Harps of the Ancient Temples] (2:05) Gail Laughton
6. Memories of Green (5:39) Vangelis
7. Blade Runner Blues (10:19) Vangelis
8. Deckard's Dream (1:12) Vangelis
9. On the Trail of Nexus 6 (5:30) Vangelis
10. If I Didn't Care (3:03) Jack Lawrence [only used in workprint]

11. Love Theme (4:57) Vangelis
12. The Prodigal Son Brings Death (3:35) Vangelis
13. Dangerous Days (1:02) Vangelis
14. Wounded Animals (10:58) Vangelis
15. Tears in Rain (2:41) Vangelis
16. End Titles (7:24) Vangelis
17. One More Kiss Dear (4:00) Skelling and Vangelis
18. Trailer and Alternate Main Titles (1:39) Robert Randles
Total disc time: 72:42

This bootleg CD of Vangelis' *Blade Runner* soundtrack surfaced in smaller spe-cialty shops a couple of days before Christmas 1993. It's unfortunate that it was not an official release, because it is clean sounding and much more comprehensive than even the 1994 "official" release!

The second bootleg soundtrack includes an eight-page booklet containing six movie stills. The cover art is from the British one-sheet movie poster that accompa-nied the 1982 release. Two of these stills are from shots that were cut from the actual film. One shows a high, downward-looking shot of Deckard's car traveling on a country road during the infamous "Ride into the Sunset"; the other shows Deckard visiting Holden at his hospital "iron lung," a photo which also ran in my *Video Watchdog* article "Do Androids Dream of Unicorns?: Seven Faces of *Blade Runner.*"

The bootleg booklet also features an article which mixes supposition (Vangelis refused to release his soundtrack because Scott used other composers' music in the film—not true) and fact (Rachael's piano piece is a variation on Chopin's Thir-teenth Nocturne).

Hardcore fans will be most interested in this CD, however, because it contains complete versions of many Vangelis *BR* tracks heard nowhere else. The producer of this bootleg (Christopher L. Shimata-Dominguez, a pseudonym) displays a keen sense of humor with his choice of name (the same as the corporation vocally adver-tising on *BR*'s blimp). His choice of a name for his record label—"Off World Music"—isn't bad, either.

Incidentally, Andrew Hoy states that this bootleg did not prompt the official *BR* soundtrack's release. "Vangelis wasn't even aware there *was* a bootleg until after his official soundtrack came out."

5) THE OFFICIAL BLADE RUNNER SOUNDTRACK

Blade Runner: Vangelis. Performed by Vangelis. Warner Brothers Music UK, Ltd., 1994. Atlantic Recording Corporation, Catalog Number 82623–2 (compact disc).

1. Main Titles (3:42)
2. Blush Response (5:47)
3. Wait for Me (5:27)
4. Rachael's Song (4:46)
5. Love Theme (4:56)
6. One More Kiss, Dear (3:58)

7. Blade Runner Blues (8:53)
8. Memories of Green (5:05)
9. Tales of the Future (4:46)
10. Damask Rose (2:32)
11. Blade Runner (End Titles) (4:40)
12. Tears in Rain (3:00)
Total disc time: 57:53

In July 1994, twelve years after the film originally came out, Vangelis finally released his Official *Blade Runner* soundtrack. He also wrote some liner notes which are printed on the enclosed twelve-page booklet. Those wanting an explanation of why this recording took so long to see the light of day, however, will have to settle for the following explanation.

"Most of the music contained in this album originates from recordings I made in London in 1982, whilst working on the score for the film BLADE RUNNER. Finding myself unable to release these recordings at the time, it is with great pleasure that I am able to do so now. Some of the pieces contained will be known to you from the Original Soundtrack of the film, whilst others are appearing here for the first time. Looking back at RIDLEY SCOTT's powerful and evocative pictures left me as stimulated as before, and made the recompiling of this music, today, an enjoyable experience." (VANGELIS Athens, April 1994)

The cover of the official soundtrack is a partial reproduction (a close-up) of the American one-sheet, showing Deckard, Rachael, and the roof of police headquarters. There's also the nicely printed booklet, which has an inner-cover photo of Vangelis himself and fifteen photos from the film. These include a couple of behind-the-scenes shots; one is an on-set still showing a smiling Ridley Scott and a grinning Harrison Ford acting as if they were the best of friends.

Also, the "lyrics" heard in "Tales of the Future" are mostly just *sounds,* not real words. "Vangelis is fascinated by phonetics," says Andrew Hoy. "So he specifically asked Mr. Demis Roussos to sing "Future" with Middle Eastern-sounding *noises,* not in any genuine language. There may be a real phrase or two, but it's mostly gobblygook."

Some of the music cues here feature dialogue and sound effects heard in the film. These are the opening track, "Main Titles" (where you can hear Deckard talking to his Esper machine), "Blush Response" (track 2), "Wait For Me" (track 3), and "Tears in Rain" (track 4, which contains Batty's famous farewell speech). "Wait For Me" is the only new composition which Vangelis created for this recording; "Blush Response," "Rachael's Theme" (track 4), and "Damask Rose" (track 10) were all originally composed for the film in 1982 but ultimately supplanted with new compositions, instead.

It's a hard call, but this writer's nomination for the album's most haunting cut is "Rachael's Theme." This cue, performed vocally by Mary Hopkin, was originally composed for the motion picture (probably for Rachael's "moving photograph" or her "Deckard humiliates me" scene). And it's wonderful.

MISCELLANEOUS MUSIC HEARD IN BLADE RUNNER ——————

I) THE BLIMP

The Japanese melody and lyrics broadcast by *Blade Runner's* advertising blimp over Sebastian's apartment building are available on compact disc. According to *Murray Chapman's Blade Runner FAQ,* they can be found on:

Japan: Traditional Vocal and Instrumental Music, Shakuhachi, Biwa, Koto, Shamisen. Performed by Ensemble Nipponia, 1976. Electra Asylum Nonesuch Records/Warner Communications Inc. Catalog Number not available (Compact disc).

The music heard coming from the blimp is produced by plucking on a traditional Japanese instrument called a "biwa." The Japanese lyrics are from a song entitled "Ogi no Mato," which is part of a larger song cycle/epic somewhat reminiscent of Shakespeare's *Romeo and Juliet* and the William Tell legend (as "Ogi no Mato" features young people from opposing clans and a crucial moment of archery). Chapman's *BR FAQ* claims that "the lyrics tell of the tragic and utter destruction of one Japanese clan by another."

2) MUSIC HEARD DURING ROY AND LEON'S WALK TO CHEW'S EYE WORKS

As the two replicants go to meet Chew, vaguely New Age-ish music is heard on the soundtrack as a horde of Asians on bicycles pass the pair. This melody is from:
    Harps of the Ancient Temples, by Gail Laughton. Chapman's *BR FAQ* states that this recording can be found in older compact disc catalogs on the Laurel label. Its catalog number is #111. No further information available (Compact disc).

3) VANGELIS MUSIC SIMILAR TO THAT OF BUT NOT HEARD IN BLADE RUNNER

Two prior Vangelis albums contain melodies and moods very similar to those found in *Blade Runner.* One is titled *Antarctica.* It was specifically recorded for a Japanese film not released in the United States. I used to have this CD, but then I sold it. Sorry. No further information available.
    The other (and most important) is 1979's *VANGELIS: Opera Sauvage,* a soundtrack for French "nature film" director Frederic Rossif, released not long after Vangelis' popular European band Aphrodite's Child had broken up. Moody, sweet, and hypnotic, *Opera Sauvage* is the closest one can get to a crypto-*Blade Runner* soundtrack.
    Two points of interest: a portion of cut number three ("L'enfant") was put to good use by Australian director Peter Weir for his 1983 Mel Gibson film *The Year of Living Dangerously.* Also on this album (track 7) is "Flamants Roses" ("Pink Flamingos"), a long composition whose central portion sounds remarkably like "Blade Runner Blues."
    VANGELIS: Opera Sauvage. Composed, arranged, produced and performed by

Vangelis. New York, New York: Polygram Records Inc., 1979. Catalog #829 663–2 Y–1 (compact disc).

4) THE INK SPOTS "IF I DIDN'T CARE"

Those fortunate enough to have seen the *Blade Runner* Workprint or a short promotional film released in 1982 trying to sell the film will also have heard the Ink Spots' sweet rendition of "If I Didn't Care," the lovely 1939 tune which Ridley Scott had originally laid over the scene where "One More Kiss, Dear" now exists in the film. ("Care" was cut when certain *BR* producers refused to pay a rights fee for the song.)

The Ink Spots were a popular black American singing quartet founded in 1934. They had a string of hits lasting up through the forties. "If I Didn't Care" is one of their most famous compositions, and can be found as track 1 on:

The Ink Spots: Greatest Hits. Original recordings performed by The Ink Spots. Universal City, California: MCA Records Inc., 1989. Catalog number MCAD–31347 (compact disc).

APPENDIX F

VIDEOGRAPHY:
BLADE RUNNER

ON TAPE, LASER DISC, AND TELEVISION

There are basically four different versions of *Blade Runner* available to the general public.

One is the R-rated original American theatrical release. The second is the unrated, slightly more violent "International Cut." The third is the R-rated "Director's Cut." The fourth is a PG-rated "Broadcast Version" of the original American theatrical release, which was edited for and occasionally appears on television. Running times for all these different versions can vary by as much as three minutes (from 114 to 117 minutes).

But what is the best way to *watch* these versions?

In a large-screen motion picture theater with a good Dolby stereo sound system, of course.

The next best way to view *BR* is on letterboxed laser disc. The Criterion Collection's supplemented "International Cut" disc and/or the Warner Brothers wide screen "Director's Cut" laser disc are the two finest entries in this format.

After laser comes videotape. Warner Home Video's letterboxed "Director's Cut" tape is the best of this bunch.

If you can't find a theater or a laser disc player or the letterboxed Director's Cut videotape (which should be in most rental stores, and clearly marked on the box as such), then your final resort is to settle for a full-frame, pan-and-scan *BR* videotape. Anything older than a 1992 tape will be this version; it will also be the unrated International Cut, as that was the only version available on video prior to 1993. Unfortunately, two-thirds of the image area will be cut off from these pan-and-scan tapes. Plus, half the time you won't be able to quite figure out what the background really looks like.

Of course, you *could* try tracking down the rare 1983 or 1987 Embassy pan-and-scan laser discs, which were the only American discs (or tapes) to contain the original 1982 American theatrical version of *Blade Runner*.

Confused? Don't be. Cataloged below are all the different varieties of *Blade Runner* to appear on video and laser disc.

Tapes are reviewed first, then lasers. Each format is further broken down to indicate which specific video or disc contains the International Cut, the Director's Cut, or the original 1982 American theatrical version. I have also listed information on the Broadcast (television) Version in a separate category at the end of this appendix.

Running times were measured from the start of the opening Ladd Company Logo to the fade out on the last end credit. Indicated aspect ratios were measured for a full, undistorted picture (all video masters for *Blade Runner* were struck from a 35mm print with an aspect ratio of 2.36:1).

Finally, as of this writing, neither the Workprint nor the various sneak preview versions of *Blade Runner* is legally available on tape or laser disc.

Happy viewing!

A) TAPES

THE INTERNATIONAL CUT

Blade Runner (videocassette recording). Los Angeles: Embassy Home Entertainment, 1983. #1380. VHS hi-fi, stereo. Pan and scan. Aspect ratio of 1.24:1. 116 min., 58 sec. Color. Not rated.

Full-frame pan-and-scan VHS copy of the International Cut.

As with all other American *BR* tapes released before January 1993, this is the NR (not rated) "International Cut" version. There is slightly more violence here than the original R-rated U.S. theatrical release.

Adds approximately fifteen seconds to four scenes with footage not seen in the original U.S. theatrical print. Extra footage includes Batty's thumbs gouging into Tyrell's eyes, Pris thrusting two fingers into Deckard's nose and raising his head off the floor, Deckard shooting Pris a third time, and two close-ups of Batty pushing a nail into and through his hand.

Blade Runner (videocassette recording). Los Angeles, California: Embassy Home Entertainment, 1986. #1380, Beta hi-fi, stereo. Pan and scan. Aspect ratio of 1.24:1. 116 min., 58 sec. Color. Not rated.

Full-frame pan-and-scan Beta copy of the International Cut, with slightly more violence than the original U.S. theatrical release. Adds approximately fifteen seconds to four scenes (footage not seen in the original U.S. theatrical print).

Blade Runner (videocassette recording). Los Angeles, California: Embassy Home Entertainment, 1986. #1380, VHS hi-fi, Dolby stereo, surround sound. Pan and scan. Aspect ratio of 1.24:1. 116 min., 58 sec. Color. Not rated.

Full-frame pan-and-scan VHS copy of the International Cut. This is the first American tape to feature Surround Sound. Slightly more violence than the original U.S. theatrical release. Adds approximately fifteen seconds to four scenes (footage not seen in the original U.S. theatrical print). Slightly better image quality than 1983 tape.

Blade Runner (videocassette recording). Los Angeles, California: Nelson Entertainment (previously Embassy Home Entertainment), 1987. #1380, VHS hi-fi, Dolby stereo, Surround Sound. Pan and scan. Aspect ratio of 1.24:1. 116 min., 58 sec. Color. Not rated.

Full-frame pan-and-scan VHS copy of the International Cut, with slightly more violence than the original U.S. theatrical release. Adds approximately fifteen seconds to four scenes (footage not seen in the original U.S. theatrical print). Same as 1986 Embassy Home Entertainment tape.

Blade Runner (videocassette recording). Los Angeles, California: New Line Home Video (Columbia TriStar Home Video, previously Nelson Home Entertainment), 1992. #1380, VHS hi-fi, Dolby stereo, Surround Sound. Pan-and-scan. Aspect ratio of 1.24:1. 116 min., 58 sec. Color. Not rated.

Advertised as "The Tenth Anniversary Edition."

When New Line Home Video unleashed this cassette in June 1992 to coincide with the tenth anniversary of *Blade Runner*'s original theatrical release, the new box art could have fooled some patrons into thinking they were buying the fabled Workprint, or perhaps, the soon-to-be-released Director's Cut. In reality, this release was neither—it was actually the same old full-frame, pan-and-scan International Cut that Embassy had been releasing for years! One early giveaway to this fact was that, although its distributor and packaging had changed, the "10th Anniversary" tape still opened with the familiar Embassy logo.

The so-called "Anniversary Edition" was only available until August 8, 1992. At that time it was put on moratorium. In fact, except for the Criterion laser discs, no other taped American copies of the International Cut are now being manufactured. This was done so that the International Cut would not conflict or compete with Ridley Scott's new, "official" version of *Blade Runner*, which was released theatrically in the fall of 1992. This version, of course, was titled the "Director's Cut" (tapes and lasers came out a year later, in 1993).

The Tenth Anniversary Edition adds approximately fifteen seconds to four scenes (footage not seen in the original U.S. theatrical print). If you don't own a laser disc player, this is *the* best way to see the International Cut at home.

THE DIRECTOR'S CUT

Blade Runner: The Director's Cut (videocassette recording). Japan: Warner Home Video, January 1993. VHS hi-fi, Dolby stereo, Surround Sound, wide screen. Color. R-rated. Number, running time and closed captioning: Unknown.

A wide-screen video version of the Director's Cut was released in Japan before America saw the same tape. It was released on January 22, 1993 (the American video came out later, on May 19), and cost ¥3800.

I have no other information on this tape.

Blade Runner: The Director's Cut (videocassette recording). Los Angeles, California: Warner Home Video, May 1993. #12682. VHS hi-fi, Dolby stereo, Surround Sound, wide screen, CC (closed caption). True aspect ratio of 2.41:1. 116 min., 6 sec. Color. R-rated.

Letterboxed version of the Director's Cut and, despite the slightly murky image (due to encoded Macrovision anticopying protection), still *the* number-one videocassette every true *Blade Runner* fan should own.

Here's where you'll find Ridley Scott's original ending, no narration, and Deckard's dream of the unicorn. The color here is also warmer than that seen on previous video versions. It does not include the extra fifteen violent seconds featured in the International Cut, however. This cassette shows at least forty percent more image than all previous pan-and-scan *Blade Runner* videotapes. In fact, this tape shows a bit more horizontal visual information (on the sides of the frame) than the expensive CAV Criterion laser disc does!

If you don't own a laser disc player, this *is the* best way to see the Director's Cut in your home.

B) LASER DISCS ———————————————

THE ORIGINAL AMERICAN THEATRICAL RELEASE

Blade Runner (laser video disc recording). Los Angeles, California: Embassy Home Entertainment, 1983. #13805, 1 disc, analog stereo, SP, extended play (CLV). Pan-and-scan. True aspect ratio 1.24:1. 116 min., 43 sec. Color. R-rated (although jacket says "NR").

BR's tangled history is amply reflected in its first laser disc pressing, because it is one of the *only* places you'll find the same print used for the original American theatrical release.

No extra violence, supplements, or other extra material here. Just a full-frame, pan-and-scan, analog stereo version of the original American theatrical print. Incidentally, side one has its time resolution in minutes; side two, for some reason, has its time resolution in seconds.

The laser disc jacket here also contains a mistake. This first *BR* laser disc is advertised as being the NR (not rated, International Cut) version. Actually, though, it's the same R-rated version released throughout America in 1982.

Blade Runner (laser video disc recording). Los Angeles, California: Embassy Home Entertainment/Nelson Entertainment, 1987. #13806. 1 disc, CX/analog stereo, Surround Sound, SP, extended play (CLV). Pan and scan. Pioneer pressing. True aspect ratio 1.24:1. 116 min., 43 sec. Color. R-rated (although jacket says "NR").

Same as the 1983 Embassy disc, but with added CX encoding. Both sides of the disc now show their time resolution in seconds.

The disc jacket here repeats the same "NR/R-rating" mistake the 1983 Embassy laser disc did. This 1987 version is also in analog (as opposed to digital) stereo. So was Embassy's 1983 disc.

The best way to see the original theatrical release at home.

Blade Runner (laser video disc recording). Japan: (Year unknown). #08JL–70008. 1 disc, digital stereo, extended play (CLV). Pan-and-scan. Color. (Pressing plant, subtitling or dubbing information, true aspect ratio, running time and rating: Unknown).

I have very little information on this Japanese pan-and-scan laser disc, other than to speculate that it is probably identical to the 1983 or 1987 Embassy laser discs of the original American theatrical print. And that it existed.

Or exists.

THE INTERNATIONAL CUT

Blade Runner (laser video disc recording). Los Angeles. California: The Criterion

Collection, 1987. #CC1120L. 2 discs, stereo, Surround Sound, full feature format (CAV), Videoscope (letterboxed), chapter stops, CX/analog stereo encoded. Six supplements. 3M pressing. True aspect ratio 2.50:1. 116 min., 58 sec. Not rated.

This widescreen version of the International Cut is one of Criterion's all-time best-selling titles, and also one of *Blade Runner*'s best laser pressings.

Includes detailed supplemental section, with: "The Syd Mead Gallery" (text explanations and visual reproductions of Mead's preproduction art); "A Fan's Notes" (William Kolb's useful, detailed, scene-by-scene overview on many different aspects of the film); "The *Blade Runner* Trivia Test" (self-explanatory, also written by Kolb); "Annotated Bibliography" (compiled by Kolb), "Syd Mead Reprise" (more Mead art, although this time viewers can press their "Play" buttons to examine illustrations instead of stepping through them frame by frame); and "Answers to the Trivia Test" (provided by Kolb, located *after* the color bars near the end of side 4, disc 2).

There are no "reel change marks" on this disc. It shows approximately forty percent more horizontal visual information than that seen on pan-and-scan *Blade Runner* videotapes; however, about ten percent of the visual information seen on the bottom of the anamorphic 35mm theatrical print is cropped off the bottom of the frame of the Criterion disc. The Criterion disc adds approximately fifteen seconds to four scenes (footage not seen in the original U.S. theatrical print).

The best way to see the International Cut in your home.

Blade Runner (laser video disc recording). Los Angeles, California: The Criterion Collection, 1987. #CC1169L. 1 disc, stereo, Surround Sound, extended play format (CLV), Videoscope (letterboxed), chapter stops, CX/analog stereo encoded. No supplements. Pioneer pressing. True aspect ratio 2.50:1. 116 min., 58 sec. Not rated.

Same wide-screen print as the CAV Criterion version, but in the CLV (extended play) format, and with no supplements. Shows approximately forty percent more horizontal visual information than that seen on pan-and-scan *Blade Runner* videotapes; however, about ten percent of the visual information is cropped off the bottom of the Criterion disc when it's compared to the anamorphic 35mm theatrical print. No reel change marks are present on this disc.

It's also cheaper than the CAV version.

Blade Runner (laser video disc recording). Japan: Warner Home Video, 1987. #NJL–20008. 2 discs, digital stereo, Surround Sound, full feature format (CAV), Videoscope (letterboxed), chapter stops, CX encoded. (Two?) supplements. Pioneer pressing. True aspect ratio 2.41:1. 116 min., 58 sec. Color. Not rated.

A Japanese pressing which was mastered from the Criterion Collection CAV *Blade Runner*. This has fewer supplements, though; primary attention is paid to the art of Syd Mead (who's quite popular in Japan).

Disc has Japanese subtitles. The picture area is somewhat reduced because of the inclusion of these subtitles, and the color is somewhat more pastel-looking than the Criterion disc. Shows no reel change marks. This is the International Cut, with slightly more violence than the original U.S. theatrical release.

Shows approximately forty percent more horizontal visual information than that seen on pan-and-scan *Blade Runner* videotapes. However, about ten percent of the visual information is cropped off the bottom of this disc when it's compared to the anamorphic 35mm theatrical print. Adds approximately 15 seconds to four scenes (footage not seen in the original U.S. theatrical print).

THE DIRECTOR'S CUT

Blade Runner: The Director's Cut (laser video disk recording). Japan: Warner Home Video laser video disc, February 1993. #NJL–12682. 1 disc, digital stereo, digital Surround Sound, CX encoded, standard play (CLV), LG-Graphics (English), CC (closed caption), letterboxed, Japanese subtitles. Pioneer pressing. True aspect ratio 2.41:1. 116 min., 12 sec. Color. R-rated.

This wide screen Japanese pressing of the Director's Cut was available in some American rental stores before the American, Warner Brothers Director's Cut laser disc was officially released. It boasts the same print seen on the U.S. laser disc version of the Warner Brothers Director's Cut (and was taken from the same video master as the Warners American DC laser disc), but unlike its American cousin, the Japanese version is in CLV. The American version is in glorious, full-featured CAV!

Color values here are "warmer" than on the Criterion disc. Japanese subtitles are added at the bottom of the frame. No reel change marks are seen. The horizontal size of the frame is slightly wider than the Criterion disc.

Blade Runner: The Director's Cut (laser video disc recording). Los Angeles, California: Warner Home Video laser video disc, May 1993. #12682. 2 discs, digital stereo, Surround Sound, digitally mastered video, CX/analog stereo encoded, CC (closed caption), full feature (CAV), wide screen (windowboxed), Chapter Stops. Pioneer pressing. True aspect ratio 2.41:1. 116 min., 6 sec. Color. R-rated.

Contains the unicorn scene, no narration, and Scott's original ending. Does not include fifteen seconds of violence seen in International Cut. No reel change marks.

The color here is warmer than that of the Criterion disc. This version also shows a bit more horizontal visual information on the sides of the frame than even the CAV Criterion disc. The best example of this widened letterboxing occurs when Rachael is at Deckard's apartment for the second time. She asks him, "Would you come after me? Hurt me?" "No, I wouldn't," Deckard replies. "I owe you one. But somebody would." At which point we can briefly see Deckard put his hand on Rachael's right shoulder (he's standing behind her).

This moment is virtually unseen in all other tape or disc versions of the film (excepting the Japanese or American wide screen Director's Cuts). It takes place on disc 2, side 3, chapter 4 ("I am the business; I owe you one"). Look for frames #12758–12796 of the Warner's Director's Cut laser disc.

Incidentally, this Deckard's-hand-on-Rachael's shoulder shot is also the only place where we see Deckard's eyes glow. Like a replicant's.

The best way to see the Director's Cut in your home, despite a very poorly placed side break on side two, which interrupts the Deckard/Zhora chase at a crucial moment.

Blade Runner: The Director's Cut (laser disc video recording). Origin of pressing company: Unknown: Warner Home Video laser video disc, March 24, 1995. #20008 LD (Catalog Number—"Laser disc Number"—4499). 1 disc, digital stereo, Dolby Surround Sound, standard play (CLV), wide screen (letterboxed), German language (dubbed or subtitled—unknown). True aspect ratio 2.35:1. 116 min., 6 sec. Color. PAL format. R-rated (Pressing plant, CX/analog availability, availability of chapter stops, all unknown).

This German-language version of the Director's Cut was released in Germany in a letterboxed CLV disc in 1995. I have very little information on it except to note that its price was 79 Deutschmarks and its format is PAL, not the United States/Japan's NTSC.

C) BROADCAST (AMERICAN TELEVISION) VERSION

Blade Runner (American television version). CBS Television Network, 1986. First broadcast February 8, 1986. Full screen, pan-and-scan, stereo. Aspect ratio of 1.24:1. 114 min., 18 sec. Edited for television. Not rated (but probably PG).

On the night of February 8, 1986, *Blade Runner* had its network television premiere. This occurred on the CBS Network, from 9:00 P.M. to 11:25 P.M., Eastern Standard Time. The print shown was a full-framed, pan-and-scan version of the original American theatrical release. However, this version was shorn of an additional two minutes and forty-two seconds of footage; what was cut was some violence and swearing. Surprisingly, the racially touchy moment when Deckard compares Bryant's use of the word "skin job" to "nigger" was left untouched.

This "broadcast version" opened with the Embassy logo; the print shown, in fact, was the same as the pan-and-scanned one used on the 1983/1987 Embassy laser discs (so if you taped *BR* that night, you have a cut-down version of the original theatrical print). This "broadcast version" occasionally still pops up on local TV stations.

(NOTE: The first *Blade Runner cable TV* broadcast I can uncover occurred in January 1984. This was on the now-defunct "Spotlight" cable network. Although a roller preceding the film claimed that it was rated R, the resultant Spotlight print was in fact the unrated International Version.)

A rumor has also arisen that when *BR* first played on American cable TV, it contained some extra words of dialogue not found in other versions. This supposedly occurred when Bryant gives Deckard the description, names, and addresses of the dead Tyrell and Sebastian over Deckard's car radio. In the cable TV version, Bryant supposedly adds ". . . and check 'em out" after he says, "I want you to go down there."

"And check 'em out" does *not* exist on the Spotlight cable TV print I have. However, if it *has* surfaced during some other cable or broadcast appearance, I would appreciate being notified of same, care of my publisher, HarperCollins.

APPENDIX G

A SHORT
BLADE RUNNER
BIBLIOGRAPHY

I had planned on reprinting, in full, William M. Kolb's superlative *Blade Runner* bibliography (a short version of which can be found in *Retrofitting Blade Runner*).

However, space limitations have prevented this. So here's the next best thing: a selection from Kolb's massive reference work that compiles a short list of those magazine articles, periodicals, and books which were most important to this author in compiling *Future Noir*.

This author heartily recommends that the reader interested in learning more about *Blade Runner* seek out these key, and essential, works.

Dick, Philip K. *Blade Runner/Do Androids Dream of Electric Sheep*. New York: Ballantine Books, 1982. Original novel on which *Blade Runner* was based.

Finch, Christopher. *Special Effects: Creating Movie Magic*. New York: Abbeville Press, 1984, pp. 186–198. Chapter on special effects in *Blade Runner*; six high-quality stills.

Friedman, Ira. ed. *Official Blade Runner Souvenir Magazine*. New York: Ira Friedman, Inc., 1982. Fourteen interviews; over 140 photos and illustrations; 68 pages.

Gader, Neil A. "The Return of Blade Runner." *The Perfect Vision* 3, no. 12 (Winter 1991/1992): 12, 14. Sidebar detailing the differences between the workprint shown at the NuArt and the 1982 theatrical release.

Goodwin, Archie. *The Official Comics Adaptation of Blade Runner*. A Marvel Super Special 1, no. 22 (September 1982). High-quality comic, 21 stills. Cover by Jim Steranko, interior art by Al Williamson, Carlos Garzon, Dan Green, Ralph Reese, and Marie Severin.

Jeter, K. W. *Blade Runner 2: The Edge Of Human*. New York: Bantam, 1995. Authorized novel/sequel picking up the "Blade Runner" story one year after the end of the plot seen in the film; hardcover.

Kerman, Judith B., ed. *Retrofitting Blade Runner: Issues in Ridley Scott's* Blade Runner *and Philip K. Dick's* Do Androids Dream of Electric Sheep. Bowling Green, Ohio: Bowling Green State University Popular Press, 1991. Excellent collection of academic essays on *Blade Runner*; 291 pages.

Kolb, William M. "Blade Runner." *Blade Runner* (laser videodisc recording). Los Angeles: The Criterion Collection, 1987. Liner notes on album jacket; analysis, bibliography, notes, and trivia test on video disc.

———. "Blade Runner: An Annotated Bibliography." *Literature/Film Quarterly* 18, no. 1 (1990): 19–64. Extensive bibliography; 2 stills.

————. "Blade Runner: The Director's Cut That Nearly Wasn't." *The Perfect Vision* 6, no. 23 (October 1994): 120–125. Article; brief credits; 2 stills.

————. "*Blade Runner* Film Notes." *Retrofitting Blade Runner: Issues in Ridley Scott's* Blade Runner *and Philip K. Dick's* Do Androids Dream of Electric Sheep. Judith B. Kerman, ed. Bowling Green, Ohio: Bowling Green State University Popular Press, 1991, pp. 154–177.

————. "Script to Screen: *Blade Runner* in Perspective." *Retrofitting* Blade Runner: Issues in Ridley Scott's Blade Runner *and Philip K. Dick's* Do Androids Dream of Electric Sheep. Judith B. Kerman, ed. Bowling Green, Ohio: Bowling Green State University Popular Press, 1991, pp. 132–153. Essay on differences between *BR* scripts and film.

————. "Bibliography." *Retrofitting* Blade Runner: Issues in Ridley Scott's Blade Runner *and Philip K. Dick's* Do Androids Dream of Electric Sheep. Judith B. Kerman, ed. Bowling Green, Ohio: Bowling Green State University Popular Press, 1991, pp. 229–272.

Lightman, Herb A. "*Blade Runner*: Special Photographic Effects." *American Cinematographer* 63, no. 7 (July 1982): 692–693, 725–732. Interview with David Dryer; extensive credits; 5 stills.

Lightman, Herb A. and Richard Patterson. "Blade Runner: Production Design and Photography." *American Cinematographer* 63, no. 7 (July 1982): 684–691, 715–725. In-depth article; 22 stills.

Lofficier, Randy and Jean-Marc. "*Blade Runner*." *Science Fiction Filmmaking in the 1980's: Interviews with Actors, Directors, Producers and Writers*, by Lee Goldberg, Randy Lofficier, Jean-Marc Lofficier and William Rabkin. Jefferson, North Carolina: McFarland & Co., 1995, pp. 23–58. Interviews with Hampton Fancher, David Peoples, Ridley Scott, and Syd Mead from *L'Ecran Fantastique* no. 26, September 1982, and *Starlog* no. 184, November 1992.

Loud, Lance. "*Blade Runner*." *Details* (October 1992): 110–15, 177. Interviews with the cast and crew; emphasis on negative aspects of production; 17 stills.

Mead, Syd. "Designing the Future." *Omni's Screen Flights/Screen Fantasies: The Future According to Science Fiction Cinema*, Danny Peary, ed. Garden City, New York: Doubleday and Co., Inc., 1984, pp. 199–213. Article; 1 still; 8 preproduction illustrations.

O'Bannon, Dan and Moebius [Jean Giraud]. "The Long Tomorrow," Parts 1 and 2. *Heavy Metal*, July and August 1977: 80–87, 65–72. Adult fantasy comic on which Scott partly based the look of *Blade Runner*.

Peary, Danny. "Blade Runner." *Cult Movies Three: Fifty More of the Classics, the Sleepers, the Weird, and the Wonderful*. New York: Fireside, 1988, pp. 32–37. Credits; synopsis and discussion; 6 stills.

————. *Guide for the Film Fanatic*. New York: Simon and Schuster, Inc., 1986, p. 58. Review.

————, ed. "Directing *Alien* and *Blade Runner*." *Omni's Screen Flights/Screen Fantasies: The Future According to Science Fiction Cinema*. Garden City, NY: Doubleday and Co., Inc., 1984, pp. 293–302. Interview with Ridley Scott; 6 stills.

Rickman, Gregg. *Philip K. Dick: In His Own Words*. Long Beach, California: Fragments West/The Valentine Press, 1984, pp. 222–236, 249–255. Correspondence and conversations with Dick.

Sammon, Paul M. "The Making of *Blade Runner*." *Cinefantastique* 12, nos. 5–6

(July-August 1982): 20–47. Comprehensive article on the making of *Blade Runner*; credits; illustrations; 83 photos.

————. "Do Androids Dream of Unicorns? The Seven Faces of *Blade Runner*." *Video Watchdog*, no. 20 (November-December 1993): 32–59. Extensive article on the different film versions of *Blade Runner*; 28 stills.

Scroggy, David, ed. Blade Runner *Sketchbook*. San Diego, California: Blue Dolphin Enterprises, Inc., 1982. Out of print book: original production designs; 95 pages.

————. *The Illustrated* Blade Runner. San Diego, California: Blue Dolphin Enterprises, Inc., 1982. Out of print book: screenplay and selected storyboards; 96 pages.

Turan, Kenneth. *"Blade Runner 2." Los Angeles Times*, September 13, 1992, *Los Angeles Times* Magazine section, pp. 18–22, 24. Article; 5 stills.

APPENDIX H

PHOTO AND SCREENPLAY
EXCERPT CREDITS

FRONT COVER PHOTOGRAPHS (CLOCKWISE FROM UPPER LEFT)

1) Harrison Ford dangles high above the mean streets of 2019 Los Angeles during his final confrontation with Rutger Hauer. Matte painting begun by Rocco Gioffre and completed by Matthew Yuricich.
2) Sean Young as the lovely replicant, Rachael.
3) Rutger Hauer as replicant leader Roy Batty steps from a VidPhon booth.
4) The twin Tyrell Pyramids loom over a futuristic industrial wasteland known as the "Hades landscape." Miniature effects Douglas Trumbull's Entertainment Effects Group (EEG).
5) Harrison Ford as Rick Deckard, replicant hunter.

BACK COVER PHOTOGRAPHS (TOP TO BOTTOM)

1) *Blade Runner* director Ridley Scott (left) coaches Rutger Hauer on how Roy Batty should look up in a glass-topped elevator after the death of Tyrell (Joe Turkel).
2) Preproduction art by Mentor Huebner, showing a Spinner flying through stormy city streets.
3) Filming the liftoff of the full-scale Spinner from the Noodle Bar on the Warner Brothers Old New York street set (note film crew lower right).

APPENDIX I

BLADE RUNNER
FILM CREDITS

A) FILM CREDITS

Note: The following contains the complete credits listed on the film—plus a few extras.

THE CAST

Deckard	HARRISON FORD
Batty	RUTGER HAUER
Rachael	SEAN YOUNG
Gaff	EDWARD JAMES OLMOS
Bryant	M. EMMET WALSH
Pris	DARYL HANNAH
Sebastian	WILLIAM SANDERSON
Leon	BRION JAMES
Tyrell	JOE TURKEL
Zhora	JOANNA CASSIDY
Chew	JAMES HONG
Holden	MORGAN PAULL
Bear	KEVIN THOMPSON
Kaiser	JOHN EDWARD ALLEN
Taffey Lewis	HY PYKE
Cambodian Lady	KIMIRO HIROSHIGE
Sushi Master	ROBERT OKAZAKI
Saleslady	CAROLYN DeMIRJIAN
Bartender #1	CHARLES KNAPP
Bartender #2	LEO GORCEY, JR.
Bartender #3	THOMAS HUTCHINSON
Show Girl	KELLY HINE
Barfly #1	SHARON HESKY
Barfly #2	ROSE MASCARI
Geisha #1	SUSAN RHEE
Geisha #2	HIROKO KIMURI
Chinese Man #1	KAI WONG
Chinese Man #2	KIT WONG
Policeman #1	HIRO OKAZAKI

Policeman #2	STEVE POPE
Policeman #3	ROBERT REITER
Stuntpersons	RAY BICKEL, JANET BRADY, DIANE CARTER, ANN CHATTERTON, GILBERT COMBS, ANTHONY COX, RITA EGLESTON, GERRY EPPER, JEANNIE EPPER, JAMES HALTY, JEFFREY IMADA, GARY McLARTY, KAREN McLARTY, BETH NUFER, ROY OGATA, BOBBY PORTER, LEE PULFORD, RUTH REDFERN, GEORGE SAWAYA, CHARLES TAMBURRO, JACK TYREE, MIKE WASHLAKE, MICHAEL ZURICH

THE CREW

Directed by	RIDLEY SCOTT
Produced by	MICHAEL DEELEY
Screenplay by	HAMPTON FANCHER and DAVID PEOPLES
Director of Photography	JORDAN CRONENWETH
Production Designed by	LAWRENCE G. PAULL
Associate Producer	IVOR POWELL
Music Composed, Arranged, Performed, and Produced by	VANGELIS
Supervising Editor	TERRY RAWLINGS
Executive Producers	BRIAN KELLY and HAMPTON FANCHER
Special Photographic Effects Supervisors	DOUGLAS TRUMBULL, RICHARD YURICICH, DAVID DRYER
Based on the Novel	"DO ANDROIDS DREAM OF ELECTRIC SHEEP" by PHILIP K. DICK
Executive in Charge of Production	C. O. ERICKSON
Production Executive	KATHERINE HABER
Unit Production Manager	JOHN W. ROGERS
First Assistant Directors	NEWTON ARNOLD, PETER CORNBERG
Second Assistant Directors	DON HAUER, MORRIS CHAPNICK, RICHARD SCHROER
Costumes Designed By	CHARLES KNODE, MICHAEL KAPLAN
Art Director	DAVID SNYDER
Visual Futurist	SYD MEAD
Additional Photography	STEVEN POSTER, BRIAN TUFANO, B.S.C.
Casting by	MIKE FENTON, JANE FEINBERG
Production Controller	STEVE WARNER
Auditor	DICK DUBUQUE
Assistant Auditor	KELLY MARSHALL
Payroll	PAULETTE FINE
Script Supervisor	ANNA MARIA QUINTANA
Production Coordinator	VICKIE ALPER

Location Manager	MICHAEL NEALE
Camera Operators	ROBERT THOMAS, S.O.C., ALBERT BETTCHER, S.O.C., DICK COLEAN
First Assistant Cameramen	MIKE GENNE, STEVE SMITH
Second Assistant Cameraman	GEORGE D. GREER
Sound Mixer	BUD ALPER
Boom Man	EUGENE BYRON ASHBROOK
Cableman	BEAU BAKER
Set Decorators	LINDA DeSCENNA, TOM ROYSDEN, LESLIE FRANKENHEIMER
Leadman	MICHAEL TAYLOR
Production Illustrators	SHERMAN LABBY, MENTOR HUEBNER, TOM SOUTHWELL
Assistant Art Director	STEPHEN DANE
Set Designers	TOM DUFFIELD, BILL SKINNER, GREG PICKRELL, CHARLES BREEN, LOUIS MANN, DAVID KLASSON
Property Master	TERRY LEWIS
Assistant Property	DAVID QUICK, ARTHUR SHIPPEE, JR., JOHN A. SCOTT III
Makeup Artist	MARVIN G. WESTMORE
Hairstylist	SHIRLEY L. PADGETT
Men's Costumers	JAMES LAPIDUS, BOBBY E. HORN
Ladies Costumers	WINNIE BROWN, LINDA A. MATTHEWS
Special Floor Effects Supervisor	TERRY FRAZEE
Special Effects Technicians	STEVE GALICH, LOGAN FRAZEE, WILLIAM G. CURTIS
Lighting Gaffer	DICK HART
Best Boy	JOSEPH W. CARDOZA, JR.
Key Grip	CAREY GRIFFITH
Best Boy Grip	ROBERT E. WINGER
Dolly Grip	DONALD A. SCHMITZ
Crab Dolly Grip	DOUGLAS G. WILLAS
Construction Coordinator	JAMES F. ORENDORF
Assistant Construction Coordinator	ALFRED J. LITTEKEN
Construction Clerk	JAMES HALE
Painting Coordinator	JAMES T. WOODS
Standby Painter	BUZZ LOMBARDO
Stunt Coordinator	GARY COMBS
Action Prop Supervisor	MIKE FINK
Action Prop Consultant	LINDA FLEISHER
Additional Casting	MARCI LIROFF
Transportation Captain	HOWARD DAVIDSON
Transportation Cocaptain	JAMES SHARP
Publicist	SAUL KAHAN
Still Photographer	STEPHEN VAUGHAN
Producer's Assistant	BRYAN HAYNES
Assistant Location Manager	GREG HAMLIN

Craft Service	MICHAEL KNUTSEN
D.G.A. Trainee	VICTORIA RHODES
Editor	MARSHA NAKASHIMA
Assistant Editor	WILLIAM ZABALA
First Assistant Editor (English Editing)	LES HEALEY
Sound Editor (English Editing)	PETER PENNELL
Dialogue Editor (English Editing)	MICHAEL HOPKINS
Assistant Sound Editor (English Editing)	JOE GALLAGHER
Assistant Dialogue Editor (English Editing)	PETER BALDOCK
Chief Dubbing Mixers (Pinewood Studios)	GRAHAM V. HARTSTONE
(Twickenham Studios)	GERRY HUMPHRIES

SPECIAL PHOTOGRAPHIC EFFECTS BY	ENTERTAINMENT EFFECTS GROUP
Director of Photography	DAVE STEWART
Optical Photography Supervisor	ROBERT HALL
Cameramen	DON BAKER, RUPERT BENSON, GLEN CAMPBELL, CHARLES COWLES, DAVID HARDBERGER, RONALD LONGO, TIMOTHY McHUGH, JOHN SEAY
Matte Artist	MATTHEW YURICICH
Additional Matte Artist	ROCCO GIOFFRE
Assistant Matte Artist	MICHELE MOEN
Matte Photography	ROBERT BAILEY, TAMA TAKAHASHI, DON JAREL
Special Camera Technician	ALAN HARDING
Optical Line up	PHILIP BARBERIO, RICHARD RIPPLE
Animation and Graphics	JOHN WASH
Effects Illustrator	TOM CRANHAM
Special Projects Consultant	WAYNE SMITH
Miniature Technician	BOB SPURLOCK
Assistant Effects Editor	MICHAEL BAKAUSKAS
Chief Model Maker	MARK STETSON
Model Makers	JERRY ALLEN, SEAN CASEY, PAUL CURLEY, LESLIE EKKER, THOMAS FIELD, VANCE FREDERICK, WILLIAM GEORGE, KRISTOPHER GREGG, ROBERT JOHNSTON, MICHAEL McMILLIAN, THOMAS PHAK, CHRISTOPHER ROSS, ROBERT WILCOX
Key Grip	PAT VAN AUKEN
Gaffer	GARY RANDALL
Film Coordinator	JACK HINKLE
Cinetechnician	GEORGE POLKINGHORNE

Still Lab	VIRGIL MIRANO
Electronic and Mechanical Design	EVANS WETMORE
Electronic Engineering	GREG McMURRY
Computer Engineering	RICHARD HOLLANDER
Special Engineering Consultants	BUD ELAM, DAVID GRAFTON
Production Office Manager	JOYCE GOLDBERG
Visual Effects Auditor	DIANA GOLD
Assistant to David Dryer	LEORA GLASS
Visual Displays by	DREAM QUEST INC.
Electron Microscope	
Photographs by	DAVID SCHARF (© 1977)
Esper Sequence by	FILMFEX & LODGE/CHEESMAN
Titles by	INTRALINK FILM GRAPHIC DESIGN

Filmed in PANAVISION®
Color by TECHNICOLOR®
Filmed at THE BURBANK STUDIOS, BURBANK, CALIFORNIA
Original Soundtrack album of music by VANGELIS
Available on POLYDOR RECORDS AND TAPES
 "Harps of the Ancient Temples" Composed and Performed by GAIL LAUGHTON
 With Thanks to WILLIAM S. BURROUGHS and ALAN E. NOURSE for the use of the title BLADE RUNNER
 A LADD COMPANY release in association with SIR RUN RUN SHAW. Through WARNER BROS. (WB). A Warner Communications Company.
 Copyright MCMLXXXII Blade Runner Partnership

B) BLADE RUNNER 35MM AND 75MM MOTION PICTURE PRINT INFORMATION

Note: The following list details the running times and technical information of four 35mm and/or 70mm motion picture versions of Blade Runner.

1) *Blade Runner*. Los Angeles, California: Warner Brothers Inc., 1982. 6 reels, color, 35mm and 70mm, 113 min. Shown in 35mm at sneak previews in Denver and Dallas in March 1982; reprised in 70mm at the Cineplex Odeon Fairfax Theater in Los Angeles on May 6, 1990.
2) *Blade Runner*. Hollywood, California: Warner Brothers Inc., 1982. 6 reels, 10,537 ft., color, 35mm Panavision, 117 min., R-rated.
3) *Blade Runner*. Los Angeles, California: Warner Brothers Inc., 1991. 6 reels, color, 35mm Panavision, 113 min., R-rated. This so-called "Workprint" was a reduction copy of the 1982 70mm Denver/Dallas Sneak Preview; its distribution was limited to the NuArt Theater in Los Angeles and the Castro Theater in San Francisco in September and October of 1991. It was rated "R" for these showings.
4) *Blade Runner: The Director's Cut*. Los Angeles, California: Warner Brothers Inc., 1992. 6 reels, 10,427 ft., color, 35mm Panavision, 116 min., R-rated.